The Quiet Wise Spirit

The
Quiet Wise Spirit

Edwin W. Smith
1876–1957
and Africa

W. John Young

EPWORTH PRESS

Copyright © W. John Young 2002

British Library Cataloguing in Publication data

A catalogue record of this book is available from the British Library

0 7162 0553 X

First published in 2002
by Epworth Press
20 Ivatt Way
Peterborough, PE3 7PG

Typeset by Regent Typesetting, London
and printed in Great Britain by
Biddles Ltd, Guildford and King's Lynn

Contents

Maps

To Hilary

Foreword

Among the more spectacular by-products of the missionary movement in the nineteenth century is the opportunity it gave to working-class men and women to break free from their economic destinies. Labourers and maidservants, mechanics and factory hands, found ways to respond to their sense of divine calling through the work of the newly formed missionary societies, and some of their names are world famous, like the Northamptonshire shoemaker William Carey, or the Dundee mill girl Mary Slessor. The Methodist movement contributed many such people, who served with faithfulness and distinction throughout the world, but whose lives have no lasting memorial. One of these was the Revd John Smith, who began his career as an agricultural labourer and rose to be General Secretary of the Primitive Methodist General Missionary Committee. John Smith worked in South Africa, where his son Edwin was born in 1876. Virtually self-educated people like John Smith read voraciously and acquired large and eclectic libraries, and their children, brought up reading their parents' books, often went to even greater achievements. So it was for Edwin W. Smith, who was to become, in 1933, the first and only missionary ever elected President of the Royal Anthropological Institute, and the foremost advocate, indeed the founder, of the study of African religion in the first half of the twentieth century. How Smith achieved this pre-eminence as an Africanist, an anthropologist, as a missiologist and as a translator, is a puzzle. He had no formal anthropological training. In fact, he had very little at all in the way of an academic education. Almost nothing was taught in his time in Methodist theological colleges which was even vaguely relevant to work overseas: no missiology, no comparative religion, no formal study of linguistics, and certainly no anthropology. John Young has been extraordinarily diligent in his quest to discover how this man emerged as a pioneer in all these fields.

At least five kinds of readers will find a rich resource in Young's work. First there is the whole Methodist community, for whom the name of Edwin W. Smith is largely unknown. Because he served the British and Foreign Bible Society (now the Bible Society), one of the great ecumenical agencies of the wider church, and later taught in the USA, Smith was never fully involved in the day-to-day activities of the circuits and the stations of Methodism. Such people are frequently neglected by their own Church, and after their deaths are too easily forgotten. But Smith remained a loyal Methodist minister to the time of his death in 1957. We should be grateful to the Epworth Press for publishing this book, thus restoring Edwin Smith to his rightful place in the gallery of those who have brought honour to the Methodist name.

Second, missiologists and students of African theology will find much to interest them in this book. When I wrote *Justice, Courtesy and Love: Theologians and Missionaries Encountering World Religions, 1846–1914,* I had to apologize that very few and far between were any references to Africa and its religious inheritance within its pages. For nineteenth-century Christians, Africa was 'the Dark Continent'. Very little respect was paid to African beliefs and practices: the key words to describe complex systems of thought were 'animism' and 'fetishism'. Africans were regarded as underdeveloped and illiterate: as savages, as members of inferior or 'lower races'. Missionaries consistently expressed their doubts whether Africans could ever become church leaders, let alone become scholars and teachers. What changes have taken place in a hundred years! Now, to be sure, the main agents in this change have been Africans themselves, and I do not wish to reinforce any patronizing imperialist assumptions that the great achievements within Africa in the twentieth century were brought about by Europeans. Yet a true reckoning of the colonial period must include figures like Smith, who resisted the prevailing views about Africans. Young shows how, as early as 1900, Smith was insisting that the sophistication of African languages indicated the presence of high intelligence and that the African people 'have a great future ahead of them'. Through his work with the Ila-speaking peoples he recognized the African gifts of accurate observation and logical argument, as well as their unusual capability for interpersonal relations, including their supreme gift of friendship. Like many others of us, Edwin Smith fell in love with Africa, and from 1915, when he returned to England for health reasons, the rest of his life was devoted to understanding and interpreting Africa. Young takes us vividly into Smith's thinking, demonstrating the extraordinary contemporary influence of books like *The Golden Stool* (1926), *African Beliefs and Christian Faith* (1936), and *African Ideas of God* (1950). My African friends assure me that such works are readily acknowledged to be the foundation of much of their present-day achievement. As early as 1926, for example, Smith was adamant that missionaries would disappear from Africa (the sooner the better, he added) and that it was therefore not their business to decide what form African Christianity should take. The third of these books is an extended refutation of the infamous question of Emil Ludwig, 'Can the untutored African conceive of God?'. Missiologists will also be intrigued by Smith's concept of the missionary as a *musemunuzhi*, a blacksmith who recasts, renews and revives old ideas. This forthright acceptance of the fulfilment theory of Christian relationship with other religions, and wholehearted commitment to the points of contact approach, was soon to be repudiated by Karl Barth and Hendrik Kraemer. In this debate there is no question but Smith stood on the side of the angels, because no true mission takes place without dialogue and a mutual respect which includes affirming the religious convictions of the other person.

Third, there is the wider academic community, especially that of the anthropologists and the professional Africanists. His first major work, *The Ila-Speaking Peoples of Northern Rhodesia*, still stands, in the words of a recent writer, as 'one of the basic documents of anthropological literature' and 'as one of the great classics of African ethnography'. Its comprehensiveness and accuracy, based as it was upon the most extensive fieldwork, still makes it a goldmine of information. (Though the book was ostensibly written with Andrew M. Dale, Young shows conclusively that Smith was responsible for 90 per cent of the text.) Young takes us into the early debates in the development of anthropology, and shows us that it was not only the missionaries who could refer glibly to 'primitive peoples', 'people of rude culture' or the 'mental outlook of savages'. These were all terms used by writers in the house bulletin of the Royal Anthropological Institute in this period. By contrast, Smith and Dale wrote 'of friends whom they respected as equals'. Happily anthropology has made great strides in the last seventy years in this respect and in many others, and into its bloodstream has certainly passed some of the profound humanity represented by Smith's two presidential addresses in 1934 and 1935. Young gives abundant evidence of a happy period when one (admittedly quite extraordinary) missionary held the highest respect of the whole anthropological community.

Fourth, all historians of race relations need to be reminded of Edwin Smith's contribution to racial justice. To be sure this contribution is implied in all the work we have just discussed, for to despise a person's religion is to despise the person himself. But even more, Smith was at the forefront of the movement to consider that all races and all cultures are equals. His experience, as an army chaplain in Belgium in 1915, of the savagery of the First World War ended any notions he may have previously entertained that Western cultures were naturally superior to others. His search for a new model of interracial relations led him to the friendship with the Ghanaian scholar James Emman Kwegyir Aggrey. Smith's *Aggrey of Africa: A Study in Black and White* (1929) was an enormously influential popularization of his ideas. Incidentally one of Young's many important discoveries, at least for me, removes a possible slur on Smith's name. About a year or so ago one of my own students, a Zulu from South Africa, had unearthed from our university library a copy of Smith's 1923 book on African religion which was entitled *The Religion of Lower Races*. I admitted to being horrified when she showed it to me and muttered something about even Smith being a child of his age. To my great relief it is clear that this was the title given by some editor at Macmillan's in New York. Smith himself apologized for the title 'which, without his knowledge or consent, was given to this book'. Much later on Smith autographed every one of his books in a New York library, except this one.

The fifth class of readers is of course the wider Christian public. Stephen Spender urged us once, by implication, to 'think continually of the truly great'. In the communion and fellowship of the saints, Edwin Smith shines as a great and splendid light. This book gives him back to us all.

Kenneth Cracknell
Brite Divinity School
Fort Worth
Texas

Acknowledgments

I am grateful to many people who have helped and encouraged me in my researches into the life and work of Edwin Smith over the last decade.

The Revd Kenneth Cracknell encouraged me in 1989 to make Edwin Smith a subject of serious study, and, twelve years later, he has most kindly agreed to contribute a Foreword to this book.

Professor Kenneth Grayston of Bristol University advised me to follow a formal course of research, and Dr Stuart Mews of Cheltenham and Gloucester College of Higher Education supervised the M.Phil. thesis on which this biography is based.

Tom Johnson of Boston University Center for African Studies and Henk van Rinsum of Utrecht University have shown great interest in this project and have made many helpful observations.

Many librarians, archivists, scholars and others kindly responded to my enquiries, and I am particularly indebted to the Methodist Missionary Society, who allowed me to use their collection of Smith Papers, and the Hartford Seminary Library, who sent me copies of Smith papers and gave permission to cite them.

The British and Foreign Bible Society granted access to their archives and permitted reference to them and to Bible Society publications.

The Revd Graham Slater, on behalf of the Epworth Press, helped me greatly with the final editing of the text.

I am deeply grateful, too, to Richard Howard-Jones, Edwin Smith's grandson, who allowed me full use of the diaries, photograph albums, Smith papers and books which he generously loaned to me. (He has now deposited most of these items in the Methodist Missionary Society Archives, thus adding considerably to an already substantial collection of Smith Papers.)

My special thanks go to my wife Hilary, to other members of my family and to many friends and church members for their interest, patience, help, support and encouragement throughout this long project.

It is good to see that recent reference works, secular and religious, have included short articles about Edwin Smith and that scholarly articles are beginning to focus on his writings. My hope is that this book will help to enhance his recovering reputation and prompt fuller study of his work.

Abbreviations and notes on the text

ABCF	*African Beliefs and Christian Faith*, 1936
'African Odyssey'	'An African Odyssey' (unpublished manuscript), 1952
Aggrey	*Aggrey of Africa*, 1929
BFBS	British and Foreign Bible Society. Also known as the Bible Society.
BM	*The Blessed Missionaries*, 1950
CMIA	*The Christian Mission in Africa*, 1926
Edinburgh 1910	World Missionary Conference, Edinburgh, June 1910
GMC	General Missionary Committee
GS	*The Golden Stool*, 1926
Handbook	*Handbook of the Ila Language*, 1907
IAI	International African Institute
IMC	International Missionary Council
IRM	*International Review of Missions*
ISP	*The Ila-Speaking Peoples of Northern Rhodesia*, with A. M. Dale, 1920
JRAI	*Journal of the Royal Anthropological Institute*
JRAS	*Journal of the Royal African Society*
Lindley	*The Life and Times of Daniel Lindley*
Lower Races	*The Religion of Lower Races*, 1923
Mabilles	*The Mabilles of Basutoland*, 1939
MAM	Methodist Archives, Manchester
MAR	Macmillan Archives, Reading
Moffat	*Robert Moffat*, 1925
Nanzela	*Nanzela: Some Personal Experiences in Central Africa*
Packmen	*Tales of God's Packmen*, 1928

Plans	*Plans and – People!,* 1948
PM	Primitive Methodist
PMQR	*Primitive Methodist Quarterly Review*
Price	*Great Lion of Bechuanaland: The Life and Times of Roger Price, Missionary,* 1957
RAI	Royal Anthropological Institute
RAS	Royal African Society
'Reminiscences'	Manuscript of reminiscences, c.1957
Secret	*The Secret of the African,* 1929
Shrine	*The Shrine of a People's Soul,* 1929
SPBSC	Smith Papers, Bible Society Archives, Cambridge
SPH	Smith Papers, Hartford Seminary Archives
SPMMS	Smith Papers, Methodist Missionary Society Archives
UCZ	United Church of Zambia
White Fields	*The Way of the White Fields in the Rhodesias,* 1928

Countries are usually referred to by their modern names, e.g. Zambia. Present-day conventions for describing African languages, for example, Tonga instead of Citonga, are observed as far as possible. I have, however, used Nanzela throughout although the present-day spelling is Nanzhila. Except where text is being quoted every effort has been made to use 'African' as an alternative to 'native'.

Edwin Smith's diaries were often in note form, so sometimes words have been added, in square brackets, to convey the sense of the quotation more smoothly. Occasional explanations have been included, also in square brackets.

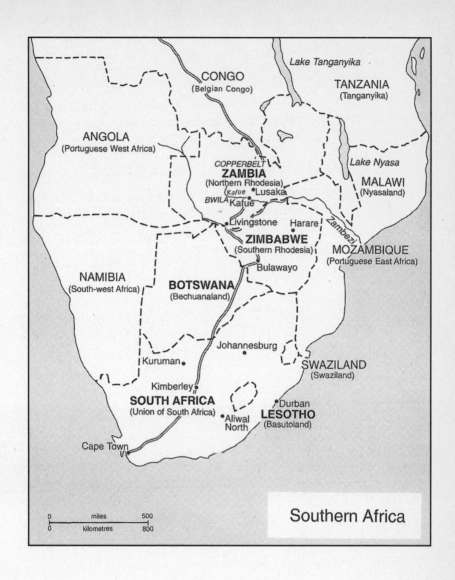

CONGO
(Belgian Congo)

Lake Tanganyika

TANZANIA
(Tanganyika)

ANGOLA
(Portuguese West Africa)

COPPERBELT

ZAMBIA
(Northern Rhodesia)

Kafue •Lusaka
BWILA •Kafue

Lake Nyasa

MALAWI
(Nyasaland)

•Livingstone   Harare•

ZIMBABWE
(Southern Rhodesia)

•Bulawayo

Zambezi

MOZAMBIQUE
(Portuguese East Africa)

NAMIBIA
(South-west Africa)

BOTSWANA
(Bechuanaland)

Johannesburg•

SWAZILAND
(Swaziland)

•Kuruman

Kimberley•

SOUTH AFRICA
(Union of South Africa)

•Durban

LESOTHO
(Basutoland)

•Aliwal
North

Cape Town

| 0 | miles | 500 |
| 0 | kilometres | 800 |

Southern Africa

Introduction

Edwin Smith, eminent in his day, was quickly forgotten after his death in 1957. Little more than ten years later, when for two years I studied religion in Africa at university, he was never mentioned. Yet, he has been described as a 'great Methodist missionary, anthropologist and pioneering Africanist',[1] and as an honoured exception to the rule that missionaries are usually poor theologians.[2] The Ila people among whom he worked nicknamed him *chitutamano*, 'man of wisdom who knows all you say'.[3]

The possible reasons for these shifting fortunes will be discussed later. There are indications, however, that the neglect of Edwin Smith may be ending. Though his name is omitted from the title and subtitle of Malcolm McVeigh's *God in Africa* (1974),[4] the book is based on his work and contains an invaluable bibliography of writings from 1920 onwards. Moreover, British Methodists like the Revd Dr Roger Peaden and the Revd Dr Martin Forward have, in their own work, found it important to be acquainted with Edwin Smith's contributions; Adrian Hastings, in his writings on religion and history in Africa, often mentions Edwin Smith, briefly but positively; and the *Dictionary of National Biography* recently added a volume entitled *Missing Persons* (1994) which contained an article on Edwin Smith. Finally, the Dutchman Henk van Rinsum, who includes Edwin Smith as a major figure in his studies, spoke on 25 February 1997 at Edinburgh University to the Centre for the Study of Christianity in a non-Western World on ' "Knowing the African": Edwin W. Smith and the invention of African Traditional Religion'. He has since published this with another article on Edwin Smith in his stimulating collection, *Slaves of Definition* (2001).[5]

I myself first heard about Edwin Smith in 1975 when, during my preparation for service in Africa, I was loaned 'Smith and Dale' on the

Ila people and language. I also read Edwin Smith's obituary in *Minutes of the Methodist Conference* for 1958, which made clear that he had achieved great eminence with little formal training. Then, in Zambia in 1977, I heard more about him and was told of a service that had been held in 1976 to mark the centenary of his birth. The UCZ archives at Kitwe, Zambia, which I was asked to arrange in 1980–1, provided yet more information; and back in Britain in the following years, I occasionally found copies of Edwin Smith's works in secondhand bookshops.

It was the positive encouragement of the Revd Kenneth Cracknell, however, which prompted me, in 1989, to prepare for serious study of Edwin Smith. The opportunity came in 1992 when I had three months of sabbatical leave. My plan was to study the Smith papers in the Methodist Missionary Society Archives as well as reading as many of his books as I could find. I also wanted to consult the Bible Society Archives but was informed that I needed permission from a living relative. Eventually, I made contact with Edwin Smith's grandson, Richard Howard-Jones, and my meeting with him in May 1992 triggered the research programme out of which this book has emerged. Mr Howard-Jones spoke about his grandfather, kindly loaned me some of his diaries, photograph albums and books, and gave me a copy of a tape on which Edwin Smith recounted early memories.

In 1992 I thought that my article, published in the *Epworth Review*,[6] would round the work off nicely. But by then I had found so much material that the idea of a fuller study began to take shape.

Edwin Smith wrote an enormous amount in books, articles, reviews, diaries, letters and manuscripts. It seems that if he was not reading he was writing, fluently and copiously. I wanted, therefore, to do two things; to tell the story of Edwin Smith's life and developing interests and to assess his significance.

The production of a thorough study of Edwin Smith is a great challenge. Anyone who reads the biographies which he wrote realizes how well he dealt with his subjects in their social, intellectual and historical contexts. I have tried to do the same for Edwin Smith himself, and this has meant covering a lot of ground. In my attempts to assess his work in African languages, religion(s), anthropology, history, translation, theology and ethics I have been deeply grateful for the help of recent scholarly studies and of consultation, wherever possible, with experts in these fields.

Edwin Smith was born in South Africa, and his religious background as the son of a Primitive Methodist missionary with progressive views is crucially important. His missionary career in Africa, where his practical and linguistic talents began to unfold, led to his efforts to understand the Ila-speaking peoples, and the study that he finally published with A. M. Dale as co-author became a classic text of anthropology. After his missionary career, he worked for the British and Foreign Bible Society (BFBS) and contributed much to translation policy. His prominent positions in the BFBS did little to restrict his interest in Africa. He joined societies, helped found the International African Institute and was honoured with the Presidency of the Royal Anthropological Institute. He met J. E. K. Aggrey, a famous African who had been on the Phelps-Stokes Commissions which investigated education in Africa; and, in writing Aggrey's life, he became more overtly committed to cooperative inter-cultural attitudes and policies, opposing cultural imperialism and pressing for active development policies. He spent a few years in the USA, where at that time African studies had a very low profile, encouraging missionaries and African Americans to value Africa and its peoples. Race relations concerned him increasingly and he came to promote a liberal, multi-racial and inclusive attitude.

Although, as we have already stressed, Edwin Smith wrote a great deal, Africa was his chief interest and most of his vast literary output was connected to some aspect of African studies.[7] His outstanding talent was for mapping out and making preliminary forays into some hitherto unexplored area – for example, African religion, African Christian theology and African symbolism. Such overviews required a broad base of information and *The Golden Stool* (1926) and, even more, his 1935 Presidential Address to the Royal Anthropological Institute, show that he was extremely well informed on all aspects of African studies, especially religion(s). I can see why Adrian Hastings speaks of the period 1925–50 as 'the age of Edwin Smith'.[8]

Edwin Smith had a missionary agenda. He argued that Christ would contribute positively to Africa and it seems that, a century after he began his missionary work, many Africans agree. His approach to missionary work, however, was unusual at the time, though not as unusual as has often been supposed. Many missionaries involved in Edinburgh 1910 showed the same enlightened, progressive outlook exemplified by Edwin Smith in Africa. It can be argued, of course, that the 'fulfilment theology' which Edwin Smith embraced was a way of justifying a takeover of African religion by Christianity.[9] His mature perspective, however, was that Christianity could be translated into African settings and that Africans could acquire and develop their own Christianity. He always believed this to be the best choice. He clearly accepted, however, that Africans had other options which would not lead to their eternal damnation. His Ila friend, Mungalo, never became a Christian, yet Edwin Smith expected to meet him in heaven. Thus the domination motif, a favourite in present-day analysis, has to be balanced by the stress on cooperation which came to the fore in the second half of Edwin Smith's adult life.

It was suggested to me at the beginning of my research that John Wesley's Arminian theology might be significant. But I found few references to Wesley in Edwin Smith's published and unpublished work. His theology, in fact, was Wesleyan in only the most general way – for example, by being eclectic and pragmatic – and was formed by using the Bible in relation to all sorts of learning. The writing of Dante Alighieri, it seems, satisfied him more than either the liberalism of the early twentieth century or the neo-orthodoxy associated with Karl Barth and Hendrik Kraemer.

Although of the old colonial order, Edwin Smith was among those who could see its end, and his studies may well have contributed to its demise. Cultural imperialism, however, has proved far more difficult to overthrow and, for this reason alone, the critique which his work contains should be more closely studied.

I

'They called me Zulu'

Edwin Smith was born in South Africa in 1876 and, although Africa affected him from the beginning, another important influence was Primitive Methodism, a nineteenth-century British religious movement in which his father, the Revd John Smith, was a leading minister.

The Primitive Methodists (PMs) emerged at the beginning of the century, spreading rapidly from the Potteries in Staffordshire and becoming influential in the industrial north and in rural East Anglia. Using open-air gatherings, developed in America and known as 'Camp Meetings', they reached working-class people in ways that other bodies failed to do, and were often involved in trade unions. They were noted for promoting teetotalism, opposing gambling and welcoming women as local preachers, as missionaries and, in the early period, as ministers. Primitive Methodism, which has been described as 'The People's Church',[1] grew in its first 100 years to more than 200,000 members.

Edwin Smith's father, John Smith (1840–1915), initially an agricultural labourer, moved at the age of fourteen to New World in the Downham Circuit and found 'a new world, for here he came into contact with the Primitive Methodists, and was soundly converted to God'.[2] He started preaching two years later and at eighteen entered the PM ministry.[3] His British circuits were mostly in East Anglia, for at that time, the 'District era' in Primitive Methodism, ministers tended to stay in the same part of the country. When in the Ely circuit (1860–2), he met Susan Collen of Soham, and married her in August 1863. After the birth of three children Susan's health failed and her death in October 1873, after a long illness, came as a great blow. Though John spoke at the time of plodding on 'in the ministry of the "holy word" for a few years at the most',[4] he was in the event very active for the next forty years.

A feature of PM life in this period was that Districts had their own emphases and the Norwich District pressed the claims of overseas missions. As far back as 1837 Yarmouth had sent a scheme to the Conference, and in 1864 it was agreed that part of the Jubilee Fund should be devoted to the formation of a mission in Port Natal, near Durban, South Africa.[5]

In 1870 this mission was opened by Henry Buckenham at Aliwal North in Cape Province, and two years later the Missionary Committee asked John Smith to work there. But 'his wife was so delicate and afflicted that she dared not undertake the voyage'.[6] After her death, however, he agreed to go and, shortly before leaving for South Africa in 1874, married his second wife, Fanny Jeary, from Martham near Great Yarmouth.[7]

Aliwal North was originally a settlement on the south bank of the Orange River founded by a Boer, Piet de Wet, and known as Buffel's Vlei.[8] In 1848, however, Sir Harry Smith, Governor of Cape Colony, established a town on the site, naming it 'Aliwal' after a village in India where he had won a battle. By 1875, 1,229 people of various races lived there.[9] Edwin,[10] the second child[11] of John Smith's second marriage, was born at the Parsonage, Aliwal North, on 7 September 1876.

The Aliwal North PM circuit had fifteen members when John Smith arrived and, as a result of his industry, church membership increased to 130 during his first tour of five years.[12] He attracted over 10 per cent of the population to his church and was so highly respected that, when the family left Aliwal North in 1879, his portrait was placed in the Reading Room alongside that of Queen Victoria.[13] In 1883, after serving in the Yarmouth and Lynn circuits of East Anglia, he returned to Aliwal North for five more years. Edwin Smith attended the local school and, at his parent's insistence, learnt Afrikaans as well as English.[14] He also heard people speaking African languages, especially Sotho. For him, however, one of the most enjoyable aspects of life at Aliwal North was the freedom to wander around the open countryside to his heart's content.

During this period the Scramble for Africa was opening the interior of Africa to Europeans who, after being involved in the coastal regions up to 1879,[15] extended their influence inland as far as Central Africa. During the early stages of the Scramble, John Smith was exercised about the position and prospects of the PM Mission at Aliwal North and 'saw no hope of any great enlargement of the sphere of operations in South Africa',[16] where there were numerous churches. He became aware, however, of other possibilities through his contacts with French missionaries from Lesotho. Impressed by their work, he wanted to emulate them and became convinced that the PMs should go where the gospel had never been heard before.

The French missionaries, who had started working among the Lozi north of the Zambezi in 1885, advised the PMs to evangelize the Lozi's neighbours, the Mashukulumbwe, or, as they called themselves, the Ila.[17] Consequently, when John Smith returned to England in 1888, he brought a scheme for a Central Africa Mission to the PM Conference, which supported his proposal, and the pioneer missionaries left England in April 1889.

When, after their two spells in Africa, the Smith family finally settled in England, Edwin Smith was sent to Elmfield College, a PM school on the outskirts of York. After the open spaces of Africa the College seemed like a prison and Edwin often broke bounds and explored the locality – conduct which, together with his boisterous behaviour in dormitory life, earned him some severe punishments. His father, apparently preoccupied with ecclesiastical and political work,[18] seemed indifferent to his misdemeanours, and his fellow pupils did not know what to make of him. 'They called me Zulu and because I came from Africa they could not understand why I was not black.'[19] When they asked him to perform a Zulu war dance he satisfied them, not having any idea what was really required, by dancing around singing an Afrikaans song. It is small wonder that Edwin Smith always regarded the 'certificate of good conduct' which he acquired as his chief trophy!

Edwin Smith learned to read well, although his education gave him a hatred of Virgil which he took decades to overcome. He did not realize that anyone had actually spoken Latin and he learnt French without ever knowing how to pronounce it, the rules of grammar being drummed into his head in order to pass the examination.[20] Since, however, he shared his father's enthusiasm for debating, he enjoyed the Elmfield Debating Society, where political subjects were frequently discussed.[21] He recalled, for example, that in his first speech he supported Stanley's cause in the Emin Pasha relief expedition (1889). The other boys criticized Stanley but Edwin Smith moved a vote of censure against Queen Victoria for not making Stanley a peer of the realm!

In 1894, when John Smith became Secretary of the PM General Missionary Committee (GMC)[22] and assumed responsibility for PM Missions as a whole, in Britain as well as Africa, the family moved to London. Edwin, who left Elmfield in 1891, at first entered business, possibly with his Uncle James in Norwich, but in London found work with a firm of estate agents in the West End. In this way, he gained invaluable experience, giving him 'insight into men and manners' and calling 'into play the exercise of punctuality, promptness and executive abilities'.[23]

Edwin Smith showed little sign of academic prowess and his failure in the Civil Service examination, for which he prepared only halfheartedly, cannot have come as a surprise. Around that time, however, his wild and restless spirit began to come under control. Although his formal studies had been unsuccessful he started to explore his father's large library. John Smith loved books and read widely: 'As soon as he was converted he threw all the energy of his strong nature into mental and spiritual culture. He began to buy books and the love of books – strong, healthy books – remains with him still.'[24] He was known, moreover, as a progressive thinker, prepared to embrace the latest ideas, Fairbairn being one of his favourite authors.[25] Edwin Smith, beginning to devour the volumes on his father's shelves, was attracted by sceptical works but found that such writings as Colenso on the Pentateuch undermined the Bible, and faith with it.

In this time of uncertainty Edwin Smith was helped by the Revd William Mincher, minister at Camden Town since 1893. Mincher, he found, had in the past experienced similar doubts but now had a joyous faith. He encouraged Edwin Smith to act on the assumption that Christianity was true and to find Christ in living. Edwin liked the text in John 7.17, 'He that shall do my will shall know the truth', and, though not convinced that Christianity was true, set out on the great adventure of living as if it was. As he himself admitted, this is a risky procedure, but he found that it worked: 'After all, Christianity is not first and foremost a dogma to be accepted but a life to be lived, and the proof of it is found in the living, in action rather than in speculation.'[26] Stirred by this all-important realization, Edwin Smith wondered what to do next, and his thoughts turned to Africa, the land of his birth. As it happened there was now an opportunity for serving Christ in the PM mission in Central Africa.

The PM missionaries who had left England in 1889 were soon caught up in the power struggles taking place around the Zambezi, especially between the Lozi and the Matabele. The Lozi king, Lewanika, held them up for a long time. Having just regretted signing away a large measure of Lozi sovereignty to Europeans, Lewanika was not kindly disposed towards these new arrivals. The missionaries could hardly have arrived at a more unsuitable time and spent over two years in

Barotseland. Eventually matters improved and the PM missionaries set off for Bwila on 6 July 1893. They took wagons where wagons had never been before and crossed rivers, gorges and boggy ground. Then, after six months: 'It was with indescribable pleasure we, in the evening of Dec. 21st, 1893, sighted the first villages in Mashukulumbweland and came in contact with these new people.'[27] They opened their first mission station at Nkala on the western side of Ila country and in 1895 started another station, Nanzela, a few miles away.

Meanwhile, young Edwin Smith was ransacking his father's library for books on African exploration. He was fascinated by all he read, and could trace, from memory, the great explorers' routes. Indeed, later in life he recalled gleefully how he once detected an error in the course of the Zambezi on a map drawn specially for his father by a leading firm of mapmakers. He acknowledged, moreover, that from his early days Africa had drawn him as the sun draws plants and that 'to return to my native land had always been a dream'.[28] This dream started to be realized in late 1894 when he was eighteen.

Edwin Smith's call to return to Africa as a missionary came while he helped his father, as he often did in the evenings, with his work as Secretary of the GMC. He was already familiar with the developing situation in South and Central Africa, but his response to it was made as he took down, at his father's dictation, an article for *The Record*, the PM missionary paper.

He said, and I wrote:

'For the first time in our history as a church, we are face to face with vast tribes of heathens, never before touched by any Christian church . . . Ponder the fact that the religion we take them is something totally different from what they have ever heard of or believed . . . Ponder the further fact that they have no written language. Their speech must be acquired and reduced to written form; then the word of God must be translated into that language. This translation, in order to be of real value, must be made from the Greek text. Until the language has been dealt with we shall remain profoundly ignorant of the inner life of these people.'

So my father went on dictating and I went on writing, and before he had finished, my mind was made up. By God's help, that should be my work: the reduction of this new language to writing. Next day, I enrolled in a Greek class at Birkbeck College, and as I went to and fro my daily work on top of a horse-drawn bus, I conned my Greek grammar.[29]

It would take more than three years of preparation before Edwin Smith could return to Africa.

2

Preparing to go to Africa

Edwin Smith's early studies were influenced by the impact of Darwin on aspects of Victorian thinking. The concept of evolution was being applied to areas other than biology – for example, the new discipline of anthropology, where E. B. Tylor (1832–1917), one of the pioneers, was interested in the origins and developments of culture and religion and J. G. Frazer (1854–1941) was beginning to gather materials for his famous *Golden Bough*.

As theologians were coming to terms with these developments and with the findings of biblical criticism, the PMs were raising the standard of their preachers. Ministerial training was now based at Hartley College, Manchester, where, from 1892, A. S. Peake introduced PM students to biblical scholarship. Before then, however, despite the denomination's reputation for narrow-mindedness, many PMs applied themselves to understanding the gospel in the light of modern knowledge.

Chester Armstrong, for example, describes two ministers who served in Northumberland at the end of the nineteenth century, one 'was an ardent lover of literature',[1] the other 'was much more a philosopher than a theologian'.[2] Such men were fed intellectually by the *Primitive Methodist Quarterly Review*, which contained learned articles and reviews of scholarly books. At a different level, the popular PM journal, the *Primitive Methodist Magazine*, offered a great variety of theological and cultural material as well as news from the Connexion and from other denominations. In short, as Edwin Smith began his studies he had the good fortune to belong to a denomination which encouraged intellectual activity.

The complete Revised Version of the English Bible was published in 1885, and Edwin used an interleaved RV when he began his preaching ministry, making notes which reflected reference to the most up-to-date scholarship. For example, he analysed Genesis in terms of the sources postulated by literary criticism and worked hard on his Greek New Testament studying significant words and summarizing biblical thought, section by section, with the help of commentaries. His notes on 'saints' in Romans 1.7[3] show that he used Sanday and Headlam's recent *International Critical Commentary on Romans* (1895). Thanks to his alert mind and a retentive memory, these studies yielded both an outline of his personal theology and a store of material for later reflection.

Edwin was influenced by his father's ideas as well as by the books in his library. John Smith, a natural leader and orator, became President of the PM Conference in 1898 and in 1900 gave the fourth Hartley Lecture, which was published as *Christ and Missions* (1900). By that time, Edwin Smith would already have been familiar with his father's thinking and in referring to it in his own Hartley Lecture, *The Golden Stool* (1926), he noted: 'I am struck, above all else, by its very modern tone . . . he set forth many of the things advocated in these pages . . . To him (as to myself) the object of the missionary work of the Church is to win for Jesus Christ the moral supremacy of the world.'[4]

In *Christ and Missions* John Smith insisted on building an indigenous church; self-governing, self-propagating, and self-supporting and rooted in African thought. He had a practical emphasis:

> The complete transformation of heathen Africa requires all the forces represented by the Christian Church . . . The ennoblement of native character and life must come by the eye and hand as well as by the head and heart.[5]

Basic to this approach to mission was the conviction that 'a well-built house, a well-kept garden, a row of trees, a spade, a plough, a plane, all help to mould the character and life of an African'.[6] John Smith wanted an African ministry in the widest sense, including teachers, catechists, evangelists and pastors and warned that 'the utmost care must be taken not to Europeanise them'.[7] He considered that the 'supreme need of a heathen world is a great host of native evangelists thoroughly versed in God's Word, its growth and structure, its style and teaching, its history and exegesis . . . '[8] and he believed that 'beyond the limits of absolute necessity, foreign assistance is a real evil'.[9] This was not new thinking. Similar ideas had been promoted by Henry Venn and others half a century earlier.[10] Theory, however, is not easily realized in practice and the dominance of missionaries frequently created dependent people. As a result autonomous churches were only established very slowly.

John Smith had other interesting ideas. He judged for example, that 'the missionary enterprise has certainly led to the recovery of the lost place of women in the Church of Jesus Christ.'[11] Indeed, woman's right to teach and preach the gospel is just the same as man's . . . it is little short of a calamity when the evangelistic fires of a Christ-like woman are smothered and quenched by a sinful deference to conventional notions of propriety.[12]

Where other religions were concerned, John Smith concluded that Christ is supreme but felt, as Edwin would point out later, that

> we must do them justice. There can be no reason why what is good in them should not be frankly recognized, and even assimilated. Their followers must not be despised or bribed, but respected and loved.[13]

Thus, through his father's progressive influence, a well-stocked library and his own studies, Edwin Smith's thinking set out in directions helpful to a prospective missionary to Africa.

Although Edwin Smith enjoyed debating, he lacked confidence in public speaking. Nevertheless, he began preaching and gave his first sermon at Camden Town on 12 September 1895. He took no more services that year but preached frequently in 1896, mainly around London at, for example, such places as Camden Town, Highbury, Caledonian Road, Marylebone and Kensington. The cause at Islington seems to have been struggling, for only two or three turned up for the evening service of 2 August 1896 and none came on 20 December! Edwin also preached in East Anglia, the region of his family origins, at Great Yarmouth (16 February) and Martham (5 April). He gave missionary sermons and used such texts as Joshua 13.1 ('there are still large areas of land to be taken over') and Psalm 68.31 ('Cush will submit herself to God').[14] To be a missionary, he needed first to become a PM minister and therefore entered the candidating procedure. After examinations, trial sermons and interviews, the PM Conference of 1897, held at Manchester, accepted him as a probationer minister. Edwin was now well motivated and his intellectual power was starting to show itself: 'He had already passed the candidates' examination, securing the first place, with 142 marks out of a possible 150.'[15]

Edwin Smith's missionary vocation was stimulated by meeting

important people from Africa. Soon after he began preaching he met Khama, the famous African chief, who came to the PMs' General Missionary Committee on Friday 4 October 1895. Edwin described events for *The Record*. The PMs thanked Khama for helping their missionaries when they travelled to Central Africa. They supported Khama's desire to have his land and other rights confirmed by the British Government and were very impressed by him: 'we believe him to be a KINGLY MAN' said H. B. Kendall, the Connexional historian.[16] Edwin and others shook 'hands with Khama, and felt it an honour to do so'.[17]

In May 1897, Edwin Smith attended the May Meeting, the chief event in the PM Missionary calendar. He was possibly on show as a missionary candidate but would have been much more interested in meeting François Coillard, of Lesotho and Barotseland, who addressed the PMs on Sunday 16 May at the Surrey Chapel, London. Edwin,

> in common with many more, came to know him personally. We recall his presence and speech at our May Meeting, when he was presented with £100 for his proposed technical school, as a slight recognition of his kindness to our pioneers.[18]

A few months later Edwin Smith celebrated his 21st birthday (7 September 1897). He had greetings and £5 from his Uncle James of Langley Abbey, Norwich.[19] His uncle also mentioned Miss Julia Fitch. She and Edwin were perhaps engaged by this time. Julia, who was two years older than Edwin, grew up as an Anglican and had found her Confirmation 'a moment of definite decision for Christ'.[20] She trained as a teacher in the village school and moved to Great Yarmouth where, staying with Primitive Methodists, she attended the Temple PM church.[21] Edwin met her when he visited that PM home. They fell in love and so began a long relationship which was only ended by Julia's death in 1952.

Edwin Smith was busy reading and writing as he prepared for his missionary work. *The Record*, September 1897, carried his article on the Christian Campaign, possibly the substance of his missionary sermon on Joshua 13.1. He compared the church to an army under Christ's leadership: 'The aim and purpose of the Christian Army is to subdue all the nations of the earth to Jesus Christ.'[22] He traced the history of mission and, after surveying the position of Christianity in 1897, asked what the PMs were doing for Africa. He admitted that they were 'doing something, though not a great deal when our resources are considered', especially as far as Central Africa was concerned: 'a vast country, almost unexplored and barely touched by the Gospel . . . Let us hasten to occupy it.'[23] Edwin described missionary work in colonial and martial tones. Stirringly, he urged his readers to 'go forward to take possession of the heathen world'.[24] His theme of domination, then prominent in his mind, was probably drawn from the colonial expansion taking place and the aggressive tradition of Protestant missionary work.

Edwin Smith realized that his theological studies needed supplementing by medical training. He 'came across an unpretentious pamphlet dealing with the work of Livingstone College', and, seeing that it was just what he wanted, sought the Missionary Committee's support. The outcome was that 'the Missionary Committee further recommended that Mr. Smith should be released from the ordinary routine of probationary work in order that he might study in the Livingstone Medical College for foreign mission work,'[25] and it became PM policy to send missionary candidates to Livingstone College for medical training.

Livingstone College was founded in 1893 to give missionaries 'a working knowledge of medicine and surgery'. This helped them but did not make them medical missionaries, and after his training Edwin realized 'the need for qualified medical men in the mission field'.[26] The College came to Stratford, East London, in 1893 and could accommodate 16 students who studied physiology and anatomy in the first term and surgery and medicine in the second. The third term was devoted to various subjects including tropical diseases, obstetrics and skin diseases. The students did first aid and practical dentistry and had clinical instruction at local hospitals. They used to visit a medical mission in Shadwell which had some connection with the College. There, after a short service, the doctors treated 'cases of disease among the poor of the East End'. At first the students observed but went on 'to take cases under the supervision of the doctor'.

They also studied Africa and its missions. Smith was busily undertaking such studies on his own initiative. He wrote about David Livingstone for *The Record* (October 1897) and thought that directly or indirectly Livingstone was largely responsible for the vastly increased knowledge of Africa that had come to Europe during the nineteenth century. For all this, Livingstone was a missionary whose policy was 'not concentration but extension'.[27] His explorations began 'with the view of finding healthy situations for mission stations'.[28] Livingstone had a broad view of missionary work in the context of 'civilising influences'[29] and was appalled by the slave trade. Smith contrasted Livingstone's methods with those of other travellers. Stanley, for example, who did great work, 'went at the head of organized expeditions, with a small regiment of soldiers to escort him . . . But Livingstone tramped thousands of miles generally unarmed and unattended save only by a few faithful followers.'[30]

Smith considered that Livingstone's success came from his way of treating Africans 'as men and brothers'. His other great strength was 'his calm trust in God . . . His constant prayer was that he might be like Christ.'[31] Smith frequently visited Livingstone's grave in Westminster Abbey and read the inscription. In imagination he saw the 'worn out figure of the great missionary kneeling at the bedside with his head buried in his hands on the pillow . . . His body rests in the Abbey, but his heart, in death as in life, is in Africa.'[32] In later writings, Smith would offer criticisms of Livingstone but always regarded Livingstone as his missionary hero and held him to be the greatest nineteenth-century missionary to Africa: 'I yield to no man, living or dead, in my admiration for the great missionary-explorer: from my youth up he has been my hero.'[33]

Edwin Smith valued his time at Livingstone College. He continued preaching in the London area and gave many missionary sermons. He read about Central Africa, and the *Primitive Methodist Magazine* of 1897 published his review article of Sir Harry Johnston's book on British Central Africa. Sir Harry was a great pioneer Africanist and wrote many books about Africa. Young Edwin Smith, twenty-one at the time, summarized the book. He included illustrations and concluded, 'We heartily commend the book to the careful study of all interested in the affairs of the Dark Continent.'[34] In the following year the same journal carried Edwin's review of M. Coillard's *On the Threshold of Central Africa*[35] and his article on Colonel St Hill Gibbons' travels in Central Africa.

Edwin Smith, with zeal, enthusiasm and not a little paternalism, looked forward to working among the Ila:

The Holy Spirit has wrought miracles in the hearts of people quite as depraved as the Mashukulumbwe . . . As we look into the future we can see thousands of them 'clothed and in their right minds, sitting at the feet of Jesus'.[36]

These articles and reviews were at the beginning of Edwin Smith's career as a literary missionary. Among his many achievements, the contribution of his writing was most notable. He penned millions of words over the next sixty years in letters, diaries, reviews, articles and books, and the accompanying research and reflection helped him to abandon the imperialistic attitudes of his youth.

When Edwin Smith set off for Africa, the Revd William Mincher wrote a short biographical sketch. He remarked that Smith was in some ways like his father but had better opportunities. Although Edwin Smith had no university education and did not learn from Dr Peake at Hartley College he attended Birkbeck College and Livingstone College and, like his father, had 'a power to form a path and resolution to follow it with a steadfastness which never wearies until the goal is reached'.[37]

The wild boy's energies were evidently channelled positively. His adventurous tendencies led him to explore Christianity, mainly with the PMs though increasingly in contact with other Christians. He read anything and everything that would help him become a literary missionary. The Bible, which he was beginning to study in depth in the original languages and in the light of contemporary ideas, became and remained a major influence. The progressive attitudes of his father and others of similar outlook were making their mark and would remain with him. He had mastered shorthand, Greek and probably Hebrew. Like David Livingstone and the explorers whom he admired, he approached challenges confidently and looked forward enthusiastically to returning to Africa, where his training would be completed by a year in Lesotho with the French missionaries.

Following Livingstone and the explorers Edwin Smith believed that 'every missionary should keep a journal, or at least a diary'.[38] He began one on leaving England on 13 August 1898. On that day he went with Julia and his mother to Waterloo station, where they met J. Murray Hofmeyr, a South African and one of Smith's fellow students at Livingstone College. Edwin then travelled with the women to Southampton. After lunch on the *Braemar Castle* Mrs Smith and Julia left, and Edwin was soon on his way back to Africa.

3

Lesotho (1898–1899)

Smith, who did not suffer from seasickness and found his fellow passengers 'a most agreeable company',[1] greatly enjoyed his voyage in the
Braemar Castle.

He had time for reading, and was glad to find James Bryce's *Impressions of South Africa* (1897) in the ship's library. The author, a brilliant
historian, jurist and Liberal politician, had recently visited southern
Africa, and both his subject and his political viewpoint appealed to
Smith. Bryce regarded Africans as inferior to Europeans but realized
that Africans would eventually dominate the region, in numbers and in
expertise, perhaps by the twenty-first century. At the same time he criticized the white man for thinking 'of the black man much as he thinks of
an ox' and for ignoring 'a native's rights when they are inconvenient to
himself'.[2]

Reading, however, did not fill all Smith's days. He joined the social
activities of the ship and, conscious of his role as a minister and a
missionary, took part in its religious life. On Sunday 21 August, he
attended an Anglican service, at which the clergyman preached what he
considered a poor sermon on Jonah. A group of Nonconformists
encouraged him to hold an evening service himself. Some good hymns
were sung and, because of the great heat, Smith only preached for 20
minutes. He thought, however, that the service went well.

The *Braemar Castle* reached Cape Town on Sunday 4 September
1898, and Smith spent a few days with his sister, Georgie, and her
family. Then, on his twenty-second birthday, 7 September, he resumed
his voyage, going around the coast as far as Port Elizabeth. A 300-mile
journey by rail brought him to his birthplace, Aliwal North, on 14
September, where he stayed for a few days with the Revd George Butt,
the Circuit Superintendent, whose son, also George, was both minister
and teacher in the circuit.

Butt senior took his young visitor around the house where he had grown up. There had been several changes. Trees had been cut down and the garden, his father's pride and joy, had been neglected. Smith was disappointed: 'no regard is paid to the aesthetic; ugly buildings are just dumped down anywhere'.[3] Such utilitarian developments contrasted with what, in his childhood, had seemed so impressive. Butt, for his part, was puzzled that Smith was going on to Lesotho instead of training at Aliwal North, where extra help was needed. There were, however, good reasons for working in Lesotho. The French missionaries, so admired by Smith's father, were well established there and familiar with the situation north of the Zambezi. In addition, though they too were Protestant, their different perspective would make a valuable contribution to Smith's training.

Nevertheless, during his brief visit Smith took note of what was happening at Aliwal North. He saw the training school which Butt had started after studying the work of the French missionaries in Lesotho. Smith watched Butt teaching and saw him in action in the industrial workshop: 'Mr B is no conventional missionary – a black coated gent with a big umbrella, spectacles, bible under arm. He works hard with his hands.'[4] He had come to Aliwal North because of his technical expertise and used his government grant of £30 per year as a master tradesman to buy equipment. The Director General of Education wanted the students to learn to design and draw plans. Butt opposed this as 'natives are no good at designing etc'. Smith qualified this by adding, 'at present anyhow'.[5]

Smith visited old friends and spent some time with the Revd John Msikinya, who impressed him greatly:

> a wonderful man; trained at Lovedale he came to Aliwal as a teacher in my father's time, and was afterwards ordained. He is a cultured man, speaking English, besides several native dialects, and being familiar with the ancient tongues.[6]

Smith did not know that he would return and spend three years at Aliwal North. So far as he was concerned he was merely passing through on the way to Lesotho, and on 17 September, he set off for Morija, the main mission station of the Paris Evangelical Mission. A long, cold, overnight journey by post cart was followed by his first, rather nervous, ride on a horse, and he reached Morija on 19 September.

At the time of Smith's arrival the Paris Evangelical Missionary Society had been in Lesotho for more than sixty-five years. Most of the missionaries were French but there were some Swiss and Italians. The dominant influence was that of the Mabille family, especially Adèle Mabille, a stately, dignified lady in her late fifties, known to the Africans as *Ma rona*, 'our mother'. Her Swiss husband, Adolphe (1836–94) had the most constructive mind in a long line of missionaries. Their son, Louis, was pastor of the Morija parish, with its extensive outstations manned by Sotho leaders. Alfred Casalis, her brother, was in charge of the Bible School. A daughter, Florence, was postmistress and ran the clinic. The Revd R. H. Dyke, husband of Aline, another daughter, was headmaster of the Normal School.

By the standards of that time, these missionaries were very enlightened. Considering themselves, and desiring the church to be, part of Lesotho they adapted themselves accordingly. Adolphe Mabille wanted a Sotho-led African Church and planned to train African evangelists and teachers from whom pastors would be recruited. He was prepared for Sotho pastors to have the same status as European missionaries 'in the pastoral office and in the future government of the Church of Lesotho'.[7] In 1898, the year Smith came to Morija and four years after Adolphe Mabille's death, such a church, the Church of Basutoland, was formed.

Smith expected to spend a year at Morija, studying Sotho and observing and participating in church life. He would then return to England to be married and to prepare for missionary service in Central Africa.

Part of his training at Morija took him into school to teach arithmetic and grammar. The missionaries were enlightened but the syllabus laid down by the Cape Colony government was not. African languages were prohibited: 'the educational value of a study of their own wonderful languages was utterly neglected'.[8] There was no instruction in gardening, practical carpentry and hygiene. Smith reflected on this years later: 'you can call this system by any name you please, but it is not education'.[9]

He was much happier with his experiences in medical work. He made his own diagnoses and dispensed medicines. He wrote to Mr Lea, a supporter of the PM Mission from Sheffield: 'I am seeking to turn to good use the training I received in medicine at Livingstone College: I am most thankful I went there, and my sphere of usefulness has been greatly extended by the knowledge I gained.'[10] He realized that a fully qualified doctor would be essential in Zambia and asked Burnett, the missionary secretary, to find one, as the medical work was very important.[11] Like many of Smith's good ideas, it took years to be realized. The doctor, Dr Gerrard, did come to Zambia but not until the Smiths finally returned to England in 1915.

The missionaries went out evangelizing from Morija on every third Sunday. On Sunday 9 October, Smith accompanied them to a hill village whose inhabitants had once been cannibals. People, many heathen, converged at 'this stronghold of Satan'. Smith was very excited and, in an article for *The Record*, described the village chief as 'a hardened heathen who is most anxious to be friendly'.[12]

Language study was the most important part of Smith's training, though learning Sotho in preparation for work in Central Africa may seem as sensible as sending an African missionary to England to learn English in preparation for going to Russia. It was not, however, as crazy as it appears because, apart from the similar structures of Bantu languages, a variety of Sotho was used in Central Africa by the Ila's overlords and neighbours, the Lozi.

Smith was taught Sotho by Akim Sello, but was powerfully stimulated by meeting (on 13 October) Jacottet, the great scholar and linguistic expert, who was examining the school. He invited Smith to visit his mission station at Thaba Bosiu and promised that there he would teach the young missionary how to acquire Ila and show him some real mission work.

There were sights to see in Lesotho, and during the school half-term holiday the young men went to the Maletsunyane and Khetane Falls. On the way, Smith noted the Sotho regard for etiquette and their puzzlement at people taking such pains ' "to go to the Falls simply to see them" '.[13] Smith and his European friends wanted to see a remarkable natural phenomenon but the Africans were more interested in the people they met and asked personal questions that were 'little short of impudent according to our English ideas'.[14] Smith was thus provided with an early example of a subject which later preoccupied him, namely, the effect of different cultural perspectives.

Smith spent a day clambering around the magnificent Maletsunyane Falls (630 feet), the highest falls in southern Africa: 'It is not too much to say we were struck dumb by the awe-inspiring spectacle . . . I cannot hope to give you an adequate idea of what I saw. To do that needs the pen of a Dante or a Milton.'[15] He and his friends also visited the Khetane Falls (430 feet), which generally attracted fewer travellers.

Smith made detailed notes of his next evangelistic outing (Sunday 30 October). He described the people, their clothes and appearance and the design of one of their huts, recording his observations without negative comment. He noted 'medicine to keep away diseases, lightning etc'. He observed hemp (i.e. cannabis) smoking and described the apparatus used by the smokers.

Smith enjoyed his life of teaching, medical work, evangelism and travel as well as language study. By mid-November he had progressed sufficiently in Sotho to make himself understood when dealing with medical cases. On Wednesday 23 November, he began preparing a sermon on Mark 2.10 in Sotho. He was also busy writing articles about his experiences as well as writing to family and friends.[16]

On one occasion Smith travelled out of the area to preach at Wepener (26 November). Though in the Aliwal North circuit, Wepener was nearer to Morija than to Aliwal North, and a visit by Smith was a convenient arrangement. He found the church leader, Hogg, at his bakehouse. Walter Hogg, an energetic Scot, had been in South Africa for seventeen years. Before that he intended becoming a missionary and enrolled at Spurgeon's college but quickly gave up the idea and returned to business. Later, when his health broke down, he went to South Africa and eventually settled at Wepener, where he built up an excellent business.[17] He led the PM cause at Wepener and maintained his missionary enthusiasm.

In South African church circles there was, at this time, a great deal of discussion about the Ethiopian movement, which was far more radical than any of the mission churches in embracing African leadership and customs. It had links with black churches in the USA, reacted to racial discrimination against Africans and led to the creation of independent African churches. The missionaries found the movement controversial and threatening, and Smith kept newspaper cuttings about it and frequently asked people for their views. It seems, however, that he did not seek the opinions of committed Ethiopians, who at that stage may not have been easy to find.

Smith asked about such things during the Christmas holidays as he travelled around the French mission stations. His tour brought him to Thaba Bosiu around lunchtime on 31 December 1898. He spent the rest of the day talking with Jacottet, and their conversation resumed the next morning until people started to come from all directions for the worship service: 'We had to do a good deal of welcoming and hand-shaking.' The service began at 10.30 a.m. with between 1,500 and 2,000 people sitting in groups under trees. Smith was introduced to a *monna moholo* (old man) who, although over 95 years of age, had walked a mile to church. At the afternoon service Smith spoke for a few minutes on 'forgetting the things that are past'. Jacottet also spoke and then the sacrament of Holy Communion was administered, the people coming forward and receiving the bread and wine from elders standing at the front. Smith learnt that the church was growing rapidly – there were 900 members and 500 new members had been added during the previous year – and he looked forward to the time when such a church would exist in Zambia.

For the rest of that day and the next morning Smith continued his conversation with Jacottet, who did most of the talking – first about languages. He explained, for example, how he had made a grammar of Serotse and Seshubia, languages used to the west of the Ila, by recording folk tales told by two students from the Zambezi; and he affirmed his deep conviction that missionaries in South Africa paid insufficient attention to language. Edwin, for his part, registered Jacottet's linguistic reputation: 'am told that he has a knowledge of 20 languages. He has a library of grammars and lexicons.'[18]

When the conversation turned to Lesotho's history, Smith's host pointed out that the French missionaries helped the country to come under British rule. He also spoke about the drink question, reporting stories about white men being drunk and policemen consuming the illicit brandy which they had confiscated. Such matters were of interest to Smith, who came from a strongly teetotal denomination and was at that time very committed to the temperance cause.[19]

Jacottet wanted a Church in South Africa for every nation, Kaffir (i.e. Xhosa), Sotho, Dutch, English. Such a view could be regarded as advocating segregation or as simply recognizing the importance of national aspirations and cultural identity. Smith was to refer to Jacottet's view many years later.[20]

Jacottet then explained his ideas on Bible translation. He believed that few men were qualified to translate the Old Testament from the Hebrew, though he considered that the Revised Version served well as a starting-point. He thought it unnecessary to translate the whole Bible: 'Found that his people read the Song of Songs more than other parts.' In his view the whole New Testament and parts of the Old Testament were sufficient. He believed that a translator should have at least five years of language study before beginning a translation and advised starting with Matthew, moving on to James and then going back to the other Gospels. Smith noted all these points for use when he would be a missionary translator.

Seen through Smith's eyes, Jacottet was an enthusiast in linguistic and cultural studies. He expressed his strong opinions fluently and forcibly. For Smith, these few days at Thaba Bosiu were the most significant part of his missionary training: 'I came away from his station fired with ambitions he had kindled within me.'[21] About ten years later he recalled this visit:

> Mr. Jacottet is one of the most erudite and versatile of men . . . It was an inspiration to sit at the feet of such a scholar. For sixteen out of the twenty-four hours we talked; at least, he did the talking, and I, except for an occasional question or remark, did the listening. I came away an enthusiast on everything relating to the Bantu, and in succeeding years have been largely engaged in following out his suggestions.[22]

Although Smith was impressed and would follow many of Jacottet's ideas, he also formed his own opinions. Jacottet's forthright views on the Drink Question soon led Smith into trouble, as we shall see.

Smith gradually worked his way back to Morija where he met J. M. Hofmeyr, his friend from Livingstone College, who was going to Malawi.[23] They enjoyed their reunion, but, for Smith and the missionary community, a more important visitor was about to arrive at Morija, François Coillard, of Lesotho and Barotseland. On 24 January Smith stretched a garland between two trees, putting the word 'welcome' on it, then went out to meet Coillard, who was accompanied by a large escort of missionaries on horseback. Coillard recognized Smith and declared, 'I never expected to see you here.' Smith was moved by the hymns, prayers and greetings on the party's arrival and the emotional meeting of Coillard and Mrs Mabille. He showed Coillard around the school and met Captain Bertrand, a Swiss officer, who came with him.[24]

Sunday 29 January was 'A great day with us at Morija', with over 3,000 people present. Captain Bertrand spoke of his impressions of the Zambezi work and of the 'Zambesias' he and Coillard had formed in Europe to pray for and support the work. Coillard then spoke 'with marvellous force and animation. He is quite a polished orator.' He addressed the chiefs and used the SVMU (Student Volunteer Missionary Union) expression, 'Make Jesus King'. He declared that when missionaries, such as Mabille, died, it was wrong to say that they had departed, for they had arrived. Smith described Coillard's sermon (on Acts 1.3) fully. Coillard explained how much had been done in Barotseland to limit the impact of witchcraft accusations. He challenged the Sotho chiefs to acknowledge Christ and called on the people to respond to the need of the Zambezi mission. About 2,000 people attended the Communion service in the afternoon, when Coillard preached on John 3.16 and about 800 communicated.

A few days later (2 February), Smith met Coillard to discuss the work north of the Zambezi. Although the PMs wanted to work near the river, Coillard made it clear that the French missionaries should pioneer the Victoria Falls area as they were there first. This, however, would become a major centre, and the PMs could move in when the population grew. Coillard thought that the railway would cross the river sixty or seventy miles downstream at a ford (Walker's Drift), and Smith gathered that there would be no objection to the PMs locating there. Smith expressed his admiration of Coillard's example and zeal, but the older man felt he had made many mistakes and wished that he could put his old head on young shoulders.

Smith made few entries in his journal for the next month. Life seemed routine. He wrote to Mr Lea of Sheffield on 19 February 1899 and explained that he and others were reading through Parker's 'Studies on Texts' on Sunday evenings. He was excused from probation examinations but was expected to study. Even in those days he had an ample library, including such books as Fairbairn's *Studies in the Life of Christ*, and needed no encouragement to read: 'I read theology steadily and regularly.'[25] He was also reading *The Life of George Pilkington* by C. F. Harford-Battersby (the founder of Livingstone College). Pilkington, a promising classical scholar, went to Uganda in 1890 and applied himself intensely to literary and evangelistic work. He used his linguistic skills in translating the Bible into Luganda but died in 1897. Smith found this story inspiring as it was so relevant to his own hopes. He thought that, if he learned one Bantu language thoroughly, he would be able to master another more easily. He wanted to make 'a comparative study of Bantu languages to some extent also, which no doubt will help me'.[26] His letter to Lea also reflected Coillard's message and SVMU sentiments, 'I have never felt Christ so near and dear to me as he is now. Oh Mr Lea "He must reign" in every heart in every land.'[27]

As well as learning from missionary experts, Smith was helped by Africans. His language teacher, Akim Sello, taught him Sotho for an hour every morning. Akim helped Smith to choose a horse. He 'paid no more than £4 for the most delightful Basuto pony that a man could wish to possess'.[28] Akim deliberately chose an animal that would only respond to being called in properly pronounced Sesuto. Thus the cost to Smith included learning the difficult q sound, for the pony's name was Qoqolosi![29] On leaving Lesotho, Smith gave Akim a Bible which remained a treasured family possession.[30]

Smith's time in Lesotho laid a foundation for his later linguistic work. He also observed the practical side of life in the buildings of the Morija mission, its houses, workshops, school and church. He was a practical man and was confident that he had, or could acquire, the skills necessary for working in a mission station in Zambia. Twenty-five years later he wrote:

> I wonder if a young missionary ever had such a delightful initiation into his work as I had. The life was brimful of interest to me. My class in the institute was devoted to me, and it was pleasant to teach such eager students. I took the opportunity of visiting the villages in company with the missionaries, and later on, alone, when I could speak to the people. My medical work took me among them a good deal, and during the holidays I rode far afield visiting nearly all the mission stations and penetrating into the interior of the country among the mountains.[31]

Satisfying and useful though it was, Smith's stay in Lesotho was curtailed by an indiscretion. A letter, in which he recounted what he had heard from Jacottet about white men being drunk, was published in the *Primitive Methodist* on 2 February and an extract appeared later in the *Express* of the Orange Free State. Sir Godfrey Lagden, the Resident Commissioner, was furious, and Smith noted, 'I have got myself into a nice mess by publicising statements without inquiring carefully into their truth.'[32] He reproached himself: 'I have never before allowed myself to publicise things without having good proof.'[33] He was summoned to Maseru to be questioned by Sir Godfrey. Smith would not reveal his source and wanted to know if his replies would be used against him. He found the interview very painful. He was told afterwards that Sir Godfrey felt hurt at the ungracious way Smith answered his questions but did not intend to proceed further. Later in the day Smith signed an apology for the officials and traders who felt aggrieved. The next day he and Goring, another missionary, visited Jacottet at Thaba Bosiu and discussed the matter with him. Another person was present, and all four signed the notes made by Goring. We do not know what the summary contained but Smith made no complaint about Jacottet and always referred to him as his revered teacher. He profited by this experience, always thereafter trying to make sure that his facts were correct.[34]

Smith felt that he had embarrassed his friends and compromised their position with the authorities so decided to leave Lesotho. Not all agreed with this decision, but it was reinforced by a request from the Revd Butt for help at Aliwal North. After six fascinating months Smith finally left Morija on Thursday 6 April 1899 with a wiser head on his young shoulders.

4

Aliwal North (1899–1902)

Instead of returning to England, as planned, and then going directly to Central Africa in 1900, Smith remained at Aliwal North. Indeed, he was unable, as we shall see, to go to Zambia until 1902, when he was an experienced minister and missionary.

His ministerial work took him around the Aliwal North circuit. On Saturday 20 May, for example, he set off for Rouxville, 22 kilometres north of Aliwal North and, with 125 members, one of the main PM centres. Despite having to ride 'Mr Butt's cart horse, a brokendown, ought-to-be-superannuated, old nag',[1] he enjoyed the ride and at Rouxville stayed with the Revd and Mrs Somngesi. They were, he learned, disappointed: first, that Somngesi, who had been accepted for the ministry in 1892, was still a probationer minister in 1899, thanks to the failure of the PM authorities to send his examination papers,[2] and secondly, that though he and his wife had been selected for the pioneer party to go to the Zambezi, he had fallen ill and been obliged to remain in South Africa.

On the evening that Smith reached Rouxville there was a church meeting for renewing the membership tickets of people from the farms. The PMs followed Methodist custom by issuing these quarterly tickets. Smith spoke and those who received tickets gave brief testimonies when their names were read out. There was also a Leaders Meeting which considered applications for baptism.[3]

All this was the prelude to Pentecost, which Smith experienced as 'a great day'. One of the services was followed by the baptism of '2 adults and 2 children, all females'. Smith addressed the candidates and the children's parents about their responsibilities and conducted the baptisms, his 'first native baptisms' in Sotho. After lunch another service was followed by Holy Communion, to which those with class tickets were admitted. Smith was impressed by the service, led by Somngesi in

Xhosa, Sotho and Dutch, with sung responses. This 'great day' ended with an evening service. The congregation filled the large church. Some white people were present and Somngesi conducted the service in Dutch. Smith's sermon on Acts 1.8 was translated into Dutch and Sotho. 'I had liberty and the translation went with a swing such as I had never experienced. The two interpreters entered thoroughly into it.'

He returned to Aliwal North on Whit Monday, a holiday. It was 24 May, the Queen's birthday. It was also, though the occasion was not, apparently, observed by the PMs, the anniversary of John Wesley's conversion. Sports were held and in the evening there was a Leaders Meeting which Smith attended. Somngesi, who came over from Rouxville, brought some Ila words for Smith from James, a worker in Zambia.[4] Smith noted them in a comparative table of Ila, English, Tonga, Xhosa and Sotho.

On another preaching trip (2 July 1899) Smith visited Zastron and conducted three services. During the afternoon service some people broke down and wept. Twenty-five years later he amplified his journal account, explaining that there was no interpreter and he could not find his notes: 'I was in a dreadful state of mind. I have always been desperately nervous in the face of an audience, even when speaking in my own language; much more so when using a foreign tongue.' He found the text in the Sotho Bible[5] and 'plunged into the sermon . . . What I said I do not know, but the people listened well and drew me on. I had not been speaking five minutes when a native woman started to weep aloud.' The emotional intensity became extreme. More women wept and one fell to the ground in a fit, so Smith brought the service to a premature close. He could neither see anything in his broken speech 'to open such sluices'[6] nor explain what had happened, and in later days Smith suppressed similar outbursts.

Some would favour such free expression of emotion as healthier and more authentically African than the controlled emphasis of Smith and other European missionaries. At such times, however, people are very open to suggestions and are easily manipulated[7] and Smith did not want the effect of his preaching to depend on crowd hysteria and altered states of consciousness.

As he travelled around Smith heard about the worsening political situation. The relationship between the British and the Dutch was strained and the British High Commissioner in South Africa, Sir Alfred Milner, was working to increase the tension and provoke a crisis. In order to prevent Kruger and his fellow Afrikaners from becoming too powerful in the Transvaal the British were promoting the position and rights of the Uitlanders, the mainly British people who had flooded into the gold-fields. At the same time they were preoccupied with the underlying issue of which side would get their hands on the gold. All in all, such a shadow was being cast over life in South Africa that Smith had to think about his personal situation.

As we have seen, he had met Julia Fitch some time before going to Africa and expected to return to England to marry her after a year in Lesotho. He now suggested to the General Missionary Committee and to Julia that she should come to Africa as soon as possible. She could then adjust to life in Africa before travelling north. Julia and the GMC agreed.

Although Julia was a mature woman of twenty-five, Edwin felt it necessary, granted the conventions of the time, to ask her parents for permission for her to come to Africa,[8] and having obtained it, looked forward eagerly to her arrival in early October. He set off for Cape Town on 29 September.[9] His train arrived early on Sunday morning (1 October), and he went to the Metropolitan Wesleyan Church to meet the minister, Mr Nuttall, with whom he discussed the wedding arrange-ments on the following evening, having spent most of the day walking around Cape Town.

Julia's ship, the *Tantallon Castle*, arrived at Cape Town as Smith went to the docks at 6 a.m. on Tuesday 3 October. Sir George White, commander of the British troops, and other officers were on the ship but Edwin only had eyes for Julia. She was escorted by Tom Raybould, another of the missionaries intended for Central Africa:

> I went aboard & had breakfast. Then we came on to the hotel: had no difficulty with the Customs. Spent morning in preparing for the wedding. After lunch Jue dressed & we drove off about two. Mr Nuttall was there & his daughter & the ceremony was soon over . . . Afterwards we returned to the hotel & after some time I took my wife for a walk in the gardens.[10]

On the previous day Smith had found some interesting papers in the library. Later, he reported that he neglected Julia for the first few days of their marriage as he studied these records. His journal, however, shows that he was not entirely neglectful and that he had exaggerated his fault. They spent a few days enjoying Cape Town and going for walks before Smith was beguiled by the archives,[11] where he and Julia copied out vocabularies made by Livingstone of languages spoken by people not far from Nanzela.

During their honeymoon Edwin and Julia visited the Missionary Institution at Wellington, 70 kilometres from Cape Town, where they met Dr Andrew Murray, famous for his books, his preaching and his involvement in the Huguenot Seminary and the Missionary Institution. Smith, impressed by Dr Murray and especially by his spirituality, included biographical information about him in an article which he sent back to England.[12]

Smith considered that, although the Missionary Institution was excellent, an ideal establishment would have a longer course of five or six years covering many subjects (e.g. church history, theology, ministerial practice, language study, Bible translation from the original languages, medicine and surgery) and providing some teaching experience. Anthropology did not feature in this ideal missionary training course, for it was only just emerging as an academic subject and Smith had yet to grasp its significance.

Edwin and Julia left Wellington on 12 October, and on 14 October reached Aliwal North, where they were to stay temporarily while preparing to set off for Zambia during the dry season, April to September 1900. Julia, who on the next day accompanied Edwin to Christchurch and the African Church, was welcomed with evident delight.

But difficult times lay ahead. The second Anglo-Boer[13] War, begun on 11 October, saw initial Afrikaner successes, and by early November 1899, Aliwal North, on the border of the Orange Free State, was full of rumours about impending invasion. The Afrikaners took the town on 13 November, to the joy of Dutch residents. With the exception of ministers, those who were unwilling to submit to Dutch rule were given fourteen days to leave, and about 600 Afrikaners remained to take charge of the town. The rest of the Afrikaner force went on and twelve days later occupied Stormberg, 65 kilometres south-south-west of Aliwal North.

African Church members, fearful of the the treatment they might expect, stole away from Aliwal North, and Europeans, anxious to avoid being compelled to fight for the Afrikaners, departed, by horse, cart and bicycle or on foot. Many Dutch residents, however, joined forces with the invaders. It was thought, nevertheless, that the war would end in two or three weeks. It continued, in the event, for more than two years.

Soon after the invasion the missionaries' house was examined by a search party. The searchers, who were cleverly steered to the Smiths' room last of all, had by this time grown tired and, being surprised to find Julia there, departed with a curse. In this way, a rifle, hidden in the roof, remained undiscovered. The missionaries, who complained to the Afrikaner leader about the search, were told that Mr Butt had been accused of supplying arms to local Africans.

Smith was unimpressed by the Afrikaners. He considered their information about the war to be lies and their system of commandeering property to be theft. The Afrikaner, he judged, wasn't 'the industrious, God-fearing brave farmer fighting for his country. We have found him to be an ignorant, thievish, lying dirty scoundrel.'[14] Although Smith often criticized the Afrikaners, he never seemed to bear any malice towards them. At times, indeed, because among them he later met many fine Christians, he defended them.

Opinion in Britain was not uniformly in favour of the war. On 24 December 1899, designated Peace Sunday, W. T. Stead wrote an article in which he argued that the war was not just and, in any case, was not being waged in a Christian spirit. He cited the treatment of prisoners, in which he considered the Afrikaners did much better than their opponents, and declared that the British had forced the Dutch in South Africa into war. Smith eventually received this article and kept a cutting in his papers.[15]

The war affected the Aliwal North circuit. There was some freedom of movement but not enough to allow visits to Rouxville or Smithfield in the Orange Free State. In Aliwal North there were fewer than half the 220 communicants attending worship before the invasion.

Smith was becoming proficient in Sotho and had been preaching in it for some time as well as using Xhosa and Dutch when necessary. He helped Julia and another missionary in training, Tom Raybould, with their Sotho studies. Moreover, Smith, who had learnt a little about teaching in Lesotho, and Julia, who was an experienced teacher, collaborated in reopening the school. Smith even learnt how to use tonic sol-fa so that he could teach singing: 'You see I'm getting on famously – having added *choir-mastering* to my other accomplishments.'[16] Among those accomplishments, as we have seen, were basic medical skills and, since the English doctor had been ordered out of Aliwal North, Smith was kept busy and his medicine chest, bought with £5 from uncle James, was put to good use. When his colleague, Tom Raybould, had pleurisy Smith was pleased to cure it before it became serious. An African lad had a fever: 'his temperature was 105 and I couldn't get it lower. I stuck at it, however, going to the location every day to see him, and at last he is quite well again.'[17]

After early setbacks, British fortunes in the war gradually changed and, with large reinforcements from home, counter-attacks were launched. Kimberley was relieved on 15 February 1900 and Ladysmith on 28 February. In the south the Afrikaners withdrew to the Orange Free State. They left Aliwal North on Saturday 10 March 1900, after wrecking and looting the railway station and government offices. On Sunday about 100 soldiers of General Brabant's Horse arrived, raced across the bridge and engaged the Afrikaner *laager* with their cannon. When the rest of Brabant's force came up a battle ensued. The towns-people converted the local school into a hospital with fifteen beds and organized themselves to look after the wounded and to supplement their rations. The graves of the soldiers who died later became an important part of the local cemetery.

Smith was glad to be rid of Afrikaner rule: 'We never want to see or have anything to do with Boers again as long as we live.'[18] He moder-ated this extreme view as time went on but was always suspicious of Afrikaner politics, which, he believed, were behind the war. In his opinion the main issue was not the Uitlander question but whether the British or the Afrikaners would rule South Africa. His experiences led him to think that Afrikaner rule would be a disaster for Africans and that therefore British rule would be preferable.[19] History has shown that Smith was right about the Afrikaners, or at least the effects of Afrikaner nationalism, but many would not share his confidence about the value of British rule in South Africa.

It was clearly an exciting time. When, however, Smith wrote about it more than twenty years later, he remarked that their problems in Aliwal North were small compared to those of people farther north 'and not to be mentioned in the same breath with what thousands of Belgians and French suffered in the Great War'.[20]

The Anglo-Boer War, as it lingered on for two more years, kept the Smiths in Aliwal North. The delay enabled Smith to gain more experi-ence as a minister and to settle down with Julia before the exacting, exhausting work in Southern Zambia.

As the threat of war died down, Smith and Raybould found, in their travels, that the people were scattered and confused and that the circuit needed to be reconstructed. It seemed, moreover, that while African and Dutch people were well served, the English were neglected and needed more ministers and services in their own language.[21] Outside the ministerial work, Smith was kept busy doing repairs and making window frames to take north; and he learnt how to make shoes, and was satisfied that he could wear them himself.[22]

Eventually there was a concentration camp at Aliwal North. Smith used to visit it but, since he wrote little in his journal during this period, we have few clues to his opinion of the later part of the war. In his old age he described the British policy of farm-burning as 'draconic'[23] but blamed the Afrikaners in the concentration camps for not attending to basic hygiene.

At the end of 1900 Smith had a holiday in Lesotho, visiting old friends and introducing Julia to them. After Christmas at Bethesda they went to Morija, where 5,000 people gathered for a special baptismal service. Several ministers spoke and twenty-three children and fifty-five adults were baptized. Nine hundred people took communion at the afternoon service. It was very impressive.[24] Smith also spoke at a service – in Sotho. He very nervous with all the experts around: 'Mr Dyke said I did very well – very correct and pronunciation and accent very good.' Smith was delighted to hear the comments of his teacher, Akim, who grasped his hands and spoke with tears in his eyes: ' "When I saw you in the pulpit I wondered who the interpreter was to be. But then I heard you speak in my own tongue. Oh sir, Oh sir, I am a happy man today!" ' 'I felt', Smith later reported, 'that I had graduated.'[25]

A guerrilla war continued, but in early 1901 the missionaries could contemplate setting off for Zambia by the middle of the year. Walter Hogg, one of the chosen group, had been back to Scotland but returned to South Africa in 1901.[26] The plan was for the Raybouls to go to Nanzela, while Smith and Hogg opened a new mission on the Zambezi at Walker's Drift. Julia, then in the early stages of pregnancy, would stay at Aliwal North until the next year.[27] Because priority was given to unloading military equipment, all their household goods from England were delayed in Algoa Bay off Port Elizabeth. But they decided that they already had enough items with them and could wait for the rest to arrive later.

With thoughts of the coming work, Smith preached at Aliwal North on 2 June 1901 on the text, 'Ethiopia their expectation', Isaiah 20.5. Ethiopia symbolized Africa. Smith realized that Africa brought hopes and disappointments. It had been damaged by wars, fear of witchcraft and the slave trade. Smith looked for a new Africa renewed, by Christ. He also suggested 'that when England has gone the way of Babylon and Rome . . . the blacks may yet be the masters of the world!'[28]

Smith and Hogg used to visit Africans in the refugee camp on the west of the town. After a farewell service there, they attended a whole series of such services around Aliwal North which proved very moving. The final Sunday meeting was so emotional that Smith did not enjoy it at all.[29]

On their way north Smith and Raybould stopped briefly at Kimberley. On hearing that Cecil Rhodes was in town, they left their cards at Rhodes' hotel and were delighted to receive an invitation to dinner. Smith treasured his memory of that meeting. The missionaries were wearing bush clothes and met Rhodes similarly attired. Everybody else was dressed formally. Apparently, Rhodes had heard about the missionaries' shabby clothing and changed from his dinner clothes. This impressed Smith.[30] It was 'the very last evening Rhodes ever spent in Kimberley . . . ', a year or so before his death on 26 March 1902.[31] Many things were discussed, including the railway, temperance and health. As Smith recalled, it was probably the 'occasion not long before Mr Rhodes' death, when, after an interview of several hours, he grasped me by the hand and said warmly: "Go on and prosper. I believe in you and your work." ' [32] Smith's meeting with Rhodes balanced all that he had read and heard about that remarkable man, and Rhodes, as he often did, left a favourable impression.

The missionaries rejoined Walter Hogg, who was already at Bulawayo, a small town with about 200 European inhabitants. They loaded their goods onto wagons, and by mid-July the party (Smith, Revd and Mrs Raybould, Walter Hogg and Daniel Mukuena) was ready to leave Bulawayo. But calamity struck. Raybould had a severe mental breakdown which was so sudden and disturbing that Smith aborted the expedition and accompanied the Rayb013;oulds to Cape Town en route for England. Mrs Raybould wrote appreciatively to the missionary secretary, Burnett: 'Mr Smith has been exceedingly kind, he has arranged everything, we have been entirely in his hands.'[33] Sadly, Raybould died in England less than three years later. Smith considered that this breakdown had been the result of excessive work. He later arranged for Raybould's affairs in Africa to be wound up.[34]

Walter Hogg, the other member of the party, went on and began working energetically at Sijoba in the hot Zambezi valley. Smith returned to Aliwal North to wait for the next travelling season. This delay must have been frustrating for him, a young man eager to get on with the job, but he used the time to continue his language studies and wrote a grammar of Sotho which, if it had not been lost, would have been his first book.[35] He also began a commentary on Mark's Gospel in Sotho.

M. Jacottet had suggested that when Smith settled in Zambia he should record Ila folklore, 'not only for its intrinsic value, but also as a means of learning the grammar'.[36] For the time being Smith studied Sotho sayings, no doubt for his grammatical work, and published his findings in a series of articles for the PM Missionary Magazine, *The Record*, as 'Sayings of the African'. In these short articles he introduced British PMs to a promising aspect of African life. Readers had already learned from the missionary at Nanzela, Revd Pickering, that African life 'is by no means attractive. The uncleanness, the dishonesty, the cruelty, the ingratitude – all this makes up a picture upon which one does not willingly dwell.'[37] Smith wanted to show another side and did this by exploring African languages:

> the languages spoken by millions of Africans . . . belong to one of the noblest divisions of language . . . these languages are soft, plaint [sic] and flexible to an unlimited extent . . . they are capable of expressing all the nicer shades of thought and feeling, and perhaps no other languages of the world are capable of more definiteness of expression.[38]

He argued that the people 'have a great future before them . . . In face of such brain power which the language reveals, the idea that they are intrinsically vastly inferior to us must be given up.'[39] Other missionaries concentrated on saving the heathen from degradation but Smith, seeing the heights already reached by Africans (e.g. Samuel Crowther, Khama, Moshoeshoe), thought it best to encourage their possibilities.

In his articles, Smith included material on Sotho proverbs and showed how preachers might use proverbs in preaching. He also looked at folktales, proverbs and names and wondered whether these sophisticated African languages were vestiges of a higher stage of civilization from which the Bantu had fallen. It may be, however, that African languages reflect a concentration of thought, energy and interest on

interpersonal and social relationships which is independent of technological development and material well-being, and that therefore there is
no need to posit a cultural and economic decline.

In the early 1900s, considerable preparations were needed for travel
to Zambia. Everything had to be assembled at Bulawayo, then trans-
ported by ox-wagons to the Zambezi and finally taken by carriers to
Nanzela, which was now Smith's destination. He relied on his father,
who always took a great interest in his work, to obtain and send suitable household goods, while the missionary committee provided useful
extra items: grist mills, doors, windows.[40] By the end of 1901 nearly
£1,000 had been spent (equivalent to £50,000, or more, 100 years
later).[41]

1902 began well. The Smiths' first child, Waldo James Thabo,[42] was
born on 2 January. Thabo, a Sotho name, means 'joy'. It was unusual
for European missionaries to give African names to their children, but
Edwin and Julia wanted to identify with their African environment.

Nanzela, their new location, had been opened in 1895 by William
Chapman, who was in England on furlough during 1900–2. Chapman
was married in 1902 and, when he returned to Zambia, he and his wife
would be the Smiths' nearest missionary neighbours, a few miles away
at Nkala.

Meanwhile, on 4 April 1902, Edwin, Julia and Thabo set off from
Aliwal North heading for Bulawayo and the Zambezi.[43]

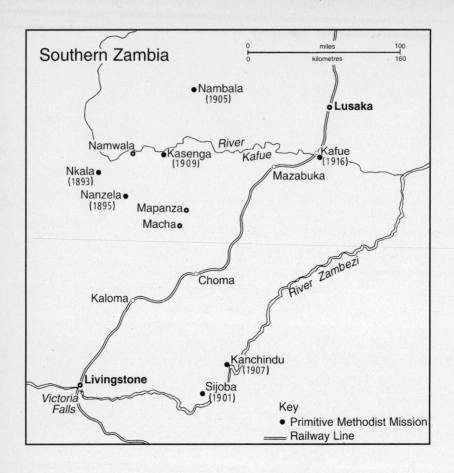

Southern Zambia

• Nambala
(1905)

○ **Lusaka**

Namwala
○

River
Kafue

Kasenga
(1909)

○ Kafue
(1916)

Nkala ●
(1893)

Mazabuka

Nanzela ●
(1895)

Mapanza ○

Macha ○

Choma ○

Kaloma ○

River Zambezi

Kanchindu
(1907)

Livingstone ○

Sijoba
(1901)

*Victoria
Falls*

Key
● Primitive Methodist Mission
━ Railway Line

0   miles   100
0   kilometres   160

5

Nanzela (1902–1907) Part 1

The Smith family went by rail as far as Bulawayo. Twelve years before, Baldwin and Buckenham had trekked from Kimberley, and in 1895 William Chapman started his wagon journey at Mafeking. These earlier expeditions took many months but the Smiths made the 300 miles from Bulawayo to the Victoria Falls in 53 days.[1]

Their party included an African teacher, Daniel Ramathe, and his family and Grey, the owner of the four wagons needed. These wagons were cumbersome, springless vehicles drawn by fourteen or sixteen oxen. They could be easily dismantled for crossing swollen rivers or other difficult places. Progress was slow because the oxen needed water and the 'road' was often rough.[2]

The Smiths' wagon was loaded high with corrugated iron. A large chest at the front (the *voorbis*) carried their food, while 'the kettle, cooking pots, a table and two chairs were tied under and on the sides of the wagon'.[3] A wooden frame laced with leather thongs served as couch by day and bed by night. To avoid the sun's heat and to allow the oxen time to graze they travelled in the early morning until sunrise and in the evening until about 10 p.m. Progress was not easy:

> Going down hill over rocky ground was rather an unpleasant sensa-
> tion, for, remember these wagons are without springs. I used to hold
> baby on the bed in the wagon while my husband held me, and he kept
> himself from falling out by planting his feet against the food-box. But
> in course of time one gets accustomed to all these little inconveniences
> and takes them as inevitable.[4]

Other inconveniences included muddy water, primitive cooking arrangements and travelling through black sand for part of the journey. The
evenings, though, were delightful: 'We would all sit on the box in front

of the wagon and feel that nothing could be compared to the calm and peace of an African forest.'[5]

They reached the Zambezi at the Victoria Falls: 'On the fiftieth day of our trek we saw signs that our trek was drawing to a close . . . we saw in the distance a huge white cloud rising between two hills.'[6] They spent a day enjoying the Falls. Smith took photographs and was 'glad to have seen the Victoria Falls before civilisation reached them'.[7]

As there was no bridge across the deep gorge below the Falls in 1902, they went four miles upstream to a drift and ferried everything across on a large steel barge. Needing to wait for porters from Nanzela, they camped near the French mission Station[8] at a small town named Livingstone. On 26 June 1902 they joined others to celebrate Edward VII's Coronation, unaware that the ceremony had been postponed because of the King's serious illness. More than forty white people and about five hundred Africans gathered[9] and Smith took part in a service which was followed by sports. He was pleased to see that some Ila men did well in the 'Native sports'.

The journey was resumed on foot. Joseph Pulinyane, the Sotho teacher at Nanzela, had sent 120 carriers for their things. At 50 pounds a man, over 2 tons of goods were carried nearly 200 miles in 12 days. Julia went by hammock and Edwin walked. He 'had been repeatedly warned by those who had the right to advise that it was fatal to try and live in the tropics without wearing wool next the skin'.[10] His advisors also suggested thick boots, rifle, binoculars, etc. A day's march through heavy sand soon convinced Smith that he had been badly advised!

The carriers regularly complained about their pay and threatened to strike if their demands were not met. Smith insisted on the standard rate, at that time about 2.5 yards of calico and one blanket, to be paid at the end of the journey.[11] The porters were testing Smith. Later, he questioned them about their behaviour and was told laughingly, 'Ushikoswe wakasukusha butale, "the rat tried his teeth on the iron" '.[12]

Smith was intensely interested in these robust Ila men and their speech: 'I thought it would be an excellent opportunity to learn something of this strange tongue.'[13] One man knew some Sotho, and Smith used this to get a foothold into Ila, especially learning the priceless phrase, *Chinzhi chechi?* ('What is this?'). 'With that question I pestered everybody . . . asking morning, noon and night, "*Chinzhi chechi?*" "*Chinzhi chechi?*" '[14] Smith was relieved to find that the people called themselves Baila and did not like the cumbersome and derogatory word Mashukulumbwe.[15]

So they came to Nanzela. The Pickerings and Chapmans were away and the Smiths' hearts sank to see the place looking 'very forsaken and desolate'.[16] In his first report to the Missionary Committee Smith remarked that all three stations north of the Zambezi had been manned by African teachers. He was unhappy about this. He had a high opinion of Africans as preachers and pastors, 'but as administrators, especially in financial matters, they are but children'.[17] Nevertheless, the school reflected 'great credit upon the native teacher'.[18]

Although Smith was very positive in his attitude to Africans, he was a man of his times and a patriotic Englishman. Nearly fifty years later he looked back and assessed his attitude when he first came among the Ila: 'from my point of view, I was indubitably, incontestably, their superior'.[19]

There is some truth in this recollection, for he was ordering Africans around, unloading his cultural baggage, introducing European civilization and dubious about African leadership. Furthermore, his articles for Primitive Methodists in Britain described the Ila as immoral and heathen. He may, however, have been too hard on himself. He was, after all, impressed by the brain power which African languages revealed.[20] But, as a patriotic and 'superior' Englishman, he was just beginning a long personal journey away from a sense of superiority.

The Nanzela buildings were on a small hill with large trees. They consisted of a small two-roomed house, some huts, a workshop and store and a church/school which seated 300 people. Some necessary renovations took several weeks to complete, then the school was reopened. Julia was impressed by Joseph Pulinyane's running of the school and, with her experience of English schools, assured Smith 'that the order is equal to anything found there'.[21]

The school was attended by about fifty pupils. Sometimes famine or other problems reduced the numbers. In 1903, Smith was pleasantly surprised 'when Chief Sezungo suggested that a number of boarders' huts should be built on the station for school children. "It is no use" said the chief, "children being here, and then returning home where they learn evil ways again. Better that they live here." '[22] Eventually, many children stayed for the school week, bringing their food with them.

The school intruded into Ila life because it took young people away from their traditional occupations of cattle-herding and out of the whole agricultural cycle from planting to harvest. This made opposition inevitable. For example, when village headmen met in 1905, ' "The speech of the day was by Mapati . . . He declared that ever since the missionaries came into the country they had been troubling the people for children . . . By the way he put it you might have thought we were ogres and lived on children." '[23] In spite of such resistance the school became established. Twenty years later more than 300 scholars were enrolled in eleven schools around Nanzela.[24]

For Julia the school was 'one of the brightest parts of our work. We are never dull because the children are always around us with their bright chatter and merry laughing ways.' The first hour was spent in singing hymns and teaching the Bible. The remaining lessons were devoted to the three Rs. Julia considered that the children were, 'superior to European children as regards behaviour'. Ila was only reduced to writing after the Smiths came to Nanzela, but in 1908 Julia observed 'that children from ten to twelve years of age could write as a composition one of their own Ila stories, and do it splendidly too, with no mistakes in grammar or spelling'. Singing was a special feature of school life: 'We often wish those at home could hear them. They take their parts splendidly, and certainly do credit to their teacher.'[25]

Julia also resumed the sewing class started by Mrs Pickering. More than twenty women, attracted by the opportunity to make and wear nice dresses, enjoyed these lessons and the conversation and singing which accompanied them. They also enjoyed having little Thabo's company, for he loved the singing, was unafraid of their black faces and smiled at everyone.

A few months after the Smiths' arrival most of the children caught measles. Joseph Pulinyane's baby, Bimbea, died and, though Edwin sent Julia and Thabo to Nkala, the little boy soon became ill. He seemed to be recovering and he and his mother returned to Nanzela 'but afterwards he took a chill, and we lost the light of our home'.[26] In her distress Julia was comforted by an African lady, Manga: 'she put her arms around me as if she had been my mother and talked to me, and although I could not understand what she said, yet it comforted me to feel that she cared and sympathized with us'.[27] Thabo died on 10 November 1902, aged ten months[28] and was buried in the little cemetery beside Bimbea. A small memorial stone with a cross marks his grave. Smith found it 'hard to have to make my own child's coffin'.[29]

After considering the situation for a few months Smith worked out three priority projects at Nanzela. The first was 'to build a comfortable house, for I knew that health in the tropics is very largely a matter of housing, and without health we could do little'.[30] He was aware of the link between mosquitoes and malaria and in 1901 had sent for galvanized netting to keep out mosquitoes and for kerosene, citing the work of Major Ross.[31]

The practical, but relatively temporary, buildings that the Smiths found at Nanzela were made from poles daubed with clay. Bricks were needed for permanent accommodation and they made some with ant-hill clay. They were unsuccessful, however, at firing these bricks and settled for sun-baked bricks, which lasted for 70 years. The brick industry began in earnest during the dry season (April to October) of 1903. They used the previous wet season (November to March) to cut trees and make planks. Brickmaking and bricklaying became major occupations. Teams of men brought water and clay, moulded the clay into bricks and laid them in rows to dry and harden. The workmen needed guidance in laying bricks because Smith's rectangular building with its straight sides was so unlike their circular houses and the winding paths and rivers. He laid the outside of a wall and his helpers laid the course of bricks behind it.

Some woodwork had been brought from South Africa, but much was done at Nanzela. Packing-cases were made into furniture. As Smith once remarked, the missionary often has 'to forsake the word of God and serve tables and not only to serve them but make them'.[32] The house had six rooms, two of them mosquito-proofed. Its thatched roof was extended by eight feet to make a verandah. It took two dry seasons to build but, when finished, Edwin and Julia 'felt as if there had never been such a house built before'.[33]

Smith was realizing

the truth of Dr Livingstone's words that a pioneer missionary must be a jack-of-all-trades and his wife a maid-of-all-work. He must be carpenter and mason, preacher and teacher, doctor and dentist, cobbler and farmer, architect and writer, judge and jury in one, and almost everything else.[34]

Smith's second project, which grew from his educational work, was 'to learn and reduce to writing the language of the people, for without that the mission could never be put on a sound footing'.[35] Sotho was not well known or accepted: 'most of the children did not understand it; a few understood it very imperfectly, and, therefore, none of them could be taught very quickly or satisfactorily'.[36] Smith applied himself to finding out the structure and vocabulary of Ila. Its intricacy and richness challenged his best abilities[37] but he persevered. The words learned by the magic phrase *Chinzhi chechi?* were noted, checked and filed alphabetically along with all the words gleaned from Smith's chattering companions on the building site.

Smith's first assistant knew some Sotho as well as Ila. Because, however, his dialect was closer to Tonga than Ila, Smith looked around and found 'a true Mwila . . . who had lived for some time at the mission'.[38] This youth, Shamatanga, impressed Smith with his intelligence, personality and eloquence. Shamatanga, from Namwala, was probably the first Ila convert. He did not wear the Ila head-cone, but with his front teeth knocked out he was distinctively Ila in appearance. Smith enjoyed Shamatanga's sense of humour and was impressed by his honesty, industry and desire for self-improvement. During Smith's first year at Nanzela Shamatanga married, settled at the mission and helped Smith with language study: 'Shamatanga is my right hand man with regard to the language.' He was willing to correct Smith's mistakes, discuss linguistic points and help him to construct a dictionary.[39]

Smith's linguistic exploration was hard work. Previous missionaries had spoken Ila but had not written it down. The Revd Pickering had described it as 'the very ugliest thing in the way of speech he had ever heard',[40] but Smith found the languages of Central Zambia 'surprisingly rich in vocabulary, and remarkably flexible and philosophical in grammar. The most delicate shades of thought can be expressed.'[41]

There were problems in learning Ila. Having heard correctly, the learner had to understand what he heard. Smith's colleague, William Chapman, had learnt the phrase for 'What is this?' He picked up a hoe, asked what it was and was told, '*Uswekonotuladibandaiamba*'. It seemed a long name. When Mr Chapman asked another man he received a longer answer. He later found that 'the first man had said, "We here call it an iamba," and the second, "And I also call it the same; there is no other name for it." '[42]

Politeness was another pitfall for the language student.

> Your African is a polite individual . . . He will not presume to correct you when he hears you make a mistake in speaking. He will rather let you go on making a fool of yourself . . . and you may go on making the same mistake for months and be none the wiser.[43]

Smith described his own mistakes. He once asked a man to remove
some maize, meaning a pile of maize cobs. However, he used the word
for maize that was still growing, so the man rooted it up and carted
it away! Again, when Smith first preached in Ila at Nkala, Chapman
asked the African teacher how he had got on. 'Very well,' was the
reply, 'only he used some words that are not necessary to be used in
church.'[44]

After a year Smith could preach without an interpreter and had made
a preliminary analysis of Ila.[45] He identified thirteen noun classifiers and
four cases (nominative, accusative, genitive and locative) and outlined
the use of pronouns, verbs and various particles. His studies enabled
him to produce Ila literature. In August 1903 he hoped to have the
Lord's Prayer, 23rd Psalm, etc. in Ila. He went on to produce a school
primer with thirty-one Old Testament stories and four Psalms. With
these, a Catechism and three school Readers, the educational and
religious work went ahead 'by leaps and bounds'.[46]

Smith then translated Mark's Gospel into Ila. Shamatanga commented on Smith's draft, and the British and Foreign Bible Society printed
500 copies of the final text.[47] The missionaries also began translating
and composing hymns: 'the astonishment of the people was very great
when we taught the first Ila hymn at Nanzela'.[48] Smith was responsible
for 78 of the 100 hymns.[49] The tunes were drawn from various sources
including Sankey and the Sotho Hymn Book. The appropriateness of
European hymn tunes to the African scene has to be questioned, though
the Africans may have modified some tunes to fit their own style of
music. Nevertheless, the missionaries were doing their best and, by the
standards of the time, their efforts were quite advanced.[50]

Meanwhile, in 1905, Smith had completed his first draft of *A Handbook of the Ila language*. His father, then living at High Wycombe,
handled the arrangements for publication in England by the Oxford
University Press. The published *Handbook* had over 250 pages of
grammatical remarks, including practical examples and suggestions for
students, followed by vocabularies, nearly 500 pages in all. It was constructed on classical lines referring to parts of speech (nouns, verbs, etc.)
and other grammatical terms such as the copula. It presented Ila dis-
junctively, i.e. the particles which make up Ila words were separated.
To take a simple example; in his 1907 *Handbook* Smith wrote, *nda
ka bona*, where *nda* indicates 'I', *ka* indicates action in the past and
bona specifies seeing as the action. The conjunctive convention, which

he adopted later, brought the particles together, writing them as
ndakabona.[51]

Smith wanted to place Ila in its linguistic context:

> For this I had proposed many notes tracing the resemblances to and
> variations from other languages, and had collected short vocabular-
> ies of the Koya, Lamba, Luba and Sodi dialects, all as yet unwritten.
> But I have been compelled by lack of space to omit this.[52]

He acknowledged help from books on other Bantu languages, including
Swahili, Zulu, Tonga and Kongo, and singled out the Revd E. Jacottet's
work on Sotho, which was formative in his study of Bantu languages.
Following Jacottet's suggestion Smith used Ila folk-tales to work out the
underlying structure. Such stories as 'The Hare Eats Lion's Children'
and 'The Tortoise and the Hare'[53] were among twenty-five folk stories
in the *Handbook*. They remain a valuable part of Ila cultural heritage.
Traditional stories are now considered important in teaching African
languages[54] – an indication that Smith's work was soundly based.

Discussing riddles was a favourite Ila pastime. Smith mentioned two
in the *Handbook*,[55] remarking that they mostly appear far-fetched to
Europeans. He also collected proverbs for use in conversation, in understanding the people and in preaching.

Smith's translation work led him to delve into African thinking and
understanding before he could put his own religious teaching into Ila.
He was learning from the Ila but was also, by his use of Ila, showing his
respect for them and their culture.

The *Handbook* was reviewed favourably in *Man*,[56] and years later
(1958) Clement Doke, a great authority on Bantu languages, regarded
it as 'still standard for the language'. He said, 'Edwin Smith showed a
sound grasp of the grammatical structure of Ila, and perhaps his greatest contribution in it was his very full treatment of the "Copula".'[57]
More recently, Ernst Wendland of the Lusaka Translation Centre of the
Bible Society of Zambia kindly gave his expert opinion on the *Handbook*. He described it as:

> a complete introductory descriptive grammar of the Ila language, one
> that includes an extensive English–Ila as well as an Ila–English
> 'Vocabulary' (I would call them both 'dictionaries' due to the quality
> and quantity of entries) . . . Smith's Handbook is incomparable and
> irreplaceable.[58]

Wendland noted that, although Smith described the language in the terms of classical language grammars, 'the accuracy (I believe), detail, and data are all present should anyone care to rewrite his results using more modern terms and a current linguistic theory'. This is possible because Smith 'dealt largely with hard, concrete data as his wealth of practical everyday examples indicate'.[59] There are those who, while acknowledging the sincere efforts of missionaries and other scholars, consider that earlier linguistic studies of African languages were too closely aligned to European-language models, so the work has to be started again, using modern (but presumably European) linguistic theories.[60] Wendland, however, was so impressed by Smith's work that he said that he would trust Smith's sample of Ila more 'than any of the typical "modern" linguistic syntactical approaches, at least those being produced for MA and PhD dissertations!'[61]

Language study was Smith's most significant achievement so far, but he had another priority project and other work to follow it.

Nanzela (1902–1907) Part 2

Smith's third priority project was evangelism, and he developed this in two ways.

His first method was to visit nearby villages on Saturdays and invite people to the Sunday service at Nanzela. Some responded and came several miles on foot. On arrival they found those who lived at the mission wearing their best clothes to mark Sunday as a special day. At that time missionaries, like other British people, took clothes, especially Sunday clothes, very seriously, and the Sotho teachers, by wearing European dress, signalled the appropriateness of clothes for Christian and 'civilized' Africans.

Smith tried to make the worship relevant by having hymns, prayers and sermon in Ila and by including African tales and proverbs in his preaching as well as incidents in people's lives. After worship there was time to discuss the sermon and the week's news, and the mission became a centre for community reflection and gossip. In the afternoon, Julia conducted a service on the lines of a Sunday school.

Smith's other evangelistic method was to hold services outside Nanzela, making day trips or weekend excursions or extended tours lasting several weeks. On these occasions, the people were amazed to hear Ila stories from books in their own language. Smith would talk about their names for God or their story about the Child of God who lived among men and was killed. He would then preach Christ. At first, however, the hearers were unresponsive and suspicious but, 'the people get to know us, and we them, and seed is sown that may be harvested in future years'.[1]

Robin Fielder, an anthropologist who came to the area in the 1960s, evaluated the PM missionaries' interaction with the Ila, mainly at Nanzela.[2] He noticed that the people around Nanzela mission were not true Ila but Lumbu who had adopted Ila ways and speech. For them the Ila were a reference group which they and Lozi migrants tried to emulate and there was an underlying Ila–Lumbu tension which remained when people became Christian.

Fielder considered that the missionaries provided personal emulatory reference groups for local people[3] by building up teams of loyal followers who had religious, educational and economic models to follow. The Lumbu, though not very responsive, were more open than the true Ila to joining a community which had leaders and followers. In addition, the true Ila were less likely to accord respect to people with few cattle. Cattle were very important in Ila culture and they would need much persuasion before considering anything that would distract them from devotion to their animals. The mission thus made less impression on the Ila than on other groups.

Smith's energetic work, especially using Ila, began a period of development for the mission, and his wider excursions broadened the mission's contacts so that the Lumbu–Ila tensions became less dominant. The Ila–European cultural divide, however, took a long time to bridge. Indeed, though the mission helped to facilitate Ila contact with European ways, which was increasing through education, trade and administration, the people remained unresponsive to the gospel.

Life at Nanzela brought frustrations, sickness, grief and joy. On 26 July 1904 the Smiths' second child was born:

on Tuesday Mrs Smith gave birth to a daughter and is doing remarkably well. The doctor was to come from Kalomo – 80 miles off but did not turn up so I had to manage the business myself with Mrs Chapman's help. She comes as 'Matsediso' – 'The mother of consolation' to occupy the place of Thabo whom we lost.[4]

Julia was unwell after giving birth and, in September 1904, she returned to England to recuperate. She took Matsediso with her and was accompanied by Mrs Chapman, who was also ill. Edwin missed Julia very much and looked forward to her return. She recovered and addressed missionary meetings in England, including the 1905 May meetings, before returning to Zambia in July. Her journey took exactly a month, for the railway now reached Kalomo, only five days' march from Nanzela. Matsi, as their little girl was always known, remained in England with relatives and grew up there.

The PM Missionary Committee ruled that the expense of Julia's return to England was the Smiths' own responsibility even though it had been undertaken under 'doctor's orders'. This matter rankled with Smith. He believed that he and Julia were being unfairly treated and applied his full literary and argumentative skills to explain the injustice they had suffered. He was still contesting the matter in 1907 when he reported dissatisfaction with the Conference's acceptance of the GMC's view that it was not responsible for the travelling expenses of missionaries invalided home by the doctor.[5] The matter was not finally resolved to his satisfaction until 1908.[6]

Medical matters were important in Central Africa. 'Every missionary must be a doctor whether he will or no.'[7] There was 'a great deal of medical work, and every day there were cases to treat'.[8] Western medicine could combat illness but it was not all-powerful, and Smith realized that Africans had medical expertise. He observed that, though Ila medicines were often charms, 'it is certain that native doctors know the medicinal uses of many plants'.[9] He knew this from experience. One day a cobra spat its venom into Smith's eye. He ran home for his gun but, since his sight was quickly affected, Shamatanga shot the snake. None of Smith's medicines relieved the intense pain. One of the Africans, therefore, fetched the local African doctor, who rubbed a preparation from the *Kabwengwe* bush around the eye and blew into it. Smith felt instant relief.

> Before, the eye was dry and burning; now the water began to flow profusely and the pain abated. For long the eye was sore but I suffered no permanent injury. They assured me that but for the old man I should have lost my eye.[10]

Alongside this local wisdom there was ignorance. Smith believed that many Ila health problems were self-inflicted through poor hygiene. Dysentery and death prevailed in one area where the water supply was contaminated during the dry season. It took a lot of persuasion before the people agreed to move nearer the Nanzela river. Smith's efforts as a hygiene reformer were usually rejected, but he hoped that the missionaries' advice would eventually be accepted.

Although physically isolated in Africa, Smith read widely. A photograph of his study at Nanzela around 1904 shows newspapers and many books. Some titles are discernible and include the *International Critical Commentary* on Romans and other commentaries. Wesley's sermons were there along with *The Philosophy of the Christian*

Religion by A. M. Fairbairn and the recently published Hastings *Dictionary of the Bible*.[11] In addition, Smith both took and contributed to the *Primitive Methodist Quarterly Review* (*PMQR*).

In April 1903 this PM theological journal carried an article by Mr W. Beckworth,[12] who criticized PM missionary work. Smith responded and in September appealed to the GMC to extend the mission. His article supported some criticisms of the work in southern Africa but answered those aimed at Zambia. Smith called for a forward policy and complained that 'the country has gone ahead, and every organisation with it, except ourselves'. North of the Zambezi 'we are faced by the astounding fact that the European staff of the mission numbers the same as when the pioneers left England over thirteen years ago'.[13] He noted the rapid advance of communications, with the weekly mail and the railway coming north of the Zambezi, and predicted the development of the copper industry and the large populations which would be attracted to the mines.

As Smith saw it, the Central African mission was being criticized as costly, remote and unproductive. He pointed out that PM mission policy was to evangelize remote places which were expensive to supply. By the time goods reached Central Africa they cost, on average, three times as much as in Britain. Moreover, it was quite normal for pioneer work to begin slowly.

In spite of the outlay Smith urged the Church to advance. The PMs, he said, had already lost splendid opportunities. The mission should now 'take possession of strategic points along the new railway', including Livingstone which, Smith believed, would become a large industrial city. In 1903 Smith expected the railway to run north of Livingstone and pass near Nanzela and Nkala before reaching 'the large copper mines in the Hook of the Kafue . . . another important sphere for mission work among both natives and men of our race'.[14] Copper mining did start in the Hook of the Kafue, but mushroomed in the 1920s around the Kafue head-waters in what is now known as the Copperbelt.[15] The railway then took a more easterly route and reached the copper mines after crossing the Batoka plateau.

Smith rightly saw the mines as places of opportunity. Surprisingly, European missionaries did not pioneer the area but, providentially, African mineworkers brought their faith from the villages to the Copperbelt. That the opportunity was exploited in the first place by Africans would have appealed to Smith.[16]

Smith also suggested that the present mission stations should extend along the Zambezi and Kafue rivers. Where these waterways met, he wanted to see 'the establishment of a thoroughly equipped technical school . . . after the style of the great institutions at Lovedale and Livingstonia'.[17] Around that time the GMC was given similar advice by Robert Coryndon, the Administrator of North Western Rhodesia, who was on leave in England in 1904. Coryndon encouraged the PMs to provide technical training and, instead of scattering many small stations around the area, to create a larger base for expansion. The GMC ignored this advice and Snelson, in his history of educational development in Zambia, criticized their shortsighted policy.[18] Without the Livingstonia type of institution the scattered stations lacked a coherent strategy and suitably trained staff. The PMs did not change their approach until a deputation visited Zambia in 1914. A training institution was then set up at Kafue, the very area Smith had suggested in 1903, and

> made more educational impact on Northern Rhodesia than twenty little mission stations each running half a dozen outschools. It is more the pity that the Kafue experiment was not begun until 1918, and was not copied elsewhere more quickly.[19]

Kafue provided trained evangelists, teachers and instructors for the mission stations. Moreover, it was near the route taken by the railway on its way north. Smith had been thinking on the right lines, but the idea took a long time to become reality.

During Smith's time in Lesotho, as we have seen, he became interested in the Ethiopian Church movement, and in 1904–5 he contributed two articles to *PMQR* about it. The first described the movement's origin and progress up to 1904. He believed that the Ethiopian Churches revealed what was going on 'in the native mind'.[20] The second paper offered a critical analysis. Smith granted that missionaries aimed to produce independent churches free of missionary control: 'The missionary, after all, is only a temporary factor in a nation's life.'[21] He felt, however, that African pastors, though great preachers and pastors, were children in financial administration. Even so it seemed to him that 'no great objection would be taken to the formation of an independent native church provided this were done in the right spirit'.[22]

Smith's main criticism of the movement was that it ran on sectarian and racial lines. He felt that African American missionaries were projecting their justified bitterness towards American whites into the South African situation, thereby fomenting racial hatred. He was also sensitive to the hurt caused to respected friends such as Coillard. Smith realized, however, that the movement provided Africans with opportunities for education and leadership which they would have missed under European control in South Africa.

When Mrs Smith and Mrs Chapman went back to England their husbands, who had seen them off from Cape Town, took a much-needed break at sea level. In early November 1904, on their way back to the Ila, they met their colleagues, Hogg and Stones, at Livingstone, discussed their work and made proposals for extension. Chapman wanted to start a new mission station north of the Kafue river. It was suggested that Hogg could start a mission farm and Smith could open another out-station. It was a stimulating time for them all.[23]

These plans suffered a serious setback, however, when Walter Hogg died suddenly on 9 February 1905, leaving a widow and four children at Sijoba.[24] It was difficult to find an immediate replacement, and although the work was continued by Ezekiel, the Sotho evangelist, expansion in the Zambezi Valley was halted for the time being.

In two of the other areas, discussion was followed by action. In April 1905 Smith accompanied Chapman across Bwila. They passed through the Mala area, went north of the Kafue river and selected a site 10 miles south of Mumbwa at Nambala. A year later Smith returned and saw how much Mr and Mrs Chapman had done. His only complaint was that, with so much practical work to do, Chapman could not consider evangelism until the mission buildings were completed. The missionaries had requested the help of an artisan but so far nobody had been sent.[25]

People drawn into Nanzela mission were involved in three types of group meeting. In the first, enquirers 'were taught what they must do and know if they wish to become real Christians'. In the second, catechumens were 'taught the first principles of religion from the catechism in Ila'.[26] In the third, members met for prayer and instruction. At first there were few members, just the Smiths and the Christians from Lesotho. Membership training went on steadily. The probationary period, from enquirer to full membership, was from four to six years, since Smith wanted converts to show 'sincerity and fidelity'.[27] These would-be Christians were trained for membership by Julia, and after her return from England plans went ahead for the first baptisms. This great event in the Church's life was held on Sunday 27 May 1906.[28]

People came from Nkala and the church was crowded. There were Ila hymns and prayers. The converts, three men and two women, were questioned, then, after saying the creed, were baptized and accepted as members. Smith and the Sotho evangelists delivered exhortations, and baptismal names were given. The men, Shamatanga, Samodike and Chikanda, took the names Pauluse, Samuele and Solomoni, and the women, Bulongo and Manga, became Maria and Matsediso. Smith's own preference, witness the names of his own children,[29] would have been for meaningful African baptismal names for each person.

On the Friday (1 June) after the baptism service Edwin and Julia set off to tour the Zambezi valley. It was time to review the position since Walter Hogg's death in February 1905. Moreover, Ezekiel Masunyane, the teacher at Sijoba, was discouraged and lonely and wrote letters in Sotho explaining his situation to Smith.

The party travelled via Kalomo and, after coming down the steep, rocky descent of 600–700 metres from the Batoka Plateau to the Zambezi Valley, reached Sijoba mission on 14 June. The mission was near the end of the long gorge below the Victoria Falls.[30] It was also close to Walker's Drift, a crossing point of the Zambezi named after Hugh Walker, who settled in southern Zambia after organizing transport to bring the police to Monze.[31]

Smith was impressed by Ezekiel's work in both school and church but considered that Walter Hogg's reports had been too optimistic. He admired Hogg and thought his efforts excellent but had a poor opinion of his linguistic performance.[32] Smith gave the matter of language careful consideration. He agreed that Ila and Tonga differed and that the Zambezi Valley Tonga differed from that spoken on the Plateau. He compared the Ila/Tonga difference to that between English dialects, say Somerset and Yorkshire. Before the advent of radio and the levelling of English dialects into regional accents this, as Smith would acknowledge years later, was a formidable difference.[33] In 1906, however, he expected Ila to become the main language of the area. His opinion, expressed in the *Handbook of the Ila Language*, that 'Ila is the most widely understood, and therefore the most useful language in North-West Rhodesia'[34] is hard to sustain. For all his sense of perspective and wide knowledge of African languages he overvalued Ila. The Tonga of the Zambezi Valley is clearly related to Ila, but the two tongues have many differences and there is much more to be said for Plateau Tonga as the main language in the large area between the Zambezi and the Kafue rivers east of Livingstone.

After a few days at Sijoba the Smiths set off for home on 18 June 1906, visiting Mwemba's area and Sinazongwe before going over the mountains and travelling via Mapanza and Mala to arrive at Nanzela on 4 July.[35]

A service was held when they called at Mala on 1 July. Afterwards, three women came and talked with Smith, having heard that he had been speaking about the Son of God and had told the story of *Mwana Leza* (Son of God) who, in the distant past, came to Lusaka, told people to stop fighting and was killed.[36] Moreover, the Smiths found that people in Mala knew about them, and that Julia was called *Mamosa*, 'the mother of kindness'.

On the strength of that visit Smith returned later in the year. He went 'for the purpose of fixing the site of the new station'[37] and chose Chitumbi, a mile from the Kafue river and two or three miles from Mala. It was about half way between Nanzela and Nambala. There were disadvantages in that the area was waterlogged for part of the year and a fully mosquito-proofed house would be essential. On the other hand, the house would be built on a spit of land which made it permanently habitable and the vicinity was well populated. Smith was accompanied by the Revd John W. Price, a new arrival in Zambia, who would be Smith's replacement at Nanzela.

The missionaries met the local leaders. Mungaila was the head chief, 'a tall, thin, oldish man, very vigorous indeed, and pleasant to converse with', but Smith questioned his sincerity. He was happier with Mungalo, 'an old man, with a face wizened and much pitted by smallpox'.[38] On the Sunday they held an informal service at which Smith, before speaking about Paul's visit to Athens, asked Mungalo about Ila names for God. Smith agreed that the Ila knew much about God but believed that they needed to know more – for example, God's holiness and love. Mungalo, he discovered, approved of missionaries because 'the Missionary is one who puts a nation to sleep'. He meant that peace came to troubled and quarrelling people, not that that they were made drowsy through boredom![39] Smith then applied to the District Administrator, A. M. Dale, for about 20 acres of land at Chitumbi.[40] Kasenga, as it was also known, would become the scene of Smith's next tour of service among those he considered the true Ila.

Smith's visit to Mala shows that he thought seriously about mission theology as well as mission policy. Significantly, he spoke about Paul's visit to Athens. On that occasion Paul had observed Athenian religion and, while respecting their knowledge and philosophy, added to it by speaking of Christ.[41] Smith followed a similar approach in Central Africa. Some might have thought this possible among Eastern religions, with their highly developed philosophies, but not in Africa. Indeed, the fulfilment theology gaining currency among missionaries was formulated in India.[42] Smith, however, was undeterred by the Ila people's apparent lack of sophistication. They had a fine language and their sayings reflected deep thought about important life issues. He adapted his message to Ila, its proverbs, etc., and to the framework of Ila thought, which he explored in depth.

In an article for *PMQR* in January 1907, for example, he offered his thoughts on Bantu religion, which he summed up as belief in God and a future life. He observed that God, under the names of *Nyambi*, *Leza* and *Mulungu* was seen as a Supreme Being and Provider. He also noticed that, although *Leza* instituted human customs, somehow 'there seems to be no connection of moral ideas with God'.[43] Again, although African prayers are made to and through the ancestral spirits, Smith noticed a few examples where the Ila prayed directly to *Leza* and concluded that Africans

> have laid hold of some essential truths. The existence of God as Creator, the need for an intermediary between man and God, the existence of a future life – these are no mean achievements of savage thought.[44]

His considered opinion was that Christian missionaries should 'seek diligently for these points of attachment and use them in the teaching of our religion . . . should ground Christian truth upon what the African has already discovered for himself . . . should follow, as far as possible his own ways of thought'.[45] Africans, though, needed to go farther in their understanding of God, and Smith believed that an ethical God would have to be introduced into African theology. His 'fulfilment theology' was a qualified acceptance of African religion, but Christianity was regarded as superior, for the 'liberal missionary creed of "fulfilment" typified the evolutionary cast of mind of the late Victorian intelligentsia'.[46]

In March 1907 Edwin and Julia returned to England on furlough. A tremendous amount had been packed into the previous few years, and it was time for change and rest. The results of this hard work were observed by the Revd G. E. Butt, Smith's former Superintendent at Aliwal North, who toured the mission in 1908 and came to Nanzela in early September:

> I began with the Mission House. The present one is the second in succession, and was built by Mr Smith. It reflects great credit on him . . . His grammar is a monument of research and industry; I go to the school and find the children reading the scripture stories he wrote; and in the services they use mostly the hymns he wrote; and then his greatest work of all is the translation of the Scripture.[47]

Unfortunately, though Julia was now a seasoned missionary who taught children, women and new converts, cultivated the garden, lived Christian kindness and was Edwin's encourager and partner in the work, there was no recognition of her contribution.

Smith had learnt much among the Ila. He still referred to them as 'savages' but recognized their abilities. He knew their language well and was beginning to understand their culture. His developing theology of mission resembled and anticipated that produced by the Edinburgh Missionary Conference a few years later in 1910. Moreover, in spite of the home committee's caution, he was eager to press on. He longed for a training institute to be started and looked forward to returning to Zambia in 1908.

7

Furlough (1907–1909)

In the nine years since Smith left for Africa, Britain had begun to change. Though travel was still dominated by railways, and bicycles were used for short journeys, in London there were motor cars and motor buses. Moreover, the 1906 election brought in a Liberal government, which 'proceeded to pass a series of social reforms which were unprecedented in scope and number'.[1] The franchise, however, was limited, though some people had multiple votes, and women remained totally excluded from voting. Perhaps most importantly, British society, still dominated by class structure, was soon to be 'subject to intense strain from forces of democracy, nationalism and economic discontent'.[2]

For the Smiths, however, furlough produced its own special stresses. Smith describes it aptly as

> that strange custom which demands that the missionary who comes back to England almost exhausted physically and mentally, and in great need of rest, should be whirled about north, south, east and west, in all weathers, cold, wet and dry, to face public audiences in a language with whose use he has become unfamiliar.[3]

It is hard, of course, to imagine Smith being idle, even given the opportunity. But quite apart from the pressure of the hectic programme, Julia probably had mixed feelings. On the one hand, having left her little girl, Matsi, in England in 1905, she must have looked forward to seeing her and other relatives again. On the other hand, she doubtless missed the warmth of Central Africa, her garden at Nanzela and her African friends.

But a furlough was undoubtedly a change, and the first part was spent in East Anglia.[4] Smith, delighted and honoured by the invitation to begin the new work at Kasenga in 1908, started to make preparations.[5]

He estimated that Kasenga mission would cost £3,650 for the first three years. The Missionary Secretary was alarmed and contacted other missionaries and missionary societies. The estimates for setting up a mission in Central Africa which they provided did not compare like for like, but the general impression was that Smith's estimate was highest by several hundred pounds. He explained why and showed that he was making economies – for example, by building the mission house himself. Smith had high standards and wanted to build a 'proper mission' at Kasenga and to do the work in the best way possible.[6] Though some may have thought his plans overambitious, he was prepared to take risks for the mission's good.

The PM Church was not rich. Most members were working-class people with modest incomes. The Central African Mission had caught the imagination in the 1890s, but fifteen years later progress seemed slow and expensive. Smith's estimate was equivalent to the total annual income of more than 30 working-class families.[7] However, Sir William Hartley, the wealthy PM benefactor, came to the rescue. He noted the estimates and offered half the proposed expenditure, whatever it happened to be between £3,000 and £4,000,[8] thus enabling plans for Kasenga mission to go ahead.

During Smith's furlough Primitive Methodism, known as a Church since 1902,[9] was celebrating its centenary as a denomination. In May 1907 a great Camp Meeting was held at Mow Cop in Staffordshire. A. T. Guttery, an outstanding PM preacher and shortly to become Missionary Secretary, was among the main speakers.[10] The celebrations took place over the next three years, and a Centenary Fund of £250,000 was proposed. Joseph Ritson's 1909 Hartley Lecture, *The Romance of Primitive Methodism*, focused on various aspects of Primitive Methodism: origins, women preachers, pursuit of learning, etc.; and a series of centenary booklets included Arthur Baldwin's *How we Entered Central Africa* and Smith's *Nanzela*.

Meanwhile, Smith travelled around Britain giving talks and lectures. One lecture, published by the PM Book Room in October 1907 and entitled 'The Secret of the African', was specifically about Ila religion. Near the beginning, citing A. M. Fairbairn in his support, Smith underlined the difficulty in understanding 'savage people'.[11] He believed, nevertheless, that, for missionaries, such understanding was essential and that the most important clue to a people's life was provided by their religion. His attitude, influenced by Rendel Harris and Longfellow, was clearly indicated. 'We shall look upon the rudest African', he wrote, 'as a brother man, a fellow-seeker for the light.'[12] Smith certainly regarded himself and other British Christians as being in the top class in God's school and Africans in the bottom class. To allow, however, that Africans were in the school at all was, at that time, a step forward.

Other observers saw Africans as hopelessly immoral. Smith had already acknowledged some bad ways[13] but insisted that there was also much 'to excite admiration and affection. You find marvellous mental capacities and many fine traits of character. And you realise that they are very far from being merely materialistic.'[14] He stressed, moreover, that 'The African looks upon the world with great awe, and for him the supernatural is as real as, if not more real than, the natural.'[15]

Smith's exposition of Ila religion began with their belief in the future life. The spirits of the dead, they believed, were found in three places: (1) beneath the earth, (2) hovering around the graves and (3) inhabiting animals. Against this background, even the apparently inhuman custom of burying a baby with its dead mother had a religious significance: 'the mother must have her child with her in the underworld'.[16]

He then discussed ancestor worship. The Ila brought prayers to respected chiefs and elders of the past and tried to keep on the right side of these ancestral spirits. There were also malignant spirits which, when manipulated by the *balozhi* or witches, wreaked havoc. Africans, therefore, believing that witchcraft caused most deaths, wanted to know, when a person died, who bewitched them; and the culprits, when discovered, would be executed.

> And so for one natural death, one other person, and it may be as many as ten persons, are killed in suspicion of having brought about the death by witchcraft . . . It has been boldly stated that the belief in witchcraft has been responsible for more deaths in Africa than even the slave trade in all its horrors.[17]

Smith saw no reality in witchcraft. Like other European observers, then and probably now, he regarded the subject as 'superstition'. Therefore, so far as he was concerned, *all* who were punished as suspected witches suffered injustice.

Smith went on to discuss the Ila concept of a High God whose chief name, *Leza*, was related to rain in that, whenever a rainstorm was imminent, the people would say, '*Wa wa Leza*', 'God is going to fall'.[18] Although *Leza* was closely associated with natural forces (e.g. wind, rainbow, thunder and lightning), he was distinct from and superior to nature. Personal names were given which showed him as 'the Creator and Sustainer and Owner of all things'.[19] *Leza*, though, was not seen as a moral God nor as being near: 'God, they say, is far removed from them. He knows nothing of them, their troubles and needs. Hence they pray to the mizhimo.'[20] These *mizhimo*, the spirits of the departed, were regarded as intermediaries between God and man.

It seemed to Smith that *Leza* resembled the Old Testament God who, as he saw it, was a tribal deity. The difference was that the Hebrew God was also holy and demanded righteousness. Smith felt that missionaries must follow the Old Testament prophets by proclaiming the moral demands of a God who is near.

He then discussed whether the *Mwana Leza* (Child of God) belief among the Ila began with David Livingstone, whose travels had taken him near Bwila, or whether, as he suspected, it was more deeply rooted in tribal lore.

Smith's treatment of Ila religion led him to consider missionary method. He continued to expound 'fulfilment theology':

> We seek to ground Christian truth upon what they already believe. We recognise there are true and false elements in all their beliefs, and while rejecting the false, we use the true as foundations for purer belief.[21]

He repeated that, difficult though it might be to achieve, a proper understanding of Ila ideas was basically important:

> you must be saturated in native lore, must know their customs and religious beliefs. You must have the power of seeing things from their point of view.[22]

After nine years in Africa Smith considered that he was just beginning to preach properly. He believed that many Ila beliefs would make good points of contact between African religion and Christianity but was convinced that Ila religion needed a stronger ethical content. Ila moral ideas were mediated by custom and taboo. Evil customs were kept firmly in place by tradition. Smith believed, therefore, that a change in their religion, the master tradition, was vital. He concluded his lecture by pointing out similarities between Africans and our Teutonic ancestors. Christianity opened a new chapter in British history which Smith saw as 'the beginning of that upward march that has placed the Anglo-Saxon race in the forefront of the nations of the earth'.[23] These words may seem to indicate a British superiority complex. It is clear, however, that Smith, who saw his forefathers' potential as having been realized through Christianity, is simply expressing the hope that Africans may have the same experience:

> They too, have magnificent possibilities. They are not always going to be hewers of wood and drawers of water . . . They have considerable mental powers. The languages they speak bear witness to that. They have the religious instinct. What they need is deliverance from their fears of the unseen and from the tyranny of custom, the purification of their religious conceptions, and above all, a moral regeneration . . . In a word they need Christ – the universal Saviour. He is Africa's only hope.[24]

The tone is condescending and reflects the ideas of social evolution. For all that, there is an underlying affirmation of Africans.

Smith's thinking can be located in its missiological context by comparison with that of another Primitive Methodist, A. S. Peake. Peake was a formidable, progressive scholar and a friend of A. M. Fairbairn. In March 1906 Peake addressed the Hartley students on our 'Responsibility to Inferior Races'. Peake opposed exploitation and racial prejudice, for 'in Christ all distinctions of race and colour are completely and for ever done away'.[25] He did not, however, allow the heathen any part in mission. As 'inferior races' they must have the opportunity to receive England's best. Peake's benevolent paternalism was progressive at the time. There were those who did not think that 'inferior races' should receive anything except exploitation. Hence, education in Africa was almost exclusively offered by Christian organizations and almost totally neglected by other agencies. Nevertheless, a one-sided missiology, as Peake's seemed to be, will ultimately be regarded as a variety of cultural imperialism. Smith's ideas were more advanced. His thinking already included respect for Africans.

Smith's ideas resemble those presented at the Edinburgh Conference of 1910, which he was unable to attend. Many delegates believed that points of contact with Christianity could be identified in what were known as animistic religions and, as examples, they mentioned belief in a higher Power, the immortality of the soul, sacrifice, the need for a mediator and the use of prayers.[26] Smith was already thinking on these lines in 1907, as were some who, from 1908 onwards, were preparing submissions for the Conference. However, in African missions the strong tendency towards cultural imperialism continued almost un-abated, and the ideas mooted at Edinburgh did not make the headway that might have been expected.[27]

Julia, who was delighted to receive a copy of Edwin's *Handbook of the Ila Language* in April 1907,[28] in the next year wrote a book herself, *Sunshine and Shade in Central Africa*. Addressed to young people and children, and illustrated by Edwin's photographs, it described the Smiths' journey to Nanzela and their life and work there from 1902 to 1907. Julia always enjoyed recalling that, though Edwin wrote many books, her book sold much better than any of his![29]

During the furlough Smith was busy, as always, reading and writing, and he contributed several articles to *PMQR*. Some were extended reviews of missionary biography: Coillard (July 1907), Holman Bentley,[30] George Grenfell,[31] and Stewart of Lovedale.[32] Smith's vision for Kafue, it should be stressed, was modelled on Lovedale.

> The future is with these Dreadnoughts of the mission-field. Every mission should have its hospital, printing press, workshops, etc., under highly trained men; then subsidiary stations in the country around . . . Such was Stewart's ideal.[33]

In these articles Smith brought models of good missionary practice before thoughtful Primitive Methodists.

Finally, in July 1909, *PMQR* published an article entitled 'Uganda: A Fairy Tale'.[34] Here Smith reviewed *Eighteen Years in Uganda and East Africa* by A. R. Tucker, Bishop of Uganda. The missionary methods in Uganda followed the principles of self-propagation, self-support and self-control and carefully avoided making 'white Africans'. Smith was particularly impressed that the Bishop 'prohibited his native teachers and evangelists from wearing European clothing, and induced them to adopt the simple flowing white Kanzu of the Arabs'.[35]

Smith, who was becoming interested in anthropology, was disap-pointed that the Bishop showed no interest in the subject and did not 'increase the world's anthropological lore by a single new fact'.[36]

However, anthropology in Uganda was already being tackled by the Revd John Roscoe, whose researches were published in 1911 as *The Baganda*. If Smith had realized this, his praise for the Ugandan Church would have been even greater.

These articles helped to build Smith's reputation as a missionary expert in African matters. They also show his interest in biography, linguistics and missiology and the beginning of his interest in anthropology.

Meanwhile, Smith's colleague, William Chapman, the most experienced PM missionary in the Central Africa field, had prepared during 1908 a report on Mission Policy. He argued that John Fell, who had just come to the Zambezi Valley, should close that work and move to Bwila. Chapman thought that Ila and Tonga differed as much as English and Dutch rather than two English dialects. He saw little point in the mission using two languages[37] and believed that it would be better to concentrate on one area. Nevertheless, the work in the Valley continued, thanks probably to John Fell's rugged determination.

The long negotiations and preparations for opening the new mission at Kasenga delayed the Smiths' return to Africa, and they spent the second half of their furlough at Swinton, between Doncaster and Barnsley, in the Mexborough circuit in South Yorkshire.

They were reminded of Africa, however, not only by recounting their experiences but by letters from friends and colleagues. There were several from John Price, one in Sotho from Kemuel Mahiritona and another in Ila from Pauluse Kaiyobe (Shamatanga). Pauluse mentioned hunger and some deaths in the area and passed on greetings. A. M. Dale, who also wrote, apologized for not writing, referred to the hunger and sent a cheque for the new mission.[38]

Near the end of 1908 it was decided that Kasenga mission could go ahead and the Mexborough circuit was asked to release Smith at the end of March 1909.

Smith's diary for 1909 has survived and gives details of his last weeks at Swinton. As well as taking Sunday services he gave lantern slide lectures, and various topics, noted on Fridays, may indicate his involvement in a literary and debating society: 'Can a man be a Christian on £1 a week?', 'Are Civic duties Christian duties?', 'Should women engage in politics?'[39] He also travelled to many places outside the circuit. His visit to Southport, from 31 January to 2 February 1909, took him to Sea View, the home of Sir William Hartley, to discuss plans for Kasenga.[40] Smith was also busy securing estimates and making orders. Calow, a pharmacist from Redcar, prepared a list of medicines to give the mission. Smith ordered tools, a water cart and other goods from Allisons, the main suppliers to the PM Mission. Then there were enquiries about a magic lantern as well as an appeal for £50 for a horse.[41]

On 31 March they 'had a splendid send off at Mexbro'[42] and on 1 April left Swinton. A good crowd gathered at the station and Smith arranged for one of the members to sell his bicycle. The impression made by Smith's short time at Swinton can be judged from the circuit's continued support for African missions. Five years later, 1913/14, PM circuits in Britain devoted 44.6 per cent of their missionary giving to the African Fund. In the Mexborough circuit, however, this was 58.4 per cent, and at the Swinton church, 71.7 per cent.[43]

The Smiths spent a few days in Norfolk, staying first with relatives at Gorleston, near Great Yarmouth. The air was bracing – 'Quite a change from smoky Swinton' – when Edwin, Julia and Mary[44] walked along the cliffs.[45] On 3 April, after Smith weighed in at 13st. 2lb. 8oz. (83.7kg.) in the market, they left Yarmouth and stayed with cousin Frank[46] at Blofield, about six miles east of Norwich. They also saw Smith's cousin Wilfred, a vet, who advised him on the care of horses and cattle.[47]

Their end-of-furlough travels took them on to Norwich for the wedding of Smith's brother Fred. Edwin Smith officiated and Matsi was a bridesmaid. After a couple of days at Norwich with Uncle James, a generous supporter of his work and an ardent PM,[48] they returned to Gorleston and stayed there until 13 April. Then Smith went to his father's home at Bush Hill Park in North London, near Enfield, to make more arrangements in London. He ordered newspapers and magazines[49] to keep him well informed about the social, political and religious world when he returned to an isolated part of Africa. There was also precious time with the family. They went to the zoo and Matsi, who saw everything and rode on an elephant, was delighted by the outing.

Then it was time to return to Africa to open Kasenga Mission. Smith's father accompanied them to Waterloo Station on 17 April. He was deeply moved and 'prayed beautifully' for them. They would never see him again. The train took them to Southampton, and 'Marie & Matsi & Mr Allison & Chapman came to the boat.'[50] Matsi, who 'stood and waved as long as the boat was in sight', stayed in Britain and would soon attend a boarding school in North Wales. For Julia the parting from her little girl was 'with much inward suffering'.

On setting off again for Africa Smith is reported to have said:

I go back to Africa without any illusions . . . I know the heartbreaking indifference to higher things we shall find at Kasenga. I know the exhausting labour, I know the weariness, lassitude, the sickness that are inevitable in such climate . . . I know it all and we have counted the cost. We put our trust in God and hope to lay the foundation of a mission that shall be fruitful of much in years to come.[51]

8

Kasenga Part 1 (1909–1910)

Progress was slow in Zambia. Around the time the Smiths returned, the PM Mission had only made about 15 full members, though 350 were registered as scholars in the schools,[1] and missionaries engaged in such work needed to be tough, resourceful characters. They needed, too, to be ready for conflict, for there was tension between the two areas covered by the mission. As we have seen, William Chapman's report on the Central African work[2] suggested that John Fell should abandon the Zambezi Valley mission, move to Ila country and learn the Ila language. Fell was neither impressed by this suggestion nor helped by Smith's Ila book in learning the language of the Valley Tonga.[3] Nicknamed *Sianguzu*, 'man of strength', Fell remained in the Valley and settled in Mwemba, where he started a school and wrote a Tonga grammar. However, there were always more PM missions and missionaries among the Ila than among the Valley Tonga in their isolated, hot Zambezi valley.

No other missions encroached on the remote areas selected by the PMs, but several settled on the plateau between the Kafue and Zambezi rivers. The Seventh Day Adventists started at Rusangu near Monze on 1 July 1905,[4] and the Jesuit Fathers settled nearby at Chikuni on 14 July 1905.[5] In the following year the Brethren in Christ, Americans from the Anabaptist–Mennonite tradition, founded Macha Mission 65 kilometres north of Choma. Finally, in May 1910, Bishop Hine of the Anglican Universities' Mission to Central Africa (UMCA) came to Livingstone[6] and, in March 1911, more than a year after Smith had suggested the site to the PM Mission,[7] the Anglicans opened a mission at Mapanza, about 20 kilometres north-east of Macha and near the southern borders of Bwila.[8] Three hundred kilometres to the west the Paris missionaries had been working among the Lozi since 1885.

The region, known in 1899 as North-Western Rhodesia, was

administered by the British South Africa Company from Kalomo until 1907 and then from Livingstone. Northern Rhodesia (now Zambia) became a political entity in 1911,[9] by which time the white population had risen from 100 in 1898[10] to 1,497. Of the Europeans over twenty, only 15 per cent were women,[11] and the only white people in Bwila were a few missionaries, officials, traders, prospectors and police/soldiers. Smith met administrative officers and was friendly with Andrew Dale, the Company magistrate at Namwala, who arrived in the territory in 1904.[12]

Although European influence was growing, the African people – the Ila around Kasenga, the Tonga on the Plateau and the Zambezi Valley and the Lozi to the west – were the chief social forces in the area.[13]

Smith's linguistic studies had already given him some understanding of the Ila people. In his next period of service he extended his grasp of their culture. The Ila-speaking peoples – a population estimated at 60,000 – were scattered over a wide area and, in marked contrast to the Europeans, women outnumbered men by three to two. Smith and his friend, Andrew Dale, gathered information from a wide area but regarded the 8,000 people near Kasenga as the most truly Ila of all.[14] All these peoples, however, spoke Ila, a variant of Tonga, and were distinctive in appearance. They wore little clothing, but men often boasted pointed head-dresses over one metre in height and adults had their upper front teeth knocked out.

Socially, the Ila were held together by common customs and kinship groups as well as by language. For practical purposes, smaller, though sizeable, regional units, the *shishi* (sing. *chishi*), gave a greater sense of belonging. Here, people lived in circular villages of thatched huts, some with more than a thousand inhabitants. Although people of one *chishi* might fight those of another, there were also shared kinship relations. These operated through clans, usually named after plants or animals. Clan members were spread throughout the *shishi* of Bwila. Fellow clan members regarded each other as kin: 'In old-time battles, if a warrior recognized an opponent to be a clansman he would refrain from attacking him.'[15] Marriage was always outside of the clan and was part of another social unit, the *Mukwashi*, the household or extended family group. Complex rules governed lineage and were tied up with a belief in reincarnation whereby certain ancestors returned in people of their own line.[16]

The Ila were fierce fighters and brave hunters. Their country was blessed with an abundance of game and the rivers swarmed with fish. They had various techniques for hunting and fishing.[17] They also practised agriculture and grew maize, sorghum and millet, which were stored in bins (*matala*), raised on stilts above the ground. Their staple foods were *inshima* (a stiff porridge) and *mabishi* (sour milk). The flour for *inshima* was prepared by a laborious process of stamping grain in a large wooden mortar. Meat, fish and various vegetables were cooked and made into a relish to eat with *inshima*. Sometimes, when the rains failed, there were food shortages, but never total starvation.

Cattle were important in Ila life and were so highly valued that it was thought cruel to use them as beasts of burden or for ploughing. Each animal was named, and much time was spent in looking after them and discussing them with friends. Cattle had secondary uses as producers of meat, milk and manure, but primarily they were 'a means of building up relationships, of acquiring influence over persons, and over the spiritual world by means of exchange and ritual involving cattle'.[18]

Interpretative anthropologists write much about the interaction of world views[19] and Smith provides an interesting example of how an individual can be affected. As he studied the Africans, his respect for them grew and he was being changed by the encounter. However, what about the Ila? How did they see and respond to Europeans? Clearly, Europeans had various agendas. They were obsessed with gadgets for hunting, thinking, travelling, measuring, treating sickness . . . In addition they brought new ways of transacting business and obtaining services (porterage, wages, money). It was thought, moreover, that Europeans came from Bulawayo[20] and obtained their goods cheaply from the seashore, where monsters had thrown them, and then sold them to Africans at high prices.[21] European reports of houses taller than three or four trees on end were considered fictional.[22] However, the first reactions of many Europeans to technological innovation, for example the railway and the aeroplane, show that these African judgments were not extraordinarily unreasonable.

The European was observed carefully. Was he a brave person? What was his clan and who were his ancestors? What power did he have with unseen forces and could he influence the fall of rain? The European missionary was a strange character. Does he

mean to make us slaves by and by? Perhaps his own country is no good, so he has come to live in ours. He may be a bad fellow; his own people may have driven him away. What is he going to get out of us? For surely some ulterior motive must influence him![23]

Whatever the Europeans' intentions, it was clear that they were going to stay for a long time and that their ways would need to be accommodated. It was therefore important to test the technical, spiritual, medical, agricultural and economic changes being introduced by Smith and others.

When Edwin and Julia returned to Central Africa, they spent a few days with Andrew Dale, who was based there at the time. Dale told Smith that Ila was being used widely. Apparently, it was becoming the language of the Batoka plateau. Anderson, the Seventh Day Adventist at Rusangu, was said to be using Smith's books.[24] Such reports about the wide use of Ila were, however, misleading. The Tonga inhabitants of the Batoka plateau, with their linguistic facility, probably responded in Ila when it was spoken to them, but it was not the area's main language. Smith seems to have heard the news he wanted to hear.

On 15 May the missionaries set off on the relatively short rail journey of 120 miles to Choma. It was nearly midnight when they arrived, to be met by Pauluse and Solomoni, who were 'glad to see us and we to see them'.[25] The following day was spent catching up on Nanzela news. After two years in England, Smith felt that his Ila was so rusty that he could hardly put a sentence together.

They spent a few days at Choma surrounded by boxes and baggage, preparing for the journey to Kasenga. Forty carriers arrived on 20 May and set off with their loads the next day. Edwin rode a horse and Julia went by hammock. After four hours they came to Walker's farm. This was the Walker of Walker's drift who came north in 1898.[26] He told Smith about his life in South Africa, offered advice about farming and donated some seeds. He arranged to bring the heavy goods to Kasenga by wagon.

The journey across the flat plateau through the dry bush took just over five days. On 25 May they reached Mala, where they were met by Mungalo and Mungaila, the local chiefs. When, on the following day, they looked at Chitumbi, the proposed site of Kasenga Mission, Smith was dubious: 'our first day's experience leads us to say we don't like it at all'.[27] The problem was that it was cut off by *vlei* (i.e. flooded ground) for much of the year and was a mile or more from the people. However, the authorities (i.e. Dale) would not allow them to settle anywhere else and Chitumbi had space for many buildings and a boarding school.

Smith was unwell with fever on Sunday 30 May but managed to hold the first service at the new mission. Some workmen came and a few Baila from the *lutanga* (cattle outpost) across the river. In the afternoon Walker arrived with his wagons and the Smiths' water cart, which rumbled in thunderously. Walker made no charge for bringing baggage and fruit trees and agreed to cut poles for building.

Building was again the first priority. Walker and Pauluse spent a day getting 257 poles, but Smith complained that many were too slender. He and his workmen built a 'grass shanty', about 12 feet by 8 feet, as a temporary residence which Smith declared 'very pleasant and cool during the day but too draughty at night'.[28]

All the time Smith was observing Ila attitudes and customs. On Friday 11 June, he was looking for good *bulongo* (clay) to plaster the walls of his buildings. He had heard that clay from a nearby ant heap was *tonda* (taboo). By this time Smith recognized and respected this aspect of Ila life. He noted several sacred places in the area including a big fig tree, said to be inhabited by Shimunenga, the local demigod. The missionaries were still feeling their way with the local Africans. Saturdays and Sundays were spent in announcing and holding services. There was always time for discussion and friendly conversation after the service. On Sunday 20 June, at Mungaila's village, Smith explained that the lads at the service were the sort needed for his school. The discussion ventured into sensitive matters when Smith's hosts asked if they should *senana* (lend wives to each other). This angered him but he was told it was only a joke. Smith's reaction did not spoil his overall relationship with them.[29]

As Mungaila accompanied him on the way home, Smith asked about a clump of trees. He was told that *Imbulumukoma*, a great two-headed snake, lived beneath them. It appeared in time of war. Smith noted that this creature was like *Itoshi* the fabulous water monsters of the rivers.[30]

When Mungalo visited the mission on Tuesday 22 June, Smith asked him about customs. Mungalo said that he knew nothing of the ant heap being *tonda*, but even if it were he could give permission to use it. Mungalo regarded Smith as a *mwami nina* (fellow chief) and was very informative about kinship, Shimunenga and related matters.

The Smiths were learning African ways, but they also had a sense of their British identity and fed it with reading matter. Julia enjoyed reading[31] and Edwin gave her all Scott's novels for her thirty-fifth birthday (6 July). They kept in touch with British and PM news through papers and other literature from home.

Building continued steadily, since the cold dry season offered ideal conditions for the work. The house, which was only intended to provide temporary accommodation, was made of poles, wattles and layers of plaster, and photographs and a sketch plan show that it consisted of a semicircle of connected thatched buildings.[32] It was, in fact, more like an African residence of several huts than a European house with several rooms under one roof.

On 7 August Smith began to arrange his study, but it was not until 22 August, after finishing the house and working on the school, that he began translating Matthew's Gospel into Ila. By October he had established a more settled pattern of study.

> Before 9 I do German. From 9–10 Bible study and am doing Ephesians now. Then rest of time am on with my article on 'African folk-tales'. In afternoon I continue this article, as soon as it is done I shall devote that time to translation.[33]

The article reviewed E. Jacottet's book, *Treasury of Basuto Lore*, vol. i: *Folk-tales* and introduced Jacottet's work to *PMQR* readers. It also set out some of Smith's ideas on the subject and these were crystallized later in a chapter of *The Ila-Speaking Peoples of Northern Rhodesia*. He mentioned an incident from the period:

> During the writing of this paper my old friend Mungalo, one of the Kasenga chiefs, came into my study and presently our talk turned to the subject of Sulwe. I made no attempt to write, but simply watched the old man's face as he told the tales. Speak of eloquence! Here was no lip-mumbling, but every muscle of face and body spoke; a vivid gesture often supplying the place of a whole sentence. Sulwe lived before us.[34]

Perhaps this was on 10 October when Mungalo attended a service at Chitumbi. Smith had known Mungalo since 1906 and the two became such firm friends that Smith dedicated his famous book *The Golden Stool* (1926) to Mungalo's memory. Mungalo was one of Smith's main informants in his study of the Ila people[35] and he was always grateful for Mungalo's help in understanding the African's soul. Smith expected to hear his greeting, '*Mulongwangu*' (my friend) on arrival at the pearly gates of heaven.[36] The old chief died in 1911.[37]

Smith translated Matthew in earnest and by 24 October reached the end of the Sermon on the Mount and declared, 'How I chafe at the restrictions of language! Quite impossible (for me anyhow) to render satisfactorily the great words of the master.'[38] He worked quickly, and on Thursday 25 November:

> This morning I completed the first draft of Matt. After dinner read chap 1 and part of 2 with Pauluse & then typed it in triplicate. Before reading with him I am carefully revising it word by word with the Greek.[39]

The missionaries clashed frequently with the General Missionary Committee. The problem lay with the organization of PM missionary work. For PMs, mission was one, whether at home or overseas. Theoretically it was a good principle; in practice it worked badly in Central Africa. The Missionary Secretary was responsible for many mission projects in Britain and Africa. Each was a separate circuit answerable to the GMC. Since Central Africa was so far away and communication was slow, trying to administer the similar Central African circuits from London was cumbersome and confusing. There was plenty of room for misunderstanding and it was easier and much quicker for the missionaries to share ideas among themselves rather than consult with the GMC. Smith had clashed with the GMC before, and there were more disagreements during his second period in Zambia. The new Missionary Secretary, the Revd Arthur T. Guttery, was highly regarded in Primitive Methodism. Like Smith, he was a minister's son and enjoyed debates at Elmfield College. Some people wondered whether he would succeed as an administrator. However, Guttery's biographer, J. G. Bowran, considered him a very successful Missionary Secretary. He opened a new mission station in Africa every year, and giving to African missions increased by 45 per cent during his five years in office.[40]

Nevertheless, Smith clashed constantly with Guttery, who soon expressed the Committee's anxiety at so much money achieving so little. Smith, for his part, tired of explaining the high cost of living in Central Africa and continued to press for a Training School at Kafue.[41]

He wanted faster progress than the GMC would or could allow. Smith appeared extravagant, but he saw the opportunities and where they were being missed, and his judgment was usually correct. A. T. Guttery became President of the PM Conference in 1916 and died in 1920, the same year as his Hartley lecture, *Christian Conversion*, was published. He was acknowledged as a great preacher, but his book shows no sign of interest in world mission.

Education was important in the mission's programme. On 6 November Smith put seats in the school building and on Sunday 7 November, a service was held, followed by medical work, still part of missionary activity. On the following Sunday he remarked that 'the school looks very nice. Lofty – seats leave plenty of room. Table on platform. Pictures hung all round walls. Very cosy and cool, I hope.'[42] The school started on Monday 22 November, and on Thursday Smith recorded that the boys were 'very enthusiastic about the school. They are very attentive and try hard to learn . . . They have built themselves huts.'[43] On the next Monday there were twenty-one pupils and by the following March forty-three boys attended school.[44]

Smith was assisted by J. K. Liphuko, an energetic Sotho teacher/ evangelist who had made good progress at Shamakunki (10 miles from Chitumbi). When Smith visited him on 25 October he was building a house and a school.[45] They discussed Sotho and Ila customs. Smith noted in his diary that Liphuko, 'Says when man becomes Xn puts away all old customs.' But, as Smith commented, 'surely not necessary – some are good'.[46]

This observation came as Smith started his serious research into Ila culture. He was already looking for points of contact between the Christian faith and African religion. Now he would go further into the social background of Ila life. Not everybody valued Ila culture. Smith's heritage as a PM, however, included respect for human rights as well as Puritan morality. PMs would have valued the Ila as fellow human beings, while being outraged by their morality and religion. Smith's colleague, the Revd William Chapman, agreed that some customs were good but saw the Ila as 'a naked, cruel, superstitious and immoral savage'.[47] He criticized polygamy, killing ('it was considered an honourable thing to have killed a fellow man'),[48] witchcraft[49] and nakedness.[50] Not many years later the missionaries of this generation would require baptismal candidates to reject praying to ancestral spirits, smoking hemp, witchcraft, mutilation of the body, etc.[51] In view of such attitudes, Smith was monumentally restrained and understanding, and helpfully dependent upon anthropology.

He became an Ordinary Fellow of the Royal Anthropological Institute (RAI) in 1909. About ten clergy, including Canon Sanday, the biblical scholar, were found among the membership of nearly 500. The Institute published a journal of its proceedings and the journal, *Man*, and these publications reflect the interests of British anthropologists. From 1907 to 1910 they included items from Africa by the Revd John Roscoe (Uganda) and the Revd W. C. Willoughby (Botswana). Anthropologists were taking an interest in Africa and missionaries were among the pioneer observers. How Smith became interested in anthropology remains uncertain, but he seems to have seen it as a necessary extension of his linguistic studies. His Ila *Handbook* was favourably reviewed in *Man*,[52] and, Smith later reported, 'it was not long before the truth . . . was forced upon us that speech can only be learnt in its cultural context . . . '.[53]

The Ila-Speaking Peoples shows that although he used informants, Smith also visited villages, observed industries and crafts and took photographs. He had already been studying the religious aspect of Ila life, had analysed folktales, a significant aspect of ethnographical study, and boasted a sound knowledge of the language. The views of influential informants were thus variously counterbalanced. On 15 August 1909 he recorded his impressions of a visit to a funeral in 'Antho. notes'.[54] This is the first indication of Smith's anthropological researches, though he could draw on his Nanzela experiences to supplement his work.[55] He and Dale read anthropological literature and

> as amateur ethnographers were very strongly influenced by Sir James Frazer. His little collection of Questions became for us a golden string leading through the maze of African life. We devoured *The Golden Bough* and the volumes on *Totemism and Exogamy*.[56]

After Dale left the BSA Company 'in 1910 and settled on a farm within sight of the Kasenga Mission',[57] he and Smith had plenty of opportunities for consultation. When Frazer's *Totemism and Exogamy* appeared in 1910, they could check his theories by their own observations and, so far as the Ila were concerned, find them wanting.[58] This shows that although the theoretical basis of their anthropology, derived from Frazer and Tylor, would soon become obsolete, their great advantage

over the armchair anthropologists was their thorough, firsthand observation. They were 'assiduous note-takers'[59] and made complete records
of all they saw and heard.

Though his life was filled with many activities, Smith's second tour
among the Ila led him into the cultural exploration that would establish
his reputation as a missionary/anthropologist.

Kasenga Part 2 (1910–1915)

In early 1910 Smith wrote, 'The Kasenga Mission, so long the object of hopes and fears is now an accomplished fact.'[1] With a European readership in mind he continued,

> We are in daily contact with heathenism in unveiled hideousness . . .
> the great bulk of them looked on with indifference or suspicion . . .
> Yet . . . they are becoming more friendly.[2]

He reported, too, the good work of Pauluse, 'our first Ila teacher', and the establishment of a school by J. K. Liphuko at Shamakunki, where he had 'a regular congregation varying from three hundred to five hundred'.[3] Smith bemoaned the limited supply of manpower and money: 'Given adequate supplies of these we could establish here the finest Mission our Church has ever had in Africa.'[4]

The night sky is a magnificent sight in the tropics but Smith was surprised to find that the Ila showed little interest in the stars. The Pleiades, which signalled the time for planting, and the Milky Way seemed to be the sum of Ila astronomy. Smith found no taboo about this and remained puzzled especially when, in May 1910, Halley's comet was seen. The Ila took little notice. Smith was amazed, 'it is certainly remarkable that the most glorious celestial phenomenon we have ever witnessed should have made so little impression'.[5] A wonder to one culture seemed unworthy of notice to another.

Another unusual phenomenon occurred around the same time. On 28 May 1910 a small earthquake approached – its tremors were felt for about thirty seconds – and then went east to the Mala villages. Smith reported that 'as the shock reached them we could hear the shrieks from the people'.[6] This event, considered a tremendous portent, provoked tales of an earthquake from days long gone which was celebrated in an old song: 'Some ascribed the shaking of the earth to Leza, others to the white men.'[7]

Whether or not these were portents, a major international event was about to take place, the World Missionary Conference held at Edinburgh in June 1910. It has been hailed as 'the birthplace of the modern ecumenical movement'[8] so its influence was massive. Two years of preparations had been led by the Executive Secretary, J. H. Oldham. Eight Commissions of twenty members were each asked to report on such topics as missionary preparation, relationships with governments and cooperation. Commission IV considered the Missionary Message to Non-Christian Religions. With respect to animism (as African religion was called), it reported that points of contact were possible, especially belief in God, immortality of the soul, sacrifice, the need for a mediator and the use of prayer.[9] As noted above (Chapters 6 and 7), Smith was already familiar with such thinking, and in later chapters we will see how he became involved in organizations that grew from Edinburgh 1910 or were sympathetic to it.

The Commissions received reports from hundreds of correspondents in many countries and churches. Sadly, however, none of the PM missionaries was consulted. Only A. T. Guttery was asked for an opinion, and that was about the Home Base of Missions. He went as a Special Delegate[10] to Edinburgh with two other PMs, the Revd J. Pickett and the formidable Mr W. Beckworth of Leeds.[11] By contrast the Wesleyans had over 40 delegates.[12]

The Revd A. T. Guttery had been GMC Secretary for two years when, a month after the Edinburgh Conference, he wrote to the missionaries in Zambia. The great themes of Edinburgh did not enter his thinking, although he did want the Mission to be self-supporting, chiefly because of the financial problem, 'a matter of great and urgent importance'.[13] The GMC 'was impressed by the great contrast in expenditure between the Missions in South Central Africa and Southern Nigeria'.[14] There was nothing new in this observation but the Missionary Secretary revived the issue. He observed that in Central Africa the missions were much less self-supporting than in Nigeria. He asked for the missionaries' views and raised the following questions:

1. Could people give free labour?
2. Are the members taught self-support?
3. Is it necessary to feed scholars?

4. Could expenditure be reduced without reducing the religious work?
5. Did the missionaries have any suggestions to offer?

Smith was first to reply (26 August 1910) and contested the matter vigorously. He explained the high cost in Central Africa, the distance from the coast and the fact that employment and voluntary labour were strange concepts to the Ila. He thought that the committee should include an advisor who had lived in the area and knew local conditions. The other missionaries sent similar replies. The strangeness of work and wages to Africans was clearer to the missionaries than to GMC members, whose lack of geographical and cultural perspective was sadly revealed in these exchanges.

Smith followed the Edinburgh spirit by attending a Missionary Conference in Umtali (in modern Zimbabwe), where he was made President of the proceedings.[15] The PM missionaries in Central Africa also held their own Conference, 3–10 August 1910, at Kasenga. Their chief suggestions for mission development, a General Superintendent and a Training Institute, were not accepted by the GMC. Smith and the other missionaries were most unhappy. He wrote again (20 October 1910) but did not send his letter. Then (10 November) he wrote that his disagreement with Guttery 'on almost everything connected with the Baila Batonga Mission is so profound that I see no use in prolonging these arguments'.[16] He felt that this difference of policy was too great for him to continue in the PM Mission. However, he would not leave until his translation work was finished, perhaps around 1913.[17] Some thought that financial misunderstandings or weariness were the cause of Smith's resignation. He pointed out in yet another letter (31 May 1911) that GMC policy was the only reason. The missionaries, who based their views on practical experience and careful thought, were not treated with the seriousness their cause merited. Home committees are subject to various pressures but 'are not so easily excused for not listening to their missionaries'.[18]

Smith worked steadily at his New Testament translation. It was essential work but had limitations:

it is not a literature written by the natives themselves, and a literature must not be an exotic but an indigenous growth . . . The time will come when in this country our conception of a great native church, self-governing, self-supporting and self-propagating will be realized.

Long before then the natives will have begun to write their own literature, and our own work will be forgotten.[19]

Smith wrote about Ila and the mission for the *Aldersgate Magazine*.[20] He also produced an *Ila Phrase Book for the use of Sportsmen and Settlers*.[21] A Book Room was started, and in 1912–13 sold Ila and Tonga school books as well as the Ila St Matthew. In addition, 'We have now sent to the press a book on Hygiene (in Ila) written by Rev. J. W. Price.'[22]

In 1912 Smith reported that the Ila New Testament, to which the Revd J. W. Price contributed translations of Acts, Philippians, 1 and 2 Timothy, Titus and Jude,[23] was now completed. Smith could not, however, return to England because a final revision was necessary and the manuscript needed to be prepared for publication. Other missionaries helped with this work. The revisers met at Kasenga, 11–13 November 1913. They discussed difficult words and agreed on the conjunctive system.[24] Each translator brought an African assistant, who had a voice in the committee. John Price, Miss Davidson (of the Brethren in Christ) and Smith (as editor) prepared the final manuscript, and the British and Foreign Bible Society agreed to 'print it, without any cost to any of the missions'.[25] It was published in 1915.

As well as translating, ministering and researching, Smith continued reading and writing. He wrote further review articles for *PMQR*. One of these, 'The South African Mission Field',[26] considered two books, *A History of Christian Missions in South Africa* by J. du Plessis and *Studies in the Evangelisation of South Africa*, by G. B. A. Gerdener, both published in 1911. Smith hoped that a forthcoming General Missionary Conference in South Africa would 'inaugurate a sane orderly advance of the Churches into the hitherto unoccupied fields north of the Zambesi'.[27] Smith, apparently following Gerdener, suggested that Churches in South Africa should combine, leaving the missionary societies to get on with evangelizing the north (i.e. Central Africa).

Smith also considered Islam's progress in Africa. He feared that, by taking over Zambia, it would be in a strategic position in relation to southern Africa. The relative claims of Christianity and Islam in Africa concerned many missionaries of that era. W. J. Platt, who years later joined Smith at the Bible Society, recalled when, in 1914, he 'offered for pioneer missionary work in West Africa. It was a neck-and-neck race – the Cross or the Crescent?'[28]

In 1912 Smith was busy building a brick house with a corrugated roof, to replace the temporary huts.[29] He and Julia also had holidays away from Kasenga. In late 1912, when they stayed with Smith's brother, John T. Smith,[30] Smith was able to visit Moffat's famous mission station at Kuruman. He admired what he saw[31] and was delighted to meet a Tswana pastor who explained the meaning of *Modimo*, the Sechuana name for God.

> He spilt a drop of oil on a piece of blotting paper, and, turning it over, showed that the oil had penetrated through. That, he said was, ho dima and Modimo was He who penetrated, permeated all things.[32]

There, in Robert Moffat's house, the pastor gave a poem-prayer, 'one of the most beautiful things I had ever heard. At the end of each stanza came the refrain: *Mma Modimo we!* . . . "Dear Mother God" '.[33] Smith reported this concept to illustrate African belief in a personal God.[34] He made no comment about the motherhood of God as though it was a familiar concept to him.

There were staffing problems when missionaries went on furlough. Since the Prices were away in 1911, the Nanzela Christians worked under Smith's supervision. Smith thought that this would 'leave the young men all the stronger in character and the Committee will then, I trust, see the necessity of establishing the training school we asked for'.[35] A. T. Guttery insisted that such an appeal to the progress of local Christians at Nanzela could not be used to 'secure the Training Institute'.[36] In a further letter Smith claimed that the conditions for the training school had already been met and that twenty young men from the area were ready to start at once. This was not accepted by Guttery and a further unhappy encounter with headquarters ensued. The confrontation was prolonged when, in early 1912, Guttery suggested that, when Chapman went on furlough in September, Smith should spend the rest of his tour at Nambala.[37] A replacement would be sent to Kasenga. Smith argued that his language study would not go well at Nambala, which was outside of true Ila country. Moreover, a newcomer would do less well at Kasenga, a new station, than at a more established mission, and so on.[38] The Secretary replied that there would be more leisure and a healthier climate at Nambala: 'your objections do not alter my opinion that it would be best for all parties'.[39] Smith suggested going to Nambala for six months,[40] and on 12 June 1913 agreed to go as requested. Then, in July, his colleague, Chapman, who was in England, advised him to stay put. The whole episode did nothing to improve Smith's opinion of the GMC and its Secretary.

Smith continued to disagree with GMC policy and remained firm about leaving the mission after his present tour of service. When, however, Guttery retired as Missionary Secretary in 1913, Smith wrote a conciliatory letter, wishing him well and promising to send a photograph album of Kasenga pictures.

By then Smith's ideas were getting through to members of the GMC. For example, the PMMS Financial Secretary, the Revd H. J. Taylor, told Smith in a letter:

> I am increasingly impressed with the need of training native agents and I heartily wish we could enter upon some bold policy such as you have on several occasions outlined. We shall not be on the highway to our best work until this is done.[41]

Smith, in cooperation with Dale, continued making notes about Ila culture. About 1913 he shared some of his researches in an article, 'The Sententious Wisdom of the African'.[42] It was a study of Ila proverbs classified as rules of conduct, cynical, fatalistic criticisms of life and clever metaphors. Smith emphasized that many sayings reflected matters expressed in folk tales and could not be understood unless the tales were also known; and he noted that the Ila were adept at 'expressing things in a roundabout way'.[43] This article was later incorporated into *ISP*,[44] but Smith gave thoughtful PMs the first opportunity to see what he had discovered.

There was at least one occasion when the Ila people responded enthusiastically to the gospel. Smith described this 'revival' in his book *The Secret of the African*.[45] Some strange events occurred around Kasenga mission in 1913. In June a leper named Mupumani from Nanzela found himself taken away during the night to meet Namulenga, the Creator, who told him to denounce witchcraft and such customs as killing cattle at funerals. Mupumani returned home as mysteriously as he had left and gave his message. People came from as far away as Ndola and Mwinilunga to hear him, but ignored his message, demanding fresh signs and wonders.

Some scoffed at Mupumani, and a member of one scoffer's household, a man from Mala, died. A local medium gave a message from

Shimunenga, the Kasenga spirit, that the man had died because some had mocked the Creator's messenger and, since they did not listen to the missionary either, they should look out! Then, a great tree which had been blown over stood upright again. Smith's scientific explanation did not commend itself to the people, who saw it as another sign: 'This accumulation of portents stirred the people to the depths of their being.'[46] Instead of the 100 people who usually attended the Sunday service Smith found himself facing more than 1,500.

> I . . . preached as I never have preached, before or since. Presently I launched an appeal for acceptance of the message I had brought . . . The whole multitude that had been listening to me intently sprang to their feet . . . and roared in chorus: 'We will accept! We will accept!' It was an overwhelming moment.[47]

After this extraordinary incident, the people 'selected their most sacred site for the building of a church and undertook to collect the material and provide the labour themselves'. Smith adds, however: 'I had to leave Kasenga for four months and the enthusiasm cooled.'[48] He could not, therefore, regard these events as a true revival.

The Wesleyan Missionary Society, which was older than that of the PMs and served in farther-flung fields, did not begin work in Zambia until 1913. Chikala, a mine-worker in Zimbabwe, was converted to Christ. He came from the Luano Valley in Zambia and wanted his own people to hear the gospel. The District Chairman, the Revd John White, explored the area in 1909, but it was not until July 1913 that the Revd S. Douglas Gray actually settled at Chipembi, north of Lusaka, among the Lenje, whose language was related to Ila and Tonga. Gray was a man

> of indefatigable energy and in the first nine months after his arrival in Northern Rhodesia he covered 800 kilometres by canoe, 1450 kilometres by bicycle, and 2100 kilometres on foot, exploring the country and learning what he could about its inhabitants.[49]

In April 1914 Gray visited Smith at Kasenga. He travelled via Kafue, where he began a journey of five days by boat up the river, a long winding journey against the current: 'Smith was delighted to see me and I have had a good time since.'[50] He was fully occupied 'working away at the Ila grammar with Smith',[51] as well as hunting and travelling about by canoe. He spent 'a very pleasant three weeks at Kasenga'[52] and went away with materials from Smith and two fine cats from Julia.

Other visitors received scholarly and practical help at Kasenga. R. Murray-Hughes usually found Smith hard at work in his study. He would discuss Ila matters with Smith and go off with 'a box of good things Mrs. Smith would have prepared for me – fresh scones, a cake, a jar of home-made jam, and a sandwich or two for the road'.[53]

The PMs had involved other missions in revising the Ila New Testament translation: 'From this successful attempt at co-operation grew the idea of regular discussion of mutual problems',[54] which bore fruit in the first General Missionary Conference, held in Livingstone. This gathering also fulfilled one of the recommendations of Edinburgh 1910, which expressed a 'strong conviction of the value of Conferences in the mission field . . . including, if possible, all the Missions working in a particular district'.[55]

Smith arrived at Livingstone in late June 1914 and joined delegates from other societies in the south and west of the country.[56] The Revd H. J. Taylor, on his deputation visit, preached on Sunday 28 June, and Smith was elected President. An address prepared by Bishop Hine, who had returned to England, was read. The Bishop 'approved co-operation with other denominations in secular matters, and in religious ones except intercommunion'.[57] Smith delivered his Presidential Address on 30 June. He had cooperation, an Edinburgh theme, in mind: 'Mr Smith said that any individual or any society which now tried to work in isolation was an anachronism. The clamant call in mission work was for co-operation.' Moreover, they, 'as a Conference, desired to co-operate with the Government'.[58] Smith also wanted to meet opposition from settlers with information about the missionaries' agenda. As reported, however, his approach, while possibly mollifying some settlers, was deeply unsatisfactory.

> None of us believes that the native is the social or should be the political, equal of ourselves. If any man says he believes in it, I ask, would he give his daughter or sister to a native? If not, to talk of social equality is nonsense. What as missionaries we do say is that white and black are equal before God, by which we mean that they should have equal opportunities of knowing his will.[59]

Smith kept no copy of his remarks and, since the *Livingstone Mail* was the voice of settler opinion,[60] this summary could reflect the paper's position rather than what he said. Certainly, the declaration about social and political equality is ironical: 'At the Old Drift Settlement (1898–1905) and in the capital, Livingstone from 1905, the Europeans seemed to live largely on whisky, and the floors of the Hotels were covered nightly with drunken, unconscious bodies.'[61] Such behaviour hardly suggests that the settlers were superior or worthy of emulation, and the credibility of Europeans was about to be undermined further by the Great War which broke out a few weeks after the meeting at Livingstone.

The printed version of Smith's Presidential Address, at a public meeting held in the High Court, was entitled 'The Bantu Conception of God'.[62] He surveyed the field widely, considering the Basuto-Bechuanaland tribes, the Zulus and the Ba-Thonga of Southern Africa. He looked north to the Baganda, by then thoroughly studied by the Revd John Roscoe, and considered the main names for God in the central Bantu region (*Mulungu*, *Nyambe* and *Leza*), which he believed had an underlying basis in nature. Although God had become somewhat remote to the Bantu, Smith concluded that, in seeking to evangelize them, their view of God was the best point of contact. He viewed the missionary as a 'smith', a *Musemunuzhi*, who recasts, renews and revives old ideas: 'We take this conception of God, and fill it with a rich energising meaning.'[63] Smith liked this description of missionary work and used it again in his famous book *The Golden Stool* (1926).[64] It came from his conversations with the Kasenga blacksmith who, when materials were in short supply, had to recycle his iron, taking something old and refashioning it.[65] Smith obtained the ear of the blacksmith when it was realized that he also was a Smith!

Discussion of Smith's paper

was enlivened by a vigorous protest by Father Torrend against one of Mr Smith's remarks that it was impossible to believe his (the Rev Father's) theory that the name Moloch was not Bantu in origin but had come down from the days when Semitic and other traders travelled in East Africa. He complimented the lecturer, however, saying that the paper was the best thing on the subject yet written.[66]

This was high praise, for Torrend was an expert in Bantu studies, especially linguistics.

Educational problems occupied much of the Conference, which urged the Government to put more money into educating Africans. These missionary conferences 'were to exercise considerable influence in the country for at least thirty years',[67] and the credit for initiating them 'must be given to the Primitive Methodists'.[68] More precisely, credit must be given to Smith, who led the Conference in these co-operative, progressive policies.

The Revd H. J. Taylor was at Livingstone as a member of the PM deputation which reviewed the work in Central Africa. He and Albert Shaw made an extensive tour. From Livingstone they went on to visit the PM mission stations among the Tonga and Ila.[69] They advised the immediate establishment of a Training Institute and, thanks to the generosity of Charles and Martha Clixby of Gainsborough, land was purchased at Kafue in 1916 and Kafue Institute, built by John Fell with the help of men from Kanchindu, was opened in 1918.[70]

Time was running out for Smith's missionary career. When the PM missionaries held their own Conference at Nanzela in 1914,[71] Smith left his colleagues with some thoughts on the 'Organization of the Mission'. He pointed out three sources of guidance: (a) the GMC, (b) the mission-aries and (c) the African Church, and said that (c) 'is the only permanent element of the three I have named'.[72] Smith did not like using denomin-ational names for the new Church and preferred some such title as the 'Church of God among the Ila, Tonga' etc. He thought it advisable to have a General Superintendent or Synod Chairman.

An industrial missionary, Till, was recruited, and by 1914 he had built a house and was cultivating 29 acres of land. His wife joined Julia in the school. Plans were made for a hospital and, before the Smiths left in March 1915, Miss Barlow, a nurse, whose nickname was *Nachimwemwe*, 'the mother of cheerfulness'[73] arrived, to be joined later in the year by Dr Herbert Gerrard, who became a legend for his medical work among the Ila.

Although Smith felt local indifference at the beginning of his time at Kasenga, he would look back on these years with happy memories, espe-cially of the Kasenga local preachers' class. This group included Paulo (i.e. Shamatanga), Peter the son of an important Nambala chief, Solomon, 'our old servant', and Jeremia from Nyasaland, of whom Smith wrote: 'He is full of force and fire, a regular Ranter.'[74] With Smith the class discussed and prayed over their texts for Sunday, and in their com-pany he extended the principle of following African ways of thinking:

half a dozen intelligent young men and I deliberately tried to find out how to relate our preaching to the actual life and thought of the people. I sat among them, not as a master but as a fellow-learner. We sought not illustrations merely, such as one might derive from fables and from the classics, but for adumbrations of Christian truth in the native religious and social practices.[75]

Smith formed the opinion early on that Kasenga life was bound up in worship of the ancestral spirit, Shimunenga. He wanted, therefore, both to turn the whole community to Christ and to build a large church directly confronting Shimunenga's sacred grove. But these plans were frustrated and, by 1915, it appeared that Shimunenga's supporters had won. Smith noted, however, that the annual festival in honour of Shimunenga had not been held that year and hoped that this was a sign of change. By that time the Baila Batonga mission had 63 members, 14 of them at Kasenga. Though progress was slow, a beginning had been made and the mission continued to grow.

Smith had to leave Shimunenga and the infant church in the hands of God and his successors, African and European, for his work in Central Africa was over. He and Julia left Kasenga in March 1915 and returned to an England now deeply embroiled in war. He was 38 years old, nearly half way through his life.

Smith achieved much as a missionary. He developed the existing mission station at Nanzela and established a new one at Kasenga. He became proficient in bricklaying, joinery and other crafts. When Dr and Mrs Gerrard came to Kasenga soon after the Smiths' departure they found not only 'an excellent bungalow gauzed to keep the mosquitoes out, but a well laid out garden with orange, lemon and grape fruit trees'.[76] In this 'industrial work' Smith followed Robert Moffat and David Livingstone and his own father. Indeed, his contributions to agriculture and the building trade would have been worthwhile in themselves.

Smith, however, contributed much more through his literary work. He reduced Ila to writing, wrote an Ila grammar and translated most of the New Testament into Ila. He produced Ila booklets, wrote most of the Ila hymns and set up a book room. This linguistic activity has already been assessed as a fine work, and other missionaries were grateful for it. The Revd and Mrs Stamp went to Zambia in 1921 and Mrs Stamp recalled:

We all, including Government officials used his book . . . In a tent I
. . . found, on my clothes, a brown 'beatily' [*sic*] looking object . . . My
husband killed it with a folded newspaper then rushed outside to ask
the boys what it was. They all called out '*Kabanza, kabanza*' [*sic*] &
he rushed in for Smith's dictionary to find it was a scorpion. We knew
the name ever after![77]

Although helpful to Europeans, Smith's linguistic work was intended to
provide the New Testament and Christian teaching for the Ila in their
own language. Then, as education brought reading, writing and practical skills, they would be able to learn more about such things for themselves.

In addition, Smith kept the Baila mission and other missionary concerns before the PM people. His wide reading, particularly in anthropology, linguistics, theology and what we would now call missiology,
was combined with careful theological study of the Bible, especially the
New Testament. Moreover, anticipating the pragmatic approach of
Church Growth writers later in the century, Smith studied the work of
great missionaries and looked for factors which accounted for their
success. This research led him to press unceasingly for a combination of
activities – industrial, medical, educational, evangelistic and literary –
based in Kafue. Kasenga, already developing on those lines, and Kafue
were modelled on Lovedale and Livingstonia. There was an African
sense of wholeness about these institutions, though Africans did not
always appreciate the industrial training.

Smith's experience and reflection led him to see the Church's life and
mission ecumenically. Influenced by the Edinburgh emphasis on cooperation and by his personal contact with Christians of other denominations, he found the divisions of European Christianity embarrassing
and inappropriate.

Smith made another exceptional contribution by becoming an
anthropologist. As a missionary, he needed to understand the culture of
the Ila as well as their language. He, therefore, became a serious fieldworker and a zealous student of the available literature in this relatively
new discipline.[78]

Anthropology also helped Smith's study of African religion, a poorly
explored subject when he began his work in Africa: 'Missionaries of this
period were ill-equipped to do more than speak of African worship in
terms of "Fetishism".'[79] An overview and bibliography of Bantu religion

by E. S. Hartland appeared in 1909 in Volume II of Hastings' *Encyclopaedia of Religion and Ethics*. By 1915, pioneer tribal monographs were appearing and 'contributed greatly, though often at a superficial level, to the knowledge of countless African religions'.[80] Smith studied the subject at first hand, read these publications as they appeared, and approached African religion more objectively and positively than many of his contemporaries. He had already written several articles on religion and would include it in *ISP*. He lacked formal training but had acquired the tools, skills and knowledge to approach African religion as both anthropologist and Christian theologian. 'Fulfilment theology' provided, for him, a very satisfactory framework for approaching African religion from the Christian point of view.

Smith's missionary role was not only as a '*musemunuzhi*' who re-forms what he finds,[81] but also as an 'understander' or 'introducer' who, coming from one group, works sympathetically with another and 'discovers the one to the other, interprets one to another'.[82] This is borne out by Smith's anthropological and other writings, where he presented Africans sympathetically to a European audience. At the same time, and with increasing care, he introduced Africans to those aspects of European life and belief which, he believed, would be useful to Africans. From his treasure store came gadgets, reading and writing, education, brick buildings and the Bible, for he was convinced that Africans should be free to receive the best that the West could offer and make something of it.

In Chapter 4 we saw that, in spite of Smith's enlightened background and education, he had considered himself superior to the Ila when he started working among them. After thirteen years, as he observed thirty-five years later, Smith's opinion had changed and matured. He realized that the Ila were intelligent, had skills which exceeded his, and spoke their intricate language with grammatical accuracy: 'As I came to know them intimately I became aware that we shared a common humanity: that behind and beneath all the dissimilarities we were akin.'[83]

This observation could have been the result of reflection, projecting later attitudes back to 1915. Memory, after all, is a reconstructive and selective activity, and Smith's report home in 1910 and his outlook, according to the newspaper reports, at the General Missionary Conference of 1914 would seem to indicate that the sense of superiority may not have been entirely eradicated before he left Africa. Nevertheless, his underlying attitude was revealed by his approach to the Ila and other African peoples, especially in his anthropology. When Elizabeth Colson introduced the 1968 edition of *ISP* she said that Smith and Dale 'wrote of friends whom they respected as their equals'.[84] This respect for Africans, sustained over many years, would undermine the superiority complex.

So powerful was the influence of Africa and its peoples on Smith that, when he left the continent, his mental furniture was largely constructed from African materials. During the next forty years his love for Africa was maintained and his knowledge and skills as an Africanist went from strength to strength.

To the Bible Society (1915–1920)

Smith's father, John Smith, retired in 1907. He remained active until 1914, preaching, speaking for the Bible Society, reading and gardening. Then, in the winter of 1914–15, he fell ill. He managed to take part in the PM Church's General Committee but, 'the following Sunday he took a chill whilst preaching, and returned to his bed never to get up again'.[1] He died on 12 February 1915 and a large crowd gathered for his funeral at Yarmouth,[2] for he was highly respected as preacher, missionary and leader. The family's grief was compounded by the death of Smith's sister, Dora, a few days later. She had worn herself out looking after her father.[3]

Smith was still away, but arrived in Britain a few weeks later on 19 April 1915.[4] He was the most likely inheritor of his father's large library of theological and African books. He needed them because most of his own had been lost at sea along with many of his papers.[5] Some papers, however, travelled with Smith and arrived safely. These included the draft manuscript for a book based on his Ila researches with Dale. Smith approached Macmillans, publishers of the classic anthropology texts of Frazer, Junod and Roscoe. His first contact was discouraging because Macmillans wanted a substantial subsidy. Smith wrote on 29 April 1915, pointing out the book's originality but regretting that neither he nor Dale could subsidize publication.

The publishers responded quickly with a suggestion for raising money by subscription.[6] Little more could be done as Smith was off to the war. He asked Macmillans to obtain an expert opinion.[7] This was done, the expert reporting

to the effect that our book is firstrate – indeed he says that it is the finest thing of the sort on an African tribe – so they are willing to publish it at their own expense, if they can get £100 from subscribers.[8]

Suggestions were offered for revision which Smith, then in France, agreed to follow.[9] The chapter on social organization was to be sent to Dr Rivers, a leading expert on this topic, for further comment.[10]

Because of the war, Smith had no time to revise his manuscript or come to terms with the loss of his father, sister and the African environment which had dominated his life for many years. Moreover, the conflict in Europe overshadowed everything. By spring 1915 hostilities had not come to the early end which had been generally expected and the stalemate of trench warfare was becoming established. Several of Smith's fellow Englishmen in Zambia, including Dale and Handley, had enlisted in the armed forces.[11] Smith himself could have gone to a circuit in Britain but, following Dale and prompted by his own patriotism, he joined the army and was in France, as a chaplain with the rank of Captain, by early June 1915.[12] He was soon posted to the Western Front in Belgium, where the British lines extended only 20–25 kilometres north of the French border, and spent most of the next three months at Elverdinge, near Ypres. It was a most unpleasant time. Smith experienced shelling, met troops in the trenches and visited the wounded and dying. He wrote letters of condolence and also had the distasteful job of censoring soldiers' correspondence.[13] He saw signs of spiritual need among the soldiers in the desperate and life-threatening conditions:

> one officer whom I found in a little broken-up dug-out said to me, 'Padre, I am glad you have come. You are the first chaplain we have had. If ever we wanted religion it is now.'[14]

Smith believed that for many 'there has now come a new determination and a desire to serve the living God'.[15]

The Ila, among whom Smith had worked, were said to be among the most savage of Africa's tribes. Now he saw how savage Europeans could be in the awful conditions of this stupid conflict. He was deeply affected by what he observed at first hand, acknowledging that his experiences in the Boer War bore no comparison to the terrible suffering of people in Belgium and France during the Great War.[16] His sense of belonging to a superior and rational civilization was being seriously challenged, and he came to loathe the war for its cruelty.[17]

By August 1915 Smith was unwell.[18] He enjoyed a few days at home at the end of the month but, by the end of the year, he had been invalided home and spent the rest of his Army service at Maidstone. He expected to have time to complete his book but, by December, he was fully occupied with chaplaincy work.[19] His friend Dale was still in a London hospital after being seriously wounded at Loos in September.[20]

Smith could not return to southern Africa because of the war and his disagreement with the PM Missionary Society,[21] and another factor now intervened: 'Diabetes prevented him from obtaining medical clearance which was a bitter disappointment.'[22] It was probably not severe at the time, but the diagnosis was alarming because insulin treatment was not introduced until after the war and early death was a likely outcome.

For the foreseeable future, then, there was no way back, but Smith could not put Africa out of his mind. Like others who have spent many years there, he was strongly attached to the continent of his birth, and he revisited Africa mentally – and, occasionally, physically – for the rest of his life. The preparation of *ISP* for publication and its subsequent influence provided a continuing point of contact over the next few years.

Smith was fortunate at this point to find employment with the British and Foreign Bible Society (BFBS), an organization which used his literary talents and enabled him to develop his interest in Africa. At the end of 1915 the Society asked the PM Church for him to be seconded as their agent in Rome.[23] Since Smith's father had supported the Society and he had himself presented his biblical translations to it and addressed meetings on its behalf, he could respond enthusiastically to this invitation.

The BFBS was founded in 1804 to encourage the circulation of Holy Scripture. By the early twentieth century it was at the centre of a worldwide network of branches and, when Smith joined in 1916, translations had been made and published in about 500 languages. It was an interdenominational, though mainly Protestant, body from the start and regarded itself as 'the visible token' of the 'deeper desire among Christians for co-operation and concord'.[24] Since missionary work and movements for cooperation among Christians were the Society's natural allies, it was well represented at Edinburgh 1910. The Revd J. H. Ritson, one of the Society's General Secretaries, 'was one of the two Clerks to the Conference'[25] and became involved in the Edinburgh Continuation Committee and the International Missionary Council. Smith, as we have seen, was already sympathetic to such ecumenical activities.

He could not, however, leave the army for this new post until June 1916.[26] Meanwhile, there had been progress over sponsorship for *ISP*. The British South Africa Company guaranteed £50 and Smith and Dale agreed to find the further £50 Macmillans required. Then, in July 1916, Smith set off for Rome, where he hoped to complete his revised manuscript.[27] First, however, he gave time to language study and, after a few months, 'was touring Sicily preaching in Italian'![28]

Italy had been in the war for just over a year when Smith arrived. Italians were finding things very difficult, with an average of 11,000 troops killed and 27,000 wounded every month.[29] Smith sensed a spiritual opportunity, for 'a new seriousness has come upon the Italian people',[30] but this opportunity would be exploited after the war by fascism.

It was said that the BFBS, a mainly Protestant organization, was regarded with suspicion in Italy, where most people were Roman Catholics. The war added complications: 'In many places fierce sermons have been preached against Protestantism. Probably for most Italians the German Emperor stands as the representative of Protestantism'.[31] It was good, therefore, that 'in the person of Edwin Smith the Society had a representative who brought a scholarly courtesy, tact born of wide study and experience and a good-humoured tolerance to the situation'.[32]

Smith's duties involved supervising Bible colporteurs and travelling on behalf of the Society: 'the Rev. E. W. Smith delivered sermons and addresses at Leghorn and Spezia in December 1917 and at Palermo, Turin, Genoa, Florence and Naples in the early spring of 1918'.[33]

When the American President, Woodrow Wilson, visited Italy, Smith publicized Bible reading. President Wilson, a Presbyterian, had given a message to American troops on the value of Bible reading. Smith had this translated into Italian: 'During President Wilson's visit to Rome we placarded the hoardings with his message, which attracted considerable attention.'[34] President Wilson, in Europe for the Versailles Peace Conference, arrived in Rome on Friday 3 January 1919. He addressed the Italian Parliament, met the Pope and held several conferences, including a meeting with American Protestants, before going on to Genoa, Milan, Turin and finally to Paris on 7 January.[35] Smith may have joined the American Protestants, for 'the Rev. E. W. Smith, had the opportunity of telling the President personally the effect his message has produced, and he expressed his gratification at the news'.[36]

Smith continued to travel widely: 'In 1920, although five months in England, he preached and lectured in Rome, Naples, Florence, Milan, Genoa, San Remo, Bordighera, Savona and Turin.'[37] He was credited with having increased the Society's circulation of Scriptures in Italy during his five years there.[38]

Smith's Christian horizons broadened in Italy, for some of the Christian denominations he encountered were new to him. He visited the Waldensian Church, which traces its history back to the twelfth century. The Methodist Episcopal Church in Italy was also informed about Bible Society work.[39] Above all, Smith met more Roman Catholics than ever before and tried hard to build good relationships with them. Both students from Roman Catholic Seminaries and Roman Catholic priests came to the Bible Society in Rome for versions in Hebrew, Greek, Arabic and Syriac. By 1919 Smith could report that, though there was opposition from many priests, the Bible Society also experienced 'friendly assistance rendered by priests of the Roman Church'.[40] Smith believed that the number of friendly priests was growing.[41]

From the Bible Society's point of view the great event of 1919 was 'the Pope's command that in the Churches in Rome the Gospel shall be read henceforth in Italian'.[42] This development was of interest to Smith because it was following Bible Society policy of making vernacular translations. Indeed, while Smith was acquiring a working knowledge of Italian, the Revised Italian New Testament was published on 1 October 1916. It was a great innovation for Italian Protestants whose Italian Bible of 1607 was translated by Giovanni Diodati (1576–1649). A pamphlet by Dr Luzzi of Florence, the chief reviser, gave the history of Italian versions and described the new one. It was not expected that the seventeenth-century version, 'which has nourished spiritual life in Italy for long generations, will be abandoned all at once'.[43]

The revised Italian version of 1916 'met with some criticism on the part of those who object to the alteration of a great national classic'.[44] Smith considered the matter and gave a lecture in Italian on 26 June 1919.[45] He mentioned English, French, Spanish and German examples of revising translations and used them to support his case for the Italian revision. Smith pointed out that the Italian Bible was a translation, whereas the other classic of Italian literature, Dante's *Divine Comedy*, was an original work which should not be altered. Translations, though, need to keep in step with changing language. As Smith told his hearers, the Bible is not intended to be a fossil but a living organism.

The mention of Dante, who is as important to Italian literature as Shakespeare is to English literature, gave Smith's lecture added interest. Dante entered the discussion because *The Divine Comedy* was written in Italian, not Latin – that is, in language accessible to ordinary people. From the time, therefore, that Smith learned Italian he was especially open to the influence – the profound and permanent spiritual influence – of Dante's writings, and he was helped by the background literature available to him, thanks to the poet's popularity in the early twentieth century.[46] For example, Hastings' *Encyclopaedia of Religion and Ethics*, one of Smith's favourite reference books, contained a survey of Dante's work and its significance.[47] It is no surprise, then, that from this time Smith began to refer to Dante in his own writing.[48]

Dante's contribution to the Italian language was not the only thing which attracted Smith to him:

1. The ordered complexity of Dante's *Divine Comedy* fascinated Smith in the same way as the languages and cultures which he had unravelled, and mastering the poem's structured system of hell, purgatory and heaven presented him with an irresistible challenge.

2. Dante's underlying notion that human wisdom is incomplete without the divine revelation in Christ accorded well with Smith's 'fulfilment theology'.

3. Smith happened upon Dante in mid-life, at a time of loss and during the Great War, itself an *Inferno* on earth: 'Midway in our life's journey, I went astray from the straight road and woke to find myself alone in a dark wood'[49] prompted serious study and led Smith on. The *Divine Comedy*, Dante's response to exile and injustice, describes a journey through hell with its vices, through a long process of purification, to a climactic revelation of divine love: 'my desire and my will were being turned like a wheel, all at one speed, by the love which moves the sun and the other stars'.[50] Aided by such a Christian perspective, Smith was enabled to link the tragic and the mystical to all areas of human knowledge.

4. Dante's numerous biblical allusions would appeal to Smith, who knew the Bible very well:

the Bible, as a text, is used or referred to by Dante as many times as Aristotle and Virgil put together, but the deep correspondences are only just becoming apparent as Dante scholarship progresses.[51]

5. *The Divine Comedy* includes the dead, or their shades, as players in the story. This was a familiar concept to Smith because, in Africa, the living dead are part of society.

6. As Dante drew upon all forms of knowledge, including the classics, to illuminate his great theme, the wholeness of his vision resonated with Smith's integrative approach and with African worldviews.

This was a difficult time for liberal Christians. Their optimism was cruelly shattered by the Great War, and the evolutionary scheme for analysing human societies received a heavy blow and was being undermined by diffusionism as an alternative explanation.[52] The concept of diffusion, that cultural change takes place though migration, had been around for some time, having been introduced by Tylor. The diffusionism, however, which flourished in Britain in the World War I era included the idea that civilization came from Egypt. Its chief supporters were able men, including the eminent W. H. R. Rivers, one of the first fieldworkers. He wrote *Kinship and Social Organisation* (1914), and part of Smith's manuscript had been sent to him. The diffusionist analysis was complex and included psychological studies. Indeed, its influence lasted longer in psychology than anthropology.

In that changing situation Smith found Dante a valued spiritual guide and source of wisdom for the next forty years.

Faced by the theology of crisis associated with the name of Karl Barth, liberal theology, at least where its emphasis on the history of religions and the social context of faith was concerned, began to decline. But it did not disappear, and many mid-twentieth century theologians would be described as 'liberal'. Many years would pass, however, before the contextual theology pioneered soon after the Great War by Ernst Troeltsch, and the positions of theologians and missionaries connected with Edinburgh 1910, were taken up again and developed.

Smith accepted that the war had forced him to revise some over-optimistic preconceptions. But, as a result of what he had already seen in Africa, he was aware of evil as well as the possibility of good, and he kept abreast of the latest thinking. The Barthian option, however, had little appeal for him. Brunner, who accepted general revelation, was the only neo-orthodox writer to interest him. Dante, on the other hand, persuaded him of the importance – and the possibility – of combining natural theology and biblical revelation, and his interest in anthropology attracted him to those who studied religious experience. Moreover, along with Marett and Rudolf Otto, who 'may to some extent be regarded as continuing and developing the tradition which Schleiermacher initiated',[53] Troeltsch and Harnack feature in his future work.

Smith continued to prepare his anthropological research for publication. He revised the chapter on social organization in the light of Dr Rivers' comments. An additional chapter on the Ila language was requested, and he wrote this after completing the revision. It was not a summary of the *Handbook* but a brief reworking of the subject in the light of further studies in linguistics, especially Bantu linguistics. This led him to favour the International Phonetic Association (IPA) alphabet. Clement Doke later described this as 'a very able chapter', and the 'following chapter, dealing with Ila proverbs, is a masterly presentation of a most interesting subject'.[54]

Since a full description of Ila life would contain sexually explicit material which, in those days, could offend some people, Smith wondered whether some passages should be in Latin.[55] He consulted Dr Peake[56] and sent copies of the passages in question. It seems that Peake judged that Latin should be used and the translation was done by Professor Conway of Manchester University.[57] Such a move appears coy nowadays, and in a new edition (1968), the Latin passages were translated back into English.

The manuscript was ready by early 1917, but publication was postponed until conditions improved.[58] At the end of 1918, circumstances were deemed suitable and Smith promised to send the manuscript with someone travelling to England.[59] At one time he considered entitling the book *The Purple Lock*, thinking this would remind people of the *The Golden Bough*.[60] The publishers were unimpressed and Smith accepted the plainer description, *The Ila-Speaking Peoples of Northern Rhodesia*, and this book made him and Dale famous.[61] Smith dealt with publication but remained in contact with Dale, who, having returned to Central Africa, sent further comments in November 1917.[62]

Smith gave more thought to Ila religion. He introduced the subject of 'dynamism' during this period (1915–19) and included a chapter on it before discussing souls, the divinities and Leza. His analysis of African religion for the next thirty years was based on this fourfold scheme.[63] He drew on R. R. Marett[64] for 'dynamism', a concept which was based on Codrington's use of *mana*, to describe Melanesian religion. It was seen as an all-pervading, impersonal power which is behind everything and which some people are believed to influence and manipulate. When people thought Smith had invented the term, he would point out that he found it in Marett and van Gennep.[65] Smith preferred 'dynamism' to 'magic' or 'fetishism', terms which he thought too derogatory.[66] The nearest Ila word for this impersonal force was *bwanga*. Its presence made things taboo or medicines potent, and those who manipulated it had to be treated with caution. Some were thought to use *bwanga* to harm their fellows, and such witchcraft was investigated and condemned. Smith realized that people could make false accusations of witchcraft to settle old scores. It was 'horrible to think of the hundreds and thousands of people who have been hurried to a violent end'[67] because of suspicion and trial by ordeal. Nevertheless, he and Dale, after their years in Africa, believed that there was something behind the belief; even though most cases were unfounded, Smith wondered whether telepathy brought harmful suggestions from a distance to trigger deadly auto-suggestions in bewitched persons. Whether telepathy was involved is uncertain, but it is known that fear and suggestion together constitute a powerful mixture.

Many of Smith's European acquaintances from Africa had perished in the war. Dale survived his serious injuries but died from blackwater fever on 1 May 1919 at Mumbwa.[68] This news 'took the spring out of the year'.[69] It was a great blow for Smith, who admired his friend. 'I will only say that of the men I have known none has come nearer my ideal of what a man should be.'[70] Smith always described their research as a joint venture and *ISP* as the book he and Dale wrote together. An analysis of its contents, however, shows that Smith was mainly responsible for over 90 per cent of the text and most of the photographs.[71]

Some PMs may have wondered why Smith devoted so much time to work which seemed far removed from his preaching vocation. Smith argued that such research would help missionaries and officials as well as academic anthropologists: 'whether one is to teach or to govern, one's first duty is to understand the people'.[72] He and Dale, who had little to help them when they came to Bwila, had to do the work themselves, and the verdict of history is that they did it very well indeed.

The Ila-Speaking Peoples, published by Macmillans in 1920, had five parts in the two volumes. The book is summarized briefly below, but has already been used in describing the Ila people and some of Smith's writings about them.

The first part covered the environment, history and physical characteristics of the Ila (Volume I, pp. 3–106). The second part described village life: building, agriculture, hunting, warfare, crafts and medicine (Volume I, pp. 109–280). Part three expounded social organization: terms of relationship, regulation of community life, etiquette, rights of property and regard for life. It also described the life cycle from birth to puberty and reviewed relations between the sexes (Volume I, p. 283 to Volume II, p. 75). Part four surveyed Ila religious life under four headings: dynamism, the doctrine of souls, the divinities and the Supreme Being, *Leza* (Volume II, pp. 79–212). Part five covered notions about time and nature, games and diversions and, in the last three chapters, the Ila language, sayings and folk-tales (Volume II, pp. 283–417).

The book was well received by anthropologists. Alice Werner in *Man* said it was 'a work which must rank with the classics of anthropology' and that 'the chapter on Social Organisation is particularly interesting'.[73] Smith was delighted with its reception and wrote to Dr Peake:

The reviewers, like yourself, have passed over the many faults of the book & have given it unstinted praise. Experts like Sir J. Frazer & Sir H. H. Johnston have written very well of it.[74]

Frazer and succeeding generations of anthropologists have praised it as a work of great quality. It came to be regarded as a 'a standard work of reference in African ethnology in the 1920's and later'.[75] It was reprinted in 1968, and Elizabeth Colson, who wrote an introduction for the new edition, described it 'as one of the basic documents of anthropological literature . . . Though they did their work before the teaching of Malinowski had set the standard for anthropological field work, they had already adopted his essential principle as their own'.[76] She showed that, although their theory of anthropology, derived from Frazer and Tylor, was outmoded by 1920, their work endured because it was comprehensive and accurate. Thus, later researchers could use *ISP*'s data to serve other interpretative schemes.

Colson judged that their account of kinship and social organization was the only part which was seriously affected by their inadequate theoretical framework. Ironically, this was where they had Rivers' expert advice, which quickly went out of fashion. As anthropology developed in the 1920s and 1930s Smith realized this and, on a visit to Zambia in 1947, made further studies of Ila social organization and set this out more clearly with special emphasis on Ila lineage, *lunungu*.[77] Colson's evaluation of the high quality of Smith's observations matches the opinion offered earlier of his linguistic work. In her view Smith and Dale 'wrote of friends whom they respected as their equals'.[78] She described *ISP* as 'one of the great classics of African ethnography . . . a precious heritage of African history'.[79]

Eighty years after its publication, *ISP* is readable and interesting. We react to Africans being called 'natives' and even more to 'backward races' or 'savages', though the latter are not often used. We should remember, however, that Smith belonged to a church whose members did not find the term 'primitive' derogatory and that occasional value judgments, such as references to some people as 'superior types' and others as 'inferior', were typical of that time. Even so, Smith's use of language compares very favourably with a revised edition of *Notes and Queries on Anthropology* produced by Section H of the British Association for the Advancement of Science in 1929. This was intended to help observers in the field, and although written nine years after *ISP*, and prepared by leading anthropologists, it had many more terms now considered inappropriate and used them more often.[80]

After *ISP*'s publication Smith was invited by Sir James Frazer to his home and became a frequent visitor. He had imagined that Sir James worked in a large room 'surrounded by thousands of books and an infinite stack of pigeon-holes into which his secretaries sorted extracts culled by them from the books'. In fact he was taken into a small room: 'It contained few printed volumes but a long line of quarto note-books . . . filled with extracts copied in his small, neat handwriting and all carefully indexed.'[81] Frazer, like many anthropologists,[82] had an anti-religious agenda but was friendly with another missionary/anthropologist, the Revd John Roscoe, whose work Smith also admired.[83]

Smith was fortunate to enter anthropology at a stimulating time of change. The theory of 'diffusion' was being tested and 'functionalism' would soon dominate: 'We were groping after a better technique. I can see now that what we were really groping for was the functional method which, to my mind, provides the best basis for a practical Anthropology.'[84] Functionalism, inspired by Malinowski, interpreted cultural institutions and customs in terms of their functions in a society. With such modifications as structural functionalism, which added social structure as a stabilizing framework, it would dominate British anthropology for a few decades. Smith was well prepared for the new anthropology because he had acquired extensive experience of field-work, one of its main features.

Smith publicized his researches by addressing the African Society on 29 October 1920 on the Ila-speaking people,[85] and Sir Harry Johnston, the famous Africanist, who chaired the meeting, said that few missionaries in Africa had done such remarkable work as Smith. Since Sir Harry was possibly more widely informed on African matters than anyone else in Britain at the time, this was a very encouraging compliment. Smith found congenial company in the African Society and, over the years, attended many of its meetings and dinners.

After World War I the Bible Society returned to an older pattern of managing its European work. Four Agencies, each covering groups of countries with cultural or linguistic affinities, were planned. In October 1920 Smith was appointed 'Superintending Secretary of the Society for France, Belgium, Spain, Portugal, French-speaking Switzerland and Italy'[86] and was commissioned

> to carry out their decisions with regard to the work of the translation, publication and distribution of the Holy Scriptures in the above countries; to act generally on their behalf in the society's business transactions and to represent it in negotiations with Church authorities.[87]

The family returned to England in early 1921 and lived at 2 Maison Dieu Road, Dover, near the harbour and with easy access to the European Continent as well as to Bible House in London.

The making of an Africanist (1921–1925)

As the Bible Society's representative for Western Europe, Smith travelled widely. In July 1921, he visited Belgium, Spain, Portugal and Italy, and in September 1921, looked after the Agency in Rome for a few weeks while the Agent, Dr Pons, recovered from illness.[1] Then, in early 1922, Smith included Corsica in his European tour. He was glad to see this 'wonderful country' and followed up his judgment that 'We ought really to be doing something in the island'[2] by making estimates in 1923 for producing Luke's Gospel in Corsican.[3]

Smith took his supervisory responsibilities seriously, looking at all aspects of Bible Society work in the countries he visited. Thus, in Belgium (May 1922) he met the colporteurs as well as addressing meetings and going to church gatherings (the Synods of the United Reformed and Missionary Churches).[4] Then, on his way to Switzerland, he visited Berlin, where he had interviews with Julius Richter (1862–1940), an expert in the history of missions, and Adolf von Harnack (1851–1930), a leading historian of Christian doctrine. These meetings suggest that Smith was developing an interest in the past, which began to bear fruit three years later with the first of his historical/biographical studies of missionary work. In 1922, however, granted his preoccupation with questions of cultural interaction, he may have regretted not seeing the renowned investigator of Christianity and its cultural setting, Ernst Troeltsch (1865–1923), who was to die shortly before Smith made a further tour of Germany.

Smith had been European Secretary of the Bible Society for about two years when, at Easter 1923, the Revd T. H. Darlow retired, after serving as Literary Superintendent since 1898.[5] Smith, who was appointed his successor, 'came to Bible House with an established literary reputation'[6] and, as his new post required, wrote extensively and edited the Bible Society's publications. There were regular monthly magazines,

The Bible in the World for adults and a children's magazine, which in 1923 was entitled *For Every Land*. In addition, an *Annual Report*, together with a readable summary known as the *Popular Report*, had to be produced. When congratulated by Dr Peake on his new appointment, Smith agreed that this great opportunity would end his wandering life for the time being.[7]

Though Smith's Bible Society work concentrated first on Italy, then on Western Europe and finally on the whole world, his special interest in Africa grew in depth and breadth, mainly through his involvement in the Royal Anthropological Institute (RAI) and the African Society.

By attending the RAI's meetings and reading anthropological literature Smith kept himself well informed in all aspects of the subject. Moreover, because *ISP* was highly regarded from the beginning, Smith was respected by anthropologists interested in Africa; and as a fieldworker he was at the cutting edge of anthropology and in tune with the functionalist method being pioneered by Malinowski. Functionalism emphasized observation in the field, regarded social activities as interdependent and became the fashionable approach over the next twenty years.

Smith kept in regular touch with key people through his membership of the African Society. This organization, now known as the Royal African Society (RAS), was founded in 1901 to continue and commemorate Mary Kingsley's work in the study of Africa, and it published the *Journal of the African Society*, later known as *African Affairs*, to which Smith contributed most of the book reviews in the early 1920s and the Editorial Notes from about 1923 until 1939. By working on these Notes, which over the years referred to most parts of Africa, Smith was able to add a grasp of economic and political considerations to his knowledge of African religion, cultures and languages.

The ecumenical missionary organization which continued the work of Edinburgh 1910 offered further opportunities for Smith to develop his knowledge and insights. At first, he was a contributor to the *International Review of Missions* (IRM), which reflected the wide interests of those who were at Edinburgh. The *IRM* was edited by J. H. Oldham,[8] the Secretary of the Edinburgh Continuation Committee, who, through his facility for making contacts and penetrating academic and political networks, obtained articles and reviews from experts in many fields of learning as well as from missionaries in many countries. He saw the potential help which anthropology could give to mission and encouraged its practitioners. Moreover, although Oldham himself had worked in India, he made sure that the *IRM* included articles and reviews on Africa. In addition to Smith, H. A. Junod, W. C. Willoughby (of Tiger Kloof) and Alice Werner (from London University), an expert on Central Africa, were among the contributors. Later, after Smith's return to Britain, he became involved in the International Missionary Council (IMC), which was established in 1921.

Henri Junod, renowned for his book, *The Life of a South African Tribe* (1912), reviewed *ISP* for the *IRM* in April 1921. He declared that this 'capital book is a complete and scientific study of a group of Bantu tribes . . . It is exactly what ethnographic science wants now.'[9] He commented, moreover, on the implied evolutionary scheme in Smith's account of Ila religion but accepted that Smith spoke of a logical rather than a historical process. Junod would have liked more information about Ila music and, perhaps most significantly, expressed the hope that Smith would draw practical conclusions to help missionaries.

Smith responded in an article for *IRM* in which he explained how African Christians could retain and transform their traditions.[10] He began with his illustration of the Kasenga blacksmith who recycled metal objects. Then, in answer to those who thought that Christ should be preached and African customs ignored, he spoke in terms of fulfilment. Accepting Justin Martyr's belief that things rightly said are the property of all Christians, he argued that Christ's light shone in Bantu hearts. Finally, taking cues from biological science, he maintained that, in order to progress, societies need variety and novelty. In this way, he distanced himself especially from those anthropologists who regarded Africans as a living cultural archive, needing to be preserved but with no right to change and develop.

Smith used psychological studies to illuminate his theme. The word 'sublimation' appealed to him. In psychoanalysis, the word referred to the expression of an instinct in a socially acceptable form. Smith, however, used the term in a different way. In his parlance, it meant using 'the experiences registered in the customs and beliefs of the native peoples as a fund for Christian ends'.[11] Sublimation, for Smith, amounted to cultural translation from one situation into another.

Smith mentioned aspects of African marriage and initiation customs which, he felt, could be taken by missionaries and 'sublimated' into African Christianity. Moreover, the African genius for friendship, expressed in the clan, could be incorporated into the Church, making it a new clan. Although Smith criticized some facets of African life, he tried above all to understand the wholeness of African life and believed that, if something is wrenched out of its context, serious damage may result. He pointed out that traditional customs

> have grown out of some felt need . . . You may repress a custom but that which is behind it will break out in another place. The custom of ukulobola, for example; missionaries have dubbed it, 'buying a wife', which it is not, and have repressed it. The motive underlying the custom simply breaks out in the absurd, ruinous, detestable practice in vogue among Christians in South Africa in compelling the bride-groom to spend large sums – perhaps all he has – upon the wedding dress and the wedding-feast.[12]

In such a situation, it was essential, Smith argued, for missionaries to be proficient in anthropology. As a Christian, however, he believed that, impressive though the work of Frazer and others might be, 'no explanation is valid which excludes the operation of the Divine Spirit'.[13]

Though Smith held that the notion of taboo, which lay behind most Bantu ethics, could be used by missionaries, he was convinced that a sense of God was yet more fundamental and that the Bantu concept of God (*Leza*, *Mulungu*, *Nyambe*), although vague, was the key element to be sublimated. 'Leza is to become the God and Father of our Lord Jesus Christ. In doing this the missionary will largely work along a path already opened up by the Bantu themselves.'[14] Smith never wavered from the conviction that African beliefs in God are the chief links between Christianity and African religions.

It may be doubted, however, whether Smith's use of the term 'sublimation' is helpful. Many traditional customs or practices could, after all, be regarded as sublimations in the psychoanalytical sense. Moreover, not everyone shared Smith's positive attitudes to African culture. Junod, for example, knew African converts who believed that their traditional games should be completely rejected.[15] Smith, by contrast, believed that elements in African culture could be given fuller significance in ways that Africans could own. The question remains whether talk of 'sublimation' is the best way to express this conviction.

If *ISP* put Smith on the map where African Studies were concerned and his article on 'Sublimation' showed how he regarded mission in an African context, his next book, *The Religion of Lower Races*, built on these writings. It was a short study of African religion, commissioned, probably as a result of Smith's association with the IMC network, by the Macmillan Company of New York and published in 1923 in a series on the world's living religions. It was a good book for its era, but Smith was increasingly troubled by the title which was given by the publishers. Indeed, as McVeigh points out, Smith apologized for it in 1928 and indicated that this title was given 'without his knowledge or consent'.[16] It is certainly totally unacceptable today.

Lower Races was based on Bantu[17] religion. In spite of Smith's later protestations, he did occasionally describe the Bantu as backward or of lower culture, and the book contains traces of evolutionary anthropology with its talk of 'survivals'. At the same time, however, Smith's high regard for Africans is clearly expressed. In his view, they needed improvement but were not savages; and he advised young missionaries, who would be impressed, he was sure, by their intelligence, to take Bantu religion seriously and study it thoroughly.

Smith's exposition of African religion expanded what he had already written. His wide reading included articles in Hastings' *Encyclopaedia of Religion and Ethics*, tribal monographs and works of anthropologists, especially the writings of R. R. Marett (1866–1943). Smith assumed that Bantu religions had many common features, and looked at Bantu culture, the concept of dynamism and the manipulation of energy, the soul and the cult of the dead. He expounded Bantu ideas about spirits of various kinds and of God who is over all, basically his triangle of Dynamism–Spirits–God which he often used to analyse African religion.

In his concluding observations Smith evaluated Bantu religion as a genuine religion with some tragically wrong aspects, e.g. witch-finding. He expected African religion to vanish through contact with Western civilization. This suggests that he was being influenced by 'the functionalist illusion . . . that because their models of society assumed equilibrium between the parts, change meant disintegration'.[18] By the early twenty-first century, however, it is clear that African religion is far more resilient and adaptable than Smith thought in 1923. Indeed, dynamism, with its charms, spells and other means of manipulating supposed unseen powers, seems to be enjoying a revival in the Western world as well.

Smith considered that Africans would gain by conversion to Islam but was confident that Christianity would provide a greater certainty of God and add a moral dimension to African lives.

He insisted that missionaries to Africa should study people with 'the same painstaking care that a chemist bestows upon a scientific investigation'.[19] As well as advising missionaries to look for points of contact with the African social and religious experience he pointed out that the best contact is 'the warm human touch'.[20] He concluded that Christlike teachers would win respect for a message that can touch every human heart.

Smith used *The Religion of Lower Races* as a textbook for his teaching,[21] perhaps at Livingstone College, the School of Oriental Studies and Selly Oak. In 1922 Clement Doke, who became an authority on Bantu languages, 'had the privilege of attending a course of lectures on African religion, which Edwin Smith gave to missionaries in London. He was most stimulating.'[22]

Edwin was promoting the study of African religion when the subject was not recognized, let alone well understood, either in missionary circles or in most churches and chapels. He was among the first to make serious contributions to what would eventually become a recognized, though often marginal, subject of study.[23]

Smith's expertise was now recognized well outside the PM community. He reviewed books on Africa for *JRAS* and other journals. In *IRM*, for example, he discussed *La Mentalité Primitive* by L. Levy-Bruhl.[24] He disagreed with Levy-Bruhl and asked, 'is it really possible to draw a hard and fast line between the mentality of "primitive" and "civilised" men. Is there really so great a gulf between the average European and the average African mind?'[25]

Smith when reviewing the later work of Canon John Roscoe[26] in many journals, criticized him for speaking of 'witch-doctors'.[27] Smith, who had once been helped by a traditional healer, did not use the expression himself and, in *ISP*, referred to 'diviners'[28] and 'doctors'.[29] In this he followed his hero, David Livingstone, who mentioned 'diviners'[30] and 'doctors' who 'generally possess some valuable knowledge, the result of long and close observation'.[31] Livingstone respected the rain-maker as a fellow doctor and recorded his discussion with one as a dialogue between a medical doctor and a rain doctor.[32] Unfortunately, however, though the African healers opposed witchcraft, it became common for them to be referred to in Europe as 'witch-doctors', a term which carried such sinister overtones that they were regarded as enemies of health. To avoid this serious confusion, Smith argued that the term 'witch-doctor' should be dropped. But alternatives, e.g. 'diviner' or 'traditional healer', took a long time to acquire a limited acceptance.

In other respects, Smith's reviews of Roscoe's work were full of praise. For example, he described *The Bakitara or Banyoro* (1923), which he reviewed for *Man*, as 'severely objective throughout' and said of its author 'He has done his work well.'[33] Being himself a proficient photographer, however, he observed 'that the photographs are not equal in quality to the text'.[34]

Smith also brought Roscoe's work, together with Frank Melland's *In Witch-Bound Africa*, to the notice of *IRM* readers and indicated that, in his view, there should soon be a conference to discuss missionary work in the light of ethnographic research and that, when it met, 'Messrs Roscoe and Melland should be among the experts invited to take part'.[35]

Smith continued writing articles for journals. The first Phelps-Stokes Commission had published its report and Dr Peake, who thought that it should be given prominence in the *Holborn Review*, asked Smith for a review article.[36] The report posed important questions about the appropriateness of Western education in Africa and suggested that the methods used to educate African Americans would be suitable. Smith did not know enough about America to comment but was 'absolutely in accord with the main theme of this Report, namely that education must be adapted to the needs of the Native'.[37] That, as Smith pointed out, left the question of what the African was to be adapted to. For example, the French method, which Smith called Aggregation, led to the students becoming French. The alternative method, which Smith called Segregation, educated Africans according to their own cultural heritages. 'Between these two extremes there is a whole gamut of possibilities, and the British way is to seek for some compromise.'[38] It was clear to Smith that the European presence in Africa would profoundly influence the future of Africans.[39]

In the 1922 article, 'Sublimation', and in *Lower Races* (1923) Smith urged missionaries to become proficient in anthropology, and wrote more fully about this relatively new discipline for the *IRM* in late 1924.[40] He pointed out that, while missionaries had gathered much of its material, anthropology could be extended to throw 'considerable light upon our own civilization and religion and should therefore be of use to all clergymen and ministers'.[41] Among missionaries, however, he noticed four attitudes to anthropology: Some neither knew nor cared about it; others were social anthropologists without realizing it; others again knew some anthropology and used it in their work; still others knew a lot about anthropology but made no use of it. After mentioning the political blunder over the Golden Stool of Ashanti,[42] Smith went on to refer to mistakes made by missionaries through not understanding African customs. For example, placing one's hands on a young person's head was not seen by Africans as a blessing but as a curse, for it indicated that they could grow no further.

Smith believed it possible to understand African minds: 'The difference between ourselves and savages is not that we are logical and they prelogical.'[43] He had witnessed many examples of logical thinking among Africans. Their different conclusions arose from their different premises, rooted in their traditional ideas and attitudes. Thus Africans would refuse to be carried on a stretcher. Such an action, being associated with the treatment of corpses, appeared to predict their death, whereas being carried in a chair did not. Given the basic convictions, the logic was flawless.

Smith granted that it was possible to be so absorbed in understanding a culture that one did not respond appropriately to the evil within it. He assumed, however, that there should be intervention, but only after the most careful assessment of the situation. Even so, intervention is dangerously close to domination, a concept which still pervades much Western thinking about Africa.

For Smith, the missionary intervenes by Christianizing African life. To Christianize, however, is not to Europeanize: 'We do not want Africans to be sham Europeans, we want them Africans.'[44] Smith then suggested how this goal might be achieved, indicating points of contact, found especially in African proverbs, folklore and customs and describing how, in the Kasenga preachers' class, he used to ask people for *Leza*'s praise names, which he saw as preparation for the gospel of Jesus Christ.

He further pointed out that there 'are indeed some New Testament texts on which it is easier to preach to Africans than to Europeans'.[45] People who believe their lives can be abstracted and hidden for safety can see what the apostle meant when he said 'Your life is hid with Christ in God.'[46] Smith clearly understood how inherited ideas shape the conceptual framework we use in interpreting our environment and how this framework can sometimes help and sometimes hinder our understanding of other cultures.

Finally, Smith advised that missionary training should include social anthropology. Colonial governments were employing anthropologists and Smith believed that anthropology was as important to missionaries.

On 8 September 1924 Smith went to a conference at High Leigh in Hertfordshire for people who were concerned about Africa. It was for him an important meeting in many ways, but not least because he met J. E. K. Aggrey. Aggrey came from Ghana (then the Gold Coast), had spent twenty years in America and was returning to his home country to work at Achimota College. He was one of the Phelps-Stokes commissioners who reported on education in Africa in 1920–1 and 1924 and had just come back from East Africa. Smith, having heard a little about him, had formed an unfavourable impression. He thought that an African who had stayed so long in the USA would want to Americanize Africa. When he met Aggrey, however, these doubts were dispelled: 'I saw in him my dearest hopes for Africa fulfilled.'[47]

In addition to this important personal contact, High Leigh bore significant organizational fruit: the Le Zoute Conference of 1926 and the International African Institute (IAI), which was formally constituted in the same year. Smith would be deeply involved in both.

Smith enjoyed reading missionary biographies, and in 1924 started a series of short biographical articles in *For Every Land* on the boyhood of great translators: Carey, Martyn, Bentley and Pilkington[48] were followed in January 1925 by two pages on Robert Moffat.[49] Smith had just finished his biography of Moffat and wrote the Preface in February 1925. *Robert Moffat: One of God's Gardeners* (1925) was dedicated to Namusa, i.e. Smith's wife Julia, another gardener. He placed Moffat's work in the historical and ethnographical setting of South Africa and wrote sympathetically and positively. He admired Moffat in many ways, not least for his achievements in language study and Bible translation, but offered a few criticisms.

He commented, for example, on Moffat's attitude to the Bechuana, especially his opinion that they were devoid of religion. Smith considered Moffat's definition of religion far too narrow. Since other Bantu peoples have a profoundly religious attitude to the world, we may expect to find the Bechuana, closely related to the Sotho, to have similar religious ideas. Moffat seemed to have ignored this possibility and, as Smith pointed out, if Moffat's writings are read carefully, it can be seen that religious beliefs and practices are being described, for example in the case of a burial.

Smith described Moffat as a pioneer and a great Bible translator along with Tyndale, Jerome and William Carey. He laid a foundation, and 'He who lays a foundation expects to see it buried beneath the edifice that is reared upon it.'[50] Moffat's good points were praised: his strength and vigour, his attractiveness, optimism and big-heartedness. Unfortunately, as Smith pointed out, Moffat's commanding presence tended to inhibit the Bechuana in their development. For all his strengths, Moffat kept power to himself. Smith believed in a greater distribution of power. He believed in self-governing, self-supporting and self-propagating churches and was influenced by his PM heritage, which emphasized an active church membership and democratic government.

Moffat was Smith's first serious historical study, and he retained a lively interest in history for the rest of his life.

Over these few years (1921–5) Smith was establishing himself as an expert on Africa. His reviews, articles and books were contributing to African studies, and the range of his African interests (cultures, languages, social conditions, history and religion) meant that he was a true Africanist. There were experts in many areas of African studies but few were building on such a broad base.

12

The complete Africanist[1] (1926)

In 1926, in addition to editing reports and magazines for the Bible Society and writing articles and reviews, Smith published two books and helped to found the International African Institute (IAI). It is difficult to imagine a more productive year.

Though outside the PM circuit system, Smith continued to write for his Church's journals and magazines and was invited to give the Hartley Lecture at the PM Conference. From 1897 to 1932, such distinguished PMs as Smith's father, John Smith, together with H. B. Kendall, A. S. Peake, A. T. Guttery and H. J. Taylor contributed to this noteworthy series. Peake remains famous and, of the others, Smith's literary legacy and scholarly reputation are the most enduring.

Like his father before him, Smith chose a missionary theme and, under the title *The Golden Stool*,[2] focused on the conflict of cultures in Africa. Sir F. D. Lugard, the famous diplomat and advocate of indirect rule, commended the volume as evidence of much reading, 'breadth of view and an insight which command admiration'.[3] Smith referred to about 150 books and articles including R. S. Rattray's 1923 book on Ashanti. Smith had met Rattray at the RAI, 'and they immediately took to each other'.[4] After reading *Ashanti*, Smith wrote his own book in three months.[5] Some of the contents had already appeared in articles or reflected his other published work, but he also introduced fresh material and made the book a comprehensive whole.

Smith was concerned that Africa's future was threatened by contact with Europeans. He had considered this briefly in *Lower Races* and in his article for *The East and the West*, April 1924. *The Golden Stool* addressed the subject thoroughly from many angles and merits serious attention as a pioneering Africanist text.

The title, which creates an association with J. G. Frazer's *Golden Bough*, referred to the Golden Stool of Ashanti. Unfortunately, it also gave the impression that Smith's book was about Ghana, though he actually used the incident to introduce his discussion of Africa as a whole. The story was as follows. The Golden Stool symbolized the Ashanti nation's soul. Nobody, not even the king, ever sat on it. The British Governor tried to take it in 1900, but the Ashanti fought rather than part with it or allow anyone to sit on it. They were defeated, but the Stool was hidden and only appeared after being desecrated twenty years later. The offenders, whose loyalty to tribal custom had faded, were tried and punished by the provincial chiefs. This time the British authorities showed no interest in acquiring the Stool because an anthropologist, Captain Rattray, had investigated Ashanti customs and explained the Stool's significance. Smith told the story to illustrate European abuse of power as well as the confusions, conflicts and changes which ocurred as cultures met in Africa, and his book went on to explore this theme.

After describing this tragic muddle, Smith recycled an article published in *Church Missionary Review*,[6] in which he surveyed the vast changes in Africa over the fifty years since his birth in 1876. He considered the debit and credit in the interaction of Africans and Europeans. Smith judged that Europeans were the chief agents of a sudden, enormous change: 'the African is being called upon to take a prodigious leap out of the prehistoric age into the twentieth century'.[7] Moreover, though he knew that African civilizations had good points and that the challenge of Africa led Livingstone, Lugard and others to noble deeds, he believed that the 'seamy side' of African life could influence Europeans negatively. In addition Europeans had done much harm – for example, by including Africans unnecessarily in the Great War, by treating them cruelly and by spreading new diseases among them. Smith concluded, 'it must be confessed that if anyone were to say that the account is against Europe then it would be difficult to contradict his statement'.[8]

Smith admired the abilities of Africans but acknowledged that they had not progressed far in European terms. Disease and isolation were doubtless partly to blame but it could also be argued that Africans had concentrated their abilities on developing complex patterns of social interaction rather than on science and technology. Whatever the case, Smith did not want Africans to be isolated but believed that they should be allowed to develop according to their abilities and traditions.

The Golden Stool continued with chapters in which Smith discussed commerce and industry, population, land and government in Africa. He soon found himself discussing race relations in South Africa, a matter of great interest to missionaries and anthropologists. J. H. Oldham had recently published *Christianity and the Race Problem* (1924). This has been described as 'the definitive study of the subject'[9] but it has also been observed that 'Oldham's ideas were by no means the common equipment of all his Christian contemporaries.'[10] Smith, however, found these ideas generally congenial but differed in one area. Oldham regarded segregation as a temporary expedient,[11] but, provided resources could be fairly divided, Smith favoured tribal kingdoms in South Africa modelled on Lesotho. As an anthropologist, he wanted to conserve African cultures but, in expressing this concern, came close to supporting separate development, and his treatment of the subject was not entirely satisfactory. Fortunately, however, he realized that, because greedy Europeans would obstruct attempts to distribute resources fairly, segregation was impractical. He offered 'thorough out-and-out Assimilation'[12] as an alternative. It was not Smith's favoured solution and could appear to suggest that Africans would assert themselves by becoming black Europeans. Moreover, Smith did not grasp, at this time, that there are other, more creative, possibilities for the European–African encounter. In due course, however, Aggrey's theme of cooperation, which was beginning to influence Smith's thinking, would reshape his approach to race relations. This would bring him much closer to J. H. Oldham, who in 1924 had declared that the 'Christian spirit, which is essentially missionary and inclusive, can never reconcile itself to any barriers which separate man from man'.[13]

The Golden Stool provides two clues that, even in 1926, Smith's practice was probably better than his theory. The book is dedicated to Andrew Dale, his collaborator in *ISP*, and to Mungalo, the chief who had helped him most to understand Ila culture. They are described – and this fact alone is significant – as 'men I was privileged to call my friends'.[14] Moreover, though a doctrinaire separatist would surely have disapproved of Dale's marriage to an Ila woman around 1912,[15] Smith said of him: 'of the men I have known none has come nearer my ideal of what a man should be'.[16]

Among liberal thinkers of those days, the South African historian W. M. Macmillan was unimpressed by anthropologists. In researching social conditions in South Africa, he had studied the papers of Dr John Philip,[17] who had advocated segregation to safeguard African life.

Smith referred to Philip in support of segregation. In Macmillan's view, however, the situation had now changed, for 'while a form of protective segregation might have been possible in the early nineteenth century, it was quite impossible in the 1920s'.[18] Macmillan, therefore, opposed the emerging functional school of anthropology with its neglect of history. Smith's regard for history was growing, but he was also heavily committed to anthropology. In time his historical studies, together with the influence of Aggrey and others, would help him find a more satisfactory theory of race relations.

In chapter 8, a revision of his article in *The East and the West*, April 1924, Smith described fully the rapid change which, he feared, would damage African societies. He saw African life as being 'at the collectivistic stage of human evolution',[19] a description which, unfortunately, could suggest that African societies were inferior. Moreover, though he thought that there was much less individualism than in Europe – 'the African acts as a part of a whole. His well-being depends on his conforming rigidly to general practice'[20] – more could have been said about the creative energy involved in the development of African social structures. In such societies, the chiefs were the traditionally authorized channels of change. European influences, however, threatened to produce greater changes by undermining the religious basis of African life, which Smith described in familiar terms: belief in a Supreme Being, survival after death and *mana* (dynamism). Africans believed that, though some rules came from God, more were laid down by the ancestors, who were closer to living beings: 'the living and the dead compose a close interdependent community, and anything which disturbs the harmony between them is regarded as a crime'.[21] Most behaviour, however, was controlled by dynamism, which exercised powerful sanctions through its charms and taboos, and all traditional morality was threatened, directly or indirectly, by European commerce, agriculture and administration.

Unscrupulous traders undoubtedly did harm, but even the best of European commerce, Smith emphasized, was a mixed blessing to Africans. When European goods were introduced, African arts and crafts were destroyed, together with the religious aspects of the skills involved and the accompanying moral sanctions. Agricultural changes were also destructive. The African sense of community ownership was undermined when individuals had their own land, and religion and morality were damaged further when land was taken away. Although other land was given in exchange, the links between present and past, living and dead (who inhabit the land of their graves), were broken and with them the ancestral moral influences. Therefore, Smith argued, the enforced removal of Africans from their land was of no advantage to the missionary, the African or the Government.

The Government brought disintegration too. It had to intervene to stop human sacrifices and cannibalism but, in doing so, struck 'at native religion which is the cement and foundation of native society. Such are the horns of the dilemma upon which the Government is impaled!'[22] Removing one problem created others. This led Smith to discuss witch-craft: 'Governments set forth proclamations for the suppression of witchcraft and, strange as it may seem, hardly anything they do causes greater resentment among the Natives.'[23] These laws prohibited witchfinding and practising witchcraft and were as foolish to Africans as banning detectives in order to stop murder would be to Europeans.

It might be supposed that Smith, a missionary, wanted the old religion replaced. His main concern, however, was that any response to Christianity should be free, not coerced by circumstances: 'I would much rather deal with people who are zealous for the old faith than with people who are shorn of all faith.'[24] He assumed, wrongly, that thanks to the influence of European individualism, African religion was doomed, and went on to consider whether other faiths could offer solutions to the serious social consequences.

He looked first at Islam and repeated and developed ideas from his *Lower Races*. He believed that Islam could do much good for Africans. Muslim missionaries were closer culturally to Africans than European Christian missionaries. Further, Islam's offer of brotherhood, which conferred equality on all nationalities, appealed strongly to Africans. Moreover, Islam's theocratic rule draws no distinction between Church and State. Smith quoted Christian writers who had observed the benefits of Islam and added that in Africa there was much to be said for the Islamic abstinence from alcohol. Finally, Islam was congenial to Africans because it permitted polygamy.[25]

Smith then indicated Islam's limitations, referring in particular to its fatalism and doctrinal rigidity. He also pointed out that although 'Muhammed undoubtedly did much for the Arabian women of his time . . . he put them – as Islam has kept them – on a very low level,'[26] and claimed that Islam had sanctioned slavery; 'it is a concomitant of Islam'.[27]

On this issue of slavery, Smith was following Samuel Zwemer, a missionary expert on Islam, who had recently mentioned 'slavery and the slave trade, which are Moslem religious privileges'.[28] In *The Spirit of Islam* (1922 edition), however, Syed Ameer Ali had already argued that Christianity was open to criticism on slavery from both the Bible and history and that Islam could show from its origins, history and practice that slavery was not of its essence.[29] Despite Smith's rash claim about slavery, however, he was generous, by the standards of the time, in his general treatment of Islam.

Nevertheless, he could not regard it as would a modern 'pluralist' in inter-faith theology. He believed, in fact, that Christianity could offer Africans much more than Islam. Despite sometimes producing confusion, it was not, in Smith's opinion, essentially disruptive but rather integrative. His ideal Christian world kept 'all the diversity that the Almighty has given to the individual peoples'.[30] He did not regard Christianity as necessarily or inevitably European. Repeatedly, he emphasized his father's position:

> our aim must be to make of the Africans not European Christians but Christians . . . and allow them to organize their faith in a manner suited to their traditions and environment.[31]

Smith admired the Church in Uganda, which had always taught Christians to regard the Church as their own. He recommended that Christianity should adapt to African cultures by using African names (his own children had African names), games, dancing, drama, African music and initiation schools. This positive evaluation of the potential of African traditions and cultures for Christians was not followed by many missionaries in those days. For example, a United Methodist traveller who visited East Africa wrote of dancing:

> The warriors came round the Mission everyday we were there and expressed their desire to arrange a dance for us. This is their form of showing hospitality . . . Much as we would have liked to have witnessed a dance, it would have been quite unseemly for a Christian Mission.[32]

Smith had no such inhibitions. Although he could not 'imagine an Anglo-Saxon dancing as a religious exercise', he could 'readily conceive of an African doing so. And why not?'[33] He noted, perceptively and with prescience, that

> Africans have also a distinct musical talent – it may well be, indeed, that they will prove to be the most gifted people in this respect . . . It is to be hoped that some day this will be, at least partially, substituted for Western music in African Churches.[34]

Later observers – for example, E. M. von Hornbostel (1933) and A. M. Jones (1958) – have written more expertly on African music, and the subject is coming into its own, with Africans playing a crucial role in its interpretation and development.[35]

African marriage customs needed sensitive discussion by Christians. Smith explained that the 'dowry' was not for buying a wife but guaranteed good treatment. Missionaries generally denounced polygamy, but Smith realized that its sudden removal would cause hardship. His own view was that the situation was analogous to that of slavery. There was no rule against it in the New Testament, but eventually it would be seen as unchristian.

Since Christianity's future in Africa should be in African hands, Smith stated that

> missionaries are not a permanent factor in the life of Africa – they will one day (the sooner the better) disappear because no longer needed. It is not their business to decide what form African Christianity shall take.[36]

He realized that missionaries had exercised too much control and had been too unsympathetic to local cultures. Smith prophesied that in 2026 many Africans would blame Europeans for letting valuable parts of African life disappear. Ironically, such things, whatever they might be, had been noted for posterity by missionary/anthropologists such as Smith, Junod and Roscoe.

Similar thinking was expressed independently by Roland Allen, who thought that missionaries had no business in judging what is fitting in Africa. Allen was 'the gadfly of missions and his criticisms were not welcomed by the mainstream'.[37] He said that if 'we want to see spontaneous expansion we must establish native churches free from our control'.[38] He considered that it was enough to teach positively, not negatively, 'and be content to wait whilst the native Christians slowly recreate their own customs'.[39] Missiologically speaking, Smith and Allen were in many ways kindred spirits. In general, however, Smith was more committed to the institutional church and the philanthropic agencies which were part of missionary endeavour, while Allen emphasized the local church and referred to the Spirit more than Smith, J. H. Oldham and other liberal missionaries.

In *The Golden Stool* Smith highlighted the dangers of cultural imperialism as well as the inevitability of change. Well-meaning travellers easily fall into the trap of assuming that the whole world should resemble their own cultures. There are many areas where the imperialistic tendency asserts itself: for example, the assumption that unmodified Western agendas of agriculture, medicine, education, economics, politics, philosophy and linguistics are the best and most appropriate for Africa.

Smith was interested in anthropology and social science. The academic anthropologists of that time explored primitive societies, as they called them, for their archaeological interest, whereas Smith, a pragmatist, sought help from the social sciences in devising strategies to cope with change. On the basis of perceived facts he expressed forthright views about the effects of European influences on Africa; and he urged his readers, having looked at the same facts, to protest vigorously when they saw injustice.

In concluding *The Golden Stool* Smith mentioned the progressive ideas expressed in his father's Hartley Lecture and indicated that he wanted his own to be seen as a sequel. He also referred to an enlarged photograph of his friend Mungalo, which had a prominent place in his study. The two men had talked together for many hours: 'Through the window of Mungalo's soul thrown open so unreservedly to me, I saw the African in all his weakness and strength.'[40] As a result, Smith declared: 'Heaven itself will be something less than heaven if I do not hear that greeting – *Mulongwangu*! – ("My friend") when I enter the pearly gates.'[41] It is clear that a form of universalism, for which the loyalty of friendship was an eternal value, lay behind Smith's assessment of non-Christian religions.

The Golden Stool shows Smith as a true Africanist, interested in Africa as a whole. Most other experts in African studies concentrated in European fashion on their own areas of expertise: languages, administration, education, missions, anthropology, history. But Smith looked at the whole picture. Of all those who studied Africa, it is probable that only Sir Harry Johnston, whose day was rapidly drawing to a close, was as well informed as Smith over the whole range of interlocking issues. Smith's comprehensive treatment made *The Golden Stool* a significant Africanist text, particularly for British colonial thinkers. He had written it as his practical response to the High Leigh meeting of 1924, where he and others decided that it was high time for much more to be done for Africa. These were early days for Western economics, education and administration in Africa. British colonies in Africa were expected to become independent, but progress was slow and 'relatively little money was spent on colonial economic development, education, public health or scientific research'.[42] Smith reviewed all these matters and the *The Golden Stool* became essential reading for colonial administrators. It is said to have been his 'most influential book . . . which went through five impressions in its first year'.[43] It was also essential reading for missionaries, and Adrian Hastings has said that 'it could well be regarded as the most authoritative textbook for African missiology in the inter-war years'.[44]

The 1924 conference at High Leigh called for positive development policies, based on scientific studies of the contact of Western civilization with African culture. A. L. Warnshuis, one of the IMC secretaries, suggested that a Bureau of African Languages and Literature be formed.[45] He, Hanns Vischer and Smith drafted this organization's first constitution. After further discussions it was formally created in 1926 as the International Institute for African Languages and Cultures, later known as the International African Institute (IAI). Within it Protestant and Roman Catholic missionaries worked with secular scholars and administrators from many countries. At an inaugural luncheon at the Savoy Hotel on 30 June 1926, Smith joined many others who were interested in Africa. He sat beside A. L. Warnshuis and opposite R. R. Marett and J. H. Oldham. The chair was taken by L. S. Amery, MP, Secretary of State for the Colonies, and many other distinguished people were present, including Sir Frederick Lugard, J. G. Frazer, Alice Werner, Dennison Ross and Hanns Vischer.[46]

A contribution from the Rockefeller Foundation of £1,000 per annum for the first five years helped the Institute to pursue research into African languages and cultures and to promote the publication of educational literature in African languages. The Institute was non-political but encouraged practical applications of the research findings as well as international cooperation in technological and other development activities.

Lord Lugard chaired the IAI Executive Council, which was formally constituted on 1 July 1926. Smith was a member of this Council along with Colonel Derendinger, Revd Father Dubois, Professor Levy-Bruhl, Professor Carl Meinhof and, inevitably, J. H. Oldham. Council meetings took Smith to many European countries over the next few years. In addition, the IAI had two Directors: Professor Diedrich Westermann of Berlin, a linguistic expert who had been a missionary in West Africa, and Professor Maurice Delafosse of École des Langues Orientales Vivantes in Paris.

The IAI created 'a style of African studies which was at the behest of the colonial system and was subsequently responsible for the type of ethnographic scrutiny to which Africans and their societies came to be subjected'.[47] It attempted to increase understanding and accelerate development within the overall colonialist agenda. It would occupy much of Smith's time and energy for the next thirty years and has been described as 'in large part his brain-child'.[48] J. H. Oldham, whose knowledge of Africa was growing rapidly, was also involved in the IAI from the beginning and became its director in the 1930s.

The High Leigh meeting also led to the IMC International Conference held at Le Zoute, Belgium, 14–21 September 1926. This was devoted exclusively to Africa, and Smith agreed to write a book on it.[49] In July a special double edition of *IRM* contained articles on the Conference themes and a poem by Arthur Shirley Cripps. Smith, as editor of *The Bible in the World*, produced a double-sized 'Special Africa Number' for September 1926. Eminent people contributed articles: Henri Junod, Alice Werner and Carl Meinhof, 'the greatest living authority on African languages'.[50] Smith provided editorial remarks and a short article, 'African Alphabets', with examples of scripts used in Africa.[51] His magazine had its own poem, 'The Language Shapers' by the Revd Philip J. Fisher, 'Dedicated to Africa's Literary Pioneers'.[52]

Smith attended Le Zoute on behalf of the Bible Society and was allowed to write about the Conference in his own way. He wrote quickly and *The Christian Mission in Africa* was published before the end of the year. The influence of African thinking can be seen in his basic conviction that, despite its bewildering variety, the New Africa must be seen as a whole. Le Zoute looked at the evangelization of Africa

and included studies on Education, Health, Land and Labour. Smith
gave a paper on the task of evangelism.[53]

While agreeing with most of the Conference statements, Smith would
have preferred clearer or different responses on some issues. On the
matter of polygamy, for example, the Conference was less tolerant than
Smith, simply affirming the lifelong and exclusive union of one man and
one woman as the Christian standard. And, where land was concerned,
the protected lands apportioned to Africans, though insufficient, were
simply accepted as a *fait accompli*:

> They did not definitely declare (as some of us would have liked them
> to declare) that the natives do not exist in Africa on sufferance but
> have definite rights in the land.[54]

Professor Westermann, IAI Director, came as a consultant, and the
establishment of the Institute was welcomed and commended to all
missions in Africa. The IAI would help missionaries to solve linguistic
problems and understand African societies. Knowledge, however, can
be misused so that with the vision of a Christian Africa Smith realized
that there was the nightmare of a selfish, grasping, soulless Africa.

Le Zoute asked for a reconsideration of 'our attitude towards some
aspects of the African's life, so that the Church might become more
deeply rooted in the nature of the people – more truly African'.[55]
That represented Smith's thinking too. He hoped he had reported the
conference fairly and made it clear when his own opinions were being
offered.

Smith met old friends at Le Zoute and made new ones from many
countries. W. C. Willoughby, whom Smith had met when Khama
visited London in 1895, had pioneered Tiger Kloof Training Institute in
South Africa and went to Hartford as a professor in 1919. He had
been investigating African religion for many years and shared many of
Smith's convictions. He was one of the main speakers at Le Zoute and
included England on his itinerary. When he visited Smith, he brought
a long manuscript which Smith recommended to Macmillans on his
behalf. The publishers, however, were not interested in this work on
African religion and returned the text to Smith.[56] The proposed book
must have been *The Soul of the Bantu*, which was published in 1928 by
Doubleday in the USA and by SCM Press in the UK.

Altogether, 1926 was a great year in Smith's life. He was prominent in setting up the IAI, and his books, *The Christian Mission in Africa* and *The Golden Stool*, showed his mastery of all aspects of African studies. He was now a complete Africanist whose opinion was sought and valued by many.

13

A magic wand (1927–1929)

When Basil Matthews reviewed the Bible Society's Popular Annual Report for 1927 (*The Immortal Story*) he said, 'Mr E. W. Smith's fountain pen is a magic wand.'[1]

Smith used that wand very creatively over the next three years, but he was also in demand as a public speaker. During 1927 and 1928, for example, he gave the Long Lectures, published as *The Secret of the African* (1929), for the Church Missionary Society (CMS). On 26 May 1927 his subject was Akan religious belief and practices, and he was surprised and dismayed when J. E. K. Aggrey, an Akan, walked in and sat down in front of him! After the lecture Aggrey spoke on the same topic. Smith wished later that he had made detailed notes of Aggrey's remarks, but at the time was too transfixed to write anything. Aggrey, then on a short visit to England, was preparing a book on race relations which he discussed with Miss Gollock, editor of the *IRM*, and others.[2]

A few weeks later Smith was again involved with the CMS, speaking at the Society's Summer School at Eastbourne over the August Bank Holiday weekend, 30 July to 1 August. At this conference he met A. G. Fraser, the first Principal of Achimota College, set up in Ghana (then Gold Coast) in 1924, and talked with him at length about the college and Aggrey, the friend and Assistant Vice-Principal, with whom Fraser worked very closely.[3] Meanwhile, Aggrey, by then in New York, was taken ill and died suddenly of meningitis on Saturday 30 July 1927. Smith knew nothing of this as he travelled slowly homeward, taking a train to Hastings and then walking along the coast to Dover. There were no newspapers on the Monday, a bank holiday, but Smith read the news the next day, 2 August, and was deeply affected:

the contrast between the smiling summertide and the rebellious grief in my soul smote me hard. To die – to be taken from his work now,

when he had refurbished his tools and was beginning to forge links
between White and Black![4]

Edwin Smith would soon become Aggrey's biographer, but, for the time
being, Bible House and his other interests kept him fully occupied.

Smith produced his fifth *Popular Annual Report* for the Bible Society
in 1927. These reports, about 100 pages in length, were written to a
formula. The prologue looked at the theme's literary and biblical background. Then, with examples from the Society's activities, it followed
the work of translators and colporteurs and included a financial report
and appeal for funds. Previously, Smith had written *The Bridge
Builders* (1923), *Like Unto Leaven* (1924), *The Seekers* (1925) and *The
Everlasting Doors* (1926). In 1927, his 'magic wand' of a pen conjured
The Immortal Story.

The Bible Society, in common with other missionary organizations,
was growing in confidence after the uncertainties produced by world-
wide economic depression. Overseas supporters helped the Bible
Society raise additional funds but, as Smith wrote in *The Bible in
the World* for January 1928, 'More than anything else, we need an
outpouring of fervent, trustful, continuous prayer.'[5] This was a new
emphasis in his missionary writings, but it never became prominent in
his thinking. Although a devout and spiritual person, Smith did not
stress intercessory prayer in the manner of evangelical missionary
societies and teachers. His liberal, intellectual approach probably
regarded consecrated human effort in God's service as more significant
than intercessory prayer. His spirituality stressed the mysticism of
Dante – and of Evelyn Underhill (1875–1941),[6] who thought that by
mysticism 'the self may be joined by love to the one eternal and ultimate
Object of love'.[7] Such mysticism opposed 'magic' (Smith's 'dynamism'),
a system of gaining power over the unseen, using either the 'prayer for
rain of orthodox Churchmen, or the consciously self-hypnotizing
devices of "New Thought" '.[8] From such a viewpoint, dreams, trances
and healings as methods of engaging with God's power were discouraged. Moreover, theologians like John Oman saw prayer, when used to
influence the invisible, as a magical and unworthy attempt to manipulate God and others,[9] while in Underhill's view the danger of 'magic'
was that it included 'all forms of self-seeking transcendentalism' which
'obtains for the self or group of selves something which it or they did
not previously possess'.[10]

Smith seems to have been part of that liberal tradition and so, while understanding the dynamic aspect of African religions, did not emphasize its possible potential as much as African Independent Churches, such as the Kimbanguists in Zaire,[11] the Independent Churches in South Africa[12] or, possibly, African members of the Methodist Church in Zambia. Smith, like many scholarly Western Christians, was wary of elements in the New Testament – for example, healings and exorcisms – which African Christians would find congenial; and though he would have accepted that intercession is closer to the main traditions of Christian life and practice, the social sciences and Dante's mysticism seem to have been more powerful influences on his thinking. Not surprisingly, therefore, instead of developing his thoughts on prayer he focused his other devotional articles for 1928 on the attributes of God.[13]

In the BFBS Popular Annual Report for that year, *The Glory of the Garden*, Smith mentioned the IMC meeting which had taken place at Jerusalem at Easter. Among other matters the question of secularism had been raised, and Smith commented that secular civilization was 'everywhere spreading like some foul, noxious weed, eating into, subverting the non-Christian religions, draining the life-blood from the Christian Church itself'.[14] Subsequent discussion of this major theological issue led to distinctions between 'secularism' and 'secularization' and to a range of evaluations of what was happening to Western society. But Smith's vivid description reflects the frustration of Christians beginning to realize that they could not check apparently relentless change.

Smith's editorial work for the Bible Society led to a book on Bible colporteurs, *Tales of God's Packmen*, which was published in mid-1928.[15] He brought together stories about colporteurs that came to him as Literary Superintendent at the Bible House. They were first published in *For Every Land* from 1926 and retold in this single volume with young people in mind. As *The Immortal Story*, his Popular Report for 1927, shows, he saw the value of story-telling. Unusually, for Smith, these stories do not take us to Africa south of the Sahara but to Russia, Korea and China. They provide, in fact, an example of his global interests and show his love for the Bible as a book for all people.

At that time the World Dominion Press was promoting world evangelization and the creation of indigenous churches. It published both the provocative writings of Roland Allen and a series of books surveying the state of God's kingdom throughout the world. By 1928, Manchuria, Amazonia and several African countries had been covered, and Smith contributed a volume on the two Rhodesias.[16] In *The Way of the White Fields in the Rhodesias*, he reviewed geographical, historical and political aspects of these countries as well the work of missions. There were many, even then, who favoured uniting the Rhodesias, but Smith preferred linking Northern Rhodesia with Tanganyika and Nyasaland, 'with a land and native policy much more favourable to the African than that which prevails in the south'.[17] He supported a segregation policy in which Africans would have their own land apportioned more equitably than hitherto.

Smith's opinion, as one who was involved in many interdenominational organizations, was that denominationalism was 'the shame of Western Christianity'.[18] He thought it would disappear as African churches became independent. In the Zambian Copperbelt, which was in its infancy when Smith wrote *White Fields*, a remarkable missionary development was initiated by African Christians who came to the copper mines from Christianized villages around Zambia. The United Missions to the Copperbelt, which led to the United Church of Zambia (UCZ), was an indigenous movement of cooperation which developed before missionary and overseas control could stifle such an initiative.[19] Though all this happened after Smith wrote his book, he had pointed out that copper mining would create a missionary opportunity.

Smith included in *White Fields* a review of literature in African languages. He thought that Bemba, 'One of the most important of the Rhodesian languages',[20] would make a good literary language for Northern Rhodesia.[21] In fact, Bemba became the main language of the Copperbelt and is used widely in Zambia, especially in the United Church of Zambia.

White Fields was mainly descriptive, but Smith occasionally offered observations and criticisms intended to nudge churches in the directions suggested at Le Zoute. His carefully gathered facts were used sixty years later to give comparative statistical data in a sociological study of the churches in Zambia.[22]

The Revd A. S. Cripps read the manuscript of *White Fields*.[23] Cripps, an eccentric poet-missionary to Zimbabwe, was a staunch defender of African rights and a great friend of the Wesleyan, John White, who also read Smith's manuscript.[24] Cripps was in England at the time[25] and his book, *An Africa for Africans*, was published in 1927. He held that

Africans should have their own territories, 'possessory segregation' as opposed to segregation 'as a *pro tempore* solution to the more immediate and pressing problems of racial friction'.[26] Smith found that Cripps objected to some of his own judgments and that,[27] unlike the liberal missionaries, had little time for 'many of the appurtances of modern missionary methods, such as committee-work' and was afraid of 'mission education becoming an arm of the State'.[28]

By this time Smith had made friends with Philip Fisher (1883–1961), a Primitive Methodist minister who, having been an army chaplain (1915–19), had served mainly in northern circuits until 1925, when he came to Kingston upon Thames.[29] This brought him into direct contact with Smith, who was nearby at Walton on Thames, and a long friendship began. Philip Fisher was a man of deep sensitivity and spiritual insight. A poet and artist, his first book was a volume of poems, *Khaki Vignettes* (1917), illustrated by himself. He wrote for the *Aldersgate Magazine* about the war poets and thought that the poems of the young men were the best, while the Poet Laureate contributed little of merit.[30] Fisher became editor of the *Methodist Leader* and thus shared a common professional interest with Smith. From time to time Smith received Fisher's poems – and cartoons: for example, a 1926 caricature of Smith sitting on an African Stool. Fisher also sent Smith his poetical Christmas greetings cards. In August 1929 he, Smith and others had a holiday in Norfolk. It was commemorated by a short poem, 'Moonlight on Barton Broad', and a letter for Smith's birthday in which Fisher wrote 'of a friendship which has meant much during recent years', and described himself as *Il Pescatore*, suggesting he shared Smith's interest in Italian and in Dante.[31]

Smith enlisted his friend in his work at Bible House. Fisher's first contribution, mentioned in the last chapter, was a poem about those who translate the Bible. He also wrote devotional articles for *The Bible in the World*, and 1928 ended with a Fisher poem for Christmas and the New Year.

The Smiths' daughter, Matsi, had been working for the *Blue Guides* in London and had settled in her own flat in London. Her fiancé, Howard Jones, had suggested that since in his work as a mycologist he travelled around the world so much, she would do well to know how to look after herself. Perhaps because Howard's father was an Anglican clergyman, he and Matsi were married at Oatlands Parish Church, near the Smith home at Walton, early in 1929. Howard, who had worked in

West Africa, soon obtained a post in the Egyptian Government Agriculture Department, and Matsi joined him in Cairo later in the year.[32]

Smith returned to a favourite theme in writing *Exploration in Africa*, which appeared in 1929. This volume in the King's Treasuries of Literature series presented the explorers, so far as possible, in their own words. A general introduction[33] was followed by nineteen extracts from famous explorers, each briefly introduced by Smith. The book was well received by *Africa*,[34] which judged the choice of extracts to be excellent. Such approval, indeed, is hardly surprising, granted Smith's long-term interest in exploration and the years he had spent in Africa. What is striking, however, is that Smith, who usually found Livingstone prosaic and restrained, thought his description of the Victoria Falls the best of the many he had read: 'not one, in my opinion equals his'.[35]

Smith made it clear that Africans, and many Arab travellers, were already familiar with what the explorers discovered[36] and highlighted African participation in the exploration. Some of the Africans were known by name, for example Mombai, Susi and Chuma, and without them nothing could have been done.

> I confess that when I follow, say, Stanley in his tremendous journey of 999 days, it is not Stanley's indomitable pluck that I admire most; it is the endurance and quenchless loyalty of his men.[37]

Twenty years later, in an unpublished manuscript on porters,[38] Smith would highlight this loyalty again; and, more recently, the African contribution has been noticed by other scholars: 'the indispensable part played by oarsmen, porters, scouts, interpreters and guides has been too quickly forgotten'.[39]

Smith, then, knew the perils and problems of travelling in Africa in the early days. His own journeys, however, led him, with the help of the human sciences, to explore African societies, their cultures and languages, and especially their religious life.

A. Victor Murray (1890–1967), a lecturer in education at the Selly Oak Colleges in Birmingham and a notable Primitive Methodist – he became Vice-President in 1932 and would be Vice-President of the Methodist Conference in 1947 – went on a long tour of Africa to study 'Native education, particularly in the training of teachers'.[40] As a result, he published *The School in the Bush* (1929). In expressing his gratitude to the many people who had assisted him in his travels and researches, he made special mention of

> the help that I have received in the writing of the book from the Rev. Edwin W. Smith. He has discussed it with me in all its stages, and it is very largely through his encouragement that I have been able to carry it through to the end.[41]

There was, however, one matter about which Smith and Murray disagreed, the question of language. Murray, after lengthy discussion, concluded that 'a language is not necessarily "the soul of a people", nor is it a necessity in order to "enshrine" such a soul'.[42] Smith, however, entitled his book on Bible translation *The Shrine of a People's Soul* (1929) and used it to fill another gap in the literature, the work of the literary missionary.[43] The missionary had been described as explorer, evangelist, educationist and doctor, but so far as Smith knew, and he knew a great deal, the literary missionary had been neglected.[44]

Smith believed that, since a person's heart is best reached through their mother tongue, it is a human tragedy if a language is lost. Powerful nations had impoverished humanity by destroying the languages and cultures of the weak. He urged missionaries, therefore, to conserve and develop languages and argued his case again in the 1930 Popular Annual Report, *In the Mother-Tongue*.

To Smith, Christianity remained exotic and foreign when it came dressed in Western forms. The mother-tongue was, he argued, the most sensible form of communication but, for practical reasons, written translations had not been made in all dialects. A major factor has been a tendency to unify dialects into one tongue, and Smith traced how English had emerged, referred to Dante's role in creating Italian out of many regional dialects, and cited 'Union Ibo' as an example from Africa. Not all such languages, however, have been produced by manipulation. Some – for example, Swahili, which Smith thought could become the language of East Africa – have developed on their own.

Smith loved language. In his early days he had been involved in literary societies, and he read widely in English literature. He respected African languages, told others about their rich vocabularies and, in his book, described his own experience of Ila, to him a marvellous language. He then went on to give advice about Bible translation. He offered three criteria: a translation must be faithful to the original text, intelligible to the readers and beautiful in style.[45] He did not require literal fidelity to the original tongues, for in some cases literalism produces the opposite of the intended meaning. Smith cited negative questions for which the answers 'Yes' or 'No' have different meanings in different languages.

Two of Smith's criteria affect the reader. W. A. Smalley, over sixty years later, remarked that Smith focused 'more fully on translation problems from the standpoint of the receptor language than did some of the biblical scholars who preceded and followed him'.[46]

Smith saw biblical revelation as progressive and to be assessed by reference to Jesus Christ.[47] Having said that, he firmly believed that all people should have an open and complete Bible. The coming independent and autonomous churches would, Smith believed, acquire spiritual and intellectual nourishment from the Bible. 'Nothing but the Scriptures can keep the younger churches tethered to the central truths of our religion. Happily the churches overseas are very largely literate, and they have access to the Bible. We have no fear of their future while this is the case.'[48]

Smith realized that what were known as 'younger churches' would make their own contributions to Bible interpretation:

> It is not the book of one race but the book of humanity, and not until all mankind interprets it in the light of various racial genius will all its meaning be revealed . . . Did not Dr Westcott say that the adequate commentary on St John would one day be written by an Indian?[49]

Shrine was well written and readable. Smith referred to many languages and translations as well as to his own experiences and knowledge of anthropology. More than twenty years later a reviewer in the then new journal *The Bible Translator* regarded it as

> a scholarly forecast of all the volumes of *The Bible Translator* yet published, written before this publication was ever thought of. In those days the American Bible Society used to urge every translator to read this book.[50]

Following Aggrey's untimely death at the age of 51, the Phelps-Stokes Trustees invited Smith to write Aggrey's biography. Many people, in Africa and elsewhere, helped him with the work, and Miss Gollock, who included a brief sketch of Aggrey in *Sons of Africa* (1928), advised

Smith throughout the project. After finishing his Popular Report for 1928, *The Glory of the Garden*, Smith met many of Aggrey's colleagues, friends and family in the USA. He visited Mrs Aggrey at her home in Salisbury, North Carolina, and went to the church, of which Aggrey was pastor, at Sandy Ridge. There he met a Mr Miller who had become a 'new man under Aggrey's influence'.[51]

Smith learnt a great deal from Aggrey. He was impressed both by him as a person and by his principle of cooperation. Aggrey rejected amalgamation as a solution to racial problems. He also rejected the conflict and hatred stirred up by the ultra-radical, Marcus Garvey. Likewise, cooperation led him to reject Gandhi's non-cooperation. Aggrey wanted blacks to become equal partners with others and, to illustrate the point, Smith quoted Aggrey's famous saying about the piano keys:

> You can play a tune of sorts on the white keys, and you can play a tune of sorts on the black keys, but for harmony you must use both the black and the white.[52]

Later, to make a similar point, Smith quoted another Aggreyism: 'If you go to Africa expecting something from us, and give us a chance to do something for you, we will give you a surprise.'[53]

In *The Golden Stool* Smith expressed his concern that the break-up of tribal life would destroy African religious concepts. But, as we have already noted, these concepts have proved much more durable than he expected in 1926. Indeed Aggrey himself provides an early indication of this resilience. Though living for twenty years in America, away from his homeland and tribe, he still held several of his early beliefs, 'some of them strangely incongruent with the scientific and Christian doctrines which he afterwards taught'.[54]

Aggrey often reflected on African religious capacities. Smith thought that African Christians would eventually show true Christianity to the whole world. By the end of the twentieth century the vigour of African Christianity[55] shows that Smith's remark was particularly prescient.

Although Aggrey was influenced by America, his worldview was essentially African. In other words it was characterized by wholeness. He recommended Christianity, education and agriculture to his people but not as separate things: 'to Aggrey they appeared a unity . . . I think that in adopting this attitude Aggrey was truly African'.[56]

Smith's *Aggrey*, which appeared in 1929, was very popular and ran to many editions. He made nothing from it because the royalties were made available to Mrs Aggrey. Through the journey and the reflection involved in writing the book, Smith came to a more favourable view of the USA and its possible usefulness to Africa, which may have kindled his desire to help African Americans in the USA itself.

Smith's Long Lectures, which Aggrey visited in 1927, were also published by the SCM Press in May 1929. Smith took the title, *The Secret of the African*, from his 1907 lecture and surveyed African religion more widely than ever before. He drew on material from South Africa, Central Africa and West Africa and used literature published during the 1920s as well as his own writings. For a survey of ancestor beliefs, he referred his readers to W. C. Willoughby's book, *The Soul of the Bantu* (1928), and described it elsewhere as 'a text-book which every candidate for African service should be bound to study'.[57]

Secret shows Smith as a phenomenologist, a student of religious experiences. He drew from Rudolf Otto's book, *The Idea of the Holy*, the description of the raw experience of religion as a sense of awe and went on to use his dynamism/spirits/God triangle to analyse African religions. He began by discussing magic and religion. Dynamism, Smith's preferred alternative to magic, responds to the incalculable by using medicines and charms to control such circumstances. Smith explained that religion and magic differ in that 'magic seeks to control, to compel; religion seeks to entreat, to persuade, to conciliate'.[58] In spite of this opinion he tended to accept dynamism as religious.

Smith also described African beliefs in ancestral and other spirits. Their various ideas about the destination of the dead suggested to him that Africans 'conceive the spirit to be capable of multi-presence'.[59] Whatever the case, he wanted his readers to realize that the spiritual world is intensely real for Africans, the living and the dead forming 'a close, interdependent community'.[60] Smith pointed out that some spirits, for example Shimunenga, are regarded with awe rather than terror and others are recognized as good. Evil spirits, however, produce fear and have to be appeased or driven away. Smith saw Christianity bringing release from such terrors.

In describing African beliefs in God, Smith chose the more experiential word, 'awareness', and tried to draw his conclusions from African experiences. Contrary to evolutionary teaching Smith saw no reason 'for dismissing as inconceivable that an uncultured people should rise to a relatively lofty conception of a God'.[61] Smith's use of 'uncultured' may offend us, but the notion that Africans have a developed concept of God should not. Nevertheless, it was often vague, especially among the Zulu and the Baganda. Smith thought that these peoples were much more aware of the ancestors of their powerful rulers than of God.

Smith had a strong conviction that belief in God was the main link between African religion and Christianity. This belief may not have been as strong or as widespread as Smith supposed. He admitted that for Africans the Supreme Being was usually seen as remote for various reasons – for example human wrongdoing or insensitivity. In general Smith considered that, for Africans, other spiritual beings were more immediate than the Supreme Being, and that therefore it was considered wise to be on good terms with them.

Although Smith described African religion respectfully, he offered a critical assessment of it on the basis of three criteria: that (a) a religion should produce the highest emotions, (b) it should rest on a rational basis and (c) it should issue in noble living. Smith expected a religion to touch a person's feelings, thoughts and actions. The meaning of the words 'highest' and 'noble' is, perhaps, less obvious today than it was when Smith carried out his assessment.

Following these criteria, he observed that dynamism can evoke noble emotions, such as bravery to overcome fear. It can also foster lower emotions, such as jealousy and malice. Smith criticized it for reasoning that like acts upon like, that the part acts on the whole and that one's desire produces the effect expressed in one's words. Smith found these illogical and rejected dynamism on the ground of an inadequate basis in reason. Dynamism's ethic was controlled by taboo and protected life and property, but when Europeans disrupted African society the controls exercised by dynamism were disrupted.

Spiritism, with its close interdependent fellowship of living and dead, provided a strong social bond, reinforced by the Africans' attachment to the land where their ancestors' bodies were buried and their spirits still hovered. Since, therefore, African spiritism, with its social benefits, would be threatened by mobility, something stronger and more universal was needed.

Finally, Smith evaluated African theism. He identified it as a vague concept, lacking a moral dimension and with little conviction that God is personal or good. Moreover, belief in God as Love was largely unknown. Smith did not hide his belief that for Africans, whose religion was being threatened, the only hope was in the gospel of Christ.

Secret was Smith's mature statement on African religion. Its approach was synthetic, drawing together beliefs from all around Africa, and it expanded and updated his previous writings. Smith knew that different beliefs were found in different areas, and his survey took him from people to people. He was looking, however, for common features and used his 'triangle' (dynamism, spirits and God) as an analytical tool. Seventy years on there is less enthusiasm for a meta-theory of African religion. The tendency is to speak of the religions of Africa. Other scholars, moreover, have preferred to write of traditional (Parrinder) or primal (Taylor) religion, and it may be granted that these terms provide 'a more positive and respectful relabelling of those religions categorized as "primitive" '.[62] They tend, however, to have pejorative overtones, whereas Smith's 'African religion' places the subject more nearly on a par with other religions.

Smith's books were travelling around the world. Probably typical of PM missionaries, Carlos Wiles (1904–95), who went to Nigeria in 1926, had copies of *The Ila-Speaking Peoples, The Religion of Lower Races, The Golden Stool* and *The Shrine of a People's Soul*;[63] and Margery Perham, when in Lesotho on her travels around Africa in 1929, discussed his *Golden Stool*: 'I borrowed it', she recalled, 'from the Resident Commissioner because I thought it would raise some general problems. It certainly does.'[64]

In the decade ending in 1929 Smith's magic wand had been very busy. He had written or edited eighteen books, eight of them over the previous two years. He was becoming well known to the churches, to anthropologists and to those who were interested in Africa. After all this work, however, and with diabetes to contend with, he needed a rest, and at the end of the year went to the Holy Land, Egypt and Sudan.

Eminent anthropologist (1930–1934)

Smith left England on 22 October 1929 on 'a trip taken by doctors' orders in search of health, and, incidentally of other things'.[1] He suffered from diabetes and overwork, and his journey around the Middle East was hardly a 'rest cure'. It was, however, a refreshing change.

Edwin and Julia went together as far as Paris and then caught trains to different places: Julia to St Raphael in the south of France and Edwin to Genoa in north-west Italy, where he boarded his ship, the *Umbria*. His trip to Egypt via Naples, Athens and Istanbul was fascinating and included meetings with Bible Society officials as well as sightseeing.

After Istanbul the *Umbria* steamed around the Turkish coast. When it anchored at Mersina, Smith visited Tarsus, St Paul's birthplace, about fifteen miles away, and was shocked to see the town's ruined buildings and general disorder. The people lived in squalor and looked miserable. Later in the day he read Ramsay's account of Tarsus.[2] The contrast between its distinguished history and present dilapidation troubled him, and he wondered how the city had fallen into such a state and why there was no monument to Paul and no Christian centre bearing his name.

Wherever he went, Smith observed the scenery and tried to sense the history, religion and current social situation of the places he saw. Not surprisingly, he was interested in changes and conflicts of cultures and had at least one research question in mind: 'One of the things I sh[ould] like to do while in Egypt is to satisfy myself as to any interactions culturally between Egyptians & Africans'.[3] In response to Elliot Smith's idea that culture diffused from Egypt, Smith listed five possibilities: similarities between Egyptian and other African cultures could point to a common ancient source, to north influencing south or vice versa, to shared contact with a passing group such as the Hamites (Smith's favoured solution), or to independent origin and development.

Smith arrived in Egypt on Saturday 9 November and stayed with his daughter, Matsi, and her husband at Maadi, a few miles south of Cairo's city centre. He saw the sights and interviewed significant people, including Dr Zwemer,[4] the chief missionary expert on Islam, who did not think that it could adapt to modern conditions. The two men visited a synagogue, where Smith saw carefully preserved manuscripts of the Pentateuch. A discussion on Palestine followed. There had been riots there the previous August and Dr Zwemer, who sympathized with the Jews, thought that if Muslims were hanged for killing Jews there would be an explosion throughout the Islamic world. 'I said, maybe,' Smith recorded, 'but if Arabs [are] guilty [they] must be punished. But justice to both sides must be done.'[5]

Smith saw many other places and met many other people. The Bishop of Sudan,[6] who remembered him from Le Zoute, encouraged him to visit Sudan. Constance Padwick of the CMS, biographer of Temple Gairdner (d. 1928), discussed translations with him. Smith saw the site of ancient Memphis and the Nile with its fertile plain. He went several times to the museum, had fascinating discussions with missionaries, and visited a bazaar and several mosques. The mosque and teaching centre of al-Azhar was especially interesting. It had been a great centre of Arabic learning and a university since AD 988. According to Smith's *Baedeker* there were 246 teachers and 4,838 students in 1926–7. The library of 52,000 volumes held 15,000 manuscripts. One magnificent copy of the Koran had large pages with letters three inches high at the top and bottom. The students came from many countries – 'A reminder that Islam professes to be universal – all brothers, one faith, one language'[7] – and Smith saw them, sitting on the ground around their teachers. Their course lasted for fifteen years. He noticed old men among the students and was told that some were so enamoured of the work that they stayed on for years after graduating.

The next phase of Smith's trip took him by overnight train to the Holy Land. He noted all he saw – people, citrus trees, olives – and related his journey to biblical scenes: 'In SW is Valley of Elah where armies of Saul & of the Philistines lay over ag[ainst] each other & David slew Goliath.'[8] At Jerusalem he was surprised by the modern buildings. He was shown around the city and came to the Holy Sepulchre: 'imitation flowers on the altar. Gaudy images of the virgin. Ghastly crucifixions . . . The whole thing a horror . . .'.[9]

Smith stayed in a hostel connected with the Anglican Cathedral and, at breakfast, heard the views of an experienced CMS missionary on the Balfour Declaration of 1917, which favoured the establishment of a Jewish national home in Palestine. The missionary considered it a disgrace to the British nation, brought about by the need for Jewish money for the war. Smith listened as she explained that making a national home for the Jews meant driving out Arabs. Before the Great War, she said, Arabs and Jews lived together amicably, but now there was hatred of Jews and the situation was very serious: 'Tears in her eyes as she spoke of the injustice done to Arabs.'[10]

Smith continued his travels by car to Haifa. It was wet, and travelling was at times difficult on the muddy roads. Smith felt that he was in biblical times: 'We could not see Anathoth – hidden behind a hill. I remembered that Peake went there so that he could tell Jeremiah in heaven that he had visited his village.'[11] At Nablus Smith met the Samaritan High Priest and learned that the Samaritan community was small, about 150 people. He saw the Samaritan Pentateuch and found that a copy, which took about five months to make, was sold for £5.

Then, travelling via Nazareth, Smith arrived at Haifa in the early evening. He found his host, Rohold, 'wholly on the side of Jews. What the truth may be I know not yet. It is very hard to get. Rohold is as fervently for Jews as Miss Hassell was for Arabs.'[12] Smith discussed the Arab/Jewish issue often and noted the strongly held opinions. If he reached a conclusion, it is not recorded in his diary.

Smith visited Damascus before returning to Galilee in early December. A well-informed German pastor showed him around Galilee and took him to a place by the lake where Jesus may have taught a great crowd from a boat. The steep bank provided favourable acoustics: 'This moved me greatly. All where we have been and are going to walk was the scene of His greatest teaching. Here he went about doing good.'[13] Smith visited Nazareth on 7 December: '*Baedeker* says that the scenery between here and Tiberias is "uninteresting". I found every inch interesting.'[14] He wished that he was an artist and could paint the scene from the hilltop at Nazareth. He saw Mount Carmel and the sea with ships at anchor at Haifa: 'What a view! As the weakening sun shines upon it, and the clouds clothe the distance with mystery, surely there is nothing more beautiful on earth.'[15] One thing jarred:

The great ecclesiastical buildings with immense white walls which crown so many of the heights, seem to me out of keeping with the scene. They give an impression of power & wealth which is repugnant.[16]

Then, travelling in a crowded taxi, Smith returned to Jerusalem. On Wednesday 11 December he visited Hebron and Bethlehem with Siraganian, the Bible Society's representative in Jerusalem. Hebron was 'one of the most ancient and famous cities in Palestine. So old, that I have been shown where Adam and Eve were buried!'[17] He was unimpressed by his visit to Bethlehem. Nevertheless, it was an 'interesting and entirely successful visit to Palestine'.[18]

Smith left for Egypt on Friday 13 December 1929. He spent Christmas with Matsi and Howard and was delighted to learn that he was going to be a grandfather the following May. He kept himself occupied as he waited to go to Sudan. One day was spent writing '10 pp. or more of Editorial Notes for African Society Journal'.[19] On another day he had a further meeting with Constance Padwick and asked her how to win Muslims for Christ. She said that in the past there was too much emphasis on polemic: 'They are won by the sheer friendliness of Christianity.'[20] Miss Padwick agreed with Smith that associating Christianity with Western civilization and the English language was a blunder. There was sure to be a reaction. Smith wanted to know whether Islam could be reformed, Miss Padwick did not think so. But she hoped that, although many Copts became Muslims, there would be mass conversions to Christ, if not of millions, at least of village communities.

After a quiet Sunday finishing a series of articles for the *Christian World*, Smith set off for Khartoum, 1,000 miles to the south, on 29 December 1929. The journey, by rail and steamboat, included a 'day of days'[21] when, after a spectacular sunset, the travellers were shown the rock temples at Abu Simbel. Smith saw the illuminated interior and was astonished at 'the labour involved & the artistic taste & capacity'.[22]

During his time at Khartoum Smith attended a dinner party at the Governor's residence overlooking the river Nile.[23] The guests included Emil Ludwig, the biographer of Bismarck, and his wife. Smith asked Mrs Ludwig how her husband managed to write so many books and found that they lived a secluded life in Switzerland. After dinner Ludwig asked Smith about the effect of missionary work on Africans. Smith spoke of release from fears by personal trust in a personal God who is like Christ. Ludwig was surprised when Smith said that Africans already believed in God: 'Seemed to think [it] could only be done by [a] philosopher. Could only say, Africans do.'[24]

Smith had many interesting visits and meetings at Khartoum, visiting 'the native village . . . Paradise compared to S. A. locations'[25] and the CMS hospital[26] with the Bishop and discussing anthropology with Hall, the Governor of Khartoum.

Before leaving Sudan on 8 January 1930 Smith met about thirty CMS and American Presbyterians missionaries and addressed them in the Cathedral's Gordon chapel on 'For Christ's sake'. Two young women told him that they had attended his lectures at the School of Oriental Studies. When Smith said goodbye to the Bishop and thanked him for his generosity, the Bishop replied, ' "It is for us to thank *you*. Your visit has been an inspiration to us all." '[27]

Smith broke his return journey at Luxor to visit the temple complexes, and at Karnak and the Valley of the Kings. He was very impressed:

> They had a genius for building, & particularly for ornamenting, these ancient Egyptians. Every available wall space is covered with hieroglyphic inscriptions & pictures of kings, & gods, slaves, battles etc etc.[28]

After a few days in Cairo with Matsi and Howard, Smith returned to England. It was 'An entirely successful trip. Laus Deo.'[29]

Smith spent three more years as the Bible Society's Literary Superintendent. His recent travels brought renewed health and provided firsthand knowledge of the Society's work in the Middle East. Articles based on the trip appeared in his magazines for 1930. He was responsible for these publications until 1932 and published three more Annual Reports and Popular Annual Reports. The Popular Annual Report for 1930 was on a subject very dear to his heart, *In the Mother-Tongue*. He had advocated vernacular versions in *Shrine* and often asked people about this matter as he travelled. Then, in 1931, his theme, *Dust of Gold*, developed a suggestion by Dr Ritson, who had retired earlier that year. He followed the usual formula but began each chapter with quotations from Karl Barth's book, *The Word of God and the Word of Man* (1925, ET 1928). Was Smith becoming a Barthian? No, but he recognized the importance of Barth, whose theme was relevant to Bible Society concerns. Smith's last Popular Annual Report, *The*

Impossible (1932), emphasized the Bible Society's pioneering activities. He asked, 'Can an African, a Chinese, an Indian really be a Christian?'[30] Some thought that such things were impossible but Smith was as deeply convinced of this possibility as he was of the primacy of the mother-tongue.

Dr Robert Kilgour retired in 1932 after supervising the Society's Bible translations for nearly 24 years, during which more than 250 new translations as well as 44 complete Bibles were produced.[31] When he retired it 'was fortunate that among his closest colleagues there was one well qualified to succeed him, in the person of the Reverend Edwin Smith'.[32] As Editorial Superintendent, Smith became responsible for the Society's translation work. He now had skills and an outlook eminently suited for such work and took on his new responsibility in 1933.

Sometime in 1930 or 1931 the Smiths moved to Chesham. As at Walton they were near the railway station. Their new home, named Kasenga after the mission station in Central Africa, consisted of a large house with a substantial garden, conservatory and greenhouse, enabling them to continue their love for gardening. There were visits from Matsi and her family and from Smith's mother, who was now approaching eighty years of age.

Smith combined anthropology and missiology in his thinking and was one of the few missionaries in the Royal Anthropological Institute. The relationship between the two groups has been described as 'ambivalent, uneasy and fraught with contradictions',[33] with anthropologists having 'a negative attitude toward missionaries'.[34] Some anthropologists, for example Sir James Frazer, were anti-religious and students could easily acquire the same bias. In the mid-1920s E. E. Evans-Pritchard, Raymond Firth, Isaac Schapera and Hortense Powdermaker made much 'of the need to keep the natives pure and undefiled by missionaries and civil servants'.[35] Missionaries, except for Edwin Smith and H. A. Junod, were regarded as enemies. The students, for their part, had to respect Smith because he was the author of *ISP*, one of their text-books.

Missionaries and anthropologists were not always at odds. Indeed, Sir James Frazer promoted Roscoe's work and cordially met Smith from time to time. In Britain the IAI brought the two groups together. This contact and cooperation has been attributed to 'the inclusion of anthropology in the preparation for mission work that arose from the collaboration of Malinowski with J. H. Oldham'.[36] Thus, in 1930, we find

Malinowski, one of the most influential anthropologists of the time, addressing a missionary lunch in London. He is reported to have said that the 'anthropologist and the missionary are exchanging experiences'. He even gave advice on missionary *praxis*: 'When it becomes a question of shaping their Christian life it is necessary to discover how much can be taken over, not destroyed.'[37] In time, however, Malinowski became more interested in analysing change.

Smith was recognized and accepted in the higher ranks of the RAI. He had already been on its Council for 1927–30[38] and served again in 1932–3. His frequent meetings with leading members of the organization, especially academic anthropologists, were useful to him, both for his Bible Society work and for the promotion of IAI concerns. The contact was also useful to the academics, who recognized Smith's breadth of knowledge and the quality of his work as a fieldworker and, despite his lack of formal qualifications, gladly used his expertise. As a result, he was an an external examiner in 1929 for Isaac Schapera's Ph.D. thesis at London[39] and examined anthropology students for Cambridge University.[40]

In 1931 Smith was awarded the Rivers medal of the RAI in recognition of his work in Africa. Then, in early 1932, he contributed to a series of lectures on Africa at the School of Oriental Studies. C. G. Seligman, R. S. Rattray and F. H. Melland were among the other lecturers. Smith's subject on 2 March was 'The Place of Folk Tales in African Life', and he argued that they contributed to recreation, and provided education in language and behaviour.[41]

Smith was so highly regarded by the RAI that at the AGM, 27 June 1933, he was elected President, the only missionary ever to be so honoured. His eminence was surely a matter of pride to his church, his family and not least to his mother, who had celebrated her eightieth birthday in December 1932. She had endured much sadness in her life, and when she died in January 1934, only three of her eight children were still living. Smith's achievements were therefore a source of special delight to her.

Smith gave his first Presidential Address, 'Anthropology and the Practical Man',[42] on 26 June 1934 and reminded the gathering that they had bestowed their highest honour on an amateur. His address was on the usefulness of anthropology for practical men – for example, colonial administrators and missionaries – and he said that the founding fathers, such as Sir E. B. Tylor, had this in mind. Sixty years later, when there were many schools of anthropology, Smith wanted anthropology to be as broadly based as possible: 'There is room for many schools. We are all in some degree believers in evolution and diffusion and, I hope, functionalism'.[43] He thought that he and Dale were really groping for the functional method, to his mind 'the best basis for a practical Anthropology'.[44] 'Functionalism' aimed to identify, by fieldwork, the functions of the elements of any social structure. It provided a framework for interpretation but tended to depict society as a house of cards which would collapse when changes occurred. It was already being modified as Malinowski and others began to take account of culture change.

Smith described how colonial administrations were seeking help from anthropologists – the Seligmans and E. E. Evans-Pritchard, for example – and hoped that anthropologists would be used in such areas as political decision-making and education. There were, however, important things to bear in mind:

> Africans have a right to be Africans. They also have a right to take over whatever they may wish from our own culture. But we have no right to impose it, to act as if all that is handed down to them from the past is valueless under the new conditions.[45]

Turning to the relevance of anthropology to missionary work, Smith argued that the practice of some anthropologists, who used their subject to further an anti-religious agenda, was inappropriate. He recognized, however, that missionary methods were not beyond criticism and offered his own assessment of missionary work:

> I think that too often missionaries have regarded themselves as agents of European civilization and have thought it part of their duty to spread the use of English language, English clothing, English music – the whole gamut of our culture.[46]

Smith, by contrast, saw Christianity as a borrower, 'always making a new body for itself':[47] 'out of the really vital elements of African life I believe the spirit of Christianity can form a body that will be at least as worthy as the European body'.[48]

He defended anthropology against the charge of being unpractical. As an external examiner at Cambridge, Smith noticed 'that the papers set in the Anthropological Tripos are largely concerned with actual questions, the chieftainship . . . '.[49] The functionalist school had the advantage of dealing 'with the living society before our eyes'.[50] He criticized Macmillan, the historian, who thought anthropology simply preserved the past, and stated that anthropology was not the enemy of progress.

Smith advised his fellow anthropologists to remember that 'whatever we do the African will decide his own destiny ultimately' and that anthropologists could only act 'in close co-operation with the African himself'.[51]

Smith urged anthropologists to be practical and the missionaries and administrators to acquire a sensitive understanding of the people they worked with. This exhortation was needed because some missionaries, administrators and educators had little time for such things, and some anthropologists saw themselves as 'engaged in pure research'.[52] Smith wanted to draw them together and did so a few weeks later when an International Conference on Anthropology and Ethnographic Sciences was held in London. There were sections dealing with physical anthropology, anthropometry, psychology, demography, religion, languages, technology and the ethnography of various areas. Smith chaired 'Section Db, Ethnography: Africa', which discussed 'certain subjects of practical importance . . . in the light of the central problem – the problem raised by the impact of Western civilisation upon African culture'.[53] It was agreed 'that the ultimate decisions will be taken by Africans',[54] and that the Africans' 'religious attitude stands first and foremost among the vital things in the African culture'.[55] Christianity, marriage laws, and witchcraft and colonial legislation were discussed with papers by R. S. Rattray, Agnes Donohugh, Cullen Young, C. P. Groves, L. S. B. Leakey, E. E. Evans-Pritchard and many others. The sessions continued in the afternoons and joint meetings with other sections (psychology, America, language, religion) were arranged for the late afternoons. Smith hoped that practical people would 'see more clearly henceforward the help that anthropology can give them in their work'.[56] Several of the papers on witchcraft were published in *Africa* at the end of 1935.

Serious study of Africa was still at an early stage. A few detailed monographs had been published, but organized research was only just beginning. IAI fellowships had enabled Margery Perham, Audrey Richards and others to do fieldwork. There was still much to do in Africa, and Smith wanted to impress this upon his fellow anthropologists. Thus, for his second presidential address (1935), 'Africa: What do we know of it?', he surveyed the whole field and identified areas for further research. It was an important and influential address. Lord Hailey, though he did not acknowledge it in his *African Survey* (1938), later stated that he had based his great work on Smith's presidential address,[57] and Sir Raymond Firth, RAI Secretary at the time, judges that this address 'did much to launch the systematic research interest in Africa which developed'[58] in the years after 1935.

It was a monumental survey of the state of African studies at the time. Smith began by acknowledging the help of experts: Miss Caton-Thompson (archaeology), Professor Ruggles Gates (genetics), Dr A. N. Tucker (linguistics), J. H. Driberg (law) and others. He then turned to Africa's geography. By 1935 only a fifth of Africa's surface had been surveyed to 1:250,000 or better. The study of soils was in its infancy. Erosion was largely the responsibility of humans, and people could correct it themselves, otherwise 'much more of Africa will degenerate into desert'.[59] He went on to review Africa's geology and to attempt a reconstruction of its history.

As for the question, 'Was Africa the cradle of the human race?', Smith concluded: 'no answer can as yet be given'.[60] He admitted that nothing was known about origins but claimed that 'we do know that some sort of man inhabited Africa very early in the Pleistocene'.[61] He stated that since 1910 opinion had changed from denying to affirming the existence of a Stone Age in Africa and, while wondering whether the Hamites were the first people to come to Africa, concluded that there was need for further evidence. He then gave his opinion on the question of races: 'We still cannot say with certainty what distinguishes, say "Negro" from "Hamite".'[62]

Smith, always interested in linguistics, discussed African languages. Classification had been attempted only over the previous half-century. Westermann, most recently, had listed three families: Khoisan, Negro (which included the Bantu languages) and Hamito-Semitic. Smith reviewed the current knowledge in each family and focused on the Bantu group of over 300 languages, a group with which he was very familiar. He sympathized

with Father Wanger in his claim . . . that we should look upon the grammar of an Ntu language from the Ntu point of view, instead of pressing it into the frame of Indo-European languages. As yet this has rarely been attempted in any printed grammar.[63]

Smith asked how far Egyptian influence penetrated other parts of Africa. His visit to Egypt had not resolved the matter. He identified a large gap in the history of most of Africa from about 3000 BC to AD 1652. One approach to the past had been made through language analysis: 'Attempts have been made to reconstruct the original Bantu tongue.'[64] From these efforts it seemed that its speakers were familiar with hippo and other large animals, had cattle but not sheep, cultivated soil and could count to at least ten. They had a notion of taboo and believed in ghosts. The past could also be approached through oral traditions which, in some places, went back to the seventeenth century.

He then reviewed the available literature on African cultures and noted that there were a few well-trained anthropologists in Africa. He hoped that they would dominate the future. Of his own work he said no more than that he 'could spend five years in a fresh examination of the people'.[65] He had published books on African religion but said that knowledge in this area was too fragmentary for comprehensive syntheses to be produced, though W. C. Willoughby's books gave useful synopses of what was known among Bantu-speaking people. Smith doubted whether six African tribes had been described to the standard he now considered possible and went on to make a series of recommendations. A handbook of tribes was needed, with summarized information and a series of synthetic and critical studies like those done by Schapera on the Khoisan. Then there should be monographs on the main ethnographic aspects of Africa:

> I mean such subjects as family life and kinship; the clan and age-grade systems; social and political organization, customary law and the chieftainship; education and the social and psychological development of children; religion; material culture; economics, agriculture and land tenure.[66]

He stressed 'the vital importance of thorough linguistic equipment'[67] and thought that ten years was needed to produce an adequate monograph. Anthropologists had to recognize and study change among Africans in contact with Europeans and vice versa. Smith suggested a few more topics for research: the effect of detribalization, migration to towns, deprivation of ancestral lands, introduction of European law, clothes, housing, tools and taxation.

The AGM was a good place to highlight Africa. Smith used the presidential address to publicize the IAI and to highlight the need for research. Because there were vast gaps in knowledge, Smith's reply to his original question, 'Africa: what do we know of it?', could only be, 'Very little as yet.'[68]

Research interest in Africa grew after 1935, and Max Gluckman, whose work in Africa and Manchester would create a whole school of anthropology devoted mainly to Central Africa, was a key figure. Gluckman, along with Z. K. Matthews, belonged to Malinowski's seminar in 1934–5,[69] so is likely to have been aware of an Africanist president of the RAI and Smith's challenge from the presidential chair. Some years later, *Seven Tribes of British Central Africa* (1951), edited by Elizabeth Colson and Max Gluckman, was dedicated with respect and admiration to Dr Edwin W. Smith and acknowledged that *ISP* 'founded modern anthropological research in British Central Africa'.[70]

Much has been done since Smith gave that address.[71] It is now confidently asserted that human life originated in Africa.[72] The influence of the Hamites and the possible spread of culture from Egypt no longer hold interest. Instead, Africa is seen as being filled with people from within, and attention is focused on humanity's journey out of Africa. The gap in historical knowledge (3000 BC to AD 1652) has to some extent been filled. Smith recognized that the base of knowledge was very low in 1935. There was insufficient evidence for firm conclusions over the whole range of African studies. What was needed was for able, trained people to get to work, and they have:

> the tradition created by the students of Malinowski (and to a lesser extent Radcliffe-Brown) established certain parameters for research, presented fieldwork in a theoretical frame, trained students in this framework and assisted them in turn to undertake fieldwork.[73]

Smith's great service was to point anthropologists to Africa, showing the limits of knowledge about Africa in 1935 and the need for research by trained workers.

African Christian theology, Bible translations and travels in India (1936–1939)

Smith was among the first to study African religion seriously. E. S. Hartland's article in Hastings' *Encyclopaedia of Religion and Ethics* (Volume II, 1909) was, in his view, the first outline of the subject. Then, in the 1920s, W. C. Willoughby began publishing the fruit of his researches.[1] At the same time, ethnographic studies – for example, R. S. Rattray's *Ashanti* (1923) and *Religion and Art in Ashanti* (1927) – showed that religion in Africa was more complex and significant than most had expected, and by the 1930s E. E. Evans-Pritchard was beginning researches which would become widely influential.

Nevertheless, in the mid-1930s, African religion was far from being recognized as a major religious tradition to be studied alongside others.[2] Smith, however, was convinced that it was central to African life and culture and, as such, of major importance.

In 'The Secret of the African' (1907) Smith regarded Europeans as in the top class of God's school and Africans in the bottom class. By 1936 he omitted such classification and said that the African fathers deserved respect for they 'like all other men, were learners in God's school'.[3] Smith had long believed that the missionaries should use elements of African culture and religion in shaping Christian worship and thought. Indeed, this conviction was fundamental to his work in Kasenga twenty-five years earlier. Now, in *African Beliefs and Christian Faith* (1936), he made a serious attempt to formulate an African Christian theology.

The IMC Committee for African Literature wanted a book for teaching Christian doctrine to African students. Smith believed it best to start with 'the African's own experience, belief and practice, and that the course should run through the Old Testament into the New'.[4] The committee members shared his view. Smith felt that his long absence from Africa disqualified him as the author and that someone in Africa writing in an African language would be much better qualified. In the 1930s, however, no-one, African or non-African, had better skills and knowledge for such a task. Smith, therefore, was overruled by his friends[5] and went on to develop a new style of theology.

ABCF, which was written in Basic English,[6] was restricted to a broad treatment of the doctrine of God, which Smith always considered the most important link between the two themes indicated by his title. That he did not cover other doctrines similarly, as he had originally hoped, enabled others, especially Africans, to make their own contributions.

Part I of *ABCF* outlined African beliefs with an emphasis on God. He saw ambivalence in African views of God. According to Smith, Africans are not clear whether God is a Person as we are persons or has unity. Further, although God has shown signs of his benevolence, life's troubles make it unclear whether he is kind and good. Africans, he said, believe that God has withdrawn and are surprised to hear that he should want to deliver us from evil. Smith used detailed examples from Africa to illustrate these points. In addition, he drew attention to the 'mother' aspect of God, which was reported from some places[7] and noted African Holy Places, Holy People and Holy Objects, which are all related to God. He concluded that Africans 'are like people walking in a half-light. What they have is, in part, a true light, but it is not enough.'[8]

Smith then presented the position in African religion, especially African theology, as he saw it.[9] There was, after all, a religious tradition to be studied, and Smith described it. But that was not the only aim of his book. He went on, therefore, to consider the Old Testament, which he believed to be relevant for African Christians, especially if teachers showed how Old Testament religion developed. Using this way of looking at the Old Testament, which another Primitive Methodist, Dr Peake, did much to popularize, Smith suggested that Africans could possibly understand the Old Testament revelation of God better than Europeans and would therefore realize that, although the Jews did well in God's school, their knowledge of him was incomplete. Africans and Jews were therefore similar in having light but not complete illumination. They both possessed traditions, history and beliefs where good was at times mixed with error. This, of course, was the first step of fulfilment theology. It affirms and validates what is so far unfulfilled and then goes on to show how the one who fulfils these hopes can bring light to all. As described in earlier chapters, 'fulfilment theology' was popular in the early twentieth century. It was accepted by many delegates at the 1910 Missionary Conference and was worked out for India by J. N. Farquhar in *The Crown of Hinduism* (1913). Smith, by adapting this theology for Africa, affirmed African religion. For example, when Jesus spoke of God as Spirit, Smith commented:

> By this word Jesus put his stamp of authority upon much of the teaching of the prophets . . . He equally puts his stamp of approval on much that Africans have said about the Highest Being – most of them, as we have seen, would not say it is possible to make a house for God or make an image of Him. God is Spirit.[10]

Fulfilment theology opened the way for dialogue by respecting other religions. As this respect grew, the fulfilment approach inevitably declined, for it seems patronizing to say that another religion needs fulfilment.

The suggestion that Jesus fulfilled more than the Old Testament prophecies was also a vulnerable point in fulfilment theology. It could be understood as implying that, since African religion and the Old Testament are alternative preparations for the gospel, the Old Testament is redundant. However, the reality, which Smith recognized, is that Jesus was Jewish and the Old Testament is necessary for understanding his ideas.[11]

Smith completed the book with specific points about Jesus' revelation of God. He claimed that these fulfilled African aspirations: God is a good, loving, kingly Father who is near and interested in us. He described Jesus' teaching on the kingdom of God as not political but a matter of the heart which 'comes in the degree in which God's desires are done among men'.[12] The Kingdom as the highest value provides a way of life for all who will enter it. To love God and other people was, said Smith, like an African regarding all others as belonging to the same clan.

He wrote of Jesus' death on the cross as a 'ray of light upon the darkest of our questions. In the great fight against evil on earth and in our hearts God is not at a distance and out of touch. He is in it with us.'[13] Smith also mentioned that the story of *Mwana Leza* (Son of God), who was killed and yet lives, had been known for many years in Central Africa. His exposition ended with what, for him, was the best part of Jesus' story: that 'the Lord Jesus is living today and that His power comes into us if our hearts are open to take it in by faith'.[14]

Smith's final quotation was from an old African woman who heard the gospel and declared: ' "There now! I was certain in my heart that there is a God like that!" The story of Jesus seemed to her to be the answer to all her questions about the Power, which she, and all of us, are conscious of.'[15] This was fulfilment indeed!

African Beliefs and Christian Faith approached theology through African ideas. Smith avoided Western theologizing as much as possible and tried to link African thinking directly to biblical concepts, and especially to those in the Gospels, which he saw as basic to Christian teaching. African Christian theology was thus worked out thoroughly for the first time, and Smith is rightly regarded as a major pioneer of the subject – the *fons et origo* of African Christian theology.[16] There can be little doubt, moreover, that the production of the book was a worthwhile venture for him and other missionaries of the IMC milieu. Even so, doubts about the enterprise may be raised from several angles.

Anti-religious observers are unhappy with this blend of African theology and Christianity. They see 'traditional African society as essentially non-religious in nature'.[17] Others, coming from the opposite direction, believe that African societies are very religious and, in contrast with Smith, assert the validity of African theology in its own right. Africans of this persuasion 'object to what they consider to be an unwarranted Christianisation of African systems of thought'.[18] Other Africans, from a Christian background, assert that they have a much deeper concept of God 'than the Christian translation for God in the Bible or other Christian literature'.[19] All these, in their varied ways, assert African culture and tradition even more strongly than Smith did.

Other thinkers criticize the enterprise in another way. Byang H. Kato, an African Evangelical, wrote *Theological Pitfalls in Africa* in 1975 and accepted that there was general revelation in African religion. He agreed that 'Christ is the fulfillment of the Old Testament and of the deep spiritual need of the human hearts, *but He is not the fulfillment of African traditional religions or any other non-Christian religion*'.[20] For Kato, as for all Evangelicals, the Old Testament is special revelation. This was also the view of the neo-orthodox theologians Kraemer, Brunner and Barth.[21] Kraemer, for example, while accepting the usefulness of anthropology and the need for an African expression of Christianity, was opposed to 'progressive missionary thinking' which appeared to take the African heritage *'primarily* as a *praeparatio evangelica'*.[22] Smith, who recognized that the Old Testament was necessary for understanding the New, saw a similarity with African tradition and, according to McVeigh, gives

> the impression that the distinction between them, as far as revelation is concerned, is one of degree not kind. It may be justified to conclude therefore that Smith identified both ancient Judaism and African Religion as general revelation, with the term special revelation confined to the gospel of Jesus Christ.[23]

Such a summary may exaggerate Smith's position, but there can be no doubt that, in making the Old Testament more inviting to Africans, he hoped to lead them to Jesus.

In this debate, then, one side would say that Smith over-valued African religion and the other that he underestimated it. Africans, however, can make their own choices and, among the numerous possibilities, they may create an understanding of Christianity that marries biblical teaching and their own concepts.

Smith's primary concern with the doctrine of God was bound up, as we have noted, with his belief that it provided the best link between African religion and Christianity. It can be argued, however, that in focusing on the highest aspect of religious development, he was led astray by evolutionary thinking. Moreover, some of those involved in religious studies maintain that he should have concentrated on the beliefs of particular societies rather than generalizing about one aspect of religion in the whole continent. In short, Smith's influence is regarded, in some quarters, as providing 'a false start from which the church in Africa has hardly yet recovered'.[24]

Nevertheless, Smith's African Christian theology endured and used most of the materials accepted as necessary fifty years later: 'the Bible and Christian tradition, the African cultural and religious heritage, and the socio-political situation in which the Church exists'.[25] His theological method, too, fits well with the advice given to African Christian theologians of the late twentieth century: to study the Bible critically, and African religions phenomenologically, and then bring the two into critical dialogue.[26] Indeed, it is interesting to compare his treatment of the subject with that of an African Christian theologian writing in 1987. Charles Nyamiti[27] argued that, although Africans can learn from the Bible, Christians can also learn about God from African tradition. Critical analysis reveals strengths and weaknesses in African religion, but among the elements which can help Christians Nyamiti cited the rich symbolism of African names for God, the feminine side of God and the possibility of conceiving God as Ancestor. In the light of such contentions, Smith was clearly aware of much that is being emphasized by contributors to African Christian theology, now regarded as an important and worthwhile and productive enterprise, more than half a century later.[28]

Alongside his own writing, Smith was busy supervising translations. The Bible Society was fortunate to have someone so knowledgeable about African languages as its Editorial Secretary, since most translations at that time – 43 out of 56 new versions published in the five years 1933–7[29] – were for Africa.

Smith also used his formidable linguistic gift to good effect, producing a tentative grammar of a language used by pygmies in the Ituri forest in the Belgian Congo: 'There was pleasurable excitement at the Bible House in London when in 1930 the news came that Canon Apolo Kivebulaya was translating the Gospel of Mark into the "Mbuti" language.'[30] Apolo, who went from Uganda as a missionary to the pygmies, encouraged 'a forest teacher called Yoasi Otubo to begin a translation of St Mark's gospel into Rumbaba. It appears that it was completed by the time Apolo died in 1933.'[31] This manuscript was found by the Revd A. B. Lloyd, who wrote a biography of Apolo. Lloyd sent a copy of the translation to the BFBS in 1934 and later brought along the original manuscript. Since it was clear that Apolo was not a linguist and that the translation was difficult to evaluate, Smith examined it closely. He first used his spare time during a year to prepare a concordance. Then, having discovered the main forms of various words, he drafted a vocabulary in July 1936.[32] Finally, he rewrote the Gospel, using what he thought should be the correct spelling and word division.

Smith had studied Bantu languages for over thirty years and saw that this language, which he named Efe, was not a Bantu tongue. After several discussions on comparative Sudanic study, he and Dr A. N. Tucker of London University[33] concluded that Efe resembled some

Sudanic languages and had Bantu features. In his grammatical notes Smith considered how sounds were probably made, and then the method of word-building. The Introduction to this unpublished manuscript was dated 7 September 1938, his 62nd birthday. His notes were intended not for publication but to be evaluated with the Dictionary and the revised version of Mark. His aim was not to unravel an unknown language but to evangelize the pygmies of the Congo forest. Smith did, however, offer his researches to the scholarly and Africanist public by reading a paper to the British Association at Cambridge, 18 August 1938, and publishing it soon afterwards in the *Journal of the Royal African Society*.[34]

By that time, indeed from August 1937, Smith was being referred to as Dr Smith. He had been awarded an honorary DD by Wesley College, Winnipeg, presumably for his contribution to African studies and missiology. Arthur Wilkes in *Mow Cop* remarked that this was 'what some British University should have done long ago'.[35] It is surprising that Smith was not honoured in Britain. He had the scholarship and was known and respected by many academics.

Smith always took into consideration the needs of those who would read Bible translations,[36] as can be seen in two aspects of his work in the 1930s.

While he was unravelling Efe, Smith was also looking at ways of translating the Bible into simplified English. At the Editorial Sub-Committee (ESC) of the BFBS on 8 November 1933 Dr Alice Werner had suggested using Basic English for people who use English as an acquired language. In late 1935 the General Committee decided that the ESC should prepare a translation of a Gospel in Basic English and circulate it for consideration during the next six months.[37] Basic English was invented in the 1920s by C. K. Ogden, who reduced English to 850 words covering most key concepts. It was claimed that these words did 'the work of the 25,000 or more which the average English adult uses in his work and play'.[38] In addition to the 850 Basic words, 50 specialized words were allowed. Basic English was not the only system available. Dr Michael West devised a form of simplified English based on the most frequently used words.

By February 1936 Smith had prepared the first six chapters of John's Gospel in both systems but wanted more time to work on them and to consult other scholars.[39] In the event, though the BFBS failed to produce a Bible in either of these simplified versions of English, Smith did publish *The Basic St John* in 1938. Moreover, Cambridge University Press produced the New Testament in Basic English (1941) and the complete *Bible in Basic English* (1949), both versions being produced by a committee under the direction of Professor S. H. Hooke of London University.[40] The Cambridge translation of John's Gospel is so close to Smith's 1938 version as to compel the conclusion that it is based on it.

Basic English has few verbs and there can be awkward circumlocutions, but this version of the Bible 'is much more valuable than might have been expected'.[41] This can easily be seen from Smith's translation of John 1.14: 'And so the Word became flesh and took a place among us for a time; and we saw his glory – such glory as is given to an only son by his father – saw it to be true and full of grace.'[42] Through his involvement in this attempt to make the Bible more easily understood, Smith contributed eventually to the *Good News Bible* and other common-language versions.

Smith's interest in accessible Bible translation is further illustrated by his tour of India for the Bible Society from November 1938 to March 1939. He was to enquire and report (a) on the campaign against illiteracy, (b) on the necessity, advisability and feasibility of producing simplified versions for adults learning to read and (c) on translation and revision:[43] 'There was never such a tour as this! I have seen more these three months than many people who have lived in India half their lives.'[44]

Smith left England on 5 October 1938. He took equipment for injecting himself with insulin and a variety of reading matter including *The Christian Message in a non-Christian World*, Hendrik Kraemer's book for the coming IMC conference at Madras, *The Mediator* by Emil Brunner and the proofs of Lord Hailey's *An African Survey*. At Port Said he met his daughter Matsi, and her younger son Richard, now four years old, who 'seems very sharp. He sits and looks at things and says little – like his grandpa.'[45] Smith gave Richard 10/- for himself and 10/- for his older brother David, aged eight.

Smith arrived in India on 29 October and set off on his travels, taking notes for his own interest as well as for his final report . On 2 November he went 80 miles by car to a Christian ashram at Poona which was run on monastic lines. The

chapel in style of Indian temple . . . Two pictures of annunciation by Indians. Angel holds a lotus: Mary dressed as Indian with flower in hair. Idea is to present Christianity in Indian forms. And by so doing to learn more of Christianity.[46]

On Sunday 6 November, however, he spoke on the Bible Society at the Church of Scotland: 'No Indianization here. Only thing Indian, was the language and saris of women. All men dressed in European style: tunes English. Nothing Indian in architecture or form of service.'[47]

By 10 November Smith was in Delhi, about 800 miles from Bombay. He was invited to a lunch: 'To my surprise one guest was C. F. Andrews. Said he had long wished to meet me. Read my books – read anything of mine he could get.'[48] Andrews (1869–1940) was influenced by Bishop Westcott and went to India as an Anglican missionary in 1904. He knew Gandhi and worked closely with the Bengali poet Rabindranath Tagore: 'Justice, courtesy, and love were the keynotes of a ministry which ended only with his death in 1940.'[49] Andrews thought that Smith should meet Gandhi. He also wanted Smith to 'go to Tambaram for the first three days for the sake of the 70 Africans, who will feel strange: thinks I would ease matters for them'.[50] Andrews was referring to the IMC conference held at Tambaram, Madras, over Christmas 1938. Smith did not follow Andrews' suggestion. In any case, the Africans needed no help. At the evening worship on Christmas day 'the African delegation provided the evening's climax . . . When they had finished, thunderous applause broke out.'[51]

Smith and Andrews spent a long time discussing Bible translation on 11 November. Andrews said that the Bengali Bible was out of date. He once got his friend Tagore to look at it: 'When he read 1 Cor xiii he shook his head, "That is not the Bengali we are reading and writing." '[52] Smith found such opinions of great value.

By 27 November he was in Allahabad (400 miles south-east of Delhi), where he preached at the Cathedral and interviewed Pandit Nehru: 'Told him I had read his pamphlet on language and was interested that he supported Basic English. What was his idea of a Basic Hindustani? Told of a series of textbooks in Basic Hindustani.'[53] On 1 December at Nagpur, in central India, Smith met Dr Mott,[54] the dynamic missionary/ecumenist, who was very complimentary about '*Aggrey* – thinks [it] the best I have done. Glad to hear of my going to USA and already plans for me to address conferences!'[55]

On the following day Smith went to see Gandhi.

We were ushered into a small unpretentious house. Gandhi was squat on the floor, a wooden support at right angles to us as we sat on floor: a thin white pillow on it. Gandhi leaned back on this when he did not lean forward talking. Dressed in loose cotton sheet. Glasses. A kindly face.

Smith went on to describe his conversation with Gandhi,

I opened by saying: 'I believe Mr Gandhi, that the father of a friend of mine was a friend of yours – Mr Doke?' 'Yes' he said, 'he was a good friend, and yours?' . . . I said I had not come to talk about Africa but about India 'We of the Bible Society are deeply interested in the campaign against illiteracy and in those questions of language and script you are now discussing . . . we are told by many that the Hindi Bible is beyond the comprehension of simple people: we do not know what to do.' G. 'Yes it is so. I have read the Bible – I have a copy here – and the style is classical. But a translation of the Bible must be in classical.' I demurred at this.[56]

They discussed dialects in England, hygiene, and various scripts, but Gandhi had no suggestions about simplified translations.

A few days later Smith was at Secunderabad (150 miles south of Nagpur) and enjoyed visiting a Harijan (outcast) village (Sunday 4 December). The congregation sang lyrics to Indian tunes, clapping their hands.

Impressed by the eager way in wh[ich] they responded and ready way they repeated things and sang lyrics. Then we marched, with drums beating, to the tank. I stepped into water and baptized each one – 20 or more – as name was called. One very old woman of 80 – others of all ages down to a baby of a few months. I did it in Sesuto and Ila.[57]

If Sotho and Ila seem inappropriate for India, they would have added to the occasion for the Indians. It suggests that Smith felt that he came there as an African.

Smith saw little evidence of Christian adaptation to Indian culture during this tour but noted what he saw. In church on Christmas day, for example, he observed that the Europeans wore Indian clothes and sat cross-legged with the others.[58]

After travelling to Darjeeling and Assam Smith went to Calcutta and nearby Santiniketan to see Andrews, who took Smith 'to pay respects to Tagore who lives in next house. Like his photos. Seated at desk, in Indian costume, writing Bengali on slips of paper.'[59] They discussed the possibility of producing a modern Bengali version of the Bible. Tagore, aged 77, said he was too old but would do 1 Corinthians 13 to show how it should be done. Dr Amiya Chakravarty was put forward to translate the Gospels, and C. F. Andrews could compare his work with the Greek.[60]

Smith went on to south India and Ceylon and left for England on 15 March. He carried the manuscript for his book, *The Mabilles*, with some suggestions for its improvement, and revised and condensed it on the voyage home. He also wrote up his official Report, in which he made the following points.

The BFBS favoured easily understandable translations: 'the simplest and best known words should be used in the idiomatic forms of the living tongue'.[61] Competent people, however, reported 'very few versions that were regarded as entirely satisfactory'.[62] Moreover, there would be imperfections as long as foreigners were in charge of translation, but Indians often felt overruled, and European translators relied too heavily on their pundits, who preferred ornate expression. Classical Hindi was loaded with Sanskrit expressions, and although Gandhi judged that the Bible, which he had read in classical Hindi translation, should be in such language, he 'thought it beyond the comprehension of common people'.[63]

Smith was convinced that simplified Gospels were essential. It was a serious matter if the Bible was largely inaccessible to ordinary people: 'My own opinion shared by many is that to teach religion through a foreign medium is a colossal blunder.'[64] His report was taken very seriously by the Bible Society. However, the outbreak of war 'necessitated the postponement of policies which only came to fruition 20 years later, long after Smith had retired. The importance of his study and recommendations has always been emphasized by his successors.'[65]

Smith's India diary contained notes, on loose sheets, of an address given at High Leigh on 20 June 1939. If one country in the world needed 'the doctrine', he observed, it was India, rent asunder by so many divisions of race, religion, politics, language and caste. By 'the doctrine' he probably meant 'the doctrine of cooperation', a major plank in Smith's thinking since *Aggrey*.

Smith's Bible Society career was coming to a close, as was another of his activities. Since the early 1920s he had been writing book reviews and editorial notes for the *Journal of the Royal African Society* (*JRAS*), although he was never its editor until 1938. As well as his paper on Efe, Smith published articles on the political scene in Africa during this period; the land issue in Kenya[66] and the future of Lesotho, Botswana and Swaziland.[67] He complained that the Government was outraging British sentiment by making racial discrimination legal in Kenya:

> from the European Reserve all Africans, and all non-Europeans, are to be excluded as land-owners, leaseholders, or tenants, while of course they will continue to be required as servants.[68]

Farther south some people wanted to transfer Lesotho, Botswana and Swaziland to the Union of South Africa. Smith, however, saw serious flaws in the case being made. In his article[69] he explained why the local people opposed it and argued that Britain should keep its pledge to act only with their consent. Smith was sure that these Africans would be far worse off under South Africa and instanced examples of oppression suffered by Africans in South Africa: 'Does one wonder that they are reluctant to place themselves under a government which treats its subject peoples in this way?'[70]

Smith's editorship was interrupted by the India tour and curtailed by his removal, as we shall see in the next chapter, to a new post in the USA. He had helped the African Society and its journal for about eighteen years, but for the immediate future it would have to do without his services.

He just managed to finish another project before leaving. It was his biography, *The Mabilles of Basutoland*. He had met members of this family in 1898–9. His researches took him in June 1937 to Basle, where he inspected Adolphe Mabille's class records. He noted that Karl Barth was lecturing in one of the rooms where Adolphe studied in 1851.[71] Smith read the available literature and studied the Paris Missionary Society's records. Mabille family members helped him and commented on his chapters. The book is interesting biographically but also because of its attention to Lesotho's history. It shows Smith's sense of historical perspective, general objectivity and generosity of spirit. He could have made many criticisms of the missionaries' methods and their strictness over such issues as African customs, but refrained from adverse comment. He emphasized the positive and wanted it to be understood that

the man and woman of whom I have written were Christian missionaries. They had as their ultimate aim a nation of Christian Basuto, a
Church co-extensive with the nation, not a dependent branch of the
Reformed Churches of France, but self-supporting, self-governing,
self-propagating.[72]

The 1930s were nearly over, and so was Smith's working life in Europe.
He could look back with pride at his achievements. He was one of the
Bible Society's chief officers and had directed its literature and translation policy. His call to translate the Bible had found much richer
fulfilment than he could ever have imagined in 1895. His literary output
of reports, biographies, religious studies and articles was prodigious
and reached a wide range of readers. The anthropologists had shown
him enormous respect and honour, and he was now becoming one of
their elder statesmen. Altogether he was an expert in all aspects of
African studies.

Europe was heading towards another Great War, and everything was
changing. He and Julia were about to leave 'Kasenga', their substantial
home and garden at Chesham. The house, however, was not empty for
long. With the advent of war, Matsi, whose husband enlisted in the
forces, returned there from Egypt with her sons, David and Richard.
By then her parents had departed to the USA on a new venture in the
service of Africa.

Professor of African studies in the USA
(1939–1944)

Smith went to America to take up a longstanding invitation to teach at the Kennedy School of Missions in the Hartford Seminary Foundation, Connecticut. Kennedy was established as a result of Edinburgh 1910, and other British missiologists had taught there earlier: W. C. Willoughby, already noted as an early expert in African studies, from 1919 to 1931, and Smith's friend C. P. Groves, since 1937.[1] Smith's invitation was a clear recognition of his world reputation in missiology, missionary education and African studies. He looked forward to it, commenting: 'I have never acted the professor before.'[2] He had, however, examined at a high level and lectured to trainee missionaries and academic bodies.

War was declared on 3 September 1939, and the Smiths set off for America on the *Aquitania* a week later. They were worried about German submarines, but the journey to New York passed without incident. Two days after reaching Hartford, Smith returned to New York with Dean Malcolm Pitt of Hartford for a meeting attended by several old friends, including Jesse Jones, the Donohughs and Dr Loram, who were all at Le Zoute thirteen years earlier. They discussed the IAI, which Mrs Donohugh and Dr Loram criticized. The Americans felt that the British despised American scholarship, and Mrs Donohugh[3] pointed out that the IAI had not given Fellowships to Americans.

Smith's teaching career began at the end of September. He taught five courses: Introduction to African studies; African culture and institutions; The Christian approach to the African; The opening up of Africa; The new Africa.[4] All went well and Smith was invited to stay at Hartford for the next academic year. He found it hard to respond to this invitation because the situation in Britain was worrying: 'I want to be sharing my country men's troubles, though I could do nothing or little

to help. I have spent sleepless nights debating the question.'[5] His uncertainty was heightened by Julia's return to England in the spring of 1940.
Her 'absence in England during the middle one of three years, made us
realize the more keenly how important an individual she is in the Smith
combination'.[6] Julia did not often appear in Edwin's writings, but her
opinion was vital, and her absence made him indecisive. He only agreed
to stay after consulting her by letter and cable.

After attending the Seminary Commencement exercises (which end
the academic year in the USA), Smith toured Canada for the Bible
Society. He arrived at Montreal on 30 May for the convocation of
McGill University but was more excited to find his aunt and cousin at
Montreal. His aunt, a fine old lady of eighty, was the widow of his
father's brother William. Smith, who enjoyed his pipe and cigars, was
irritated that she did not allow smoking in the house but pleased that
she showed him pictures of his paternal grandparents. While in
Montreal, on 31 May, Smith met local Bible Society supporters and was
introduced as someone who 'must have been born near Babel!'.[7] He
went on to address Bible Society meetings in Quebec and Toronto and
followed his usual practice of keeping records of places and people he
saw. Thus, at Brantford, when shown the Iroquois Indian Reservation,
he made detailed notes about the way the Indians were governed,
educated, etc.

From Toronto, a 36-hour train journey took him to Winnipeg to the
home of his brother, Jack, who was 'in a very bad state of health'[8] and
to Wesley College. Smith was unimpressed by the college; 'Looks a
dingy 3rd rate place.'[9] Nevertheless, it had awarded him a doctorate,
albeit to 'Edwin H. Smith'. He ensured that his name was correctly
recorded and promised to send his parchment for correction and his
books for the library.

Smith then made a special journey across Lake Winnipeg to Norway
House for celebrations to commemorate the pioneering work of James
Evans. In 1840 Evans had reduced the Cree language to writing, and
Smith had written about his syllabic writing system in *Shrine*.[10] At the
centenary service, Cree and English Bibles were presented to the church
and received by Smith, who conducted a dedication service. A portrait
of Evans was unveiled, together with a bronze tablet for the Evans
Memorial Church, and the celebrations were completed with an Evans
Pageant in four scenes.

Smith continued his travels across Canada and spoke for the Bible

Society at many places. At Edmonton, he met a man who was at Aliwal North in 1901 and told Smith of his 'vivid gratitude to Jue and me for our hospitality. Had been converted 3 months when he came to A. N. Our example turned him towards missionary work.'[11]

News from Europe continued to be worrying. It was not long after Dunkirk and a few days after the Germans occupied Paris. British troops were being evacuated from France, and Hitler, it seemed, would soon invade Britain. Not surprisingly, Edwin's uncertainty increased, and it did not help him that Julia's replies to his letters, taking eleven days by airmail and nearly a month by sea, had to find him as he travelled about.

After addressing Bible Society supporters at Calgary on 27 June, Smith went south to see his brother Stanley, who lived near Fort Macleod. It was over thirty years since he had seen Stanley, who proved to be so much thinner and smaller than he expected that he hardly recognized him. Stanley was a prosperous farmer and had started his sons and sons-in-law in businesses or farms. Smith spent two days travelling around with his brother, enjoying the scenery (the Rocky Mountains) and visiting nephews and nieces. Stanley encouraged Edwin to remain in the USA and offered a home for the grandsons if they came over.

Smith then resumed his journey. He was sorry to leave the lovely area but continued by train across the Rocky Mountains and arrived at Vancouver on 5 July to find a letter from Julia: 'Also a cable from her that she is sailing end of July with the boys. Great news'.[12] In fact, the boys remained in England when Julia returned to the USA.

When Smith reached the USA, at Seattle, he was shocked to hear of his brother Jack's death. He wondered whether to return to Winnipeg for the funeral but, concluding that he could not arrive in time, set off for Los Angeles and the long journey across the USA to Hartford. War news remained depressing, but hearing Churchill's speech on the radio 'put heart'[13] into him. Moreover, when he broke his journey at the Grand Canyon, he described it – and we must remember that he had seen many remarkable sights during his life – as 'One of the Supreme things of the earth.'[14] He arrived back at Hartford on 21 July, where he found 'all very quiet'.[15]

A few months later, in October 1940, Smith addressed the Fellowship of Professors of Missions at Princeton, New Jersey.[16] His subject was 'Association and Assimilation in the Christian Mission'. He compared missions and colonial policies and argued that the French colonial policy of 'assimilation' (i.e. to French culture) worked against local languages and cultures. Britain's pragmatic colonial policy, which led to indirect rule, was paralleled by the missionary movement's latest policy, offered at Madras in 1938, which asked for indigenous expressions of the faith and was 'in effect a condemnation of much in the past and present practice of missions'.[17] Smith gave examples;

> When I travelled through India and Ceylon two years ago, I was amazed at the little that has been done to naturalize Christianity . . . Almost uniformly the music was European; the hymns translations; the men usually dressed in European coats and trousers – the women more becomingly retained their beautiful Indian costume . . . Almost always the church was of western architecture . . .[18]

He also referred to Africa:

> Again it is horrifying to hear from a missionary from West Africa that not a single African Christian leader in his area believes it possible for an African to be at once African and Christian.[19]

Smith wanted Christianity to adapt to local cultures, not displace them. Indeed, 'our duty is to release Christianity from the fetters of western civilisation'.[20]

He pursued these and other themes in the Powell Lectures, given at the Canadian School of Missions, Toronto, in 1940. They were revised and published with additions in 1946 as *Knowing the African*. He drew on his wide reading, experience and previous writings to advise missionaries on theological and practical matters.

Smith believed that, although Christian work must touch all human needs, agricultural, industrial, commercial or political issues are not themselves the objective of Christian mission. Missionaries, therefore, had to beware of exploitation – for example, by colonial governments seeking to propagate their national culture. For Western culture and Christianity are not identical. Yet, in Smith's considered opinion, the missionary enterprise itself was palpably impregnated with a superiority complex, and the danger was that those who rebelled against Western imperialism would discard Christianity too. The post-colonial age had not yet arrived, but Smith, especially after his visit to India, could see it coming. Therefore, one of the supreme needs of the day was 'to purge our missionary enterprise of all taint of cultural imperialism'.[21] Our first principle 'is Christ; not western civilisation'.[22] He repeated what he said in 1934 to the RAI: 'out of the really vital elements of African life I believe the spirit of Christianity can form a body that will be at least as worthy as the European body'.[23]

Smith believed this harmonized with the conclusions of Tambaram, 1938. But though he would have accepted, perhaps with some modifications, the conference's assertion of the 'finality and absoluteness of the Christian faith in the face of any of its rivals, and as the only hope for the world',[24] he preferred to highlight its stress on the importance of literature and the need for Christianity to adapt to the local cultures.

After his cautions on cultural imperialism, Smith discussed whether conversion is for groups or for individuals only. Troeltsch and Brunner taught unqualified individualism as the gospel's outstanding ethic. Smith thought they knew better than that, for there is truth and error in both individualism and collectivism. He believed that the perfect synthesis is found in the kingdom of God, 'that state of life in which God will have supreme control'.[25] He mentioned with approval how corporate individualism was expressed by the Tambaram Council: 'when we find the kingdom of God we find ourselves.'[26]

Smith then returned to a favourite theme and encouraged missionaries to think anthropologically. He thought that perhaps half the troubles between white and black in Africa could be traced to misunderstandings of language or customs. For example, in some cultures spitting is not an insult but a sign of gratitude. He pointed out that Africans have powerful logical abilities and that European and American life have numerous pre-logical features. He considered that the main differences between Africans and Europeans were social. Because our different premises are derived from different social traditions it takes 'careful, painstaking, sympathetic study'[27] to build bridges between people of different cultural backgrounds. Smith highlighted a vital skill for this understanding, learning a language, which he always considered the partner of anthropology.

He then explained that African social solidarity never completely overcomes the desire to explore. It was not, after all, contact with Europeans alone which was affecting Africans; their chiefs and prophets were also effecting change, especially through their methods of consulting both the living and the dead. Anthropology could study such changes as they happened, and Smith made sure that his readers knew about the leading role which the IAI was playing in researching them.

Smith advised missionaries to be thoroughly acquainted with marriage customs and family structures, since their significance in Africa can hardly be exaggerated. He had little to add to his previous ideas on *uku-lobola* (misnamed 'bride-price'), polygamy and incorporating the traditional marriage meal in Christian ceremonies. He also offered guidance about African religion to would-be missionaries. He pointed out that in Africa almost everything is religious in some way and followed his usual scheme: dynamism, ancestor worship and theism. He noted that, although the ancestor cult seemed to be declining in the growing cities of Africa, dynamism with its charms and talismans was flourishing. This argument, which went against the view, expressed in *The Golden Stool*, that dynamism was doomed by changes to tribal life, shows that Smith was prepared to modify his ideas in the light of new information.

Some critics had argued that Smith was wrong to use the vague theism of Africans in his theory and practice of mission because it was less effective in African life than the ancestor cult. He was unrepentant:

> I still believe that in presenting Christianity to the African one should begin where the African has left off: and that it is for us to develop all the rich promise that lies in their awareness, however vague it may be, of a Supreme Being.[28]

Smith went on to emphasize indigenous African educational practices which provided 'a genuine education'.[29] He noted that Baden Powell used Zulu ideas for his scouting movement and argued that traditional education and modern schooling should be combined to conserve the values of both.

He repeated his ideas on the usefulness of African folk-tales and then considered literature for Africa. He called for literary missionaries who could write books and edit newspapers. There was great potential in African traditions and stories, which should be written down as faithfully as possible. Above all, literature for Africa should be produced by Africans, and therefore 'now we must look to the training, and the encouragement, of African authors'.[30] He had no doubt about the literary talent of Africans – a view which has been confirmed by the subsequent development of African literature[31] – and mentioned examples of their work.

Smith concluded with thoughts that may have been repeated frequently in the classroom and elsewhere:

> During the past fifty years I have often been pained, and tempted not so much to despair as to furious anger, by contemplating the injustice meted out to Africans by my fellow white men. I believe that a better day has dawned.[32]

Africans, he was convinced, were coming into their own 'as men and women with gifts of personality and leadership to be respected and fostered'.[33]

Smith's next project was a biography of Daniel Lindley, an American who ministered among both Zulus and Dutch South Africans. Others had attempted this, most recently Dr C. T. Loram, who came from South Africa to teach at Yale University. Unfortunately, Dr Loram died soon after beginning this work.[34] Daniel Lindley was Mrs Anson Phelps-Stokes's grandfather, and Smith, by this time a friend of the family, was in the right place at the right time and had more or less completed the biography by May 1942, though the long delay in publishing enabled him to make revisions when he visited South Africa in 1946–7.

During the college vacations Smith made fact-finding journeys. In September 1942 he toured the deep South to study rural industry and education. His destination was Tuskegee Institute in Alabama, famous for its contribution to African American education. There he saw the George Washington Carver Museum and was impressed by the 'very wonderful collection of the things the old negro chemist had produced from peanuts, sweet potatoes, clays etc'.[35]

Sunday 6 September was one of Smith's 'great' days. Kelly, an assistant chaplain at Tuskegee, took him to a country church at Camp Hill 20–25 miles away. They arrived while the Sunday school, attended by many adults, was in session. The service proper began at 11 a.m. with the congregation going outside to a pool, where Kelly baptized about twenty young people. All then returned to the church for the communion service. The singing was unimpressive until the congregation started on spirituals. Smith asked for 'Swing Low' and found it 'very touching'. The pastor's prayer 'soon became rhythmic, like a song: "Heavenly Father" every few words'. Smith 'was asked to read a lesson, pray and speak a bit'. He noticed how fervent it all was, 'People enter into [the] service.'[36]

When Smith returned to Tuskegee in the evening this great day was completed by discussing the religious situation with Richardson, the chaplain. The day's experiences led to a conversation about music. Richardson's opinion was that African Americans had often despised spirituals but reacted favourably after seeing how whites had esteemed them. Smith also heard that very little religious music was being created because musical talent was being absorbed by secular music. He then had a long discussion about Tuskegee with its president. He was impressed by President Patterson's views, especially on race relations. There was a long way to go towards political and economic equality: 'Nothing more true than what B. W. [Booker T. Washington] said about holding man in ditch. – South suffers.'[37]

Arrangements had been made for Smith to visit farms with Mrs Williams, 'a fascinating Negro woman from Washington – a dietitian in Federal service'.[38] They met groups of farmers with Thurston, an agricultural officer, who was reorganizing farmers' clubs with the aim of maximizing production. At one meeting, attended by people in ragged clothing, Smith heard how the community was struggling because of poor cotton crops. The meeting closed with singing and a benediction and, before leaving, Smith gave a short speech about Africa.

As they travelled he saw on a large plantation the shacks in which labourers lived: 'horrible places, closed in by fields up to the doors. No gardens.'[39] Mrs Williams thought that the people only differed from slaves in not being bought or sold. However, few improvements could be made because of the owners' power. Some were said to be Representatives and Senators. This was Mrs Williams's first visit to the South and she found that in Mississippi blacks and whites were separated by a curtain in diners. She felt this deeply and told Smith that she found it hard to get hotel places and could not enter good restaurants.

Back at Tuskegee Smith met Dr Work, aged 76, who had 70,000 references for a bibliography of writings by African Americans. He was unusual in having a vote[40] and showed Smith the Alabama voting laws. He explained that the franchise was controlled by the governor's registrar. Dr Work considered that black people joined emotional sects because the white churches were becoming intellectualist. Meanwhile, in rural areas, community leadership was passing from the Church into the hands of teachers and agriculturalists, who were closer to the people than pastors.[41]

Before leaving Tuskegee Smith spoke further with Richardson, who had written a paper on Negro Christianity, which (he maintained) came in different forms, ranging from intellectual to emotional, and labelled, by Smith, as Upper Few, Middle Few and Lower Few.[42]

Smith's travels then took him to Montgomery, 50 miles west of Tuskegee, on a two-day excursion. Mr Street, an African American, was his driver. When they stopped for lunch on 11 September Smith wanted Street to eat with him 'but he explained it is impossible here for a negro to eat with a white man'.[43] Smith was extremely disappointed. Street asked about India and was surprised when Smith told him about caste.

Race problems continued to be in Smith's mind when, on Sunday 13 September, he attended a service for dedicating two flags, the Christian flag and the National flag. In the light of recent experiences much of what he heard smacked of hypocrisy:

> The foundations of this Republic are builded on the Christian teaching that every man is of infinite value in the sight of God . . . one nation, indivisible with liberty and justice for all.[44]

A judge spoke of no man being condemned without the judgment of a jury: 'I wanted to ask about the 132 lynchings in Alabama between 1900–31.'[45]

In the evening he visited a black congregation. Every taxi driver professed not to know where it was: 'I got one finally by naming not the Church, but the Madison Av. and Ripley St corner.'[46] Few people were present at first, but others kept arriving until there were thirty or forty altogether. The presiding elder preached. He began quietly and worked himself into a frenzy. Smith was glad that he went. He noticed that the people were nicely dressed and observed that 'in worship as in other things – dress, speech, they assimilate'.[47]

From Montgomery Smith went on to Nashville. He first visited Scarritt college for Christian workers and heard that it would be impossible to have blacks in the college or whites would not come. He toured Nashville, saw several places of education and met Dr Jones, a white Quaker, the President of Fisk University. Fisk was started after the Civil War by philanthropists helped by General Clinton B. Fisk. Dr Jones, a graduate of Hartford, became President in 1926. 'Fisk', said Smith, 'is an island: their own laws and customs. No colour bar: white and black live side by side, eat together, dance together.'[48] Smith was surprised and delighted to find such a place. A student took him around, showing him the excellent collection of black writings and portraits of Wilberforce, Shaftesbury, Livingstone and Queen Victoria. At lunch with Dr Jones, Smith 'told him about *"The Religion of <u>Lower</u> Races"* '.[49] The dreadful title imposed on his book was still a sore point.

Smith left Nashville for Hartford on 17 September 1942, and chatted on the train with two educated white men. They discussed race relations, and Smith was given various reasons for the colour line. He was told there was trouble when blacks crossed it. When he pointed out that the meanest white would not eat with an educated black he was told that black people were syphilitic, unclean, etc. etc.: 'Yet, said I, you allow them to cook your food and nurse your children.'[50] Smith then asked why distinctions were made in a democratic country whose creed is that all men are created equal. He heard that it was not a matter of superiority or inferiority but that the two are different: 'Take a cow and a horse: you milk a cow: you race horses: they are different – one not superior to other.'[51] Smith tried to explain that, since cows and horses are different species which will not interbreed but blacks and whites are not different species, the analogy is false. Smith was amazed that they were unconvinced: 'I was too flabbergasted to continue the argument. What can be said to such men? Christian professors in reputable colleges!!'[52]

Now in his fourth year in the USA, Smith spoke on Bible translation to the Hartford Oriental Society on 9 November 1942.[53] His ideas had already been expressed in *Shrine*: translations should be faithful to the original, intelligible and beautiful. He noted the Summer Institute of Linguistics (SIL), now eight years old, but thought it insufficient because there was no insistence on the original languages and six weeks was, in Smith's opinion, too short for training translators. He advocated a specialist department for translation. Students would need to be competent in biblical languages and a modern language other than English. However, SIL rightly put phonetic study of languages at the forefront and flourished in the second half of the twentieth century.

Smith suggested that students should practise translating into Basic English because this made the translator break up a passage into its elements. Naturally, anthropology, biblical and ethnic, was essential: 'words have no meaning apart from their context'.[54] He repeated his long-held views: 'All versions of Scripture made by foreigners are provisional . . . The time will come when translation and revision will fall entirely into the hands of native scholars.'[55]

In his teaching career Smith inspired his students with his love for Africa. Bill and Zilpha Booth studied Bantu linguistics at Hartford with him in 1943. Booth recalled that a dozen students were preparing to learn six different Bantu languages:

> His task was to help us acquire enough understanding of the structure of our particular language to be able to go on, with the help of local informers, and learn the language properly in the field.[56]

There were no grammars for these languages but

> Using an English concordance and all the Bantu Bibles in turn, Dr Smith worked up class notes and vocabularies for us, figuring out, from his knowledge of other Bantu languages, sufficient details to give us vocabularies, basics of grammar, exercises, phonetics, pronunciation – an incredibly complex and valuable accomplishment ... his knowledge of Bantu linguistics was enormous.[57]

Booth also recalled an amusing incident:

> Our class with Smith met in a room on the ground floor of Avery Hall, a neo-gothic building with tall, low windows. One warm spring day I was a bit late getting to class, and seeing the window open, I took the short cut and vaulted in the window. The class exploded in hilarious laughter which left me puzzled until someone explained that Dr Smith, noting the open window, had just advised the class to build their churches and schools with high windows to prevent Africans from using them as doors.[58]

He described Smith as a wise man devoted to his students and with a deep love for Africa. He also pointed out that Smith's opposition to cultural imperialism and his deep respect for African peoples and their cultures were very unusual at that time.

Early in 1943 Smith was contemplating the future. He had stayed much longer than the one year originally intended and felt homesick and tired. It was time to retire from responsibilities. He also regretted not being with his own people in the war. He was uncertain about returning home but, feeling that it was wrong to keep the Kennedy School in suspense, decided to leave Hartford in May 1943. There remained one possible reason for staying in the States: 'A scheme is being set afoot to establish an Institute of African Studies and I have been asked to remain in America for a year to organise it – the Institute I mean.'[59] He did not want to be misunderstood if, having left Hartford after expressing the desire to return to England, he then accepted this new appointment:

> All my life I have been devoted to Africa; and if now at the end I could render another service – and such a service as helping to set up an Institute for the study of Africa in this country – I should not be justified in turning from it.[60]

Smith's contribution to the Kennedy School of Missions was noted in a brief piece on his time there:

> By his scholarly interests and authorship, attested by a number of volumes, by his linguistic abilities and his pioneering in Basic English, by his profound understanding of African life and culture, by his depth of spiritual insight, and by his genial good humor, he has endeared himself to one and all and made a very significant contribution to the training of future leaders for Christian work in Africa and elsewhere.[61]

Smith remained in the USA and taught at Fisk University as a consultant in charge of African studies. He spent June 1943 visiting significant places and people, discussing the scheme and gathering ideas for the Fisk project.

After attending a luncheon on 9 June in New York to honour the Liberian President, Smith visited a branch of the New York Library where Reddick, 'an intelligent negro', was in charge. He had written a thesis on how white school books bolster the anti-black tradition and was fully in sympathy with the Fisk scheme. Smith noted, 'The collection is very good. Not all my books. *Mabilles* & *Moffat* & *ISP* missing.' He autographed copies of his books, 'Except *Lower Races* – I declined and told him the story.'[62] The title had troubled him for a long time and he made sure that people knew that he had not given it.

A few days later Smith was at the Pennsylvania University Museum in Philadelphia. He saw how the African Department was organized and was promised the extended loan of African artefacts for Fisk. He went from there to Howard University, Washington, a leading centre of black higher education and met eminent black academics such as Dr Rayford W. Logan[63] and Mordecai Johnson ('a remarkable man'). Johnson agreed that the Fisk course should be objective but, as he pointed out, 'in human affairs, where emotions are aroused, it is not easy to be objective'.[64] They discussed colonial policy, and Smith heard that Britain lacked action and planning with respect to Africa.

After consultations with Ralph Bunche, who became famous for his work for the UN, Smith went to Atlanta, where he was met by W. E. B. Du Bois,[65] with whom he spent the evening: 'a delightful companion, courteous, merry, human'.[66] Du Bois looked at Smith's plan for Fisk with interest and thought Smith was doing too much. As well as being an expert in sociology, Du Bois was a graduate of Fisk and knowledgeable about all the places and subjects Smith mentioned. Smith also met other Atlanta University teachers, including Ira Reid, who impressed him greatly. On 23 June he visited Reid's seminar, where several students were talking about black communities, festivals, etc. Smith was asked to speak, so talked about *matushi*, 'curses'.[67] They also discussed how a person should respond in an alien group. Smith heard that 'nigger', 'negra' and 'negress' were unacceptable terms. Du Bois told him not to say 'your people' when talking to blacks and had found some objections to 'negro'. Smith thought that Du Bois had mellowed in his attitude to segregation. While he did not approve of it, he saw that it could not be destroyed by agitation and argument, so accepted it as a fact and then worked for the best in every aspect of life.

The Fisk Program of African Studies was set up after this wide consultation. In a small introductory booklet, Mark Hanna Watkins, Professor of Anthropology and Sociology, described the Program and explained that it built on what had already been done in his department. The staff members included Smith and others who had been in various parts of Africa. Professor Watkins had written a grammar of Chichewa, and Dr Lorenzo D. Turner was particularly interested in survivals of African languages in the New World.

Smith contributed a short paper, 'The Significance of a Program of African Studies'. He pointed out that up to then 'American Negroes have cherished no pride in their ancestry', largely because their origins had been widely denigrated. Indeed, those who wanted to salve their consciences over slavery and keep a servile black population liked to represent the African American 'as having been redeemed from the utter degradation of life in Africa'. Smith, by contrast, argued strongly that it was 'a mistake to exaggerate the degradation of the native African'. He wanted African Americans to value their African origins. Immense study had been devoted to Africa and showed that 'the more we know the more reason we have to respect the Africans'.

Smith hoped that Fisk graduates would do anthropological fieldwork in Africa and that there would be exchanges between Fisk and African colleges which 'would give admirable opportunities for the initiation of American students into African life'. He also hoped that African Americans would use their training in the development of African countries:

> All such workers, in addition to their professional training as teachers, doctors and so on, need to have specific training in African sociology, linguistics, economics, etc., if they are to fit into the African environment and render effective service.[68]

Smith enjoyed his five years in the USA. He trained missionaries, continued writing, gave talks and made fascinating journeys. But, as his diaries make all too clear, he was deeply saddened by the racist attitudes that he frequently encountered.

He made every effort, therefore, both to change existing attitudes and to promote knowledge and understanding of African cultures. It was an uphill struggle on both fronts. On the one hand, many white people, Christians among them, would have been offended by his affection and respect for Africans and their diaspora relatives in the USA. On the other hand, as Emory Ross, African Secretary of the North American Missionary Conference, pointed out, 'apart from the missionary societies, interest in African Studies was confined to a relatively small group in America'.[69]

But Smith, we may be sure, was well pleased to make any contribution that he could.

Return to Britain. Revisiting Africa
(1944–1948)

After the D-Day landings in early June 1944, the war was entering its final phase and the Smiths were able to return home in mid-July.

In a letter to Malcolm Pitt of Hartford, Smith described how he was settling down. He wanted to enjoy his library and garden but had little leisure. 'Kasenga' was a large house, and Smith spent much time 'repairing things and getting the wilderness of a garden into shape again'. He did some fire-watching and Air Raid Precautions duties; his societies welcomed him back and put him on committees; and Lord Lugard wanted him to take on the editorship of *Africa*. Smith was giving talks about life in the USA and found, as he explained to Malcolm Pitt, that the 'unfortunate actions of some of your men in relation to the Negro soldiers over here'[1] had quickened interest in American racial problems.

On 7 December 1944 Smith attended a meeting of the Royal African Society. After a lull in activity during the intense part of the war the Society was restarting and used the opportunity to welcome Smith back from the USA and to present him with the last of its eight Silver Medals.[2] In the absence of the aged Lord Lugard, who sent a telegram, Lord Hailey, famous for his *African Survey* (1938), presented the medal 'for services to Africa'. He spoke about Smith's work, the editorial notes which for sixteen years he had produced for the society's journal and his writings: 'Lord Hailey said how much he himself had been influenced, before he had taken any practical part in African affairs, by Edwin Smith's book, *The Golden Stool*.'[3] He described Smith's 1935 Presidential Address to the RAI as 'a monumental account of the sociological aspects of African research'[4] and acknowledged that he owed to Edwin Smith his conviction that, whatever the British people tried to do in and for Africa, nothing could be accomplished without the willing cooperation of the African people or without, on our part, a real understanding of their institutions.[5]

He concluded: 'He has made a contribution to Africa which few can equal; and in presenting him with this medal the Society may feel that in honouring him it has honoured the Society.'[6] Sir Hanns Vischer then paid tribute to the help which Smith gave twenty years earlier to the Advisory Committee for Education in the Colonies. He spoke of Smith's modesty and his 'fundamental attitude towards the African as a fellow human being'.[7]

Smith concluded his response by saying, 'Africa and her peoples have been my greatest interest, and if you were to open me up you would find "Africa" written on my heart.'[8]

The IAI was returning to life, and Smith agreed to become editor of *Africa*, the institute's journal. Thanks to his experience with the Bible Society he was well qualified for such work and over the next three years 'threw himself with characteristic energy into making *Africa* a forum of considered opinion on the social problems of African development'.[9] He reviewed books – in Portuguese, Spanish, French and Italian as well as English – and was impressed by the French edition of *Bantu Philosophy* by the Roman Catholic missionary Placide Tempels:

> This long review reflects our sense of the importance of this little book. We wish that it might be translated into English, widely circulated, and its theories submitted to close scrutiny all over the Bantu field.[10]

It has been said of the Frazer Lectures at Liverpool University that 'the lecturers have been among the most eminent anthropologists in the world'.[11] It is therefore a mark of Smith's growing recognition that he was invited to contribute to the series, and he delivered his lecture, which was published as *Plans and – People! A Dynamic Science of Man in the Service of Africa* (1948) on 23 October 1946.

Having surveyed the changes in anthropology since Frazer's inaugural lecture in 1908, Smith argued that Frazer's devotion to the past had to be supplemented by studying rapid changes in contemporary societies and the effects of contacts between cultures. Smith considered that these developments should be studied by anthropologists who could advise on further changes: 'Who are more fitted – it is asked – to take place in social engineering than men and women who are trained to observe social facts and trends?'[12] Such a question may seem naive, but Smith knew very well 'that science divorced from ethics might be the enemy of mankind'.[13] The atomic bomb had recently shown the destructive potential of science. Thus, he added, conclusions drawn from careful fieldwork need to be supplemented by value-premises.[14] He declared his own belief in the kingdom of God as the best value for social development but was sure that there was enough common ground in values for many people to work together.

In *The Golden Stool* (1926) Smith had criticized Europe's contribution to African development. Now he believed that social research would spur the government into action, for it had done little so far. Quoting the example of Nigeria he said, 'you cannot build a nation on three shillings a head'.[15] He welcomed the 1940 Development and Welfare Act as a sign of the government's good intentions.

In his 1934 Presidential Address Smith concluded that it was for government officials and others to apply the results of anthropological research. Now, in *Plans and – People!* he regarded anthropology as an applied subject, able to engage in social engineering. In the event, however, anthropology did not follow this path. Its usefulness for understanding humankind was acknowledged, but after World War II its development was controlled by universities, where theoretical interests dominated. Moreover, the Association of Social Anthropologists, set up in 1946, excluded all but professional teachers of the subject. Finally, a combination of attitudes hampered the realization of Smith's hopes: anthropologists were not disposed to take responsibility for political actions, and colonial officials did not welcome interference from anthropologists.[16]

Shortly after the Frazer Lecture and nearly two years into his editorship of *Africa*, Smith made an eight-month tour of southern Africa,[17] sailing from Liverpool on the SS *Nestor*.

Smith got to know his fellow passengers, some from Zambia: 'a man got up and greeted me: I knew his face, much altered and when he said: "Tagart", I remembered.'[18] E. S. B. Tagart, a barrister, went to northeastern Rhodesia as Assistant Collector for the BSA Co. in 1902. He became Secretary for Native Affairs when Northern Rhodesia came under the British Crown in 1924.[19] Tagart joined the Royal Anthropological Institute in 1915[20] and the Royal African Society in 1929.[21] Now crippled with arthritis, he was on his way to retire in South Africa. He and his second wife Betty were to provide Smith with a base in Cape Town on his visits to South Africa.

Smith arrived at Cape Town on 30 November 1946. It was over thirty years since he was last in southern Africa. During that time he had read nearly everything written about the peoples and politics of the whole continent and had written much himself.

Now, he wanted to see for himself what was really happening, especially in what was known as Native Affairs, and to interview Africans as well as white officials and missionaries. The officials who met him said he would be given 'the fullest opportunity of seeing any aspects of Native life or administration that he might wish to study'.[22] He was anxious, too, to revisit his birthplace, Aliwal North, and to fit in a tour of Zambia, scene of most of his missionary work. At the same time, his Lindley research continued, revisions being made before publication in 1949, and he was always on the lookout for articles for *Africa*.

Smith spent his first week observing the 'locations' or housing estates for Africans. Of the African settlement at Windermere, which he visited with a police escort, he wrote: 'Why Windermere & why Kensington, the adjoining area? A misnomer, if ever there was one . . . A more horrible human habitation surely doesn't exist on earth.'[23] The situation depressed Brownlee of the Native Affairs Department (NAD).

Smith went from Cape Town to stay at Ficksburg near Lesotho, with Mrs Dyke and Mrs Flor Mabille, members of the Mabilles family. He fitted in a quick tour of Lesotho and saw how much Morija Mission had changed since 1898. Then, after Christmas at Ficksburg, Smith went north to Johannesburg. He discussed linguistics with C. M. Doke[24] and met Dr Ashton, Welfare Officer of the NAD in Johannesburg, who took Smith to see African dwellings on 30 December.[25] They first visited the 'barracks – euphemistically called Hostels for single men employed in town'.[26] One held about 4,000 men, including 200 in 'the "Black Hole of Calcutta" – [an] underground place intended for bicycles'.[27] Another hostel, not yet finished, was more commodious and 'when it is laid out in grass & trees planted will be as pleasant as one can expect'.[28] However, it had a dump on one side and a slum where the men visited prostitutes on another.

Then they came to the 'locations', estates of small houses with limited amenities. The tenants paid rates on the same basis as whites but did not enjoy the same benefits. The locations were surrounded by squatter settlements. For example, after seeing Orlando West with 7,400 people in 'neat cottages', Smith went through 'Shanty town, another squatter movement . . . 30,000 people . . . Shelters made of breeze blocks without mortar.'[29] In other places homes were made from sacks. Ashton thought the housing schemes were 'merely dumping grounds for Natives: no provision made for amenities'.[30] Smith noted, 'These locations are 12–15 miles out of J'burg. People have to travel so far to work & cost has to come out of their wages.'[31]

On the way back to Johannesburg they passed through 'Sophia Town, a slum built on elevation from which glorious view is secured . . . Passed a large Anglican Mission which A. says does good work.'[32] The Anglican Mission was where Trevor Huddleston worked and, though Sophiatown was, on the face of it, mostly a slum, it was 'not a "location" '.[33] It 'had a special character . . . It was both bohemian and conventional, lively and sedate.'[34]

Smith went on to Zululand and visited the Adams Mission Reserve, near Durban: 'Booth and his wife were there whom I had as students at Hartford. Living in house nearby with Zulus to learn language.'[35] He saw Lindley's house in Inanda on 12 January: 'Three Zulus came to talk to me. Dr Gumede, whom I met at Kingsmead in 1926(?).'[36] They spent some time discussing Daniel Lindley. Smith met and sought the opinion of many Africans as he travelled. He met Chief Luthuli, who became prominent in the ANC and spoke warmly of Smith's *Aggrey*. Then, on 25 January, Smith went to see Chief Mshiyeni, who had been acting Paramount Chief of the Zulus. He was given African beer which he deemed excellent. The chief told him about famous Zulus and he stayed for lunch, though the chief and his wife did not eat with their European visitor. They did, however, give Smith their autographs for his grandson Richard. The chief was building a brick chapel: 'Behind [the] altar semi-circularly inscribed: *Unkulunkulu nthando*: God is love.'[37]

From Zululand Smith made his way along the north of Lesotho to the Methodist mission at Thaba Nchu. He arranged to see the African Nationalist leader, Dr James Moroka: 'He came and had tea with me.'[38] Dr Moroka was educated at Lovedale, had studied medicine in Scotland and had now built up a huge medical practice: 'Says he has even more European than African patients.'[39] The doctor did not believe that all people were equal[40] but experienced no colour bar except with regard to the vote. Smith found this outrageous: 'Moroka is a fully qualified

medico . . . respected by white and black . . . has property – is wealthy
. . . yet has no voice in public affairs . . . cannot cast a vote in municipal,
provincial or parliamentary elections.'[41] Dr Moroka saw no logic in
what was happening and, together with other educated men, was deter-
mined to fight this ban. Smith said, 'If I were in your position I would
fight like hell.'[42] Some whites were afraid that Africans who got power
would be anti-white and destroy civilization: ' "This is our country" he
said "as well as of the whites and we should work together for the common good".'[43] Dr Moroka was a member of the Native Representative
Council for Transvaal, a body which was in abeyance at the time. The
members were unhappy to have no more than an advisory function.

Because the British royal family was paying a state visit, officials in
the south were not immediately free to see Smith. He therefore toured
the far north of the country and spent a few days at Johannesburg, seeing Professor Doke and Dr Ashton and meeting Rheinallt Jones of the
Institute of Race Relations, and Senator Edgar Brookes, another of
the white liberals. He then visited the west of the country and was
thrilled to see Mabotsa, the site of Livingstone's first mission station.[44]
At Taungs, 45 miles north of Kimberley, he had a discussion with the
chief's secretary and a member of the Representative Council. Part of the
conversation 'was in Sotho: and the Secretary said: "What astonishes
me is that a gentleman from England should know our language." '[45]
Smith produced a similar reaction at the tribal school: 'On the board in
one classroom was a Sotho poem, part of which I read – to the astonishment of the pupils.'[46]

The British royal family had now left the south, and Smith made his
way via Bloemfontein and Zastron to Ciskei and Transkei. He accumu-
lated more facts from officials, missionaries, farmers and anyone else
who could inform him and paid close attention to rural and urban
conditions:

a wonderful drive along a rough road high above the Orange. Far
below some fields on the bank . . . Towering above us on the right
were steep mountains, sheer rock and bushes, no grass. The slopes
below are dreadfully eroded . . . The erosion is heart-breaking . . .
Forty years ago, this was one of the best cattle countries, but now
cattle look thin and stunted.[47]

Travelling on, he met two distinguished Africans, Dr Bokwe and

Professor Jabavu. He asked the former about the Representative Council and was told that the members wanted executive powers and above all the franchise so as 'to share with whites in the functions of government'.[48] When Margery Perham visited South Africa in 1929, she described Professor Jabavu as 'perhaps the most famous living South African native'.[49] In response to Smith's questioning, the Professor said that the situation was deteriorating: 'Jabavu spoke of [the] humiliation he felt today in PO when white clerk chatted [a] long time with [a] white man and ignored the waiting natives.'[50] The Professor said that the government could appoint an African to fill a vacancy on the Native Affairs Commission. He was delighted that the King and Queen had shaken hands with him and other Africans on their recent visit to Lovedale: ' "Why can't all whites show the same feelings?" '[51]

Smith visited Lovedale, the famous mission station near Alice, and went on to the Methodist Institution at Healdtown. He met the governor, Grant, who had been at the anthropological congress in 1934, and S. M. Mokitimi, house master and chaplain, whom Edwin had met in 1939. Mokitimi had reviewed *The Mabilles* in Sotho newspapers and was highly regarded by Grant[52] and Nelson Mandela.[53] The Methodist Church in South Africa would make him its first African President in 1964.[54] Mrs Mokitimi was the daughter of Smith's Sotho teacher, Akim Sello: 'She says her father always spoke well of my Sotho and ability to learn.'[55] Smith found Mokitimi 'sane, level-headed. Says he keeps to Aggrey's doctrine of co-operation – the black and white keys.'[56]

Smith met more white people. At Rhodes University at Grahamstown on 13 March he came across Monica Wilson, 'whom I was pleased to see again'.[57] She had been one of the IAI's research fellows and, with Godfrey, her late husband, had directed the Rhodes–Livingstone Institute before the war. She spoke of Z. K. Matthews as one whom most whites would accept were he to be made principal of Fort Hare. She said that there were many pressures on black leaders to move away from cooperation. Smith learnt of her research interests in relationships among the Nyakyusa, especially kinship, chiefs and people and religion:[58] 'Godfrey was keen on symbolism and being [a] poet at heart could appreciate it. She promised to write for Africa an article on Symbolism.'[59]

Back in Cape Town on 16 March, Smith met D. L. Smit, chairman of the Native Affairs Commission, and broached the subject of appointing an African as a fifth member. Smit agreed but had to consider the political implications. He said that Z. K. Matthews, probably the most obvious candidate, could talk in extreme terms in the Native Representative Council. Smit took him to see J. H. Hofmeyr, a leading liberal politician, who had heard of Smith's books. Smith explained, 'I had come to S. A. to see things for myself & that IAI had given six months leave.'[60] He instanced illogicalities – for example, a well-educated black doctor who had no vote – and expressed the view that Africans were being pushed up with one hand and held down with the other. Hofmeyr thought that the UN had made things difficult in that the National Party's reaction was to make white people fearful of a black majority. He said they were going to use this fear to make the colour bar an issue for the next election.

After meeting this highly intelligent and liberal politician, Smith had a shock. He met Major van der Byl, cabinet minister for native affairs, and listened, apparently with much forbearance:

He started by saying: 'This is our country. We were here first (in the old colony, I interjected). When our fathers landed the Bantu were on the other side of the Fish River' (I might have said, if prior arrival gives right to a country then this belongs to Hottentots and Bushmen – but I didn't and merely said: 'I am familiar with the history.'[61]

Smith debated some points and doubted whether assimilation once started could be stopped. The Major was sure that intermarriage could not be tolerated: 'He repeated the old cliché: "Brother in Christ, but not brother-in-law".'[62] The minister said that his job was to prepare Africans for the future. Smith pointed out that many Africans were now well prepared, 'educated, good worthy citizens, who are outside the political system'.[63] They were frustrated. The minister agreed but argued against any franchise for Africans. He said that it was ridiculous to give uneducated Africans the vote. He would not, however, give educated Africans the vote either, since no such discrimination had ever been imposed on whites. The minister must have realized that, if educational tests were applied, some whites would lose their vote. In any case, white people would not vote for a party that supported an African franchise. He finished by saying that communism was the real danger. It was out to destroy the British Empire through its keystone, South Africa. Smith told his friend Tagart about this meeting and 'he thought I must be very disappointed: the Minister had talked childishly'.[64]

Smith also lunched at the Houses of Parliament with General Smuts and others. When he entered the conversation he 'reminded Smuts that he had said segregation is dead. He confirmed this. "Development on their own lines", [is] also dead.'⁶⁵ Smuts said that Africans must be drawn into the system, beginning with economics. 'He said he didn't believe in equality . . . What he stands for is justice for all.'⁶⁶ For Smith, the discussion started to become interesting when Smuts said that civilization got going among *superior races* while Africans remained stagnant. Unfortunately, there was no time to discuss this. Smith told Smuts of his origins and their proximity in the Boer War. In parting Smuts said, ' "My heart warms to you because you were born at Aliwal." '⁶⁷

Smith completed his observations of native affairs by going east again, to Transkei and Pondoland. By 29 March at Port St John's he stated his analysis of the situation in native policy thus: 'Lack of definite long term policy felt by D.Cs. – they don't know what they are striving towards.'⁶⁸ He later published his conclusion that the Native Affairs Department was 'more liberal in its administration than Parliament is in its legislation'.⁶⁹ He offered this opinion after he had been all over South Africa, seeing things for himself and meeting Africans, officials, academics and politicians of various opinions.

Throughout South Africa Smith found people who valued his *Aggrey* and asked him to autograph their copy. Some had read *African Beliefs*. At Umtata 'I told one clerk that I was author of *Aggrey*. The news soon spread and I was asked to meet some of the men.'⁷⁰ They discussed 'initiation' and gave various opinions. Smith asked if Aggrey's principle of the piano keys still held good and was told that white people did not cooperate. A man asked about 'witch doctors'. Smith did not accept the term and they had a long discussion about 'traditional healers'. At the end one man was heard to say, ' "That hour has been well spent." '⁷¹

Having completed his fact-finding mission Smith visited his birth-place, Aliwal North. It was greatly changed: 'I set out to explore this strange city – so it appeared to me: I could recognise nothing until I came to the Post Office: . . . new shops and garages. The Public school I attended is superseded by newer buildings.'⁷² He went to the parsonage and was sad to see the neglected garden: 'A general air of neglect pervades what I remember, in father's time, as a small paradise.'⁷³ In the library he saw 'Father's portrait in one room – it looked fresh. No name attached . . . found three of my books on the shelves.'⁷⁴ Then on

Saturday 5 April he was off again by train heading for Thaba Nchu. The next day was Easter Sunday and Smith attended an evening service. The preacher

> Says he intentionally does not simplify his English: students wish him not to. If they don't know the words they will find the meaning. They will undoubtedly have many questions after this sermon . . . Singing is good but all English hymns . . . why do they waste their fine voices on English pieces?[75]

Smith asked later for a Sotho hymn and 'it was grand'.[76]

After a couple of days at Ficksburg with Mrs Dyke he set off for Zambia on 9 April. He met his nieces at Kimberley and went on to Lusaka, after a short stop at Bulawayo. He was back in Zambia, looking forward intently to seeing the Ila people. He had an anthropological as well as a nostalgic interest in this journey. There were some things to add to *ISP*. One of his stock questions on this part of the tour was to ask Ila people about their lineage. This topic was of great interest to anthropologists of the day[77] and, as will be seen, Smith frequently asked people about their *lunungu*. This word was used for the long branching stem of pumpkin and melon and so was used for lineage.[78]

Before going to Bwila, Smith went to the Copperbelt, which did not exist when he was in Zambia. At Luanshya he met a young missionary named Macpherson who said that 'several teachers asked him to get my books – *Xn Beliefs – Secret of the African*: he did so; and they read them. They bring up for discussion things I wrote.'[79] Fergus Macpherson was one of Smith's admirers. His missionary leader in Scotland, Matthew Faulds, had advised him that Edwin Smith and Roland Allen were important missionary thinkers. Macpherson had read *Shrine*, *Secret* and *ABCF* and was excited to hear of Smith's visit from the Revd John Shaw, a Methodist missionary, who drove them around. For him, it was a very memorable occasion indeed.[80]

After conversations and a visit to a copper mine, Smith made his way back to Lusaka. He stopped at Kabwe to meet Douglas Gray, who had stayed at Kasenga in 1914. It was sad to see Gray appear so old at 63. He also met Gray's daughter, a doctor, and her husband, Merfyn Temple, who was recovering from pleurisy: 'a young man with ideas'.[81] Then Smith went to Chipembi, famous for its girls' school. He thought the school syllabus inappropriate, and his visit did not go down well with the local missionaries: 'He stayed on the ex Wesleyan Mission of Chipembi where he was not very popular. They thought him somewhat arrogant.'[82]

On Saturday 26 April 1947 Smith began the fifth volume of his diary.

> This is the day when I approach the climax of my long tour: a visit to Bwila where I spent the happiest periods of my life – I begin with some things that have been told of the Baila lately. J. R. Shaw, ex-chaplain of the NRR, says that whenever you met a particularly fine NCO he was almost certain to be a Mwila or Ngoni.[83]

On the way to Bwila, Smith attended the prize-giving at Kafue mission, the fruit of Smith's thinking and pressure. He presented the prizes and spoke of old times and Aggrey's message. Ernest Stamp, who felt disappointed about the work in Bwila, was asked by Smith where the missionaries had failed. Stamp, who went to Zambia in 1921, thought 'we have underestimated depravity of [the] people'.[84] Mrs Stamp remembered

> Mr Smith's visit to Kafue while we were there . . . I remember how impatient he was with anything not kept up that he had started. My husband thought he was putting too much into his visit and rather overtiring himself.[85]

On Sunday he attended the school service and heard the 'Tonga hymns which grated on my ears because [the] stress did not fall in keeping with music – futula for futula etc.'[86] Many were translations of English hymns. Smith met Cecil Hopgood: 'He is the linguistic expert, but could throw no light on *lunungu* etc . . . Is as taciturn as ever.'[87] Smith addressed the schoolboys on Monday and told them how Ila words were first written down and then had a long chat with the headmaster, Robinson Nabulyato,[88] who furnished Smith with plenty of information on *lunungu* etc.

Smith left Kafue 'with growing sense of disappointment . . . am I to regret ever coming back to NR?'[89] and arrived at Namwala in the late afternoon. When he was taken to Kasenga he did not recognize the region as there were more trees, including a patch of eucalyptus.

The next day they looked around:

Went first to my old house. Needs doing up but structure looks sound. Particularly pleased to see how the arches have stood – one in bedroom has a crack ... Surroundings of house disgraceful ... where my beautiful garden was is a desert. A few silver oaks and nothing else. All fruit trees gone: where years ago we had more fruit than we could do with, and supplied the countryside – citrus, peaches, guavas, bananas, pines – there is nothing.[90]

Much building had been done, including a hospital, but the 'whole aspect of the place unkempt'.[91] He visited the village where Mungaila had lived, and people gathered round asking, 'who is the white man who speaks Ila?'[92] He amused them by saying '*Matako a mweenzu makadikwa.*'[93] Smith asked if Shimunenga's place was still honoured, and they all went to see it. He saw Solomon's neat house and the oven where he made bread. Solomon, he was glad to say, 'looks hale and hearty, slightly grey beard. Says Pauluse is dead, Samuel, Ngwalungwalu & Mwanapobola still alive at Lubwe & Nanzela.'[94] At one village, a 'woman looked hard and wouldn't believe until I took off my helmet. Asked after Namusa. Indeed everybody did. I was identified as Mulumi a Namusa.'[95] Smith had to explain that he was not a spirit but a real person and was delighted to find that he could still speak Ila after thirty years' absence. He gave Solomon his suit, a shirt and £1 for his wife and went on to discuss *lunungu* with the teacher at Maala, who added to Smith's knowledge of the topic. Then, in the evening, the Chitumbi Christians sang two of Smith's hymns and he gave a short address in Ila.

Nanzela was the next place to see and, after staying briefly at Namwala and having discussions with officials on Ila health, fertility, education, etc., he set off on a bumpy journey of five hours which brought him to Nanzela at 13.40 on 3 May. His old house had been turned into a school, but the walls were sound. The church still had the pulpit he had made. Then he 'visited Thabo's and Edwin Price's graves, all in order under the sausage tree.'[96]

A group of men came to see him:

They said one man was Thomas Mwanapobola. Only on close examination did I know him. Face wizened, doubled with pain in back, very deaf, like Egyptian mummy. Pained me to the heart to see my dear old friend in this condition.[97]

He gave Thomas a white suit. Another old friend, Pauluse Kaiyobe, or Shamatanga, Smith's informant in linguistic and cultural matters, was dead. Smith met his widow, Naomi, who wept when Smith spoke of her husband as his dear friend. It was an emotional time, and so was a reunion with Mr and Mrs David Mubitana, who came to help when the truck was bogged down on the way back to Namwala.[98]

Smith set off the next day for Choma. He stopped at the Anglican mission at Mapanza for a cup of tea and autographed a copy of *ISP*: 'Father Jones has studied Tonga music . . . He undertook to write an article for *Africa* on the subject.'[99] The Revd E. G. Nightingale, the Methodist District Chairman, came from Lusaka, met Smith at Choma and took him to Masuku mission to see Matthew Lucheya, an Ila minister. Lucheya had read *ISP* and said that it was very accurate: 'Found things in it he did not know but when [he] asked old men they confirmed what we wrote.'[100] Nightingale asked Smith for his impressions of Kasenga: 'I said I was profoundly disappointed . . . and that goes for every place I have been to.'[101] Smith could not see any success for the mission among the Bantu Botatwe when there was not a missionary who could hold a conversation in the vernacular. Such a claim was not actually true because Cecil Hopgood was highly proficient in Tonga. Smith, however, was not impressed by the linguistic performance of the missionaries he met. He criticized the policy of stationing African ministers outside their own language area and suggested that he should come there himself if his wife's health permitted. Eventually, he left Zambia after a few days in Livingstone: 'Shall I ever see it again? Not likely.'[102]

The visit to Bwila was a bitter disappointment to Smith, who may have expected too much from his successors. He did, however, find it useful anthropologically, and after returning from Zambia gave a paper, 'The Ba-Ila Revisited', to the Royal Anthropological Institute on 18 November 1947.[103] His anthropological observations were later published in two articles in *African Studies*.[104] He included an account of Ila history which had been collected by the Revd L. W. S. Price and noted changes since 1902. The Ila headdresses were no longer to be seen. He thought that the villages were dirtier than in the old days, though Ila teachers disputed this. European clothes were widely used and the language was being influenced by English. He was distressed, perhaps needlessly, by the thought that the Ila still had fertility problems.[105]

Of all the changes since 1902 the development of local government under indirect rule was the most influential. When Smith remembered how hard it had been to persuade people to let their children attend school, he was surprised to learn that the Ila were the first people in British Africa to start compulsory education. Unfortunately, able people then left the rural areas. He thought that an education tailored to the local economy and focused on the area's natural resources was badly needed.

Smith was well aware of faults in *ISP*, especially its discussion of social organization, and he hoped that proper studies would be made. For the time being, however, he submitted notes based on his recent visit and drew on the writing of Evans-Pritchard and others to interpret his findings about the clan and family structure of Ila life. He explained the main terms and where further research was needed. He had been interested in *lunungu*, lineage, as he travelled. The word had not appeared in his published vocabulary, but he had used it to translate 'seed' in Romans 9.7. He found that, though it meant seed, especially of the pumpkin, it also included the pumpkin's long branching stem and thus could refer to human lineage. His informants gave diverse opinions, some asserting that descent is patrilineal and others that it is matrilineal. It was clear that the subject was important in social life. People in the same *lunungu* and in the same generation or in the two following generations could not intermarry. The *lunungu* also had a religious function and controlled which ancestors a man or woman could pray to.

As he travelled south, Smith stopped at Bulawayo, where he met the Revd A. J. Haile, Superintendent of the London Missionary Society (LMS), who had some archives for Smith to see. Haile thought that Smith should follow the LMS's suggestion and write a life of Roger Price, a son-in-law of Robert Moffat. The very next day, however, having met a son of Roger Price, who said that his sister in South Africa was collecting material about their father, Smith considered withdrawing from this project.

On his return to Cape Town Smith met white advocates of African rights. Mrs Ballinger, one of the most forceful of them, impressed Smith immensely by her 'passion, thoughtfulness – power of expression'.[106] She felt that, though the NAD officials did good work, they did not touch the deepest problems of African aspirations. Her husband was secretary/organizer of the Friends of Africa, a society chaired by D. M.

Buchanan, another of Smith's friends. Like them, Smith was very concerned about the political developments taking place in South Africa.
On 8 May 1947, Smuts presented a statement to African leaders on the
future of native policy. Smith made notes of this and of an African
National Congress meeting on 19 May which decided that the proposals
were unacceptable.

Smith discussed his notes on *lunungu* etc. with Professor Schapera,
who suggested that Smith should take his place when he went on leave
from July to November 1948: 'a very attractive proposition'.[107]

On 10 June Smith wound up his tour by looking again at
Windermere: 'I wanted to see it in wintry conditions. Once again I
entered the stockade: more filthy than ever, owing to the rains . . . I said
this is the worst place I have seen in the Union.'[108] This was one of his
last impressions before leaving South Africa. He had seen things for
himself and heard numerous opinions from a wide range of people. He
then had a wonderful voyage, reading a novel a day and writing notes
for *Africa* and arrived back at Chesham on 27 June 1947.

By this time Smith knew Geoffrey Parrinder, a Methodist minister
who had served in West Africa and had submitted a comprehensive
study of religion in that region for a Ph.D. at London University. Smith
and E. O. James were his examiners.[109] Smith contributed a foreword
(dated 15 September 1947) to the published version, *West African
Religion* (1949). He noted that Parrinder offered a synthesis and felt
that the time was now ripe for such studies. He hoped that Parrinder
would go on to investigate how African Christianity had developed,
and wondered how the new religion had been coloured by the old:

> Aggrey, we know always thought of God as Father–Mother, or
> rather Mother–Father: and I doubt not that this sense of the mother-
> hood of God lingered on from his early training in a pagan family.
> Christians may thus be enriched from pagan sources.[110]

Smith's hopes were not disappointed. Geoffrey Parrinder wrote more
about African religions and coined the expression 'African traditional
religion'. Moreover, he became one of the leading teachers in comparative religion, his academic reputation and influence being greater than
Smith's and his interests wider. But he always acknowledged his great
respect for Edwin Smith.[111]

In the spring of 1948 the Smiths moved from Chesham to Deal,[112] nearer to Matsi, who was now living in that area. Their retirement home was the Old Watch House on the sea front. 'Kasenga' with its large garden may have been too big, for both of them had health problems. For this reason he wound up his job as editor of *Africa* and was succeeded by Daryll Forde, who led the IAI and its journal into a new era of research and publication.

The Blessed Missionaries (1948–1950)

Towards the end of 1948 Smith returned to southern Africa to gather material for a biography of the Welsh missionary and son-in-law of Robert Moffat, Roger Price (1834–1900).[1] In the previous year, as we have seen, Smith had been told that Price's daughter, Miss Christian Price, had already embarked on this task. It turned out that she was working on her mother's diaries and willingly agreed to let Smith write her father's life story.

Because Julia, like her husband, was a diabetic and did not enjoy good health in her old age, Edwin was sad to leave her in England: 'I feel very unhappy about it. Fear I am making the biggest mistake of my life in taking this trip.'[2] Perhaps he wondered whether he would see her again.

On the sea journey, Smith took his usual keen interest in his fellow passengers. They included his Methodist friends from Thaba Nchu, Revd and Mrs William Illsley, who were returning from leave in Britain. They invited Smith to spend Christmas with them.[3] The MP for Aliwal North was on board and, in view of the political developments in South Africa, Smith asked him what was meant by apartheid. He was told that the National Party did 'not want to "suppress" the natives. But must preserve "White Supremacy".'[4] The MP seemed 'to think everybody Communists who are against [the] colour bar and described Mr and Mrs Ballinger as communists'.[5] Smith knew the Ballingers and had been impressed by Mrs Ballinger's strength of character and intellect. He asked the MP whether the National Party 'intended to take [the] franchise from Africans. Yes, decidedly, he said.' Smith thought it strange to be committed to take away something that had not been given. He also learnt that Africans would be taught trades but not 'in competition with Whites'.[6] The MP later called another of Smith's friends, D. Buchanan, KC, ' "a white Kaffir" ',[7] a term of abuse.

After a few days in Cape Town Smith went to George, 240 miles to the east, and for the first time met Miss Price. She was 'not at all the formidable woman I feared: about 67, kindly face'.[8] He plunged into the Price papers, taking notes from Mrs Price's diaries. Then, on 1 December, Miss Price had a sudden, severe stroke, and to the shock of her illness – she was little better when Smith left for Cape Town on 4 December – was added the distressing news that J. H. Hofmeyr had died. Smith considered the loss of Hofmeyr's intellectual power a serious blow to South Africa and not simply to the liberal wing of the United Party.

While Smith was at Cape Town, on 13 December, he received an invitation from the university to give the Phelps-Stokes Lectures in 1949. He discussed the subject and dates for these lectures with university officials, accepted Isaac Schapera's suggestion that he should consider the missionary contribution to race relations, and indicated that he would approach the topic both historically and anthropologically.

His friend Tagart remarked:

'Many people think that missionaries are in a bag and all come out alike. Whereas they differ as much at least as D.O.'s and governors or African chiefs.' Very well I said I will quote you to that effect.[9]

During the rest of his stay, Smith's conversations and reading were focused on Christian attitudes to race relations in southern Africa, alongside his Roger Price researches.

Christmas was spent, as planned, with the Illsleys at Thaba Nchu. Smith met an Afrikaner official who 'left a very favourable impression on my mind . . . really interested in Africans'.[10] Smith wondered, though, whether the man would sit at meals with Africans. That was the test. Leslie Hewson, Methodist tutor from Grahamstown, also spent Christmas with the Illsleys. He said that Smith's Africanizing ideas attracted him but he was sceptical about carrying them out among detribalized people.

On Christmas Day Smith attended church services. He was well pleased with Hewson's preaching at the Methodist church but, in his judgment, a service at the hospital was less satisfactory. Smith noted the incongruity of Father Christmas and wondered whether the northern church had any relevant Christmas message for an old Sotho man with a broken arm.

Smith met Africans as well as Europeans interested in African studies. At Bloemfontein he came across the Methodist minister, Revd Litheko, who was chaplain of the Orange Free State branch of the National Congress:

> their meetings open with a sermon . . . He stands for co-operation: opposed to those who say must have no dealings with whites . . . Accepts Aggrey's doctrine . . . people do not advance in isolation. Fatal for Africans to separate from Europeans.[11]

Another African approached Smith and asked:

> 'Are you the Dr Smith who used to be at Morija?' – 'Yes, 50 years ago' – 'Do you remember Akim Sello?' – 'Yes: he taught me Sesuto' – 'I'm his son: & before he died (1946?) he gave me the Bible which you gave him.' He was overjoyed to meet me.[12]

The names mentioned in Smith's travels read like a list from a *Who's Who* of African affairs. He passed his own test of eating with Africans on 28 December, at a dinner party with Dr Moroka and Z. K. Matthews and their wives. These highly qualified Africans were involved in political movements in South Africa. Matthews was Hofmeyr's 'intellectual equal'.[13] He would suggest the Freedom Charter for a multi-racial, democratic South Africa.[14] Smith asked him why he was not to be Principal of Fort Hare and was told that he would be next time. Dr Moroka thought that the government would not allow such an appointment because it 'would mean putting whites under a black'.[15] Smith discussed with these eminent men the lectures he was preparing. Matthews thought that the church was not bold enough: 'They have actually put cooperation into practice; but seem afraid to let their voice be heard lest [they] should lose support in what [they are] doing.'[16] When Smith asked about the future of Africans in South Africa, Matthews said that Africans would become acculturated but not cease to be African. He expected some separate development but not an imposed segregation. The language, he thought, would be revived as a unified Bantu tongue. Smith elicited their views on forms of government. Matthews said that some people had hoped that Hofmeyr would start a party to fight for cooperation: 'But his loyalty to Smuts prevented his breaking away.'[17] This was why Matthews had opposed Hofmeyr at a crucial meeting in 1946. He would later remark:

That a man of such liberal attitudes and one on whom Africans had pinned their hopes for the future, could allow himself to be used to make such an ineffectual statement was bitterly disappointing.[18]

Smith continued his travels on 5 January 1949 and at Johannesburg met his friend Clement Doke, who made some suggestions for the lectures. In a further conversation, on 7 January, Smith learned that Doke's attempt to get B. W. Vilakazi recognized as a university lecturer on the grounds of his scholarship, his success in work, and his authorship of five books, had been frustrated by a minority.

Smith then visited his nieces Mary and Ruth, who lived near Postmasburg on the edge of the Kalahari. It was a quiet place, and he would have been bored out of his mind without his lectures to think about. He saw his brother J. T.'s house, 'where Jue and I visited in 1913 (?)'.[19] An old Afrikaner said that Smith was like his brother J. T., who 'did so much for [the] Farmers' Association. Mainly instrumental in getting the F. A. Hall built, which still stands.'[20] Another brother, Sydney Baldwin Smith, had been reported missing in France in October 1916 aged 32, and Smith saw the brass memorial plate at St Catherine's Church.[21]

After staying with his relatives, Smith went on 7 February 1949 to Kuruman, where he visited Moffat's house, saw Roger Price's grave and made several journeys around the area, seeing the countryside and talking with old men about Roger Price. His research tour then took him to Zimbabwe (Southern Rhodesia) and the Central African Archives, where he read the Moffat papers and letters of Roger Price. The Methodist District Chairman, Herbert Carter, invited Smith to stay with his family. They discussed race relations, and Smith learned that the 'basis of S. R. native policy is segregation'.[22] The Methodists, however, expected Africans to come wholly into the European system. The chairman was sure that a trained African was the equal of a European. Smith learnt that church organization was English with a few local modifications: 'Africans bring in own nuances such as all shaking hands after Communion.'[23] Smith described his forthcoming lectures and asked Carter 'to define right race relations. He thinks Aggrey's simile of the Piano Keys is over-quoted. Says there is a gamut: – Dominance – modified dominance – trusteeship – partnership – friendship. Right relation is friendship . . . '.[24] Aggrey's saying actually made a lasting impression in Zimbabwe for, in 1991, Crispen C. G. Mazobere of the

Methodist Church in Zimbabwe paraphrased it after stating: 'The Methodist Church in Zimbabwe has learnt and by God's grace is trying to live by Dr K. Aggrey's wise declaration.'[25]

Smith liked being with Herbert Carter, who had been in Zimbabwe for more than thirty years. On Monday 7 March, Carter took him to a school:

> It is the first secondary school for Africans . . . Carter says he had a long hard fight . . . ?9 years to get his proposal accepted: Huggins was at first opposed. Idea seems to have been that Africans don't need higher education.[26]

Smith's stock question on his travels was based on Professor Hoernlé's remark that missionaries were muddle-headed in their race policy.[27] He used it to canvass opinions on the subject.

On 16 March he lunched with Revd St John Evans, director of missions for the diocese and formerly in Ghana. They last met when Smith took the chair at the RAI and Evans read a paper. Smith discussed his lectures and raised the subject of muddle-headedness. Evans agreed that there was no long-term policy and revealed that the Church was not immune from the colour bar and its illogicalities; for example, 'Evans says he has seen [a] child brought into church for baptism by a "nannie" who held it till she handed it to mother for presentation. Parents would not tolerate Africans in church services.'[28] Evans saw that 'separatist churches are a criticism of the church; on 2 lines: (a) a protest against withholding privileges and responsibilities from Africans; (b) a protest against an exclusive European presentation of Christianity'.[29] They discussed African customs and agreed that only Africans could decide what customs to preserve: 'He instanced dances. Some of these seem innocent enough to us, yet Africans may detect obscene suggestions that are not apparent to us.'[30]

Smith spent a short time at Bulawayo, where he interviewed Robert Price about his father. He found out little and went on to Palapye in Botswana, where he preached on 27 March at the church which Khama built. To the people's surprise and delight he gave the benediction in Sotho. The regent, Tshekedi, met him and said he had read Smith's books so there was no need for an introduction.

Smith then travelled south and visited Tiger Kloof Institute at Easter. He had been overdoing things and felt very ill when he came to Kimberley. He spent a few days in hospital, suffering from angina.

Visitors came from the local church, and his relatives in the area came to see him. After this rest Smith went to Cape Town, stayed with the Tagarts and worked on his lectures for the next six weeks.

He gave the first lecture on Tuesday 14 June 1949. There was 'great excitement today over the Citizenship Bill', so the audience 'was as good as to be expected with big protest meetings on'.[31] The bill in question affected British migrants by increasing the waiting period for them to qualify for citizenship from two to five years.[32] More oppressive measures affecting the African population were on the way. By that time, the process by which the National Party was changing the *de facto* segregation in South Africa to a *de jure* system was only just beginning.

A larger audience attended the second lecture. Douglas Buchanan, who took the chair, said, 'You will be Public Enemy No 1 after this.'[33] The third lecture, on 22 June, was chaired by Isaac Schapera and attracted a small audience, but Smith felt that the last one, on 23 June, went well. He set off for home the following day and was back in Deal on 8 July.

An expanded form of the lectures was published in 1950 as *The Blessed Missionaries* (BM). Smith dedicated the book to the Tagarts, and a Foreword was provided by Sir Herbert Stanley, a former colonial governor. The printed lectures show that Smith had read widely on the subject and was well aware of the latest developments in South African politics. At least one scholar has been misled by Smith's title, noting it as another example of missionary hagiography.[34] The title refers, however, to a saying of Sir Harry Smith, Governor of Cape Colony (1847–52), who, when he received a strongly worded protest from the French missionaries in Lesotho, 'labelled it "The Blessed Missionaries' Statement"'.[35] The lectures therefore deal with the missionaries as blessed nuisances down the years and with the contemporary relevance of their contribution to the social situation in South Africa.

Smith described South Africa as a multi-racial, multi-cultural society with a policy of creating a united nation. Although, for the next forty years, South Africa departed from this ideal, there were liberal South Africans who shared Smith's belief that the right race relations were friendly cooperation and partnership on the basis of mutual respect. Another option, self-determination, conserving traditional values and customs, seemed a good ideal, and *apartheid*, as separation, appeared to offer a way of realizing it. Smith, however, saw it as entirely impracticable in South Africa. Separation, for which Smith had once argued in

The Golden Stool, was no longer possible, and he now considered cooperation a far better option, based on the democratic idea of equality of opportunity. In his lectures Smith wanted to evaluate the Church's past and present contributions and to suggest how it could promote cooperation in the future.

The first chapter, presumably the first lecture, was entitled 'The Introducers'. In earlier years he had used the illustration of the Kasenga blacksmith to depict the missionary as one who recycles existing ideas to form something new. The notion of an 'Introducer' came into the picture when he worked for the Bible Society.[36] It was borrowed from *The Friendly Road* by Ray Stannard Baker (1870–1946) writing under the pseudonym David Grayson. Baker, an investigative journalist and biographer of Woodrow Wilson, was a 'progressive' who saw his life's work as being a 'maker of understandings'.[37] His explorations of the colour line and of industrial and spiritual unrest were all of a piece with the homespun tales of the Grayson books. He and Smith shared an emphasis on the importance of understanding. According to Smith, the missionary comes from one culture, sympathetically understands another and introduces the two cultures to each other. This idea of the missionary as a person between the cultures prepared the way for later thinkers. 'Understanding' turns out to be important in the method of inter-faith dialogue which became popular towards the end of the twentieth century.[38]

Smith showed that missionaries took a leading part in bringing about an understanding of Africa. They explored its geography, its cultures and, as 90 per cent of Dr Doke's huge personal library of books on African languages revealed, its languages. Smith had great respect for African languages and suggested that Bantu languages should be taught in schools to white children: 'I defy anyone to study a Bantu language thoroughly and retain an opinion that Africans are innately inferior to Europeans in intellect.'[39] In this way language studies would foster right relations between peoples.

Missionaries had also helped the development of anthropology. Though many missionaries had made negative, subjective evaluations of Africans, others had gone far towards producing objective studies. Smith listed many of the books that had been written, modestly omitting *ISP*, and reminded his readers that missionaries, Roman Catholic and Protestant, had joined with anthropologists to establish the International African Institute.

Smith believed that reason, by exposing racism as combining false thought and wrong attitudes, afforded the best opposition to it. It is arguable, however, that such a liberal approach is unrealistic and that, as a social scientist and advocate of social engineering, he should have pressed more strongly for creating social structures that would facilitate inter-racial cooperation.

In his previous writings Smith had promoted the Africanization of Christianity. Now he heard that, because of cultural changes, Africans should accept European ideas and institutions. But, as Smith pointed out, Africans do not simply absorb or borrow, they also transform what they receive 'to produce something which did not exist before'.[40] This important point has been noted again in recent religious studies: 'the African expression of religious experience is geared to finding new clusters of meaning, embracing new concepts and religions, but in embracing them, reshaping them'.[41]

Most early missionaries introduced European clothes, houses and culture, but they also supported local languages and leadership. They were pathfinders in social welfare (education, agriculture, medicine, etc.) for Africans. Smith, however, pointed out that, because many trades were monopolized by whites, educated and trained Africans were often prevented from expressing their skills. Not surprisingly, there was bitterness and many turned to Communism. Smith argued that, since Christianity is opposed to injustice, Christian Africans were right to protest against oppression.

The second lecture moved naturally to the question of human rights. South Africa shared a dilemma with the USA which proclaimed human rights unequivocally in the Declaration of Independence and, as Smith had witnessed, denied them to black Americans. In South Africa there may have been a desire to act justly towards non-Europeans but there was no knowledge of what was due to them. Missionaries had often been hated for taking up the rights of subject peoples. Smith traced the race problem to the introduction of slavery to South Africa in 1658. There was no caste-society in those days. Indeed, a Hottentot girl's marriage to a European in 1662 was a great social event. But by the early nineteenth century a missionary's marriage to a woman of Malagasy extraction was universally disapproved. This change in attitude came about, Smith believed, when the attitude to slaves, as property, was transferred to black people. A class of indentured servants was thus created and missionaries, who began to address their grievances,

became alienated from the colonists. Smith highlighted the LMS superintendent, John Philip, who spoke for the underprivileged. Philip probably knew more about living conditions in southern Africa than any
other person of his day. He believed in the equality of white and black
and only advocated segregation as a provisional measure, for his ideal
was integration.

The third lecture, on 'Political Parsons', dealt with land. Smith illustrated, by reference to several tribes, how Africans had been deprived of
land. Missionaries helped to combat such practices, but some white
people in South Africa thought that the separate existence of such areas
as Lesotho and Botswana was monstrous. Africans in those lands, however, dreaded entering the Union, and Smith repeated his opinion of ten
years earlier that, as long as South Africa continued as it was, their
apprehension was entirely justified.

The last lecture focused on 'Principles and Policies'. Professor
Hoernlé had alleged that the Christian Church was muddled about the
ideal relationship between the ethnic groups in South Africa. Smith
agreed that there was disunity among Christians. Nevertheless, as one
African Christian leader told him, there are guiding principles which, if
practised, would lead to a solution: Christian teaching on the sanctity
of personality, on brotherhood and on corporate personality, as illustrated by St Paul's teaching on the Church as the body of Christ in
which all belong to each other. Smith referred to the recent (1948) book
on Independent African Churches by Bengt Sundkler.[42] Sundkler
showed that such movements, despite their eccentricities, exposed the
Church's denominationalism, racism and cultural imperialism. He gave
examples of all these faults and showed how the independent churches
tried to express their devotion in an African way.

Some churches (Roman Catholic, Anglican, Methodist and Congre-
gational) had, in theory at least, no colour line. The Dutch Reformed
Church, however, had developed ecclesiastical apartheid over the nineteenth century. If this precedent were followed, each group would have
its own church. Smith mentioned his teacher, Jacottet, who argued that
European and African churches should be separate, not only to respect
European feelings towards Africans but also to enable Africans to
develop fully as African Christians. Smith agreed that such indigenous
churches offered Africans scope for leadership and resisted extreme
syncretism but, appealing to St Paul, who ruled out parallel churches
for Jews and Gentiles, he argued strongly for a church which drew

people together. He then spoke of the Church as an integrating factor in African social life. The Church synthesizes the old tribal collectivism and the new urban individualism and, in South Africa, becomes a place for all ethnic groups to find their spiritual home. Although much progress had been made, it 'will be a great step forward when worshipping together, which is now sporadic, becomes general' and 'when nobody is shocked to see an African clergyman in the pulpit, at the reading desk, and at the Communion rail'.[43]

Smith based his doctrine of the Church on what he called a Christian humanism. He agreed with scientists in regarding humanity as one species and physically related to the rest of creation, yet he also saw humans as offspring of God. He accepted that sin corrupts human life, and introduced the life and teaching of Christ as a sign of hope. Since Christ revealed the fatherhood of God and the brotherhood of man, colour discrimination was unacceptable. Therefore, white Christians, who used Scripture ingeniously to deny their kinship with blacks, were rationalizing their contempt for other races.

Many white South Africans would have found Smith's dream a nightmare. He agreed that in many societies inequality seems self-evident. He cited India, but recognized that Africa too provided examples: 'A Zulu would never put a Bushman on an equality with himself.'[44] He then told of his own experience among the Baila, maintaining that he and they were united in their humanity but separated by their environment and tradition. For Smith, likeness and unlikeness were the pre-conditions for cooperation, and he referred to Brunner as supporting his argument. Since, for Christians, individuals who differ in ability are equal in human dignity, cooperation is of key importance in drawing people together and solving social problems.

> In conclusion, Smith acknowledged how difficult it would be to realize his challenging ideal of Christian society. If South Africa, he said, can establish a community in which the several ethnical groups can live in harmony, and cooperation for the common good, she will deserve, and receive, the admiration and thanks of the whole world. If we cannot – what then? We shall certainly not be able to assume the moral leadership of the New Africa.[45]

The Blessed Missionaries represents Smith's mature thoughts on matters which had occupied him for many years. He drew into a balanced synthesis, as he had to, his ideas on cultural integrity, culture change and inter-racial cooperation. He knew about the inhumanity of whites towards blacks but, drawing on the resources of Christian theology, looked to change the situation. For many years events were controlled by a very different philosophy, and it seemed that his hopes would never be realized. After more than forty years, however, his view has prevailed. While it was relatively easy for Smith to formulate and affirm his ideal, it is striking that in 1964 Nelson Mandela expressed his own long-standing vision in similar terms: 'I have cherished the ideal of a democratic and free society in which all persons live together in harmony and with equal opportunities.'[46] In 1949, when Smith was presenting his thoughts, few white people in South Africa were willing to take them seriously. By the beginning of the twenty-first century, however, South Africa has been given a new chance to earn the admiration of the whole world.

After this 1948–9 trip to Africa, Smith edited a symposium on *African Ideas of God*. The IAI produced similar works on aspects of African social anthropology,[47] but *African Ideas* was produced not by professional anthropologists but by missionaries from several parts of Africa. Following the Smith agenda, they included notes about the environment, culture and religion of the people. Smith was probably gathering materials for his contributions on his recent tours of South Africa, especially in 1946–7. He wrote the Preface in September 1949, soon after his most recent visit and regretted that much valuable material had to be omitted because of the post-war restrictions on paper.

Smith's introductory chapter considered the problems and methodology of such an enterprise. There were the pitfalls of reading-in what is not there and of reading-out what is not indigenous. He warned researchers to be cautious in using etymological studies and advised them to investigate the praise-names, proverbs, legends, myths and prayers of Africans. He knew that Africans could think abstractly but that, more commonly, their life and religion was saturated with symbols, which people could interpret freely. The book was about African theism, but Smith reminded his readers of the larger religious context, which included dynamism and spiritism.

By that time the work of Placide Tempels was becoming known. Smith commended it as an 'effort to demonstrate that Africans have a philosophy that is not irrational and that offers a coherent explanation of their religion, law and ethics'.[48] He disagreed about dynamism, which

Tempels saw as many forces rather than one. He was convinced, however, that Tempels was 'on the right lines'.[49]

Smith took issue with another Africanist, J. H. Driberg, who thought that African belief in God was mainly dynamistic. Smith outlined criteria for belief in a High God rather than a dynamistic, impersonal cosmic *mana*, and argued that they were met by the evidence presented in *African Ideas*.

Smith regarded spiritism of two types, (a) nature spirits and (b) ancestors who are in constant interplay with the living, as central to African religion. He held, moreover, that the second kind of spiritism, so important to Africans, illustrated a deep human belief in survival after death. He believed, however, that although Africans saw dynamism and spiritism as useful and significant, they did not find them fully satisfying, since 'they do not meet all the facts, nor adequately solve the problems of life'.[50] He therefore turned to African belief in God.

Smith thought that Africans could have conceived the idea of God from their own natural curiosity and the sense of wonder which their myths and praise-names express. He thus disagreed with Barth, who held that there was no knowledge of God outside of the revelation of God in Jesus Christ: 'Apart from and without Jesus Christ we can say nothing at all about God and man and their relationship one with another.'[51] Although Barth was becoming influential in Britain, Smith preferred Brunner, who, he said, 'rightly maintains that a general revelation is an integral part of Christian doctrine'.[52] Smith then argued that belief in a general revelation is consistent with Scripture and defended the use of African names for God in Bible translations. He said that in the Bible existing words – for example *theos* – were taken over but given new meaning through their particular use. Moreover, in the Teutonic world the same thing happened with the word *god*. It followed, therefore, that in Africa local personal names – for example, *Leza* – could properly be used.

African Ideas, as we have indicated, was written by and for missionaries. Some secular reviewers – for example, Phyllis Kaberry in *Africa* 21 and R. G. Lienhardt in *Man* (1950) – were unenthusiastic about it. Lienhardt thought that the Christian view of the authors needed to be made more explicit, and Kaberry that there should have been much more about the African social context. Neither point was altogether fair. Social background was included and, but for the tight restriction on paper, would no doubt have figured more prominently; and the missionary status of the writers and the overall missionary agenda were clearly indicated. The symposium concentrated, in short, on those things which Smith believed to be most useful to missionaries. But, by indicating with commendable objectivity that there were other aspects of African religion, Smith's introduction placed the concept of God firmly in perspective. James Welch in *African Affairs* thought the book added to knowledge and raised questions for anthropology and the comparative study of religions: 'Dr Edwin Smith, in causing this book to be written has added to our indebtedness to him about things African.'[53] Two decades later, E. G. Parrinder, one of the contributors, said that it was accepted that most 'African peoples have had a belief in a Supreme Being' and the 'symposium *African Ideas of God* did much to establish this finally'.[54]

Smith's other contributions to the symposium were notes on three Bantu names for God and a wide-ranging article on 'The Idea of God among South African Tribes'.[55] He had recently made two long tours around the areas involved and read everything of note about these peoples, their cultures, history and languages. He used material he had already published in *The Secret of the African* (1929) and had no hesitation in mentioning, as he had in 1924 in *Moffat*, examples of God being called mother by Tswana people. It is unlikely, indeed impossible, that such a concept would have come via Christian missionaries.[56] Gabriel Setiloane, a Tswana Christian, thought that some titles for God mentioned by Smith may have reflected Christian influence,[57] but freely mentioned Smith's reference to God as mother.[58] Smith, after surveying numerous peoples, concluded that among the southern Bantu 'the Supreme Being is overshadowed by the ancestral gods – is indeed pushed so far to the circumference of their thought that often his very name is forgotten.'[59] Yet he agreed with Junod that the concept was not wholly foreign and was easily accepted by these people: ' "It seems as if one were telling them an old story, with which they had been quite familiar but had now half forgotten." '[60] If that is so, the article did not establish that belief in God was strong in all areas but showed that it was possible to revive the notion, if it had faded, or to introduce it, if it was unknown. The concept of God could therefore be more useful for missionary work than may appear at first sight.

Smith was criticized by F. B. Welbourn, who considered his emphasis on the High God an error. Welbourn believed that Smith gave the Church in Africa a false start from which it had hardly recovered by

1974. As he saw it, Smith ignored the differences which he knew existed in African societies and made generalizations which could not be sustained. He also considered that Smith failed to come to terms with the corporateness and wholeness of African life, where sacred and secular were not separated. Welbourn called for studies of religion in the setting of particular societies.[61] Like those mentioned above, such criticisms were not altogether fair. Smith was fully aware that, in Africa, religion and life are intimately connected; and because he realized the importance, for Africans, of the community, *African Ideas* looked at the social context. In focusing on God, Smith was acting as a missiologist and seeking a point of contact by which Christianity might establish itself among many African peoples. His way of drawing things together, of seeking consensus, of integrating his African studies, suggests that Smith was more deeply influenced by African holistic thinking than Welbourn realized.

Smith's chapter on South Africa was cited by Gabriel Setiloane and Janet Hodgson,[62] who, in their studies of ideas of God among South African peoples, closely follow the range of topics that Smith considered relevant. The only major weakness in this and Smith's other studies of religion up to this time was the lack of any detailed analysis of rituals, such as rites of passage. He was, however, thinking about the matter.

Last years in Deal (1951–1957)

In his late seventies, Smith's mind remained active and, in his writing, he was always looking for areas overlooked by others. As a result he began to develop, in 1951, a theme which he had touched on, in 1928, in his book on exploration in Africa. The new manuscript, which unfortunately failed to find a publisher, was about African porters, and most of his information was drawn from the writings of great explorers: for example, Burton, Speke, Grant and Stanley.

Smith began by quoting from A. S. Cripps's poem, 'To My Carriers' and explained that it was 'time they had a book to themselves'.[1] He recalled his own experiences of porters, their resilience, playfulness and awkwardness, and described the discipline, sometimes brutal, dealt out by the explorers. The porters needed their own leaders to maintain order, and Smith, having selected two of the most famous, Mombai (Bombay) and Mabruki, who appeared in the accounts of many explorers, wove his story around them. Together with the Baldwin diaries, which Smith edited, this manuscript provides invaluable archive material for future researchers.

Smith spent early 1952 preparing for the fourth Henry Myers Lecture.[2] His distinguished predecessors were A. R. Radcliffe-Brown, Raymond Firth and E. O. James, and the invitation to contribute to the series, which related anthropology to religion, constituted further recognition of Smith's eminence in his field.

His chosen subject was African symbolism. Symbolism was already being addressed by serious students of religion. Mircea Eliade, for example, who wrote *Images and Symbols* (1952; ET 1961) had been considering symbolism for some time. But Smith's decision to tackle the subject may have been triggered by a conversation a few years earlier with Monica Wilson. In due course her studies of the Nyakyusa of Zambia would pay close attention to symbolism in their culture, and

V. W. Turner would dedicate his book *The Forest of Symbols* (1967) to her. These anthropologists examined symbolism in particular cultures, but Smith was concerned, before symbolism had been widely researched in Africa, to produce an overview of the subject. His bibliography of over a hundred works, almost half of them published since 1942, included writings by philosophers, linguists, psychologists, sociologists, anthropologists and students of religion. Three early writings of Geoffrey Parrinder were listed, as well as four titles by Max Gluckman and five by E. E. Evans-Pritchard.

Smith's fundamental premise was that most symbolism is based on analogy. He observed that science uses symbols to explain its subject, whether for non-specialists or for scientists themselves. He considered that religious symbols attempt to express the religious experiences which are so vital for all religions. Smith thought that the most contemplative of mystics and the strictest of Puritans were subject to the same compulsion to express religion and values symbolically. Dante, for example, was a master of symbolism who, at the end of his great poem, *The Divine Comedy*, spoke of God's glory, the love which moved the sun and the other stars,[3] as a circle of light.

Smith realized that it is too easy to read one's own interpretation into symbols and that, because symbols carry emotional power, they act as charms to many people, including those European Christians who see magical power in their sacraments.

He then turned to symbolism in Africa, using recent literature in African studies as well as his own experiences. He began with verbal symbolism, referring to African sayings and prayers and the symbolic structure of African conversation. He also mentioned names, which are very meaningful to Africans, praise-titles, full of metaphors, being given to chiefs or to the Supreme Power. Smith, who had used such titles as evidence of the theology of traditional African religion, did not believe that Africans confused their symbols with God.

A discussion of non-verbal symbolism followed. Colours are meaningful and Smith was surprised to find that many Africans gave black a negative value. He noted that a whole message is conveyed by the colours worked into a Zulu girl's beadwork. He also mentioned the variety of number symbolism. Some regarded the number seven with the same dread that many Europeans feel for thirteen, while others considered it sacrosanct. African art, too, is rich in symbolism, and he pointed out that Picasso drew inspiration from the Congo. Smith mentioned costumes and masks, 'macabre masterpieces', and wondered whether they were intended to inspire terror and a sense of mystery.

Actions are often symbolic: 'All over Africa you will find actions which have a meaning beyond themselves.'[4] Smith used van Gennep's analogy of passing through doors from room to room to describe the African's journey through life. *Rites de passage* mark each change. Smith felt that a whole book was needed for this subject, and briefly discussed initiations and marriage. Fuller study was done, in due course, by post-war anthropologists, especially by Victor Turner (1920–83), who began, in 1964, to take van Gennep's approach seriously. Turner focused on the liminal, or threshold-crossing, period as critical in these rites of passage.[5]

Smith went on to discuss African mythology as a symbolic philosophy. He used three of Jung's archetypes to represent the subject diagrammatically as a triangle: Sky at the apex, and Earth and Wise Old Man as the base. In this way, the Supreme Power, the fertility of the soil and the chief as representative of the people are symbolized. Between God and earth are the nature spirits, and between God and man there are the ancestors. Along with a concept of an Earth-Mother, all are intimately connected in the African's world.

Smith emphasized the earth's importance for Africans. He believed that Europeans had never fully realized that the taking away of their soil was, for Africans, close to sacrilege. He pointed out that the chief was often the priest of the land and that the Lozi king's common title, *Litunga*, means 'earth'. He showed that land, nation and chief are symbolically renewed in the Swazi ceremony of *Incwala*, held over several days in connection with the first-fruits.

In conclusion, Smith drew attention to the interweaving of symbols and their compelling emotional power. He said that Africans believe that words are 'like missiles' to be treated with care. Witchcraft and sorcery are seen as controlling the occult energy which operates in animals, people and rituals. Smith did not like the term 'magic', and thought it was time to give it a decent burial. As we know, he preferred to use 'dynamism', which he here attributed to van Gennep; and, though still claiming to be an evolutionist, he observed that in Africa 'dynamism, spiritism and theism – exist side by side or interwoven into one whole'.[6]

Smith agreed with A. N. Whitehead that symbolism always survives attempts to remove it. Moreover, he described in a few sentences what would now be called 'paradigm shifts', in which the intellectual and

Sky = Supreme Being

Divinities

nature spirits   ancestors

Earth-Mother

Earth = fertility   Wise Old Man = chief = people

Smith's use of Jungian archetypes to illustrate African symbolism.

social structures which support symbols are undermined and there is uncertainty and chaos until new convictions find new symbolic expression. Repeating his view that the rapid changes taking place in Africa were creating this kind of situation, he wondered how the future would turn out. Would dynamism and the ancestor cult be dropped and with them the old symbolism and values? Would Africans reshape European symbols? Would African Christians reinterpret old symbols? These were stimulating and important questions, and much of the future would depend on how they were answered. Although Smith did not try to predict the outcome, he saw the issues clearly.

All in all, Smith paid much more attention than previously to ritual and to the wholeness of African life and thought, and this wide-ranging lecture, given before researchers in Africa concentrated on its theme, shows that Smith discerned the possibilities of African studies and the direction that they had to take.

The year 1952 ended sadly. Julia, who had been in poor health for some time, was admitted to the Victoria Hospital at Deal for surgery. Because of her weak heart, any such procedure was bound to be risky, and she died, soon after the operation, on 17 December 1952. Smith wrote to Mrs Capen, one of their friends at Hartford, 'She was the pluckiest woman I ever knew . . . I feel lost without her.'[7] After fifty-three years of married life this 'was a heavy blow'.[8] Smith always turned to her for support and advice in important decisions. He was the famous Africanist, but, to Africans, Julia was *Mamosa*, 'mother of kindness'. The Smiths were happy together, though Julia had to endure many separations during her married life. At such times she received numerous letters, certainly informative and descriptive, from Smith's 'magic wand' of a pen.

On 18 December 1953, a day after the anniversary of Julia's death, Smith left for a last visit to Africa. He took his manuscripts for 'Roger

Price' and 'An African Odyssey' which had not yet found publishers. The sea journey took him to the east coast of Africa via the Suez Canal. There were two Roman Catholic priests who 'have my *Knowing the African* on board & are reading it'.[9] One said it was the policy of his mission among the Tumbuka. There were frequent stops. Many people joined the ship at Mombasa, 'including Bedford and his family – wife & 3 daughters, on [the] way to England'.[10] The Revd F. J. Bedford (1909–69) was responsible for Bible Society work in East Africa. From the Primitive Methodist tradition, he had been at Kafue and Mufulira in Zambia. He became responsible for Africanizing the Society's work in East Africa. He was influenced by Smith and possessed many of his books.[11] Through Bedford's contacts Smith went sightseeing around Zanzibar on Tuesday 19 January. It was a 'great day' and among other things he saw, at the museum, a volume of letters by the explorer Speke.

When they came to Durban, some of Smith's views were reported in the *Natal Mercury*.[12] The unrest in Africa, he believed, was inspired by Communists who found 'Africa's frustrated millions' a ' "happy hunting ground" '. Cooperation and advancement were the only viable future policies. Repression of Africans he thought would be self-destructive for the whites:

> You cannot go on denying people their rights without hurting your-self. You cannot expect the White men to come into Africa, ordering the Native to do this and that, taking away from him a large propor-tion of his land, . . . and expect to get no reaction.[13]

Smith mentioned Africans who were better qualified to vote than some white people and stated that unless these educated Africans were enfranchised the volcano would blow up. He repeated his view that all races in South Africa needed to find some way of living together in har-mony. Smith's vision of cooperation, however, was out of tune with the thinking of most South African whites at the time. His Phelps-Stokes Lectures, *The Blessed Missionaries*, advocated cooperation but, as we saw earlier, had not been well attended; and he would learn, when he reached Cape Town, that only a quarter of the print run of 2,000 had been sold.

Smith was still at Durban on the Sunday and, with the Bedfords, attended West Street Methodist church. The minister, Revd S. B. Sudbury, introduced them to the congregation and said that *The*

Golden Stool had directed him to Africa. Sudbury became the secretary of the South African Methodist Conference and was one of many whose vision was influenced by Smith.[14]

Smith eventually disembarked at Cape Town and met Edward and Betty Tagart and old friends in the political and academic communities. He visited Parliament and spoke with Dr D. L. Smit, Secretary for Native Affairs, who felt that he could not do constructive work under the National Party. Dr Smit took him to hear part of the debate on the Communism Bill. This bill gave the government minister power to declare that a person was a communist, with no right of appeal.

Smith met leading anthropologists, and on 13 February had dinner at the home of Monica Wilson. He learned that she was looking at Nyakyusa symbolism, had joined the Liberal Party and was much concerned with African rights.

He heard some adverse opinions of Heaton Nicholls, a friend from Zambia days. He did not jump to conclusions, however, but found out for himself where Nicholls stood. On 19 February, when Nicholls was speaking at the University Summer School about the United Federal Party, Smith questioned him about apartheid and related matters. Nicholls was against Africans having the franchise on educational grounds but was vague about what to substitute for it. Nevertheless, he opposed apartheid because it regarded non-Europeans as a sub-species.

Smith spent March and early April with his relatives near Kuruman and at Kimberley. He checked a few details for his book on Roger Price. Otherwise, it was a leisurely time. He read many books and was often absorbed in Dante's *Divine Comedy*. At Kimberley the mayor arranged a town tour for him. He saw the Great Hole, the Kimberley mine, and at the Sanatorium, which had once been an hotel, he recalled his dinner with Rhodes.

Smith then made his way to Grahamstown, where he met Leslie Hewson, Methodist tutor at Rhodes University since 1947, and learnt that his books would be used in a course on comparative religion. Smith also attended Philip Mayer's inaugural lecture as Professor of Anthropology at Rhodes University. The subject was 'Witches'. Smith considered it a good lecture badly delivered.[15] He later met Mayer, who felt the social pressures of the time. If he met educated Africans, he was at risk of being 'named' by the authorities. As Professor of Anthropology, however, he could not stand aloof from Africans.

The leading anthropologist, Radcliffe-Brown, was also there to give the Lugard Lecture. Smith met him on 11 May and they discussed Lugard's policy of dual mandate. Radcliffe-Brown said that it failed because it was contradictory. He also said that development on one's own lines was absurd and that no anthropologist could subscribe to it. Smith, who believed that there was great potential in African cultures, noted the latter statement without comment.

On 14 May Smith visited the Hewsons for supper and addressed Leslie Hewson's theological students. His thoughts were well received. Then, at 9.30 p.m., they all listened to a radio talk which Smith had recorded earlier.

He returned to Cape Town on 19 May, spent a few days with friends and relatives and left Africa for the last time[16] on Wednesday 26 May 1954. As usual he noted the conversations of the fellow passengers whom he met. On 4 June he was introduced to the Revd J. V. Taylor, who was returning to Britain from Uganda with his family, and sought his opinion on events there. John Taylor, whose thinking about Africa had been influenced by several of Smith's books, remembered meeting 'a quiet and modest man with the far-away, brooding look which Africa gives to the eyes of those who love her'.[17] He looked on Smith as a great authority on African religion: 'At that stage I regarded myself as entirely a pupil in his company.'[18] Subsequently, John Taylor has achieved eminence as a writer and Anglican bishop. His early books were devoted to African themes,[19] and he considered that Smith, and Cullen Young, must have laid the foundations for his future insights about Africa. Although, in *The Primal Vision* (1963), one of his most acclaimed works, John Taylor relied more heavily on B. A. Pauw, Godfrey Lienhardt and Monica Wilson, he also drew directly on Smith's idea of dynamism. He saw Smith as 'a pioneer among serious writers on African spirituality who were themselves committed Christians'.[20]

When Smith returned to Deal, he addressed a Christian Fellowship group on South Africa. He outlined the situation and, though unsure whether the heterogeneous masses could form one nation, indicated the steps needing to be taken to achieve unification, including educational and economic development, removal of the colour bar and creation of equal political and social rights. He also showed how integration was resisted, especially by apartheid, explained the policies of the political parties and described other areas of life in South Africa.

Geoffrey Parrinder, by that time Lecturer in Religious Studies at the University of Ibadan in Nigeria, was one of the many people who visited

Smith in the Old Watch House, Deal. Smith, prompted by his late son-in-law's links with West Africa and by his own interest in Parrinder's work, had decided to bequeath some of his books to Ibadan University. Parrinder, who went to look over Smith's substantial library, enjoyed the study, 'with its walls lined with books, but with a telescope before the window to watch ships going up and down the Channel'.[21]

Merfyn Temple was another visitor. He had been ill when Smith visited Zambia in 1947, but would have known about him through his father-in-law, Revd S. Douglas Gray, who visited the Smiths at Kasenga in 1914, and his father, who was one of the Bible Society secretaries. During the day he spent in Deal, he realized for himself that he 'was in the presence of a man who had a deep understanding of African ways'.[22]

Contacts with Smith are still remembered by those who belonged to the local Methodist congregation. Mrs June Smedley, for example, recalls that, as a Methodist teenager in Deal, she occasionally delivered messages to Dr Smith. Her mother told her not to stay and make herself a nuisance. Nevertheless, she looked forward to being invited in for a cup of tea and being allowed to look at the passing ships through his telescope. She was fascinated by the huge collection of books and by what he told her about his experiences of Africa. But what impressed her most was his demeanour: 'He never talked down to me but always treated me with a quiet courtesy and respect.'

His stories and remarks about African languages, some of which she heard in chapel, made a deep impression on her. She found his sermon on the names of Christ particularly memorable. In it he mentioned some of the names he had been given in Africa including *chitutamano*, with its double meaning. As Smith liked to say, it could mean 'the silent cunning devil' or 'the quiet clever spirit'. The people of one village had regarded him with suspicion, for they had heard that *chitutamano* was coming and understood the word in the first sense. June Smedley, however, thought that, understood in the second way, it provided the perfect description of Edwin Smith: 'He seemed to me to have a quiet, gentle humility, was certainly a very clever man, and had a great spirituality.'[23] Her opinion accords well with that given by many others of Smith as quiet, modest, wise and spiritual.

The Revd Hedley Lyddon came to Deal as a probationer minister and met Smith frequently. The older man told his African stories and encouraged his young colleague to study. Indeed, Lyddon regarded Smith as his mentor as he set out in the ministry. Both he and his wife found Smith a 'real gentleman' who treated others with great respect.[24]

Smith's life of Roger Price, *Great Lion of Bechuanaland*, was not published until 1956. It was a large book, and in writing it Smith not only followed Price's footsteps in Africa but also visited the Brecon area of South Wales to learn about his early life. None of Smith's biographies was about an Englishman, and none of the missionaries was a Methodist. Price was a Welsh Independent of the warm Calvinistic tradition generated by the eighteenth-century revival. His mother tongue was Welsh and he had to learn English before going to Africa. He mastered it quickly and, in due course, became equally fluent in the Tswana language of southern Africa. Smith took the title from the name *Tau e Tona*, 'Great Lion', which the Africans gave to Roger Price. Isaac Schapera, who reviewed the book for *Africa*, remarked that Smith had made 'many outstanding contributions to African studies'. These included 'notable missionary biographies'. His only criticisms were (a) the need for more about the extent of religious change during Price's missionary career and (b) some revision to the conclusions of Smith's careful summary of published material about Sebitwane and the Makololo. The volume gave 'further cause to admire and welcome his scholarship and industry'.[25]

In 1957, in conjunction with a tape recording which his grandson, Richard, persuaded him to make, Smith started, but sadly never completed, a potentially invaluable autobiographical sketch. He also reviewed for *Africa* a new edition of Lord Hailey's massive (1,676-page) *African Survey*. After commenting that the first edition had 'ushered in a new era of African history',[26] he offered a few criticisms of details in the new version, indicated that, in his judgment, the Christian Church and Islam merited a chapter each and expressed the wish that he might live a hundred years in order to see what results the interaction of African and Western traditions would produce.

Unfortunately, he only lived for a few more days. He was a victim of the influenza epidemic which affected many people that winter. Pneumonia followed and, despite treatment in hospital, he died on 23 December 1957.

The funeral service at the local crematorium was conducted by the Methodist superintendent, the Revd Crowson Muncey, and obituaries appeared in many publications. In Deal, according to the local newspaper, no commemoration of his life was planned.[27] At Bible House, however, a memorial service on 22 January 1958 was conducted by the Revd Dr Ronald Spivey, minister of Wesley's Chapel, City Road. The high commissioner of Rhodesia and Nyasaland was present along with fellow ministers and representatives of learned societies. Professor Schapera, Revd Phil Fisher and Dr Platt of the Bible Society gave addresses: 'The distinguished gathering of friends and colleagues in many fields was a most worthy tribute to the labours and character of so notable a figure.'[28]

Conclusion: Edwin Smith's contribution

It is hardly surprising that Smith, born in South Africa of missionary parents and possessing a love for Africa and a fascination with languages, should have found his vocation as a literary missionary. What is truly remarkable, however, is the fact that, as his talents were stimulated and his interests broadened, he was able to make so substantial a contribution across the full range of African studies. Was there, indeed, any other person so expert in so many parts of African studies as well as the field as a whole? Anthropology in British Central Africa – he was the founder. Research interest in Africa – he set it going in earnest. African traditional religion – he outlined its chief characteristics. African Christian theology – he was its *'fons et origo'*. In addition, he was president of the RAI, wrote editorial notes for the RAS and articulated the needs which the IAI fulfilled.

His influence was clearly both wide and deep, and our final task must be to understand why his importance has not been generally recognized. But first his achievements need to be recapitulated in some detail.

His contributions to the study of religion in Africa were made in several ways. In his anthropological writings, beginning with *ISP* (1920) and concluding with his Henry Myers Lecture of 1952, he insisted that African religion is worthy of serious study and not to be dismissed. His own researches were respected by his fellow anthropologists, and his mature thinking on the subject was fed by their work. He was certainly one of the earliest anthropological contributors to the study of religion in Africa, and he remained an informed student and prolific expositor of the subject. Colson, in her introduction to the 1968 edition of *ISP*, remarked that what he wrote in 1920 on Ila religion had deficiencies but in some respects was 'very much in line with contemporary work on African religion'.[1] Nevertheless, after 1950, British anthropologists had a narrower focus than Smith, being content to leave God out of their studies and concentrating on ritual symbolism, ancestor worship and witchcraft.[2]

Smith did much to publicize African religion from 1920 to 1950. He had access to networks with worldwide interests: the International Missionary Council, the British and Foreign Bible Society, the Royal African Society, the Royal Anthropological Institute and the International African Institute. Through them he brought the subject to the attention of those who could otherwise despise or at least fail to notice it. He was recognized as the leading British expert in this field, and in 1960 W. T. Harris and E. G. Parrinder wrote of 'Dr Edwin Smith, the greatest authority on African religion in this country'.[3]

His work in African religion went back to 1907 and matured from 1923–52. Up to the end of World War II he used his triangle, God–spirits–dynamism, as a framework for analysis. This broadened, however, in the post-war years and, in the light of new approaches, he concentrated more on accurate description. Nevertheless, he still aimed for synthesis and generalization and thought that, with sufficient knowledge, it would be possible to produce a theoretical framework which made sense of the whole of African religious experience. The richness of detail in local and area studies, however, has made it increasingly difficult to offer adequate generalizations, and attempts to produce a synthetic picture have largely been abandoned. Even so, Smith's headings – of God, ancestors and other spirits, dynamism – along with his later awareness of ritual symbolism have helped to elucidate a great deal of religion in Africa and other places. With good reason, therefore, it can be claimed that he founded the study of religion in Africa as a serious academic discipline and helped to give the religion itself a recognized place among world faiths.

Smith's contribution to the development of African Christian theology was surprisingly fruitful. It was not entirely original, in that he used the 'fulfilment' model designed in India. But his contention that it is possible to be truly African and truly Christian was certainly not generally accepted, in theory or practice, in his day. After the Le Zoute conference of 1926, however, Protestant thinkers began to move with Smith towards greater sympathy for African traditions. *African Beliefs and Christian Faith* (1936) sought to blend African and biblical beliefs and, perhaps more than anyone else alive at the time, Smith had the range of expertise needed for the task. He was thoroughly acquainted with the Bible, its original languages and theology. Translation, from language to language and from culture to culture, was his stock in trade. Most importantly, he was thoroughly versed in African cultures, languages and religious traditions and was utterly convinced that New Testament Christianity could be married to African beliefs to make African Christianity.

The subsequent development of African Christian theology may have been inhibited by the dominance of Barthian theology, with its negative view of natural religion, during the period 1935–60. The main influence here was Hendrik Kraemer, whose book *The Christian Message in a Non-Christian World* (1938) was prepared for that year's World Missionary Conference at Madras. The Barthian style of missiology respected other cultures and rejected cultural imperialism, but it argued that 'there are no bridges from human religious consciousness to the reality in Christ'.[4] This would have been a temporary hindrance, for, since 1960, African Christian theology has advanced enormously. Tempels' work was the trigger for Roman Catholics and was supported by a remarkable speech of Pope Paul VI, who insisted that an African Christianity was essential.[5] By that time, however, many European missionaries and African Christians, having read Smith's books or heard him lecture, were influenced by his approach. Eugene A. Nida, an American who was prominent in raising the profile of accessible Bible translation in conjunction with anthropology since World War II, 'was amazed at the number of people in Africa . . . who had been significantly influenced by Edwin Smith's writings and teaching'.[6] Today Africans have become the chief practitioners of this kind of theology, much of which proceeds, ironically, in apparent ignorance of Smith's pioneer efforts.

Christianity has now settled in Africa and is part of the African religious tradition. The historical process by which this happened has been studied for some time, and Smith's friend, C. P. Groves, wrote the history of Christianity in Africa in great detail. Smith was also interested in this field and contributed to historical studies, mainly through his biographies. His subjects, apart from Aggrey, were all missionaries in southern Africa but, since he set them in their historical, social and religious contexts, his books are widely informative. The historical aspect dominated another of his works, *The Blessed Missionaries*, where he looked at Christianity and race relations in South Africa. *African Ideas of God* had an historical agenda, too, in that it attempted to establish how Africans thought about God before the arrival of Christianity.

Smith used and advocated a contextual theology of mission. His approach, emphasizing how important it is to understand people, their language and culture, is commonplace in mission studies today. In the early part of the twentieth century, however, it was a novelty. Edinburgh 1910 and other IMC meetings provided a forum for fresh approaches, and Le Zoute (1926) was a watershed in Protestant thinking. Smith continually emphasized and advocated understanding and adaptation as the proper missionary approach. By 1926, indeed, he could see the need for radical contextualization, and by 1946 he was outspoken in his condemnation of cultural imperialism. Unfortunately, many others lacked Smith's awareness, and much missionary work continued to transplant and impose attitudes and customs which were not essential to the gospel of Christ. Indeed, the missiology of context and adaptation, although taught, has not been widely practised. Missionaries, after all, may feel their religious and cultural identity threatened by change, and it is easier, in any case, to impose unmodified doctrines, structures, attitudes and methods than to find or create new and appropriate expressions of the faith. Moreover, some cultural imports are received enthusiastically because they immediately appear suitable, while others are accepted because time and use have obscured their strangeness. Nevertheless, 'cultural imperialism' produces change by domination and manipulation rather than by friendship and cooperation and must, therefore, be eliminated.

It is not easy, of course, to transform attitudes. In politics, commerce, education, language, sport, philosophy and development, as well as religion in Africa, Westerners have assumed that they know what is best for Africans. Many missionaries and inter-cultural workers, however, have been helped, directly or indirectly by Smith's approach. One of Smith's distinguished missionary successors, the Revd Dr Colin Morris, heard of Smith when he went to work in Zambia:

> That led me to his books which taught me to take African culture and religion seriously on their own terms and not to regard them negatively as part of the old paganism to be swept away without evaluation.[7]

Smith did not expect cultures in contact with each other to remain unchanged. When cultural imperialism is removed and replaced by mutual respect and cooperation, creative possibilities emerge. Smith's mature view was that Christian mission proceeds best by conversation and dialogue. The missionary introduces the Christian faith to other cultures. If the meeting is fruitful, new Christian communities are created and need to work with existing churches in a cooperative, diverse and ever-changing network.

Translation was part of Smith's missiology. He began as a Bible translator, and much of his subsequent work flowed from trying to work out what translation involves. He studied the Bible carefully and was well versed in its teaching. He saw the Bible and the faith which comes from it as translatable into the languages and cultures of the world. He believed that missionaries should learn languages thoroughly, and he practised what he preached. He was in charge of the Bible Society's translation department for many years and his views and policies favoured translations which are accessible to readers/hearers. His report on translations in India influenced policy for future Indian translations, and his experiment with Basic English paved the way for subsequent versions in simplified English. Thus his mark is on much that happened in this field for the rest of the century.

Although Smith achieved so much in various aspects of religious studies (African religion, church history, African Christian theology, missiology and Bible translation) he was also eminent as an anthropologist in his own right. He had a good collaborator in A. M. Dale and, although he always acknowledged his friend's part in producing *ISP*, one of the great ethnographic texts, he was himself responsible for most of it. As time passed and new methods of ethnographic research emerged, Smith became aware of *ISP*'s deficiencies, and made some improvements a quarter of a century later. Nevertheless, Colson and Gluckman dedicated their book *Seven Tribes of Central Africa* (1951) 'with respect and admiration to Dr Edwin W. Smith'. They said that *ISP* 'founded modern anthropological research in British Central Africa'.[8]

Smith helped the development of anthropology in the UK by his participation in the Royal Anthropological Society, which elected him President (1933–5) and was influenced by his Presidential Address for 1935, with its emphasis on the need for more research in Africa. It was remarkable that he, a missionary, was so highly honoured by the RAI. He became chief of this hostile tribe and was highly respected for his contribution. Later RAI presidents agreed that his 1935 address was very influential. H. J. Braunholtz described it as 'a monumental survey, summarizing our knowledge to date of the geography, prehistory, ethnology and linguistics of the continent';[9] and Sir Raymond Firth noted that the 1935 address 'did much to launch the systematic research interest in Africa'[10] which developed in the following decades. H. J. Braunholtz also remarked that, as President of the RAI, Smith's 'conduct of its affairs inspired general admiration and respect'.[11]

Anthropology in Africa was furthered by the International African Institute. Smith was one of the founders and made a significant contribution to its work. He helped to draft its constitution and wrote its first history in 1934. He edited *Africa*, when the institute was re-establishing its work after World War II, and was involved in various IAI enterprises: 'It was at Edwin Smith's suggestion that the Institute organized and obtained international support for the Northern Bantu borderland linguistic field survey.'[12]

Smith's approach was integrative. *The Golden Stool* (1926)and his 1935 Presidential Address show that he considered African studies as a whole. If wholeness is a characteristic of African thinking then Smith was clearly influenced by Africans through his years of personal contact with them.

As an expert in many aspects of African studies Smith was one of the great pioneer Africanists. Through his societies (RAS, RAI and IAI) Smith did all he could as a literary man to promote the good of Africa through information and suggestions to people who wielded power. Although he valued debate and was very interested in politics, he was not himself a politician or diplomat. As a Christian worker, he led and organized people throughout his career. But it was as as a scholar and thinker that he took his place in the scheme of African studies. He was no power broker in religion and politics, but his opinion was always available to and welcomed by those who made the policies.

In spite of his reputation and eminence Smith has been ignored and neglected in every area that he explored with such skill and versatility. For example, a book entitled *Anthropological Studies of Religion* by Brian Morris (1987) treats its subject without mentioning Smith at all. Why this neglect? There are many possible reasons. In anthropology he would be seen as a representative of organized religion. Although his qualities were clear enough to his illustrious contemporaries, later anthropologists could marginalize him as a missionary and therefore of no consequence.

Smith was by nature a scholar and writer but had no academic training and never attended university. His scholarship was recognized in that major universities engaged him to examine anthropology students. The fact, however, that he never held an academic post in the UK would have counted against him, especially in the professional, academic era of anthropology which followed World War II.

Moreover, Smith epitomized the Primitive Methodist tradition at a time when Wesleyans were influencing the direction of Methodism after the union in 1932. Again, most of his work was not for the Methodist public and none of his biographies was about a British Methodist missionary. All this may account for his lack of recognition among Methodists in general, though enthusiasts about Africa or Primitive Methodism still revere the name of Edwin Smith.

Once African countries achieved political independence, the writings of Christian missionaries attracted little interest. The influence of other Western ideologies tended to belittle the contribution of Western Christians and it would not occur to modern Africans that anything useful could be found in that period. When, therefore, an extract from *The Golden Stool* (1926) was read to a Zambian secondary school teacher in 1995 he was astonished that someone held such modern ideas in the 1920s. In addition, educated African élites became so Westernized that they despised both their origins and their traditions in religion, education, agriculture and medicine. Smith, however, supported both tradition and progress from a Christian perspective. His views could be, and were, ignored by those of other ideologies and those intoxicated by the Western materialistic dream.

Smith was part of the foundations of modern African studies. As he himself pointed out long ago, foundations are lost to sight when something substantial is built. That is the nature of things. His books are now increasingly difficult to acquire and have been superseded by modern volumes. In that sense, there is nothing unusual about his loss of fame. The contributions of thousands of brilliant people are buried in the same way. A little research, however, reveals the extent and quality of his influence.

Finally, some reasons for Smith's present obscurity could be described as accidental. The title, *Religion of Lower Races* (1923), is held against him, but it reflected his publishers' thinking rather than his. *The Secret of the African* and *Knowing the African* are also thought to be strange titles these days. Such matters weigh heavily and enable him to be dismissed by those who do not bother to read his books or do not have access to his writings.

Another unfortunate accident was that Malcolm McVeigh's *God in Africa* (1974), a major thematic study of Smith's religious thinking, did not mention him in either its title or sub-title. As noted earlier this was not McVeigh's intention, but an opportunity to highlight Smith was missed. McVeigh was puzzled, nevertheless, by Smith's disappearance from the scene and by the fact that he 'was not accorded the world-wide acclaim that he merited'.[13]

It is to be hoped that this and other studies will help to redress the balance and that Smith's valuable and influential work will be recognized again. Modern researchers may not share his methods. Nevertheless, his industry, attitude and pioneering explorations helped to produce a more sympathetic view of Africa and Africans among Westerners. He advanced views that were ahead of his time, especially in religion, theology of mission and inter-cultural relations. His pleas for cooperation and an end to cultural imperialism need to be heeded continually. His insistence on the sophistication of African languages and the importance of learning them curbs the predatory instinct of English-language speakers and should be taken to heart. His willingness to tolerate experiences, customs and practices that were far different from his own marks him out as unusual among missionaries of his time. He was *chitutamano*, 'the quiet wise spirit' of African studies.

Notes

Introduction

1. Cracknell, Kenneth, *Towards a New Relationship*, London: Epworth, 1986, p. 182.
2. Parrinder, E. G., 'Learning from Other Faiths, VI: African Religion', *Expository Times*, August 1972, p. 327.
3. Revd M. S. Lucheya, Centenary Address 1976, unpublished MS. Edwin Smith's discussion of this nickname is mentioned later in this book.
4. 'I would have listed him in the title of my book or at a minimum the sub-title, but sometimes publishers just go and do their own thing'; letter from M. McVeigh to the author, 17 February 1994. See also note 13, Chapter 20.
5. Rinsum, Henk J. van, *Slaves of Definition: In Quest of the Unbeliever and the Ignoramus*, Maastricht: Shaker Publications BV, 2001.
6. Young, W. John, 'Edwin Smith: Pioneer Explorer in African Christian Theology', *Epworth Review*, May 1993, pp. 80–8.
7. On his work as an Africanist, see Young, W. John, 'The Integrative Vision of a Pioneer Africanist: Edwin W. Smith (1876–1957)', unpublished M.Phil. thesis, University of Bristol, 1997.
8. Hastings, Adrian, *African Catholicism: Essays in Discovery*, London: SCM Press, 1989, p. 25.
9. Rinsum, Henk J. van, ' "Knowing the African": Edwin W. Smith and the Invention of African Traditional Religion', in van Rinsum, *Slaves of Definition*, pp. 26f.

Chapter 1

1. Turner, John M., *The People's Church: Primitive Methodism, from Counter-Culture to Transformer of Values*, Englesea Brook, 1994.
2. *Aldersgate Magazine*, 1899, p. 4.
3. *Aldersgate Magazine*, 1899, p. 4.
4. *Primitive Methodist Magazine*, 1875, pp. 374f. Susan was 28 years old.
5. R. E. Davies et al. (eds), *A History of Methodism in Great Britain*, vol. iii, London: Epworth, 1983, p. 176. Although Primitive Methodism evangelized enthusiastically in Britain it responded more slowly than other churches to the claims of world mission. The Wesleyans, for example, began their Missionary Society in 1813. The PMs did have churches in Canada, the USA, Australia and

New Zealand, but these were for settlers rather than for reaching hitherto unevangelized people. Their Missionary Society dated from 1837 but their missions to West and South Africa did not begin until 1870.

6. Smith, John, 'The Early Days of our Mission in South Africa', ch. 1, *Aldersgate Magazine*, c.1906, SPMMS.

7. St Catherine's House Register, marriage registered in the quarter April to June 1874; the Jeary family was from Martham and a sister married H. J. Waters, Edwin Smith's uncle James. James Tilby in his family tree of descendants of William Smith has traced this to 7 April 1874 at the Primitive Methodist church, Catfield, Norfolk.

8. *Mabilles*, p. 109.

9. Smith, John, 'The Early Days of our Mission in South Africa', ch. 2, *Aldersgate Magazine*, c.1906, p. 799, SPMMS.

10. What was Edwin W. Smith's middle name? Some say William and some Williams.

A. William:
a. Biographical details in his writing in the Bible he owned and used from the 1890s.
b. The Bible Society Personnel file.
c. Letter of April 1921 appointing him to be the Bible Society's Superintending Secretary for Western Europe.
d. His baptism and marriage certificates.
e. Death certificate of Julia Smith.
f. Death certificate of Edwin William Smith.
g. The Methodist obituary in *Minutes of Conference*, 1958.

B. Williams:
a. The Anthropological obituaries (Forde in *Africa*, April 1958; Schapera in *Man*, 1959).
b. *The Times* obituary, 28 December 1957.
c. Rotberg in his book *Christian Missionaries and the Creation of Northern Rhodesia 1880–1924*, Princeton: Princeton University Press, 1965, consistently used Edwin Williams Smith.
d. His grandson volunteered the information that Williams is the correct name.

The evidence in the public domain is A.g, B.a, B.b, B.c. On the basis of this with B.d, I thought that Williams was probably correct. However, I then came across A.a–e, all generated before his death, which decisively prove that it is William. He was known in the family circle as 'Ted'.

11. A daughter, Lititia Gertrude, was born 27 November 1875 and died about 1877. Tilbe, Jim, 'The Descendants of William Smith', ongoing genealogical information.

12. Kendall, H. B., *The Origin and History of the Primitive Methodist Church*, vol. ii, London, 1906, p. 497.

13. Smith, John, 'Early Days of our Mission in South Africa', introductory chapter, *Aldersgate Magazine*, c.1906, p. 624, SPMMS.

14. *African Affairs*, October 1923, p. 60.
15. Oliver, R., and Fage, J. D., *A Short History of Africa*, Harmondsworth: Penguin, 1966, p. 183.
16. Kendall, *The Origin*, vol. ii, p. 502.
17. Bolink, P., *Towards Church Union in Zambia*, Franeker: Wever, 1967, pp. 68f. The PMs did not know then that the Lozi, who considered themselves overlords of the Ila, used Mashukulumbwe as a term of disparagement. Smith, Edwin W., and Dale, Andrew M., *The Ila-Speaking Peoples of Northern Rhodesia*, London: Macmillan, 1920 (*ISP*), p. xxv, see also p. xxvii, 'Ila is a root-word, and is not, from the native point of view, complete without a prefix.' Mwila (= mu-ila) means a single person of the tribe; Ba-ila, more than one person; Bwila (= bu-ila) is the name of the country.
18. Ecclesiastical and secular politics. When John Smith returned to England he was elected to the Yarmouth School Board and there was a suggestion that he should stand for Parliament, presumably as a Liberal candidate. Tribute by A. T. W. (Arthur Watson) in a cutting from a *Primitive Methodist Magazine*, 1890, 449f, SPMMS, Fiche 578.
19. Smith, Edwin W., tape recording of early memories, *c.*1957. Much of the material in this section comes from this tape. He used a typescript of reminiscences for the tape. I refer to it as 'Reminiscences'. It goes farther than the tape but breaks off around 1902.
20. Smith, Edwin W., *The Shrine of a People's Soul*, London: Church Missionary Society, 1929 (*Shrine*), p. 98.
21. Bowran, John G., *Life of A. T. Guttery*, London: Holborn Publishing House, n.d., p. 23.
22. Leary, W., *Directory of P.M. Ministers and their Circuits*, Loughborough: Teamprint, 1990, p. 190.
23. 'Smith, Edwin W.', by W. Mincher, 1898, cutting, probably from the *Record*, SPMMS, Fiche 578.
24. *Aldersgate Magazine*, 1899, p. 4.
25. Tribute to John Smith by W. A. Hammond, 18 February 1915. Cutting in writer's possession, ?PM Leader.
26. Smith, Edwin W., tape and 'Reminiscences', SPMMS.
27. Baldwin, Arthur, *How we entered Central Africa*, *c.*1907, p. 8.
28. Tape and 'Reminiscences'.
29. Tape and 'Reminiscences'.

Chapter 2

1. Armstrong, Chester, *Pilgrimage from Nenthead*, London, 1938, p. 111.
2. Armstrong, *Pilgrimage from Nenthead*, p. 115.
3. Notes on Romans 1.17, on interleaved pages of Edwin Smith's Bible.
4. Smith, Edwin W., *The Golden Stool*, London: Holborn Publishing House, 1926 (*GS*), p. 314.
5. Quoted in *GS*, pp. 314f.
6. Smith, John, *Christ and Missions*, London: Primitive Methodist Publishing

House, 1900, p. 62.

7. Smith, *Christ and Missions*, p. 73.

8. Smith, *Christ and Missions*, p. 75.

9. Smith, *Christ and Missions*, p. 75.

10. Cf. Warren, M., *To Apply the Gospel*, Grand Rapids: Eerdmans, 1971.

11. Smith, *Christ and Missions*, p. 81.

12. Smith, *Christ and Missions*, pp. 83–4.

13. Smith, *Christ and Missions*, p. 158.

14. I am most grateful to Mrs June Smedley for the information in these two paragraphs and for other references to his preaching which are drawn from Edwin Smith's Bible in her possession.

15. Report of Conference, *Primitive Methodist World*, 1897, SPMMS, Fiche 576.

16. *The Record*, November 1895, p. 166.

17. *The Record*, November 1895, p. 170.

18. *PMQR*, July 1907, p. 476.

19. Mr H. J. Waters, see Scotland, N., *Methodism and the Revolt of the Field*, Gloucester: Alan Sutton, 1981, p. 223.

20. SPMMS, Fiche 586.

21. SPMMS, Fiche 586.

22. *The Record*, September 1897.

23. *The Record*, September 1897.

24. *The Record*, September 1897.

25. Report of Conference, *Primitive Methodist World*, 1897, SPMMS, Fiche 576.

26. Article on Livingstone College, ?*Primitive Methodist Magazine*, 1898, SPMMS, Fiche 577.

27. Article on Livingstone College.

28. Article on Livingstone College.

29. Article on Livingstone College.

30. Article on Livingstone College.

31. Article on Livingstone College.

32. Article on Livingstone College.

33. Smith, Edwin W., *Great Lion of Bechuanaland*, London: Independent Press, 1957, p. xi, Foreword, 7 September 1956.

34. *Primitive Methodist Magazine*, 1897, p. 758.

35. *Primitive Methodist Magazine*, 1898, pp. 37–43.

36. *Primitive Methodist Magazine*, 1898, p. 694.

37. Mincher, W., 1898, SPMMS, Fiche 578.

38. Smith, Edwin W., 'Leaves from My Journal', *Aldersgate Magazine*, August 1924, p. 558.

Chapter 3

1. *The Primitive Methodist*, 27 October 1898, SPMMS, Fiche 576.

2. Bryce, James, *Impressions of South Africa*, London: Macmillan, 1897, p. 463.

3. Journal, SPMMS, Fiche 570.

4. SPMMS, Fiches 570, 578.

5. SPMMS, Fiche 570.
6. 'A visit to Aliwal North, South Africa', SPMMS, Fiche 578.
7. *Mabilles*, p. 130.
8. Smith, Edwin W., 'Education of the African', *Holborn Review*, July 1923, pp. 310f.
9. Smith, 'Education of the African', p. 311.
10. EWS to Mr Lea, 19 February 1899, SPMMS.
11. Letter, 10 November 1899, SPMMS.
12. 'Among the "Cannibals"', *The Record*, January 1899.
13. *Aldersgate Magazine*, February 1899, p. 107.
14. *Aldersgate Magazine*, February 1899, p. 106.
15. *Aldersgate Magazine*, February 1899, p. 107.
16. For example, on 9 November he wrote to many members of his family: Father, Fred (brother), Mother, Dora (sister), Jue (his fiancée), Jack (brother) and Georgie (sister).
17. Journal and cuttings, photograph album, SPMMS.
18. SPMMS, Fiche 571.
19. His uncle James, a Primitive Methodist preacher, 'was forthright in temperance work'. Scotland, N., *Methodism and the Revolt of the Field*, Gloucester: Alan Sutton, 1981, p. 167.
20. e.g. *BM*, p. 115.
21. 'Leaves from my Journal – I', *Aldersgate Magazine*, 1924, SPMMS, Fiche 569. Cf. 'Reminiscences'.
22. Smith, Edwin W., 'African Folk-Tales', *PMQR*, April 1910, p. 234.
23. J. Murray Hofmeyr went to Malawi and later entered NE Zambia in mid-1902, Sampson, R., *They Came to Northern Rhodesia*, Lusaka, 1956. He had died by 1946.
24. Journal, 25 January 1899, SPMMS, Fiche 571.
25. EWS to Burnett, 21 March 1900, SPMMS.
26. EWS, letter to Mr Lea, 19 February 1899, SPMMS, Fiche 653.
27. EWS, letter to Mr Lea, 19 February 1899, SPMMS, Fiche 653.
28. *Mabilles*, p. 110.
29. Family recollection, R. Howard-Jones, also 'Leaves from my Journal – I', *Aldersgate Magazine*, 1924, SPMMS, Fiche 569.
30. E. W. Smith, unpublished diary, 28 December 1948, SPMMS.
31. 'Leaves from my Journal', *Aldersgate Magazine*, 1924, SPMMS, Fiche 569.
32. Journal, 11 March 1899, SPMMS, Fiche 571.
33. Journal, 11 March 1899, SPMMS, Fiche 571.
34. 'Leaves from my Journal', *Aldersgate Magazine*, 1924, SPMMS, Fiche 569.

Chapter 4

1. Journal, 20 May 1899, SPMMS, Fiche 571.
2. Somngesi was actually ordained on 19 August 1899, three months after Smith's visit, SPMMS, Fiche 578.
3. A Leaders Meeting was the chief meeting for the spiritual and disciplinary

government of the local church.

4. 24 May 1899, SPMMS, Fiche 571. James, presumably James Tozzo, an evangelist to the Ila.
5. Luke 15.32, Edwin Smith's Bible, in loc.
6. 'Leaves from my Journal – II', *Aldersgate Magazine*, 1924, pp. 631–2, SPMMS, Fiche 569.
7. Cf. Sargant, W., *Battle for the Mind*, London: Heinemann, 1957; Temple, R., *Open to Suggestion*, Wellingborough: Aquarian Press, 1989.
8. Journal, 23 June 1899, SPMMS, Fiche 572.
9. Smith's diary was out of sequence for a few days. He left Aliwal North on Friday 28 September according to his journal, 29 September in fact, SPMMS, Fiche 572.
10. Journal, 3 October 1899, SPMMS, Fiche 572; cf. also SPMMS, Fiche 578, where Julia is described as daughter of J. Fitch, Esq., of Dalham, Newmarket; she was born in 1874.
11. 'Leaves from my Journal – II', *Aldersgate Magazine*, 1924, p. 633, SPMMS, Fiche 569; Journal, SPMMS, Fiche 572.
12. 'A Visit to Wellington, Cape Colony', SPMMS, Fiche 579.
13. In this chapter the term 'Boer' has been replaced by 'Afrikaner', except when used by Edwin Smith and his contemporaries and in the expression 'Anglo-Boer War'.
14. Letter to his mother, 13 March 1900, SPMMS.
15. SPMMS, Fiche 578.
16. Letter to his mother, 13 March 1900.
17. Letter to his mother, 13 March 1900.
18. Probably in the *Cape Times*, SPMMS, Fiche 578.
19. SPMMS, Fiche 579.
20. 'Leaves from my Journal – II', *Aldersgate Magazine*, 1924, SPMMS, Fiche 569.
21. SPMMS, Fiche 580.
22. E. W. Smith to Burnett, no date, SPMMS.
23. 'Reminiscences', ch. 3, p. 23.
24. E. W. Smith to Lea, 2 February 1901, SPMMS.
25. 'Reminiscences', ch. 3, p. 27, SPMMS.
26. Hogg's wife had died, cf. his testimony 'As I was mourning . . . ', SPMMS, Fiche 582. In Scotland he met Miss McHendrie, who would come to Africa in 1902 to marry him.
27. 'Leaves from my Journal – III', *Aldersgate Magazine*, 1924, p. 719, SPMMS, Fiche 569.
28. SPMMS, Fiche 582.
29. SPMMS, Fiche 582.
30. 'Reminiscences'; family memory.
31. Smith, Edwin W., 'Cecil Rhodes', *PMQR*, c.1911, p. 420, SPMMS.
32. Smith, Edwin W., 'Stewart of Lovedale', *PMQR*, January 1909, p. 15, SPMMS.
33. Mrs Raybould to Burnett, 24 July 1901, SPMMS.
34. SPMMS, Fiche 558.

35. 'Leaves from my Journal – III', *Aldersgate Magazine*, 1924, p. 723, SPMMS, Fiche 569.
36. *Shrine*, p. 126.
37. 'Sayings of the African', article 1, SPMMS.
38. 'Sayings of the African', article 1, SPMMS.
39. 'Sayings of the African', article 1, SPMMS.
40. E. W. Smith to General Missionary Committee (GMC), 22 March 1901, SPMMS .
41. E. W. Smith to Burnett, 18 October 1901, SPMMS.
42. Family register in Edwin Smith's Bible.
43. From a series of articles on the work of the mission, in the *Aldersgate Magazine*, 1911.

Chapter 5

1. *GS*, p. 31.
2. Smith, Edwin W., *The Life and Times of Daniel Lindley*, London: Epworth, 1949, pp. 65f.
3. Smith, Julia A., *Sunshine and Shade in Central Africa*, Primitive Methodist Publishing House, 1908, p. 8.
4. Smith, Julia, *Sunshine and Shade*, pp. 8f.
5. Smith, Julia, *Sunshine and Shade*, p. 11.
6. 'Leaves from my Journal – IV', *Aldersgate Magazine*, January 1925, p. 25, SPMMS, Fiche 569.
7. 'Leaves from my Journal – IV', *Aldersgate Magazine*, January 1925, p. 25, SPMMS, Fiche 569.
8. EWS to R. W. Burnett, 14 June 1902, SPMMS, Fiche 584.
9. *The Primitive Methodist*, 4 December 1902, SPMMS, Fiche 584.
10. MS of 'Leaves from my Journal – V', SPMMS, Fiche 568.
11. Nanzela accounts, 16 November 1902, UCZ Archives, Kitwe, Zambia; *The Primitive Methodist*, 27 December 1902, SPMMS, Fiche 584.
12. 'African Odyssey', p. 43, SPMMS; 'Leaves from my Journal – V', SPMMS, Fiche 568.
13. *Shrine*, p. 24. Ila culture and its setting among other peoples in Zambia will be described in Chapter 8 when Smith went to Kasenga, among those he believed to be the true Ila.
14. *Shrine*, p. 25.
15. *The Primitive Methodist*, 11 December 1902, SPMMS, Fiche 584; it is now conventional to say Ila, though strictly speaking the people are Baila, the country Bwila and the language Cila, pronounced cheela.
16. Smith, Julia, *Sunshine and Shade*, p. 19.
17. Smith, E. W., 'Article on the Ethiopian Church Movement, Second Paper', *PMQR*, *c.*1905, p. 504, SPMMS.
18. Station Report, September 1902, SPMMS. The Sotho teachers should be regarded as African missionaries, and their work has been neglected in mission studies.

19. *BM*, pp. 135f.; van Rinsum, Henk J., *Slaves of Definition*, Maastricht: Shaker Publishing, 2001, pp. 55ff., shows that this sense of superiority was prominent when Smith wrote to Primitive Methodist readers in Britain about the Ila; cf. also Cocks, Paul, 'Muzemunuzhi: Edwin Smith and the Restoration and Fulfillment of African Society and Religion', *Patterns of Prejudice* 35.2 (2001).
20. 'Sayings of the African', *c.*1902, Article 1, SPMMS.
21. Letter to GMC, *Herald/Record*, 3 September 1902, SPMMS, Fiche 584.
22. Fielder, R. J., in Snelson, P. D., *Educational Development in Northern Rhodesia 1883–1945*, Lusaka: Neczam, 1974, p. 52.
23. Fielder, in Snelson, *Educational Development*, p. 53.
24. Education Report, December 1925, UCZ Archives, Kitwe.
25. All quotations in this paragraph from Smith, Julia, *Sunshine and Shade*, pp. 36f.
26. Smith, Julia, *Sunshine and Shade*, p. 26.
27. Smith, Julia, *Sunshine and Shade*, p. 26.
28. Inscription on grave, E. W. Smith, unpublished photograph album, SPMMS.
29. Smith, Edwin W., *Nanzela: Some Personal Experiences in Central Africa*, London: Edwin Dalton, n.d., *c.*1908 (*Nanzela*), p. 2.
30. *Nanzela*, pp. 2, 3.
31. EWS to R. W. Burnett, 1 November 1901, SPMMS. Smith received a journal called *Climate*, in which such matters were raised.
32. *Aldersgate Magazine*, *c.*1909–10, p. 224.
33. Smith, Julia, *Sunshine and Shade*, p. 31.
34. *Nanzela*, p. 3.
35. *Nanzela*, p. 3.
36. Smith, Julia, *Sunshine and Shade*, p. 22.
37. *BM*, p. 136.
38. *Handbook*, p. v.
39. 'A Letter from Nanzela, "The Father of Melons"', ?*Herald*, *c.*1903, SPMMS, Fiche 585.
40. *Aldersgate Magazine*, *c.*1909–10, pp. 380ff., SPMMS.
41. *Aldersgate Magazine*, *c.*1909–10, pp. 380ff., SPMMS.
42. Cited in *Shrine*, p. 14.
43. *Aldersgate Magazine*, *c.*1909–10, pp. 380ff.
44. *Nanzela*, p. 11.
45. SPMMS, Fiches 545, 546.
46. Smith, Julia, *Sunshine and Shade*, p. 32.
47. Roe, J. M., *A History of the British and Foreign Bible Society, 1905–1954*, London: British and Foreign Bible Society, 1964, p. 43.
48. Smith, Julia, *Sunshine and Shade*, p. 32.
49. SPMMS, Fiches 574, 575.
50. When Smith presented his papers to the Archives (1950s) he inserted this remark: 'This is the first attempt to produce a HYMN BOOK in the ILA language of Northern Rhodesia. The result, it must be confessed, is somewhat crude; but it served its purpose.' SPMMS, Fiche 543.
51. Smith was following the usage then current with Sotho, his first African

language; see obituary of Edwin Smith by Clement P. Doke, *African Studies* 17.2 (1958), p. 116. The disjunctive form continued in Sotho, e.g. *Suto-English Phrase-Book*, Morija, 1983.

52. *Handbook*, p. vi.
53. *Handbook*, pp. 115–18.
54. Awoniyi, T. A., *The Teaching of African Languages*, London: Hodder & Stoughton, 1982, pp. 99–102.
55. *Handbook*, p. 334.
56. By Ralph Durand, *Man*, 1907, §80.
57. Obituary of Edwin Smith by Clement P. Doke, *African Studies* 17.2 (1958), p. 116.
58. Letter to the writer from Ernst Wendland, 12 September 1994.
59. Letter to the writer from Ernst Wendland, 12 September 1994.
60. Sow, A. I., and Abdulaziz, M. H., in UNESCO *General History of Africa*, viii: *Africa Since 1935*, Oxford: Heinemann, 1993, ch. 18, pp. 522ff; also Awoniyi, *Teaching*, p. 18.
61. Letter to the writer from Ernst Wendland, 12 September 1994.

Chapter 6

1. *Nanzela*, p. 15.
2. Fielder, R. J., 'Social Change among the Ila-Speaking Peoples of Northern Rhodesia: With Particular Reference to their Relations with the Primitive Methodist Mission', unpublished MA thesis, University of Manchester, 1965.
3. Fielder, 'Social Change', ch. 7.
4. EWS to Revd Pickett, 28 July 1904, SPMMS.
5. EWS to GMC, 5 September 1907, SPMMS.
6. EWS to Revd Pickett, 6 January 1908, SPMMS.
7. *Nanzela*, p. 5.
8. Smith, Julia, *Sunshine and Shade*, p. 33.
9. *Nanzela*, p. 6.
10. *Nanzela*, pp. 6, 7; cf. *ISP*, vol. ii, p. 246; *For Every Land*, February 1925, pp. 9, 10.
11. Smith family papers, photograph albums, SPMMS.
12. A prominent, eloquent, lay leader from Leeds who was involved in many aspects of the church's life including the African missions, Wilkes, A., and Lovatt, J., *Mow Cop*, Leominster: The Orphans' Printing Press, n.d (*c.*1943), p. 185; Barber, B. A., *A Methodist Pageant*, London: Holborn, 1932, pp. 275f.
13. *PMQR*, January 1904, pp. 4f.
14. *PMQR*, January 1904, p. 14.
15. Taylor, John V., and Lehmann, Dorothea, *Christians of the Copperbelt*, London: SCM Press, 1961, pp. 9f.; Kay, G., *A Social Geography of Zambia*, London: University of London Press, 1967, p. 31.
16. Taylor and Lehmann, *Christians of the Copperbelt*, pp. 33–7.
17. Taylor and Lehmann, *Christians of the Copperbelt*, pp. 33–7.
18. Snelson, P. D., *Educational Development in Northern Rhodesia 1883–1945*,

Lusaka: Neczam, 1974, p. 55.

19. Snelson, *Educational Development*, p. 57.

20. *PMQR, c.*1905, p. 331, SPMMS.

21. *PMQR, c.*1905, p. 505, SPMMS.

22. *PMQR, c.*1905, p. 505, SPMMS.

23. The *Herald, c.*February 1905, SPMMS, Fiche 587; E. W. Smith photograph collection, SPMMS.

24. Three daughters, Janet, Jean and Lizzie from Hogg's first marriage came to Zambia with Mrs Nellie Hogg in 1902. Another child was born from their short marriage. One of the daughters, Janet, married into the Walker family, of Walker's Drift & Choma. Sampson, R., *They Came to Northern Rhodesia*, Lusaka, 1956, pp. 17, 34; Photograph collection, SPMMS.

25. Articles in the *Herald*, and *Aldersgate Magazine*, June/July 1907, SPMMS, Fiche 594.

26. Smith, Julia, *Sunshine and Shade*, p. 38.

27. *Nanzela*, p. 16.

28. The baptism service is described in SPMMS, Fiches 543, 593.

29. *GS*, pp. 273f.

30. The PM mission in the Zambezi Valley is described and analysed in Luig, Ulrich, *Conversion as a Social Process: A History of Missionary Christianity among the Valley Tonga, Zambia*, Hamburg: LIT, 1997.

31. Sampson, *They Came*, p. 34.

32. Correspondence of EWS with Revd Pickett, 1906, SPMMS.

33. 'I remember visiting a remote village on the borders of Lancashire and Yorkshire where I was totally unable to understand what was said to me; I might have been in a foreign land', *Shrine*, p. 50.

34. *Handbook*, p. 1.

35. Photograph collection, SPMMS.

36. Photograph collection, SPMMS.

37. EWS to GMC, 18 December 1906, SPMMS, Fiche 560.

38. *The Herald, c.*April 1907, SPMMS, Fiche 594.

39. *The Herald, c.*April 1907, SPMMS, Fiche 594.

40. December 1906, SPMMS.

41. Acts 17.16–34.

42. Farquhar, J. N., *The Crown of Hinduism*, London: Oxford University Press, 1913; Andrews, C. F., *The Renaissance in India*, London: United Council for Missionary Education, 1914; cf. Stanley, B., *The Bible and the Flag*, Leicester: Apollos, 1990, p. 164.

43. *PMQR*, January 1907, p. 30.

44. *PMQR*, January 1907, p. 31.

45. *PMQR*, January 1907, p. 31.

46. Stanley, *The Bible and the Flag*, p. 164; cf. also, McVeigh, M. J., *God in Africa: Conceptions of God in African Traditional Religion and Christianity*, Cape Cod, Mass.: Claude Starke, 1974, pp. 157ff.

47. Butt, G. E., *My Travels in North West Rhodesia*, London: E. Dalton, p. 155.

Chapter 7

1. Marwick, A., *Britain in the Century of Total War*, Harmondsworth: Pelican, 1968, p. 33.
2. Marwick, *Britain in the Century of Total War*, p. 47.
3. Smith, Edwin W., *Robert Moffat*, London: SCM Press, 1925, p. 183.
4. SPMMS, Fiche 561.
5. GMC to EWS, 25 July 1907, SPMMS, Fiche 561.
6. EWS to GMC, 18 July 1907.
7. See Bédarida, F., *A Social History of England, 1851–1975*, ET A. S. Forster, London: Methuen, 1979, p. 217.
8. GMC to EWS, 7 August 1907, SPMMS, Fiche 561.
9. Kendall, H. B., *History of the Primitive Methodist Church*, London: Primitive Methodist Publishing House, 1919, p. 134.
10. Wilkes, A., and Lovatt, J., *Mow Cop*, Leominster: Orphans' Printing Press, n.d (*c*.1943), p. 203; Bowran, J. G., *The Life of Arthur Thomas Guttery D.D.*, London: Holborn Publishing House, n.d., pp. 130f.
11. A. M. Fairbairn (1838–1912) had been to India and had many books on non-Christian religions. He 'knew that he would have to work out his systematic teaching in the context of religious plurality'. (Kenneth Cracknell, *Justice, Courtesy and Love: Five Early Scottish Contributions to the Theology of Inter-Faith Dialogue*, St Colm's Public Lecture 1991, p. 9). He was closely associated with the Primitive Methodist A. S. Peake at Mansfield College from 1890–2. Smith had at least two of Fairbairn's books and it is probable that many suggestions were planted in his mind through reading them.
12. Smith, Edwin W., 'The Secret of the African', Primitive Methodist Book Room, October 1907, p. 4.
13. e.g. 'killing infants who are born with certain irregularities', *Nanzela*, p. 8.
14. *Nanzela*, p. 5.
15. *Nanzela*, pp. 5, 6.
16. Smith, 'Secret', p. 9.
17. Smith, 'Secret', p. 17.
18. Smith, 'Secret', p. 18.
19. Smith, 'Secret', p. 20.
20. Smith, 'Secret', p. 21.
21. Smith, 'Secret', p. 21.
22. Smith, 'Secret', p. 25.
23. Smith, 'Secret', p. 31.
24. Smith, 'Secret', p. 32.
25. A. S. Peake, 'Our Responsibility to Inferior Races' (delivered 8 March 1906), in *Plain Thoughts on Great Subjects*, London: Allenson, n.d., p. 146.
26. Edinburgh 1910, *Report of Commission IV*, London: Oliphant, Anderson & Ferrier, 1910, ch. 2.
27. It may have been hindered by several factors: World War I, the subsequent continued colonialism with slow development policies, missionaries becoming absorbed by colonial attitudes and the rise of Barthianism.

28. Copy in possession of R. Howard-Jones. 1,000 copies were printed by Oxford University Press. It was published on 11 April 1907 at 15 shillings net. Smith had two copies interleaved, and his Bible rebound by the Press, letter to author from OUP, 3 November 1994.

29. Family memory, Richard Howard-Jones.

30. *PMQR*, 1907, pp. 613–30.

31. *PMQR*, 1908, pp. 601–15.

32. *PMQR*, 1909, pp. 1–18.

33. *PMQR*, 1909, p. 11.

34. *PMQR*, 1909, pp. 385–401.

35. *PMQR*, 1909, p. 400.

36. *PMQR*, 1909, p. 386.

37. Chapman report, no date, *c.*mid-1908, SPMMS, Fiches 563, 564.

38. SPMMS, Fiche 564.

39. Diary, 1909, SPMMS, uncited quotations come from this source.

40. Also SPMMS, Fiche 565.

41. SPMMS, Fiches 565, 566.

42. Diary, 1 April 1909, SPMMS.

43. *Primitive Methodist Missionary Society, Seventy First Annual Report*, London: Primitive Methodist Publishing House, 1914, pp. 137, 138, 217, 223, 224.

44. Possibly Julia's sister.

45. Diary, 2 April 1909, SPMMS.

46. Mr F. Waters, see letter to Allison, 2 April 1909, SPMMS, Fiche 566. Frank and Wilfred were sons of H. J. Waters, Smith's uncle James. H. J. Waters and John Smith married two sisters of the Jeary family of Martham, which, in the 1870s, was in the Yarmouth circuit. Letters to author from Mr A. Waters, Mr J. Waters.

47. Wilfred was a veterinary surgeon, as was his own son, Jim. Letter to author from Jim Waters.

48. H. J. Waters, Ambleside, Snape Road, Norwich, SPMMS, Fiche 596. Uncle James was an active PM, a local preacher, union leader, auctioneer and alderman. Waters correspondence; Scotland, Nigel, *Methodism and the Revolt of the Field: A Study of the Methodist Contribution to Agricultural Trade Unionism in East Anglia, 1872–96*, Gloucester: Alan Sutton, 1981, pp. 167, 223.

49. These included: 1 *Aldersgate* (The PM Magazine), 1 *Morning* (The PM Magazine for Young People), 1 *Quarterly Review* (The PM Theological Journal), 2 *Heralds* (The PM Missionary Magazine), *The Times Weekly Edition, Punch, The Christian World Pulpit, Review of Reviews, Expository Times* and *The Hibbert Journal* (A journal of philosophy and theology); Diary, April 1909, SPMMS.

50. Marie could be Marie Fitch, also a teacher, see SPMMS, Fiche 596.

51. UCZ Archives, Kafue, from Baldwin, A., *A Missionary Outpost in Central Africa*, London, 1914.

Chapter 8

1. UCZ Archives, Kitwe, File 575.
2. *c.*1908, UCZ Archives, File 813, see SPMMS, Fiche 564.
3. Report of William Chapman, *c.*1908, SPMMS, Fiche 564. Fell's Tonga grammar was, however, very much on the lines of Smith's book.
4. Snelson, Peter Desmond, *Educational Development in Northern Rhodesia, 1883–1945*, Lusaka: Neczam, 1974, pp. 94f; *Seventh-day Adventist Encyclopedia*, Washington DC, 1976, p. 1639.
5. Lane, W., *Jesuits in Zambia, 1880–1991*, Lusaka, 1991, p. 9; Snelson, *Educational Development*, pp. 85f.
6. Snelson, *Educational Development*, p. 102.
7. A. T. Guttery to EWS, 31 January 1910, SPMMS.
8. Snelson, *Educational Development*, p. 103.
9. Kay, George, *A Social Geography of Zambia: A Survey of Population Patterns in a Developing Country*, London: University of London Press, 1971, p. 16.
10. Needham, D. E., *From Iron Age to Independence: A History of Central Africa*, London: Longman, 1974, p. 138.
11. Kay, *Social Geography*, pp. 26–9.
12. *ISP*, vol. i, p. ix.
13. These peoples have been described by anthropologists. Max Gluckman, who researched the Lozi, went on to head the Manchester school of anthropology with its emphasis on Central Africa (Kuper, A., *Anthropology and Anthropologists: The Modern British School*, London: Routledge, 1983, pp. 128f., 142ff.). Elizabeth Colson (of the Manchester school) studied the various Tonga groups during the third quarter of the twentieth century ('The Plateau Tonga of Northern Rhodesia', in Colson, E., and Gluckman, M. (eds), *Seven Tribes of British Central Africa*, London: Oxford University Press, 1951/60; *Marriage and the Family among the Plateau Tonga of Northern Rhodesia*, 1958; *The Social Organisation of the Gwembe Tonga*, 1960; *The Plateau Tonga of Northern Rhodesia (Zambia): Social and Religious Studies*, 1962). A generation earlier, in the first quarter of the twentieth century, the classic Ila study was made by Smith and his friend Andrew Dale. Fifty years later Robin Fielder, another Manchester-trained anthropologist, made further researches among the Ila, especially around Nanzela (Fielder, Robin J., 'Social Change among the Ila-Speaking Peoples of Northern Rhodesia: With Particular Reference to their Relations with the Primitive Methodist Mission (PMM)', unpublished MA thesis, University of Manchester, 1965.)
14. *ISP*, vol. i, pp. 331ff.
15. Smith, Edwin W., 'Addendum to the "Ila-Speaking Peoples of Northern Rhodesia", Part II', *African Studies*, June 1949, p. 54.
16. Ila religious beliefs, ancestor worship and Leza, have been described in Chapter 7. What Smith later called 'dynamism', involving witchcraft, taboos and the use of talismans and medicines, is discussed in Chapter 10.
17. *ISP*, vol. i, pp. 153–69.
18. Fielder, 'Social Change', p. 17.

19. Comaroff, John and Jean, *Of Revelation and Revolution*, Chicago: University of Chicago Press, 1991; Clifford, James, *Person and Myth: Maurice Leenhardt in the Melanesian World*, Durham, N.C.: Duke University Press, 1982.

20. *ISP*, vol. ii, p. 223.

21. *ISP*, vol. ii, p. 223.

22. *ISP*, vol. ii, p. 223.

23. Chapman, William, *A Pathfinder in Central Africa*, London: Hammond, 1910, pp. 151f.

24. Diary, 12 May 1909, SPMMS. William Harrison Anderson (1870–1950) was the pioneer SDA missionary in Zambia; Snelson, *Educational Development*, pp. 94f.

25. Diary, 16 May 1909, SPMMS.

26. When W. H. Anderson came that way in 1903 to find somewhere to establish a mission he 'almost died of dysentery, but was nursed back to health by a certain Mr Walker of Choma'; *SDA Encyclopedia*, 1976, p. 1639.

27. Diary, 26 May 1909, SPMMS.

28. Diary, 1 June 1909, SPMMS.

29. Fielder mentions a similar incident concerning Smith as recounted by Revd John Price where Mungalo is specified, this could be the story recorded here, or part of the incident mentioned above. Fielder, 'Social Change', p. 274.

30. Strangely, Smith did not mention this in *ISP*.

31. In *Sunshine and Shade* she said, 'We have a good library, and the characters in Scott, Lytton, George Eliot, and Dickens and Jane Austen seem to be quite old friends of ours', p. 86.

32. SPMMS, Fiche 563; Photograph collection, SPMMS.

33. Diary, 11 October 1909, SPMMS.

34. *PMQR*, April 1910, p. 243.

35. *ISP*, vol. i, p. xii.

36. *GS*, p. 325.

37. *ISP*, vol. i, p. 55.

38. Diary, 24 October 1909, SPMMS.

39. Diary, 25 November 1909, SPMMS.

40. Bowran, J. G., *The Life of Arthur Thomas Guttery D.D.*, London: Holborn Publishing House, n.d., pp. 18–24, 110–37.

41. EWS to A. T. Guttery, 10 September 1910, 6 February 1913, SPMMS, Fiches 595–9.

42. Diary, 14 November 1909. Smith obtained a series of pictures from the Religious Tract Society. We would probably consider them inappropriate for the African context today and would point to the wall paintings of Africanized scenes in the life of Christ by the African artist Nsama (c.1970) which hang in the chapel of Njase Girls Secondary School in Choma as more appropriate.

43. Diary, 25 November 1909, SPMMS.

44. *Sixty Seventh Annual Report of the Primitive Methodist Missionary Society*, p. lxvi.

45. By March 1910 there were 19 boarders and a regular congregation varying from three hundred to five hundred, PMMS *Annual Report 1910*, p. lxvi.

46. Diary, 25 October 1909, SPMMS.
47. Chapman, *Pathfinder*, p. 307.
48. Chapman, *Pathfinder*, p. 212.
49. Chapman, *Pathfinder*, p. 326.
50. Chapman, *Pathfinder*, p. 131.
51. Minutes of Synod at Kafue, 1919, UCZ Archives, Kitwe, File 494.
52. *Man*, 1907, §80.
53. Smith, Edwin W., 'Anthropology and the Practical Man', Presidential Address, Journal of the Royal Anthropological Institute, 1934, p. xvi.
54. Diary, 15 August 1909, SPMMS.
55. Diary, 15 August 1909, SPMMS.
56. *Plans*, p. 7.
57. *ISP*, vol. i, p. x.
58. 'We cannot indeed find in the facts before us any reason to support any of the current theories as to the origin of Totemism', *ISP*, vol. i, p. 291.
59. *ISP*, vol. i, p. xi.

Chapter 9

1. PMMS, *Annual Report 1910*, p. lxvi.
2. PMMS, *Annual Report 1910*, p. lxvi. Edwin Smith's reports and articles in the *Herald*, especially in the earlier part of his missionary service, present a more negative view of the Ila than his other writings and show that his sense of superiority continued for a long time, cf. van Rinsum, Henk J., *Slaves of Definition*, Maaschricht: Shaker Publishing, 2001, pp. 55ff.
3. PMMS, *Annual Report 1910*, pp. lxvi, lxvii.
4. PMMS, *Annual Report 1910*, p. lxvii.
5. *ISP*, vol. i, pp. 219–20.
6. *ISP*, vol. ii, p. 222.
7. *ISP*, vol. ii, p. 222.
8. Latourrette, K. S., in Rouse, R., and Neill, S. C. (eds), *A History of the Ecumenical Movement, 1517–1948*, London: SPCK, 1967, p. 362.
9. World Missionary Conference 1910, *Report of Commission IV*, pp. 25–7.
10. World Missionary Conference 1910, *History and Records*, vol. ix, p. 40.
11. World Missionary Conference 1910, *History and Records*, vol. ix, p. 47.
12. World Missionary Conference 1910, *History and Records*, vol. ix, p. 51.
13. A. T. Guttery to EWS, 29 July 1910, SPMMS, Fiche 567.
14. A. T. Guttery to EWS, 29 July 1910, SPMMS, Fiche 567.
15. A. T. Guttery to EWS, 9 August 1910, SPMMS, Fiche 596.
16. EWS to A. T. Guttery, 10 November 1910, SPMMS, Fiche 596
17. EWS to GMC, 10 March 1911, SPMMS, Fiche 597.
18. Cracknell, K., *Justice, Courtesy and Love: Theologians and Missionaries Encountering World Religions, 1846–1914*, London: Epworth, 1995, p. 125.
19. *Aldersgate Magazine*, 1911, pp. 485ff.
20. 'The Story of our Central African Mission, ch. X, A Sketch of Missionary Activity', *Aldersgate Magazine*, 1911, pp. 224ff; 'The Story of our Central

African Mission, ch. XI, Missionary Activity', *Aldersgate Magazine*, 1911, pp. 296ff; 'The Story of our Central African Mission, ch. XII, The Beginnings of the Ila Language', *Aldersgate Magazine*, 1911, pp. 380ff and pp. 485ff.

21. The 'Administration Press', Livingstone, 1911. This was expanded in 1914 with grammatical notes as *Ila Made Easy*.

22. National Archives of Zambia, NAZ/KSF/3/2/1 Annual Reports, Namwala District, 1912–1915; Report for 1912–13 of The Primitive Methodist Mission. I am indebted to Tom Johnson for this reference. The hygiene book was not published until 1915, Smith Edwin W., *The Way of the White Fields in the Rhodesias: A survey of Christian Enterprise in Northern and Southern Rhodesia*, London: World Dominion Press, p. 109.

23. *White Fields*, p. 109.

24. See above, Chapter 5.

25. *Primitive Methodist Missionary Society, Seventy First Annual Report*, 1 April 1913 to 31 March 1914, p. lxxix.

26. 'The South African Mission Field', *PMQR*, January 1913, pp. 105–22, SPMMS.

27. 'South African Mission Field', p. 109. In a handwritten note commenting on the word 'recent' in the text, Smith pointed out that he had written before the Conference expressing his hope about it, 'But all in vain!' The Conference was held 3–8 July 1912, so the article was most probably published in 1913 though written in the first part of 1912.

28. Platt, W. J., *From Fetish to Faith*, London: Cargate, 1935, p. 5.

29. EWS to A. T. Guttery, 15 June 1912, SPMMS, Fiche 598.

30. Diary, 29 January 1949, SPMMS, where Smith has 'Through Lohathla we turned R & then took road to N. Passed thro Lomoteng [?Lomoleng – JY] farm & saw J. T.'s house where Jue and I visited in 1913?'

31. Smith, Edwin W., *Robert Moffat: One of God's Gardeners*, London: SCM Press, 1928, p. 9. Moffat was a gardener and brought his gardening to Africa. Smith's father, who began life as an agricultural worker, was a keen gardener. Edwin and Julia Smith both did a lot of gardening.

32. *Moffat*, p. 108; cf. 'Presidential Address', 1915, p. 6.

33. *Moffat*, p. 109; 'Presidential Address'.

34. Cf. also Smith, Edwin W. (ed.), *African Ideas of God*, London: Edinburgh House Press, 1950, p. 122.

35. EWS to A. T. Guttery, 1 July 1911, SPMMS, Fiche 597.

36. A. T. Guttery to EWS, 31 July 1911, SPMMS, Fiche 597.

37. Chapman had only been back to Africa for two years. Mrs Chapman seems not to have come with him in 1910 – she had to leave Zambia in 1907 when there were disturbances at Nambala – perhaps fear prevented her return.

38. EWS to A. T. Guttery, GMC, 30 March, 15 June and 14 September 1912, SPMMS, Fiche 598.

39. A. T. Guttery to EWS, 15 July 12, also 15 October 1912, 12 March 1913, SPMMS, Fiche 599.

40. EWS to GMC, 8 February 1913, SPMMS, Fiche 599.

41. H. J. Taylor to EWS, 7 February 1912, SPMMS, Fiche 598.

42. 'The Sententious Wisdom of the African', *PMQR*, ?April 1913, pp. 225–37; I am uncertain about the date. It has Northern Rhodesia, which suggests it was after 1911. In Smith's bound volume of articles, now in SPMMS, it was placed after the article on S. African missions also from Northern Rhodesia, but before one on Rhodes from North Western Rhodesia. On balance I think 1913 for this article.

43. Smith, 'Sententious Wisdom of the African', p. 237.

44. *ISP*, vol. ii, pp. 311–24, which is almost identical to the article.

45. *Secret*, pp. 9–15; cf. *ISP*, vol. ii, pp. 147–52.

46. *Secret*, p. 14.

47. *Secret*, p. 15.

48. *Primitive Methodist Missionary Society, Seventy First Annual Report*, 1 April 1913 to 31 March 1914, p. lxxviii.

49. Snelson, Peter Desmond, *Educational Development in Northern Rhodesia, 1883–1945*, Lusaka: Neczam, 1974, p. 114. For the story of the Wesleyan Mission in Zambia see Gray, S. D., *Frontiers of the Kingdom in Rhodesia*, London: Cargate, 1929; Johnson, K., 'Now the Word Doth Swiftly Run', in Nightingale, E. G. (ed.), *The Widening Way*, London: Cargate, 1952.

50. 'Extracts from the papers of Rev. Sydney Douglas Gray, pioneer missionary in Central Africa 1883–1964', collected by Revd Merfyn Temple, n.d., p. 51, referred to as Gray, 'Extracts'. The Lenje language used at Chipembi was one of the Bantu Botatwe group which includes Ila and Tonga. I thank the Revd Merfyn Temple for providing me with this information.

51. Gray, 'Extracts', p. 51.

52. Gray, 'Extracts', p. 53.

53. R. Murray-Hughes, 'Missionaries I Have Known', *Northern Rhodesia Journal*, 111.6 (1958), p. 511.

54. Snelson, *Educational Development*, p. 127.

55. *World Missionary Conference, 1910, vol. VIII*, p. 141.

56. PMs, Paris Evangelical Mission, Brethren in Christ, UMCA, Wesleyan Methodists, Roman Catholics.

57. Livingstone St Andrew's Log Book, 29 June 1914. I owe these references and quotations to Revd D. G. Whitehead, Livingstone.

58. From the *Livingstone Mail*, in Livingstone St Andrew's Log Book, 30 June 1914.

59. From the *Livingstone Mail*, in Livingstone St Andrew's Log Book, 30 June 1914.

60. Cf. 'Leopold Moore versus the Chartered Company', *Northern Rhodesia Journal*, 4.3 (1960), pp. 219ff.

61. Letter to writer from the Revd D. G. Whitehead, 17 March 1995.

62. 'The Bantu Conception of God: A Lecture Delivered at the First General Missionary Conference of North Western Rhodesia, by Revd E. W. Smith, the President', July 1914, SPMMS.

63. Smith, 'The Bantu Conception of God', p. 40.

64. *GS*, p. 261.

65. *ISP*, vol. i, pp. 212–13.

66. From the *Livingstone Mail*, in Livingstone St Andrew's Log Book, 30 June 1914.
67. Snelson, *Educational Development*, p. 127.
68. Snelson, *Educational Development*, p. 127.
69. Taylor, H. J., *From Cape Town to Kafue*, London: Hammond, 1915.
70. Kafue School Archives, Kafue; Syabbalo, E., and Syatakali, J., *Mukristo Muzambezi*, United Church of Zambia, n.d., p. 12; interview with Johane Syamayuwa.
71. UCZ Archives, Kitwe, File 622; either the reports are undated or I did not note the dates.
72. UCZ Archives, Kitwe, File 622.
73. PMMS *Annual Report 1915*, p. lv.
74. PMMS *Annual Report 1915*, p. lv.
75. *IRM*, October 1924, pp. 529–30.
76. Memories of Mrs Doris Gerrard, in *The Go-Between, Magazine of the Leominster, Presteigne and Kington Methodist Circuit*, October 1994.
77. Letter from Mrs Stamp to the writer, 15 July 1994, cf. *Handbook*, p. 407, which has *kabanzi*; Torrend, J., *An English–Vernacular Dictionary of the Bantu-Botatwe Dialects of Northern Rhodesia*, 1931/67, has *kabanze*, though the 'e' is pronounced 'a' as in hay. However, Mrs Stamp remembered it pretty well in her late nineties!
78. Smith, 'Presidential Address', 1934, p. xvi.
79. Cracknell, *Justice, Courtesy and Love*, p. 376.
80. Grottanelli. V., 'African Religions: History of Study', in M. Eliade (ed.), *Encyclopedia of Religion*, New York: Macmillan, 1987, vol. i, p. 93.
81. *GS*, p. 261.
82. *BM*, p. 1.
83. *BM*, p. 136.
84. Colson, E., 'Introduction' to the 1968 edition of *ISP*, p. 6.

Chapter 10

1. Cutting, apparently from the *PM Leader*, 18 February 1915, article by W. A. Hammond.
2. PM *Minutes of Conference*, 1915, p. 44.
3. *Aldersgate Magazine*, 1915, pp. 575–6; Edwin Smith, 'Tribute to mother'; Smith's mother lived on into the 1930s, (Smith photograph album; 'Tribute to mother'), SPMMS.
4. Diary, 1915, SPMMS.
5. 'Leaves from my Journal – I', SPMMS, Fiche 569.
6. This is apparent from Smith's correspondence, EWS to Macmillan, 9 June 1915, also 1 May 1915, MAR.
7. EWS to Macmillan, 1 May 1915, MAR.
8. Diary, 6 June 1915, SPMMS.
9. EWS to Macmillan, 6 June 1916, MAR.
10. On Rivers see Kuklick, H., *The Savage Within: The Social History of British*

Anthropology 1885–1945, Cambridge: Cambridge University Press, 1993, pp. 119–81; Gregory, R. L., *Oxford Companion to the Mind*, Oxford: Oxford University Press, 1987, p. 686; Sills, D. L. (ed.), *International Dictionary of the Social Sciences*, New York, 1969, vol. xiii, pp 526–8.

11. *ISP*, vol. i, p. xiv.
12. EWS to Macmillan, 6 June 1915, c/o The Base Commandant, Havre, MAR.
13. Diary, 18 June 1915, SPMMS.
14. *The Bible in the World*, 1916, p. 112.
15. *The Bible in the World*, 1916, p. 112.
16. 'Leaves from my Journal – II', SPMMS, Fiche 569.
17. Diary, 10 July 1915, SPMMS.
18. Diary, 9 August 1915, SPMMS.
19. EWS to Macmillan, 23 November 1915, MAR.
20. EWS to Macmillan, 15 December, 1915, MAR; *ISP*, vol. i, p. x.
21. Letter from E. G. Parrinder to writer, 5 November 1977, see also Ch. 9.
22. McVeigh, M., *God in Africa: Conceptions of God in African Traditional Religion and Christianity*, Cape Cod, Mass.: Claude Starke, 1974, p. 2.
23. Letter from BFBS, 30 December 1915, SPMMS, Fiche 666.
24. *A Fountain Unsealed: A Popular Illustrated Report of the British and Foreign Bible Society 1910–1911*, p. 42.
25. Roe, James Moulton, *A History of The British and Foreign Bible Society, 1905–54*, London: British and Foreign Bible Society, 1965, p. 36.
26. BFBS, *112th Annual Report*, for year ending March 1916.
27. BFBS, *112th Annual Report*, for year ending March 1916.
28. Obituary by Clement Doke, 'Dr Edwin W. Smith', *African Studies* 17.2 (1958), p. 116.
29. Gallo, M., *Mussolini's Italy: Twenty Years of the Fascist Era*, London: Abelard-Schuman, 1974, p. 49.
30. BFBS, *113th Annual Report*, for the year ending March 1917, p. 43.
31. BFBS, *113th Annual Report*, for the year ending March 1917, p. 44.
32. Roe, *History*, p. 278.
33. BFBS, *114th Annual Report*, for year ending March 1918, p. 39.
34. BFBS, *115th Annual Report*, for year ending March 1919, p. 40.
35. Link, Arthur S. (ed.), *The Papers of Woodrow Wilson*, Princeton: Princeton University Press, 1986, vol. liii, pp. 597–634.
36. BFBS, *115th Annual Report*, for year ending March 1919, p. 40.
37. BFBS, *117th Annual Report*, for year ending March 1921, p. 26.
38. BFBS, *117th Annual Report*, for year ending March 1921, p. 33.
39. BFBS, *116th Annual Report*, for year ending March 1920, p. 38.
40. BFBS, *115th Annual Report*, for year ending March 1919, p. 45.
41. BFBS, *115th Annual Report*, for year ending March 1919, p. 45.
42. BFBS, *116th Annual Report*, for year ending March 1920, p. 37.
43. BFBS, *113th Annual Report*, for year ending March 1917, p. 45.
44. BFBS, *116th Annual Report*, for year ending March 1920, p. 38.
45. Smith, Edwin W., 'La Bibbia in Italia', 1919, SPMMS.
46. Hastings, James (ed.), *Encyclopaedia of Religion and Ethics*, Edinburgh: T. & T.

Clark, vol. iv, 1911, p. 399.

47. Hastings, *Encyclopaedia of Religion and Ethics*, vol. iv, pp. 394–9.

48. Here and there he mentioned Dante in his writing: in a review of Papini's *Life of Christ* (*Outward Bound*, June 1923, p. 667), in a Bible Society magazine (*Bible in the World*, July 1923, p. 97; November 1923, p. 162), in an article for the *Holborn Review* ('The Avengers', *Holborn Review*, January 1925, pp. 12, 13), in a book on Bible translation (*Shrine*, pp. 76, 77), in his packing list for a trip to India (Diary, 1938), in the dedication of a book, (Smith, Edwin W., *The Life and Times of Daniel Lindley*, 1949), in an erudite lecture on African Symbolism (Henry Myers Lecture, 1952, p. 17). 'Next to the Bible he loved Dante and studied him deeply' (*Minutes of the Methodist Conference, 1958*, p. 183).

49. Dante, *Inferno*, i.1–3, trans. John Ciardi, New Brunswick: Rutgers University Press, 1954.

50. Dante, *Paradiso*, xxxiii.143–5, trans. C. H. Sisson, Oxford: Oxford University Press, 1980.

51. Higgins, D. H., 'Introduction and Notes' to Dante Alighieri, *The Divine Comedy*, trans. C. H. Sisson, Oxford: Oxford University Press, 1993, p. 21.

52. Sharpe, E. J., *Comparative Religion: A History*, London: Duckworth, 1975, p. 172.

53. Macquarrie, J., *Twentieth-Century Religious Thought*, London: SCM Press, 1988, p. 210.

54. Doke, C. M., 'Dr Edwin W. Smith', *African Studies* 17.2, p. 116.

55. EWS to A. S. Peake, 27 November 1916, MAM, Peake Papers, IV 1642.

56. EWS to A. S. Peake, 27 November 1916, MAM. Julia had relayed a message from Smith to Peake; he also asked after Peake's health, which had not been good when Smith last saw him. L. S. Peake, in *Arthur Samuel Peake*, London: Hodder & Stoughton, 1930, refers to a 'serious breakdown in 1915', so possibly Smith saw Peake then. Earlier (1907) Peake had reviewed the *Handbook* favourably, see EWS to A. S. Peake, 31 May 1907, MAM, Peake Papers, IV 1641.

57. *ISP*, vol. i, p. xiv.

58. EWS to Macmillans, 12 February 1917, MAR.

59. EWS to Macmillans, 14 December 1918, MAR.

60. EWS to Macmillans, 2 January 1919, MAR.

61. EWS to Macmillans, 10 February 1919, MAR.

62. Cf *ISP*, vol. i, p. 412; vol. ii, pp. 75, 110.

63. Smith usually followed a threefold scheme, dynamism, spirits, God, where the two middle terms of his analysis of Ila religion are put together under 'spirits'.

64. R. R. Marett, *The Threshold of Religion*, London: Methuen, 1909/14, and Marett's article on Mana in Hastings, *Encyclopaedia of Religion and Ethics*, vol. viii, pp. 375ff.

65. *Secret*, p. 46; 'African Symbolism', Henry Myers Lecture, 1952, p. 34.

66. Cf. *ISP*, vol. ii, p. 80.

67. *ISP*, vol. ii, p. 97.

68. A son was born after Dale's death, letter to author from Hugh Macmillan, 10

September 1994; M. Temple, *New Hope for Africa*, Reading: Taurus Publishing, 1991, pp. 96f.

69. *ISP*, vol. i, p. xv.
70. *ISP*, vol. i, p. xv.
71. Allowing for blank pages, there are about 830 pages of text including photographs. Chapters for which Smith had primary responsibility were marked *, Dale's by **. Where both had a share then * **, or ** * depending who had the main share. Three chapters are marked ** (32pp., 3.9 per cent) and 2 ** * (35pp., 4.2 per cent). Two have * ** (34pp., 4.1 per cent). Twenty-one chapters are marked *, including the whole of Volume II (415 pp.). Smith thus had major responsibility for around 92 per cent of the text. He took 139 (81.3 per cent) of the 171 photographs.
72. *ISP*, vol. i, p. ix.
73. *Man*, 1921, §73.
74. EWS to A. S. Peake, 28 December 1920, MAM, Peake Papers IV 1644.
75. Letter to author from Sir Raymond Firth, 28 June 1994.
76. Colson, 'Introduction', p. 1.
77. 'Addendum to the "The Ila-Speaking Peoples of Northern Rhodesia" ', *African Studies* 8.1 (March 1949), pp. 1–9, and 8.2 (June 1949), pp. 53–61.
78. Colson, 'Introduction', p. 6.
79. Colson, 'Introduction', p. 1.
80. 'savage people' (*Notes and Queries on Anthropology*, London: The Royal Anthropological Institute, 1929, p. 24), 'higher races' (p. 30), 'People of rude culture' (p. 40), 'people of low culture' (p. 45), 'primitive peoples' (pp. 72, 87), 'The Mental Outlook of Savages' (p. 180), and so on.
81. *Plans – and People!*, p. 7.
82. Kuklick, *Savage*, pp. 78ff.
83. Ackerman, R., *J. G. Frazer: His Life and Work*, Cambridge: Cambridge University Press, 1987, pp. 210–11.
84. Smith, Edwin W., 'Presidential Address: Anthropology and the Practical Man', *Journal of the Royal Anthropological Institute of Great Britain and Ireland* 64 (1934), p. xvi.
85. *Journal of the African Society*, 1920–1, pp. 89ff.
86. Memo of 21 April 1921, SPBSC.
87. Memo of 21 April 1921, SPBSC.

Chapter 11

1. BFBS, *Annual Report 1922*, pp. 36, 37, 48, 57.
2. Letter, 7 November 1921, SPBSC.
3. EWS to J. H. Ritson, 4 November 1922 and 28 December 1923, SPBSC.
4. BFBS, *Annual Report 1922*, p. 28.
5. Roe, James Moulton, *A History of The British and Foreign Bible Society, 1905–54*, London: British and Foreign Bible Society, 1965, pp. 59, 230.
6. Roe, *History*, p. 230.
7. EWS to A. S. Peake, 26 February 1923, MAM, Peake Papers.

8. On Oldham, see Clements, Keith, *Faith on the Frontier: A Life of J. H. Oldham*, Edinburgh: T. & T. Clark, 1999. This is a very detailed study of Oldham. There is no mention of E. W. Smith.
9. *IRM*, April 1922, p. 278.
10. 'The Sublimation of Bantu Life and Thought', *IRM*, January 1922, pp. 83–95.
11. Smith, 'Sublimation', p. 87.
12. Smith, 'Sublimation', p. 87.
13. Smith, 'Sublimation', p. 92.
14. Smith, 'Sublimation', p. 95.
15. 'Should Heathen Games be Preserved in a Christian Community? A Bantu Speaks', *IRM*, 1920, pp. 274ff.
16. *White Fields*, p. 23.
17. 'Bantu' describes many peoples across Africa south of the Sahara who speak Bantu languages. It is not meant to carry the derogatory overtones often used to demean Africans in South Africa.
18. Kuper, A., *Anthropology and Anthropologists: The Modern British School*, London: Routledge, 1983, p. 106.
19. *Lower Races*, 74.
20. *Lower Races*, 74.
21. Letter of 11 August 1923, MAR.
22. Obituary by Clement Doke, 'Dr Edwin W. Smith', *African Studies* 17.2 (1958), p. 117.
23. W. C. Willoughby of Hartford Seminary, another who took African religion seriously, could have been invited to write this book on African religion but he was busy preparing another book, also published in 1923, *Race Problems in the New Africa*.
24. *IRM*, 1923, pp. 133–5.
25. *IRM*, 1923, pp. 134–5.
26. Canon John Roscoe, a friend of J. G. Frazer, had written *The Baganda* (1911). Roscoe was in England from 1909 but returned to Uganda in 1919–20 for further fieldwork and published three books, 1923–4. In 1923 he gave the second Frazer Lecture.
27. *Journal of the African Society* 23 (1923), p. 76.
28. *ISP*, vol. i, pp. 265–72.
29. *ISP*, vol. i, pp. 272–80.
30. Livingstone, D., *Missionary Travels*, 1857, p. 372.
31. Livingstone, *Missionary Travels*, p. 114.
32. Livingstone, *Missionary Travels*, pp. 20–2.
33. *Man*, 1924, §73.
34. *Man*, 1924, §73.
35. *IRM*, 1924, p. 131.
36. 'Education of the African', *Holborn Review*, July 1923, pp. 302–14; cf. EWS to A. S. Peake, 26 February 1923, MAM, Peake Papers.
37. Smith, 'Education of the African', p. 306.
38. Smith, 'Education of the African', p. 314.
39. Other articles included two to the *Church Missionary Review* on the long

relationship between the Church Missionary Society and the BFBS: 'An Unbroken Fellowship: The Story of 120 Years' Close Co-operation', *Church Missionary Review* 74 (December 1923), pp. 212–20 and *Church Missionary Review* 75 (March 1924), pp. 18–26. A third article in *Church Missionary Review* for December 1925, 'These Fifty Years', was largely incorporated into a chapter of *The Golden Stool* (1926). The same happened to an article on the disintegration of African society which appeared in the SPG Review *The East and the West* in April 1924.

The PM *Aldersgate Magazine* for 1924 published a series entitled 'Leaves from my Journal' which shed light on Smith's experiences as a missionary from 1898 to 1902 and were based on his original diary, a valuable and detailed source, rather than later recollections.

40. Smith, Edwin W., 'Social Anthropology and Missionary Work', *IRM*, October 1924, pp. 518–31.
41. Smith, 'Social Anthropology and Missionary Work', p. 518.
42. See Chapter 12.
43. Smith, 'Social Anthropology and Missionary Work', p. 523.
44. Smith, 'Social Anthropology and Missionary Work', p. 528.
45. Smith, 'Social Anthropology and Missionary Work', p. 530.
46. Smith, 'Social Anthropology and Missionary Work', p. 530.
47. *Aggrey*, p. 231.
48. *For Every Land*, 1924, pp. 49f., 57f., 65f., 89f.
49. *For Every Land*, 1925, pp. 1f.
50. *Moffat*, p. 245.

Chapter 12

1. Af·ri·can·ist \-nist\ n. (1895): a specialist in African languages or culture, *Webster's Dictionary*.
2. *GS*, pp. xvi, 328.
3. *GS*, p. viii.
4. Machin, Noel, ' "Government Anthropologist", A Life of R. S. Rattray', Centre for Social Anthropology and Computing, The University of Kent at Canterbury, 1998, p. 122.
5. *Africa*, 1945, p. 89.
6. 'These Fifty Years in Africa', *Church Missionary Review*, December 1925, pp. 296–308.
7. *GS*, p. 53.
8. *GS*, p. 71.
9. Oliver, J., *The Church and Social Order*, London: Mowbray, 1968, pp. 171f.; the subject was also addressed by W. C. Willoughby, *The Race Problem in the New Africa*, London: SCM Press, 1923, and Basil Mathews, *The Clash of Colour*, London: Edinburgh House Press, 1925.
10. Oliver, *Church and Social Order*, p. 172.
11. Oldham, J. H., *Christianity and the Race Problem*, London: SCM Press, 1924, p. 175.

12. *GS*, p. 186.

13. Oldham, *Christianity and the Race Problem*, p. 175.

14. *GS*, dedication page.

15. Letter from Andrew Mapani Dale to author, 26 May 1995.

16. *ISP*, vol. i, p. xv.

17. John Philip (1775–1851) was Superintendent of the London Missionary Society in South Africa from 1819.

18. Macmillan, H., and Marks, S. (eds), *Africa and Empire: W. M. Macmillan, Historian and Social Critic*, Aldershot: Gower, 1989, p. 72.

19. *GS*, p. 188.

20. *GS*, p. 188.

21. *GS*, p. 192.

22. *GS*, p. 210

23. *GS*, p. 210

24. *GS*, p. 203.

25. *GS*, p.233, quoted from E. W. Blyden (1832–1912) Blyden, who had held similar views on the relevance of Islam to Africa, may have influenced Smith's thought here. I owe this observation to Dr Kevin Ward of Leeds University.

26. *GS*, p. 240.

27. *GS*, p. 242.

28. 'The British Empire and Islam', *The East and the West*, 22.86 (April 1924), p. 115.

29. Syed Ameer Ali, *The Spirit of Islam*, London: Chatto & Windus, 1922 edition, 258–67; I am grateful to the Revd Dr Martin Forward for pointing me to this.

30. *GS*, p. 259.

31. *GS*, p. 263.

32. Butler, Mrs T., *Missions as I Saw Them*, London: Seeley, Service & Co, 1924, p. 260.

33. *GS*, pp. 274f.

34. *GS*, p. 275.

35. See *UNESCO General History of Africa*, vol. viii, ed. Mazrui, A. A., Oxford: Heinemann, 1993, pp. 605–15, for further information and bibliographical notes.

36. *GS*, pp. 281f.

37. Phillips, J. M., and Coote, R. T., *Towards the 21st Century in Christian Mission*, Grand Rapids: Eerdmans, 1993, p. 228.

38. Allen, R., *The Spontaneous Expansion of the Church*, London: World Dominion Press, 1927, p. 5.

39. Allen, *Spontaneous Expansion*, p. 79.

40. *GS*, p. 325.

41. *GS*, p. 325.

42. Farmer, A., *Britain: Foreign and Imperial Affairs 1919–39*, London: Hodder & Stoughton, 1992, pp. 63f.

43. Peel, J. D. Y., in Nicholls, C. S. (ed.), *Dictionary of National Biography, Missing Persons*, Oxford: Oxford University Press, 1993, p. 612.

44. Hastings, A., *The Church in Africa: 1450–1950*, Oxford: Oxford University Press, 1994, p. 553.
45. Hogg, W. R., *Ecumenical Foundations*, New York: Harper, 1952, p. 231. Born in 1877, Warnshuis was an American who had served in China. He became an IMC co-secretary with Oldham in 1921.
46. Seating plan for the luncheon, SPMMS.
47. Sow, A. I., and Abdulaziz, M. H., in *UNESCO General History of Africa*, vol. viii. Oxford: Heinemann, 1993, p. 526.
48. Hastings, *The Church in Africa*, p. 553.
49. Smith, Edwin W., *The Christian Mission in Africa*, London: International Missionary Council, 1926, p. v. Cited as *CMIA*.
50. *The Bible in the World*, September 1926, p. 152.
51. *The Bible in the World*, September 1926, pp. 155–7.
52. *The Bible in the World*, September 1926, p. 144; Smith used two of these verses, taken from a book by Fisher, to head a chapter of his last book, *Great Lion of Bechuanaland*, London: Independent Press, 1957, p. 307.
53. *CMIA*, pp. 38ff.
54. *CMIA*, p. 89.
55. *CMIA*, p. 106.
56. EWS to Macmillans, 24 November and 8 December 1926, MAR.

Chapter 13

1. *The Bible in the World*, 1927, p. 150.
2. *Aggrey*, pp. 271–3; Gollock, G. A., *Sons of Africa*, London: SCM Press, 1928; New York: Negro Universities Press, 1969, p. 151.
3. *Aggrey*, pp. 230, 286; 'Aggrey and Fraser: a Unique Photograph', *African Affairs* 94.374 (1995), pp. 87–9.
4. *Aggrey*, p. 280.
5. *The Bible in the World*, 1928, p. 1.
6. Underhill, E., *Mysticism*, 12th edn, London: Methuen, 1930; *Concerning the Inner Life*; *The Spiritual Life* (1937); etc.
7. Underhill, *Mysticism*, p. 71.
8. Underhill, *Mysticism*, p. 71. By 'New Thought' Underhill meant those, especially occultists, who tried to influence the world by their thought and will.
9. See e.g. Oman, J., *Grace and Personality*, Cambridge: Cambridge University Press, 1925 edn, p. 176.
10. Underhill, *Mysticism*, p. 71.
11. McVeigh, M., *God in Africa: Conceptions of God in African Traditional Religion and Christianity*, Cape Cod, Mass.: Claude Starke, 1974, pp. 175ff.
12. Sundkler, B. G. M., *Bantu Prophets in South Africa*, London: Oxford University Press, 1961, pp. 220ff.
13. 'The Love of God and the Patience of God', p. 17; 'The God of Hope', p. 33; 'The God of Peace', p. 65; 'The God of all Grace', p. 113; and 'The God of Love', p. 161; all in *The Bible in the World*, 1928.
14. *The Glory of the Garden*, p. 13.

15. *Tales of God's Packmen*, London: British and Foreign Bible Society 1928, referred as Packmen.
16. *The Way of the White Fields in the Rhodesias*, London: World Dominion Press, 1928.
17. *White Fields*, p. 48.
18. *White Fields*, p. 152.
19. Taylor, J. V., and Lehmann, D.A., *Christians of the Copperbelt: The Growth of the Church in the Copperbelt*, London: SCM Press, 1961, p. 37.
20. *White Fields*, p. 103.
21. *White Fields*, p. 164.
22. Henkel, R., *Christian Missions in Africa: A Social Geographical Study of the Impact of their Activities in Zambia*, Berlin: Reimer, 1989.
23. Steele, M., 'With Hope Unconquered and Unconquerable: Arthur Shearly Cripps, 1869–1952', in Ranger, T. O., and Weller, J. (eds), *Themes in the Christian History of Central Africa*, London: Heinemann, 1975, pp. 152–74. Also, Steere, Douglas V., *God's Irregular: Arthur Shearly Cripps, A Rhodesian Epic*, London: SPCK, 1973.
24. *White Fields*, Author's Preface.
25. Steele, *With Hope*, p. 153.
26. Steele, *With Hope*, p. 157.
27. *White Fields*, p. vi. These are not specified but were probably on the issues of land and segregation.
28. Steele, *With Hope*, p. 158.
29. Leary, W., *Directory of Primitive Methodist Ministers and their Circuits*, Loughborough: Teamprint, 1990, p. 73; *Minutes and Yearbook of the Methodist Conference*, 1961, p. 232.
30. *Aldersgate Magazine*, 1922, pp. 608–10.
31. Smith photograph collection, SPMMS.
32. Interview with R. Howard-Jones, 27 September 1995.
33. *Exploration in Africa*, pp. 5–11.
34. *Africa* 3 (1930), p. 127.
35. *Exploration in Africa*, p. 9.
36. *Exploration in Africa*, p. 6.
37. *Exploration in Africa*, pp. 10f.
38. Smith, Edwin W., 'An African Odyssey, The Story of Two Porters, Mombai and Mubruki', unpublished MS, 1951.
39. A. Hugon, *The Exploration of Africa, from Cairo to the Cape*, London: Thames & Hudson, 1993, p. 122.
40. Murray, A. V., *The School in the Bush: A Critical Study of the Theory and practice of Education in Africa*, London: Longman, 1929, p. vii.
41. Murray, *The School in the Bush*, p. xiii.
42. Murray, *The School in the Bush*, p. 145.
43. The title, as Smith mentioned 20 years later, was adapted from a book by Oliver Wendell Holmes, *The Professor at the Breakfast Table*, London: J. M. Dent & Co. 1859/1902, p. 40; cf. *Africa* 18, p. 75; Smith referred to this idea

in *Handbook*, p. vii, and *Lower Races*, p. 73; Victor Murray in Murray, A. V., *The School in the Bush*, p. 143, traced the idea to Hegel.

44. This aspect of mission is easily overlooked. David Bosch's almost comprehensive work on missiology, *Transforming Mission* (1991), omits Bible translation, though W. A. Smalley in *Translation as Mission* (1991) gave the matter the attention it deserves.

45. *Shrine*, p. 152.

46. Smalley, *Translation as Mission*, pp. 67f.

47. *Shrine*, p. 193; this was a common view at the time and popularized by A. S. Peake, for example, *The Bible, its Origin, its Significance, and its Abiding Worth*, London: Hodder & Stoughton, 1913, p. 190.

48. *Shrine*, p. 202.

49. *Shrine*, pp. 202–3; the reference to Westcott is hard to track down. Cracknell (1995) could find no reference to it in the bishop's writings but noted that it had been mentioned by C. F. Andrews and wondered whether it could have been oral tradition. Since Andrews regarded 'the talks I had with Bishop Westcott, during our walks over the Yorkshire moors' (Andrews, C. F., *What I Owe to Christ*, London: Hodder & Stoughton, 1932, p. 166) as of great value in his preparation for going to India, this is probable.

50. *The Bible Translator* 4 (1953), p. 143.

51. *Aggrey*, p. 89.

52. *Aggrey*, p. 123.

53. *Aggrey*, p. 224.

54. *Aggrey*, p. 31.

55. See Gifford, Paul, 'Recent Developments in African Christianity', *African Affairs* 93 (1994), pp. 513–34.

56. *Aggrey*, p. 137.

57. *IRM*, 18.70 (April 1929).

58. *Secret*, p. 40.

59. *Secret*, p. 62.

60. *Secret*, p. 63.

61. *Secret*, p. 71.

62. Shaw, R., 'The Invention of African Traditional Religion', *Religion* 20 (1990), p. 341.

63. List of African books left by Carlos Wiles, letter of D. G. Davies to author, 28 October 1995.

64. Perham, M., *African Apprenticeship*, London: Faber, 1974, p. 104.

Chapter 14

1. Edwin Smith, unpublished travel diary, 1929–30, 24 October 1929 (Diary). His diary dates occasionally get out of step with the actual date. I cite Smith's date for the sake of reference.

2. Presumably in *The Cities of St Paul*, London, 1907.

3. Diary, 9 November 1929.

4. Samuel Zwemer (1867–1952) was a missionary to Islam and edited *The*

Muslim World from 1911. He was based in Cairo from 1913 to 1929. Douglas, J. D., *New International Dictionary of the Christian Church*, London: Paternoster, 1974, p. 1072.

5. Diary, 11 November 1929.
6. Bishop Gwynne had been the Bishop of Sudan from 1908. Egypt was included in 1920, *The Church Directory and Almanack 1929*, London: John Hart & Co., 1928, p. 70.
7. Diary, 20 November 1929.
8. Diary, 27 November 1929.
9. Diary, 27 November 1929.
10. Diary, 28 November 1929
11. Diary, 30 November 1929.
12. Diary, 30 November 1929.
13. Diary, 6 December 1929.
14. Diary, 7 December 1929
15. Diary, 7 December 1929.
16. Diary, 7 December 1929.
17. Diary, 11 December 1929
18. Diary, 13 December 1929
19. Diary, Tuesday 18 December 1929; Tuesday was actually 17 December.
20. Diary, 28 December 1929
21. Diary, 31 December 1929.
22. Diary, 31 December 1929.
23. 'The Civilisation of Africa' (1930), in *From Cape to Cairo*, 1982 Railway Video. A few minutes of this film shows vividly the railway and steamboat journey between Khartoum and Cairo.
24. Diary, 4 January 1930; cf. Smith, Edwin W. (ed.), *African Ideas of God*, London: Edinburgh House Press, 1950, p. 1.
25. Diary, 2 January 1930.
26. Diary, 6 January 1930; *The Bible in the World*, 1930, p. 63.
27. Diary, 8 January 1930.
28. Diary, 12 January 1930.
29. Diary, 25 January 1930.
30. *The Impossible*, p. 54.
31. Roe, *History*, p. 247.
32. Roe, *History*, p. 247.
33. van der Geest, S., 'Anthropologists and Missionaries: Brothers under the Skin', *Man* n.s. 25 (1990), p. 588.
34. 'Anthropologists versus Missionaries', in Stipe, C. E., *Current Anthropology* 21.2 (April 1980), p. 165.
35. Powdermaker, H., *Stranger and Friend: The Way of an Anthropologist*, London: Secker & Warburg, 1967, p. 42.
36. Lucy Mair, 'Comments on "Anthropologists versus Missionaries"', in Stipe, C. E., *Current Anthropology*, 21.2 (April 1980), p. 172.
37. *Methodist Recorder*, 15 May 1930, p. 20.

38. *JRAI*, 1927, p. 2; 1928, p. ii; 1929, p. ii.
39. Letter to author from I. Schapera, 8 August 1992.
40. Presidential Address, 1934, 'Anthropology and the Practical Man', *JRAI* 64 (1934), p. xxxi.
41. *Man*, 1932, p. 119; *JRAI*, 1932, p. v.
42. 'Anthropology and the Practical Man', pp xiii-xxxvii.
43. 'Anthropology and the Practical Man', p. xv.
44. 'Anthropology and the Practical Man', p. xvi.
45. 'Anthropology and the Practical Man', p. xxi.
46. 'Anthropology and the Practical Man', pp. xxvif.
47. 'Anthropology and the Practical Man', p. xxvii.
48. 'Anthropology and the Practical Man', p. xxvii.
49. 'Anthropology and the Practical Man', p. xxxi.
50. 'Anthropology and the Practical Man', p. xxxi.
51. 'Anthropology and the Practical Man', p. xxxvii.
52. Goody, J., *The Expansive Moment: Anthropology in Britain and Africa 1918–1970*, Cambridge: Cambridge University Press, 1995, p. 74.
53. *Man*, 1934, §169.
54. *Man*, 1934, §169.
55. *Man*, 1934, §169.
56. *Man*, 1934, §169.
57. *Africa* 15 (1945), p. 89.
58. Letter to author from Sir Raymond Firth, 28 June 1994.
59. 'Presidential Address 1935: Africa: What do we know of it?' *JRAI*, 1935, p. 6.
60. 'Presidential Address 1935', p. 17.
61. 'Presidential Address 1935', p. 18.
62. 'Presidential Address 1935', p. 38.
63. 'Presidential Address 1935', p. 47.
64. 'Presidential Address 1935', p. 58.
65. 'Presidential Address 1935', p. 70.
66. 'Presidential Address 1935', p. 78.
67. 'Presidential Address 1935', p. 78.
68. 'Presidential Address 1935', p. 81.
69. Macmillan, H., 'Return to the Malungwana Drift', *African Affairs* 94 (1995), p. 62.
70. Colson E., and Gluckman M. (eds), *Seven Tribes of British Central Africa*, London: Oxford University Press, 1951, p. ix.
71. The achievements of anthropology in Africa are described in Goody, *Expansive Moment*, pp. 87–117.
72. For example, Oliver, R., *The African Experience*, London: Pimlico, 1991, pp. 1ff.
73. Goody, *Expansive Moment*, p. 117.

Chapter 15

1. *The Soul of the Bantu* (1928); *Nature Worship and Taboo* (1932).
2. This can be demonstrated by sampling the literature on comparative religion

published since 1925; *A Short Comparative History of Religions* by T. H. Robinson (1926/1951) had a few passing references to Africa. Africa was not considered in F. H. Smith *The Elements of Comparative Theology* (1937), E. O. James *Comparative Religion* (1938) and A. C. Bouquet, *Comparative Religion* (1941). The later, but patchy, acceptance of African religion for study will be examined when *African Ideas of God* (1950) is reviewed.

3. Smith, Edwin W., *African Beliefs and Christian Faith*, London: United Society for Christian Literature, 1936, p. 26; referred to as *ABCF*.

4. *ABCF*, p. 11.

5. Other possible candidates would be Cullen Young and Dr Westermann.

6. Basic English was a form of English recently devised to help those whose mother-tongue was not English. See below.

7. *ABCF*, pp. 52f.

8. *ABCF*, p. 80.

9. The terms 'African theology' and 'African Christian theology' should be distinguished. Smith and others have pointed out that Africans believed in God before Christianity arrived. 'African Christian theology' has usually described Christian theology done in an African style.

10. *ABCF*, p. 155.

11. *ABCF*, p. 149. 'Fulfilment theology' is discussed in Sharpe, E. J., *Not to Destroy but to Fulfil: The Contribution of J. N. Farquhar to Protestant Missionary Thought in India before 1914*, Uppsala: Almqvist & Wiksells Boktryckeri AB, 1965; Malcolm McVeigh analysed Smith's concept of fulfilment in *God in Africa*, Cape Cod: Claude Starke, 1974, pp. 157–62, and thought that Christianity offered an answer to the African question of God's absence. However, Smith regarded this as a misconception and held that God is actually very near and has not gone away, *ABCF*, p. 157.

12. *ABCF*, p. 172.

13. *ABCF*, p. 189.

14. *ABCF*, p. 192.

15. *ABCF*, p. 192.

16. Schofeleers, M., 'Black and African Theology in Southern Africa: A Controversy Re-examined', *Journal of Religion in Africa*, June 1988, p. 120.

17. Ward, K., 'Even God Is Not Wise Enough . . . ', *Epworth Review*, January 1994, p. 95.

18. Ward, 'Even God . . . ', p. 95.

19. Setiloane, G., 'Where Are We in African Theology', in Appiah-Kubi, K., and Torres, S. (eds), *African Theology en Route*, Maryknoll, New York: Orbis, 1979, p. 60.

20. Kato, Byang H., *Theological Pitfalls in Africa*, Kisumu, Kenya: Evangel, 1975, p. 155.

21. McVeigh, *God in Africa*, p. 162.

22. Kraemer, H., *The Christian Message in a Non-Christian World*, London: Edinburgh House Press, 1938, p. 338.

23. McVeigh, *God in Africa*, p. 83.

24. Review of McVeigh's *God in Africa* by Welbourn, F. B., *Journal of Religion in Africa*, 1974, p. 141. Welbourn liked to point out exceptions to any generalizations about Africa, especially about God. He emphasized social studies, and one would have thought that he would be more in sympathy with Edwin Smith.

25. Parratt, J. (ed.), *A Reader in African Christian Theology*, London: SPCK, 1987, p. 149.

26. In Parratt, *Reader*, pp. 29–35.

27. Included in Parratt, *Reader*, pp. 58–66.

28. See bibliographies in Gibellini, R. (ed.), *Paths of African Theology*, London: SCM Press, 1994, and Martey, M., *African Theology: Inculturation and Liberation*, Maryknoll, New York: Orbis, 1993.

29. Roe, James Moulton, *A History of The British and Foreign Bible Society, 1905–54*, London: British and Foreign Bible Society, 1965, p. 391.

30. 'A Tentative Grammar of the Efe or Mbuti Language', p. 1, SPBSC.

31. Luck, A., *African Saint*, London: SCM Press, 1963, pp. 137f.; it seems that this was the Efe translation Edwin was referring to, whatever Rumbaba or Mbuti might be.

32. Efe–English Vocabulary, SPBSC.

33. 'A Tentative Grammar of the Efe or Mbuti Language', p. 23, SPBSC.

34. 'The Language of Pygmies of the Ituri', *JRAS* 37 (October 1938), pp. 464–70.

35. In Wilkes, Arthur, and Lovatt, Joseph, *Mow Cop and the Camp Meeting Movement: Sketches of Primitive Methodism*, Leominster: Orphans' Printing Press, 1942, p. 114. I contacted the Canadian College but was unable to discover exactly when and why he received the degree.

36. Smalley, W. A., *Translation as Mission*, Macon: Mercer, 1991, pp. 67f.

37. ESC minutes, 9 October 1935, Bible Society Archives.

38. Myers, A., *Basic and the Teaching of English in India*, Bombay: The Times of India Press, 1938, p. 51.

39. ESC minutes, 4 February 1936, Bible Society Archives.

40. Note at front of *Bible in Basic English*, 1949; a notice for *The Basic Bible* in Myers, A., *Basic and the Teaching of English in India*, p. 353, lists W. R. Matthews, Dean of St Paul's, Professors W. O. E. Oesterley and T. H. Robinson, along with Smith and others, in supporting S. H. Hooke in this project.

41. Bruce, F. F., *The English Bible*, London: Lutterworth, 1961, p. 174.

42. Smith, Edwin W., *The Basic St. John*, London: Trench, Trubner & Co., 1938, p. 17; *The Bible in Basic English*, Cambridge: Cambridge University Press, 1949, p. 770, is word for word the same as Smith's version, along with verses 12, 13 and 15–18.

43. Report of Visit to India, p. 1, SPBSC.

44. EWS to Bible Society, 30 January 1939, SPBSC.

45. Diary, 1938–9, vol. i, p. 9, SPBSC.

46. Diary, 1938–9, vol. i, p. 38, SPBSC.

47. Diary, 1938–9, vol. i, p. 50, SPBSC.

48. Diary, 1938–9, vol. i, p. 69, SPBSC.

49. Cracknell, K., *Justice, Courtesy and Love: Five Early Scottish Contributions to*

the Theology of Inter-Faith Dialogue, St Colm's Public Lecture, 1991, p. 173; Cracknell has a short section on Andrews, pp. 173–80; also Chaturvedi, B., and Sykes, M., *Charles Freer Andrews*, New York: Harper, 1950; Cox, Jeffrey, 'C. F. Andrews and the Failure of the Modern Missionary Movement', in Mews, S., (ed.), *Modern Religious Rebels*, London: Epworth, 1993, pp. 226–44. Andrews wrote an autobiography, *What I Owe to Christ*, London: Hodder & Stoughton, 1932, and numerous other works.

50. Diary, 1938–9, vol. i, p. 70, SPBSC.
51. Hogg, W. R., *Ecumenical Foundations*, New York: Harper, 1952, p. 292.
52. Diary, 1938–9, vol. i, p. 76, SPBSC.
53. Diary, 1938–9, vol. i, p. 140, SPBSC.
54. John R. Mott (1865–1955), 'the pioneer of the modern ecumenical movement', Rouse, R., and Neill, S. C. (eds), *A History of the Ecumenical Movement, 1517–1948*, London: SPCK, 1967, p. 331.
55. Diary, 1938–9, vol. i, p. 159, SPBSC.
56. Diary, 1938–9, vol. i, pp. 160, 161, SPBSC.
57. Diary, 1938–9, vol. i, p. 178, SPBSC.
58. Diary, 1938–9, vol. ii, p. 50, SPBSC.
59. Diary, 1938–9, vol. iii, p. 31, SPBSC.
60. Report of Visit to India, p. 59.
61. Report of Visit to India, p. 9.
62. Report of Visit to India, p. 10.
63. Report of Visit to India, p. 39.
64. Report of Visit to India, p. 154
65. Roe, *History*, p. 367.
66. Smith, Edwin W., 'Land in Kenya', *JRAS* 35 (July 1936), pp. 246–50.
67. Smith, Edwin W., 'The South African Protectorates', *JRAS* 37 (April 1938), pp. 199–205.
68. Smith, 'Land in Kenya', p. 249.
69. Smith, 'South African Protectorates', pp. 199–205.
70. Smith, 'South African Protectorates', p. 205.
71. *Mabilles*, pp. 73–4.
72. *Mabilles*, p. 9.

Chapter 16

1. C. P. Groves, (1887–1973) was from the PM tradition and returned from the USA to Kingsmead, the Missionary Training College in Birmingham, where he had been a tutor since 1926. One of the few PM missionaries from an academic background, Groves had been an outstanding missionary-educator in Nigeria from 1911 to 1924. His immense scholarship earned him the title, 'Eusebius of Africa'. He later wrote a monumental 4-volume history, *The Planting of Christianity in Africa* (1948–58); *Minutes of the Methodist Conference*, 1973, pp. 143–4.
2. EWS to Capen, 20 June 1939, Smith Papers, Hartford, 21637. Cited below as SPH with number of paper.

3. Agnes Donohugh was an anthropologist as well as being involved in the missionary enterprise; List of Members of the American Anthropological Association in *American Anthropologist* 43 (1941), p. 140.

4. SPH, 21645.

5. EWS to M. Pitt, 13 June 1940, SPH, 21653.

6. SPH, 21708.

7. Diary, 31 May 1940.

8. Diary, 10 June 1940.

9. Diary, 13 June 1940.

10. *Shrine*, pp. 110f.

11. Diary, 25 June 1940.

12. Diary, 5 July 1940.

13. Diary, Sunday 14 July 1940; Churchill in his speech on that day said ' "This is the War of the Unknown Warrior, but let all strive, without failing in faith or in duty, and the dark curse of Hitler will be lifted from our age." ' Quoted in Gilbert, M., *The Second World War*, London: Fontana, 1990, p. 110.

14. Diary, 17/18 July 1940.

15. Diary, 21 July 1940.

16. 'Association and Assimilation in the Christian Mission', *IRM* 30 (1941), pp. 324–36.

17. *IRM* 30 (1941), p. 329.

18. *IRM* 30 (1941), p. 331. He did note a few examples of Indian styles when he went to India.

19. *IRM* 30 (1941), p. 331.

20. *IRM* 30 (1941), p. 336.

21. Smith, *Knowing the African*, p. 18.

22. Smith, *Knowing the African*, p. 18.

23. Smith, *Knowing the African*, p. 20; cf. 1934 Presidential Address, see above, ch. 14.

24. Till, B., *The Churches Search for Unity*, Harmondsworth: Penguin, 1972, p. 198.

25. Smith, *Knowing the African*, p. 26, quoting Troeltsch.

26. Smith, *Knowing the African*, p. 28.

27. Smith, *Knowing the African*, p. 43.

28. Smith, *Knowing the African*, p. 120.

29. Smith, *Knowing the African*, p. 140.

30. Smith, *Knowing the African*, p. 189.

31. *UNESCO General History of Africa*, vol. viii: *Africa Since 1935*, ed. Mazrui, A. A., Oxford: Heinemann, 1993, pp. 553–81.

32. Smith, *Knowing the African*, p. 192.

33. Smith, *Knowing the African*, p. 192.

34. Dr Loram was one of the Phelps-Stokes commissioners in 1920–1 and 1924. Smith had consulted him about Aggrey's visit to South Africa and, as we have seen, he met Smith in September 1939.

35. Diary, 5 September 1942.

36. Diary, 6 September 1942.

37. Diary, 7 September 1942. B. W.; i.e. Booker T. Washington, the founder and first principal of Tuskegee.
38. Diary, 7 September 1942.
39. Diary, 8 September 1942.
40. Southern blacks had the franchise for nearly 25 years after the end of slavery. From 1890 this was drastically reduced. In Louisana 99 per cent of black voters lost the right to vote between 1897 and 1904; Giliomee, H., 'The Non-Racial Franchise and Afrikaner and Coloured Identities, 1910–1994', *African Affairs* 94 (1995), pp. 199f; Quarles, B., *The Negro in the Making of America*, New York: Collier, 1964, p. 145.
41. K. S. Latourette refers bibliographically to Work, Monroe N., as editor *Negro Year Book*, 1931–1932, Tuskegee, 1931. Latourette, K. S., *Christianity in a Revolutionary Age*, vol. v, New York: Harper & Row, 1962, p. 551. W. E. B. Du Bois referred to 'Monroe Work, now at Tuskegee Institute', in *Dusk of Dawn* (1940), printed in *Du Bois*, Literary Classics of the United States, 1986, pp. 615f.
42. K. S. Latourette refers bibliographically to Richardson, Harry V., *Dark Glory. A Picture of the the Church among Negroes in the Rural South*, New York, 1947, cites it several times and describes it as 'An able survey.' Latourette, *Christianity in a Revolutionary Age*, vol. v, p. 547; citations, pp. 55–8.
43. Diary, 11 September 1942.
44. Diary, 13 September 1942.
45. Diary, 13 September 1942.
46. Diary, 13 September 1942.
47. Diary, 13 September 1942.
48. Diary, 16 September 1942.
49. Diary, 16 September 1942.
50. Diary, 17 September 1942.
51. Diary, 17 September 1942.
52. Diary, 17 September 1942; see *BM*, p. 123.
53. Smith, Edwin W., 'A School for Translators', *IRM*, July 1945, pp. 243–52.
54. Smith, 'School for Translators', p. 250.
55. Smith, 'School for Translators', p. 252.
56. Letter to author from B. Booth, 6 March 1993.
57. Letter to author from B. Booth, 6 March 1993.
58. Letter to author from B. Booth, 6 March 1993.
59. EWS to Barstow, 24 February 1943, SPH, 21687.
60. EWS to Barstow, 24 February 1943, SPH, 21687.
61. May 1943, SPH, 21708.
62. Diary, 9 June 1943.
63. R. W. Logan was a major African American scholar and wrote *The Negro in American Life and Thought: The Nadir, 1877–1901*, New York, 1954. He edited, with Michael R. Winston, *Dictionary of American Negro Biography*, New York, 1982.
64. Diary, 17 June 1943.
65. W. E. B. Du Bois (1868–1963), the famous black American intellectual who

had been very influential in the National Association for the Advancement of Colored People (NAACP) as well as sociological study.

66. Diary, 21 June 1943.
67. See *ISP*, vol. i, p. 375.
68. Quotations in this section come from the Fisk booklet.
69. Reported in *Africa*, 1945, p. 144. American anthropologists still relied heavily on British studies of Africa. They were largely occupied in researching Native American cultures on their own continent. This can be seen by consulting the Bibliography in Goldenweiser, A., *Anthropology: An Introduction to Primitive Culture*, London: Harrap, 1937, pp. 529–37; *American Anthropologist* 44 (1942), pp. 527ff., reviewed 'Anthropology Offerings in American Undergraduate Colleges' and showed, p. 529, that there were 4 courses on Africa, 2 on African languages and 70 on American Indians.

Chapter 17

1. Quotations in this section are from: EWS to M. Pitt, 8 November 1944, SPH, 21702.
2. *Africa*, 1945, pp. 88f.; *JRAS*, 1945, p. 8. See also Robinson, K., 'The Society's Medals', *African Affairs* 85.338 (January 1986). Other recipients were R. S. Rattray (1925), Alice Werner (1931) and Margery Perham (1941).
3. *Africa*, 1945, p. 89.
4. *Africa*, 1945, p. 89.
5. *Africa*, 1945, p. 89.
6. *JRAS*, 1945, p. 8.
7. *JRAS*, 1945, p. 8.
8. *JRAS*, 1945, p. 8.
9. *Africa* 18 (October 1948), p. 241.
10. *Africa* 16 (1946), pp. 199ff; cf. Smith, Edwin W. (ed.), *African Ideas of God*, London: Edinburgh House Press, 1950, pp. 17ff.
11. Ackerman, R., *J. G. Frazer, His Life and Work*, Cambridge: Cambridge University Press, 1987, p. 288.
12. *Plans and – People!*, London: Lutterworth, 1948, p. 21.
13. *Plans and – People!*, p. 55.
14. *Plans and – People!*, pp. 62–3.
15. *Plans and – People!*, p. 25.
16. See Evans-Pritchard, E. E., *Social Anthropology*, London: Cohen & West, 1951, pp. 109ff; Kuper, A., *Anthropology and Anthropologists: The Modern British School*, London: Routledge, 1983, pp. 112ff; Goody, J., *The Expansive Moment: Anthropology in Britain and Africa 1918–1970*, Cambridge: Cambridge University Press, 1995, pp. 77ff.
17. Smith kept detailed notes of people he met, places visited and things he did. This record filled over five notebooks, more than 200,000 words or nearly 1,000 words per day.
18. Diary 1946–7, vol. i, p. 5.
19. *Who was Who, 1951–1960*, London, 1961; Sampson, R., *They came to*

Northern Rhodesia, Lusaka, 1956, p. 32.

20. *JRAI*, roll of members in issues after 1915.
21. Minute book of RAS
22. Diary 1946–7, vol. i, p. 29.
23. Diary 1946–7, vol. i, p. 42.
24. Diary 1946–7, vol. i, p. 131; Doke was one of the leading experts in Bantu languages. An article by Doke, 'The Basis of Bantu Literature', appeared in *Africa* 18 (1948), pp. 284–301.
25. Ashton's research interests included Lesotho; an article by him, 'Democracy and Indirect Rule', concentrated on Lesotho and Botswana and appeared in *Africa*, October 1947. He published a book, *The Basuto*, London: Oxford University Press, 1952.
26. Diary 1946–7, vol. i, p. 141.
27. Diary 1946–7, vol. i, p. 141.
28. Diary 1946–7, vol. i, p. 142.
29. Diary 1946–7, vol. i, p. 146.
30. Diary 1946–7, vol. i, p. 146.
31. Diary 1946–7, vol. i, p. 146.
32. Diary 1946–7, vol. i, p. 148.
33. Huddleston, T., *Naught For Your Comfort*, London: Collins, 1956, p. 123.
34. Mandela, N. R., *Long Walk to Freedom: The Autobiography of Nelson Mandela*, London: Abacus, 1995, pp. 178–9.
35. Diary 1946–7, vol. ii, p. 14. See Chapter 16.
36. Diary 1946–7, vol. ii, p. 27; Wood, H. G., *John William Hoyland of Kingsmead*, London: SPCK, 1931. Innes Gumede is shown in a photograph of Kingsmead Group of 1926, opposite p. 216.
37. Diary 1946–7, vol. ii, p. 104; also Smith, *African Ideas*, p. 102.
38. Diary 1946–7, vol. iii, p. 1.
39. Diary 1946–7, vol. iii, p. 2, 15 February 1947.
40. Diary 1946–7, vol. iii, p. 3; see also Mandela, *Long Walk*, p. 158.
41. Diary 1946–7, vol. iii, p. 3.
42. Diary 1946–7, vol. iii, p. 3.
43. Diary 1946–7, vol. iii, p. 4.
44. Diary 1946–7, vol. iii, p. 128, 1 March.
45. Diary 1946–7, vol. iii, p. 144, 3 March.
46. Diary 1946–7, vol. iii, p. 145, 3 March.
47. Diary 1946–7, vol. iii, p. 161, 6 March.
48. Diary 1946–7, vol. iii, p. 195, 10 March.
49. Perham, Margery, *African Apprenticeship*, London: Faber, 1974, p. 53; D. D. T. Jabavu has been thoroughly studied recently by Catherine Higgs, *The Ghost of Equality: The Public Lives of D. D. T. Jabavu of South Africa, 1885–1959*, Athens, Ohio: Ohio University Press, 1997.
50. Diary 1946–7, vol. iii, p. 195, 10 March 1947.
51. Diary 1946–7, vol. iii, p. 196, 10 March 1947.
52. Diary 1946–7, vol. iv, p. 8, 12 March 1947.

53. Mandela, *Long Walk*, pp. 45f.
54. Garrett, A. E. F. (ed.), *South African Methodism: Her Missionary Witness*, Cape Town: Methodist Publishing House, n.d., p. viii.
55. Diary 1946–7, vol. iv, p. 8, 12 March 1947.
56. Diary 1946–7, vol. iv, pp. 8, 9, 12 March 1947.
57. Diary 1946–7, vol. iv, p. 15, 13 March 1947.
58. She contributed a paper, 'Nyakyusa Kinship', for Radcliffe-Brown, A. R., and Forde, D. (eds), *African Systems of Kinship and Marriage*, London: Oxford University Press, 1950, pp. 111–39.
59. Diary 1946–7, vol. iv, pp. 18, 19, 13 March 1947. Smith took up the theme of African Symbolism in his Henry Myers Lecture five years later.
60. Diary 1946–7, vol. iv, p. 37.
61. Diary 1946–7, vol. iv, p. 57, 24 March 1947.
62. Diary 1946–7, vol. iv, p. 60, 24 March 1947.
63. Diary 1946–7, vol. iv, p. 60, 24 March 1947.
64. Diary 1946–7, vol. iv, p. 62, 24 March 1947.
65. Diary 1946–7, vol. iv, p. 65, 24 March 1947.
66. Diary 1946–7, vol. iv, p. 66, 24 March 1947.
67. Diary 1946–7, vol. iv, p. 67, 24 March 1947.
68. Diary 1946–7, vol. iv, p. 101, 29 March 1947.
69. *Africa* XVII, 1947, 282.
70. Diary 1946–7, vol. iv, p. 112, 1 April 1947. Aggrey had addressed a meeting at Umtata, *Aggrey*, pp. 178ff.
71. Diary 1946–7, vol. iv, p. 112, 1 April 1947.
72. Diary 1946–7, vol. iv, p. 122f., 3 April 1947.
73. Diary 1946–7, vol. iv, p. 125, 3 April 1947.
74. Diary 1946–7, vol. iv, p. 126, 3 April 1947.
75. Diary 1946–7, vol. iv, p. 134, 6 April 1947.
76. Diary 1946–7, vol. iv, p. 135, 6 April 1947.
77. See Goody, *Expansive Moment*, pp. 88ff.
78. *African Studies* 8.2 (June 1949), p. 56.
79. Diary 1946–7, vol. iv, p. 168, April 19 1947.
80. Telephone interview with Revd Fergus Macpherson, 1 December 1995.
81. Diary 1946–7, vol. iv, p. 190, 23 April 1947. Merfyn's father was one of the secretaries of the Bible Society and his brothers James and David also served in Zambia.
82. Letter to author from Mrs Muriel Stamp, 15 July 1994.
83. Diary 1946–7, vol. v, p. 1, 26 April 1947.
84. Diary 1946–7, vol. v, p. 9, 26 April 1947.
85. Letter to author from Mrs Muriel Stamp, 15 July 1994.
86. Diary 1946–7, vol. v, p. 9, 27 April 1947.
87. Diary 1946–7, vol. v, p. 12, 27 April 1947.
88. Nabulyato became Speaker of the Zambian Parliament.
89. Diary 1946–7, vol. v, pp. 16–17, 28 April 1947.
90. Diary 1946–7, vol. v, pp. 24–5, 30 April 1947.
91. Diary 1946–7, vol. v, p. 26.

92. Diary 1946–7, vol. v, p. 29.
93. Diary 1946–7, vol. v, p. 31, 30 April 1947; see *ISP*, vol. ii, p. 312, 'the buttocks of a friend are made to sit upon'.
94. Diary 1946–7, vol. v, pp. 32–3, 30 April 1947.
95. Diary 1946–7, vol. v, p. 33, 30 April 1947. Smith was bald when he served in Zambia over 30 years earlier.
96. Diary 1946–7, vol. v, p. 50, 3 May 1947.
97. Diary 1946–7, vol. v, p. 51, 3 May 1947.
98. Diary 1946–7, vol. v, p. 58, 4 May 1947.
99. Diary 1946–7, vol. v, p. 64, 5 May 1947; A. M. Jones contributed an article on 'The Kalimba of the Lala Tribe, Northern Rhodesia', *Africa* 20 (1950), pp. 324ff.
100. Diary 1946–7, vol. v, p. 77, 9 May 1947.
101. Diary 1946–7, vol. v, p. 79, 10 May 1947.
102. Diary 1946–7, vol. v, p. 92, 13 May 1947. He may have made another visit in the mid-1950s.
103. *JRAI* 75.2 (1947), p. 98. Dr Audrey Richards used this paper in her article in *African Systems of Kinship and Marriage*; Richards, A. I., 'Some Types of Family Structure amongst the Central Bantu', in Radcliffe-Brown, A. R., and Forde, Daryll (eds), *African Systems of Kinship and Marriage*, London: Oxford University Press, 1950, p. 236.
104. *African Studies*, March 1949, pp. 1–9; June 1949, pp. 53–61.
105. Johnson, Tom, 'A Vanishing People?', unpublished draft, 1995, shows that the Ila continued without much diminution despite these anxieties. Medical treatment of venereal disease contributed to a higher fertility rate.
106. Diary 1946–7, vol. v, p. 129, 1 May 1947.
107. Diary 1946–7, vol. vi, p. 4, 28 May 1947. I wrote to Professor Schapera, but he could not remember any of the meetings reported by Smith.
108. Diary 1946–7, vol. vi, p. 51, 10 June 1947.
109. *Epworth Review*, January 1995, p. 31.
110. Smith, Edwin W., Foreword to Parrinder, G., *West African Religion*, London: Epworth, 1949, p. xii.
111. For example, 'I would like to pay tribute, as Tom Harris himself did, to the memory of Dr Edwin W. Smith, who gave personal encouragement to us both.' Harris, W. T., and Parrinder, E. G., *The Christian Approach to the Animist*, London: Edinburgh House Press, 1960, p. 8. Also 'Dr Edwin Smith, the greatest authority on African religion in this country', p. 26.
112. Telephone conversation with Mrs M. Bell of Chesham, 4 March 1996. Matsi's husband had been killed in an aircraft crash in 1945.

Chapter 18

1. Smith, Edwin W., *Great Lion of Bechuanaland: The Life and Times of Roger Price, Missionary*, London: Independent Press, 1957 (*Price*), pp. xf.
2. Diary, 28 October 1948, SPMMS; for this diary references are to date only.
3. William Illsley (1895–1975) was from a Primitive Methodist family. He and

his wife had settled in South Africa in 1922 and he would become President of the Methodist Church in South Africa in 1956. Both became vigorous opponents of apartheid and promoted African rights. Letter to author from Mrs C. Harris, 23 March 1996; *Methodist Recorder*, 15 February 1996; information in Circuit Plan of Rosebank Circuit, Cape Town, August to October 1972, held by Mrs Harris; two cuttings from *Cape Times*: (a) from Mrs C. Harris, (b) in author's collection.

4. Diary, 3 November 1948; Smith used the term 'Nationalists', but to save confusion with other nationalist movements I have used National Party, as the Afrikaner nationalists became known.
5. Diary, 3 November 1948.
6. Diary, 4, 5 November 1948.
7. Diary, 10 November 1948.
8. Diary, 20 November 1948.
9. Diary, 15 December 1948; see *BM*.
10. Diary, 24 December 1948.
11. Diary, 24 December 1948.
12. Diary, 28 December 1948.
13. Paton, A., *Hofmeyr*, Cape Town: Oxford University Press, 1964, p. 438.
14. Matthews, Z. K., *Freedom for my People*, Claremont, South Africa: David Philip, 1983, p. 176; Mandela, Nelson, *Long Walk to Freedom: The Autobiography of Nelson Mandela*, London: Abacus, 1995, p. 199.
15. Diary, 28 December 1948; when Dent resigned, Matthews was still not made Principal, Matthews, *Freedom*, p. 192
16. Diary, 28 December 1948.
17. Diary, 28 December 1948.
18. Matthews, *Freedom*, p. 149.
19. Diary, 29 January 1949; J. T. was an older half-brother, John T., who was now dead.
20. Diary, 29 January 1949.
21. Diary, 31 January 1949. This would have been one of Smith's younger brothers, see tribute to his mother, *c.*January 1934, SPMMS.
22. Diary, 1 March 1949.
23. Diary, 1 March 1949.
24. Diary, 6 March 1949.
25. Mazobere, C. C. G., 'Christian Theology of Mission', in Banana, C. S. (ed.), *A Century of Methodism in Zimbabwe 1891–1991*, Harare, 1991, p. 167.
26. Diary, 7 March 1949.
27. *BM*, p. 103. Hoernlé gave the previous Phelps-Stokes Lectures in 1939, published as *South African Native Policy and the Liberal Spirit*, Johannesburg: Witwatersrand University Press, 1945, though this was not the source of the 'muddle-headedness' remark.
28. Diary, 16 March 1949.
29. Diary, 16 March 1949.
30. Diary, 16 March 1949.
31. Diary, 14 June 1949.

32. Smuts, J. C., *Jan Christian Smuts*, London: Cassell, 1952, p. 520.

33. Diary, 16 June 1949.

34. Kalu, Ogbu U., in Appiah-Kubi, Kofi, and Torres, Sergio (eds), *African Theology en Route*, Maryknoll, New York: Orbis Books, 1979, p. 14, described one work as 'a panegyric of the missionaries', then in a related foot-note on p. 21 writes, 'See also E. W. Smith, *The Blessed Missionaries*.'

35. *BM*, p. v.

36. Chapter title in *The Everlasting Doors*, BFBS *Popular Annual Report* for 1926.

37. Baker, R. S., *American Chronicle*, New York: C. Scribner's Sons, 1945, p. 133.

38. Cracknell, K., *Towards a New Relationship*, London: Epworth, 1986, pp. 118ff.

39. *BM*, p. 6.

40. *BM*, p. 22.

41. van Beek, Walter E. A., and Blakely, Thomas D., 'Introduction', in Blakely, Thomas D., van Beek, Walter E. A., and Thomson, Dennis L. (eds), *Religion in Africa*, London: James Currey, 1994.

42. Sundkler, B. G., *Bantu Prophets in South Africa*, London: Oxford University Press, 1948.

43. *BM*, p. 120.

44. *BM*, p. 135.

45. *BM*, p. 142.

46. Mandela, *Long Walk*, p. 438.

47. Fortes, M., and Evans-Pritchard, E. E., *African Political Systems*, London: Oxford University Press, 1940, and Radcliffe-Brown, A. R., and Forde, Daryll (eds), *African Systems of Kinship and Marriage*, London: Oxford University Press, 1950.

48. Smith, *African Ideas*, p. 17.

49. Smith, *African Ideas*, p. 19.

50. Smith, *African Ideas*, p. 29.

51. In Gollwitzer, H. (ed.), *Karl Barth's Church Dogmatics*, selections, Edinburgh: T. & T. Clark, 1961, p. 50; from IV/1, p. 45.

52. Smith, *African Ideas*, p. 32.

53. *African Affairs* 49 (July 1950), p. 353.

54. Parrinder, E. G., *Religion in Africa*, Harmondsworth: Penguin, 1969, p. 39.

55. Smith, *African Ideas*, pp. 78–134.

56. Smith, *African Ideas*, p. 122; cf. *Moffat*, p. 109.

57. Setiloane, G. M., *The Image of God among the Sotho-Tswana*, Rotterdam: Balkema, 1976, p. 79.

58. Setiloane, *Image of God*, p. 81.

59. Smith, *African Ideas*, p. 133.

60. Smith, *African Ideas*, p. 133, quoting Junod, H. A., *The Life of a South African Tribe*, London: Macmillan, 1927, p. 449.

61. Review by Welbourn, F. B., of McVeigh, M., *God in Africa* (1974), in *Journal of Religion in Africa*, 1974, pp. 140ff. See above, Chapter 15.

62. For example, Hodgson, Janet, *The God of the Xhosa*, Cape Town: Oxford University Press, 1982, p. 96; Setiloane, *Image of God*, pp. 79f., 270f.

Chapter 19

1. Smith, Edwin W., 'An African Odyssey', unpublished manuscript, 1952, Introduction, p. 2, SPMMS.

2. 'African Symbolism', Henry Myers Lecture, *JRAI* 82 (1952), pp. 13–37. Given at the Royal Anthropological Institute on 27 May 1952.

3. See Dante, *Paradiso*, XXXIII.

4. Smith, 'African Symbolism', p. 28.

5. Turner, V. W., 'Betwixt and Between: The Liminal Period', in *Rites of Passage*, 1964. Reprinted in Turner, V. W., *The Forest of Symbols: Aspects of Ndembu Ritual*, New York: Cornell University Press, 1967.

6. Smith, 'African Symbolism', p. 35.

7. Edwin Smith to Mrs Capen, 22 December 1952, SPH, 21702.

8. Obituary by Clement Doke, 'Dr Edwin W. Smith', *African Studies* 17.2 (1958), p. 117.

9. Diary, 6 January 1954.

10. Diary, 17 January 1954.

11. Letter to author from Mrs Priscilla Hannam, 15 January 1995.

12. Smith's cutting has 30/1/52 written on it. However, the days and dates of events on the reverse of the same cutting show that this must have been 1954.

13. *Natal Mercury*, 30 January 1954.

14. See Garrett, A. E. F. (ed.), *South African Methodism: Her Missionary Witness*, Cape Town: Methodist Publishing House, n.d., pp. 133ff., where Sudbury advocated cooperation and unity between churches and peoples.

15. See Marwick, Max (ed.), *Witchcraft and Sorcery: Selected Readings* 2nd edn, Harmondsworth: Penguin, 1982, pp. 54ff. for the text of lecture.

16. This is how Smith understood the situation. I have heard that Smith went to Africa again in 1955–6. Although I suspect that informants were thinking of his earlier visits, it remains a possibility.

17. Letter to writer from J. V. Taylor, 20 March 1993.

18. Letter to writer from J. V. Taylor, 20 March 1993.

19. Taylor, John V., *Christianity and Politics in Africa* (1957); *The Growth of the Church in Buganda* (1958); *Christians of the Copperbelt*, with Dorothea Lehmann (1961); and *The Primal Vision* (1963).

20. Letter to writer from J. V. Taylor, 20 March 1993.

21. Letter to writer from G. Parrinder, 30 May 1992.

22. Letter to writer from Revd Merfyn Temple, 17 June 1992.

23. Quotations from letter to writer from Mrs J. Smedley, 19 November 1992.

24. Interview with Revd and Mrs H. P. Lyddon, 26 September 1998.

25. *Africa* 28 (April 1958), p. 171.

26. *Africa* 28 (April 1958), p. 168.

27. I received this information in 1999 from the Revd Dennis Fowler of Sandwich.

28. *One Hundred and Fifty-Third Report of the British and Foreign Bible Society for the Year Ending December 31st 1957*, p. 15.

Chapter 20

1. Colson, E., 'Introduction', *ISP*, 1968 edn, p. 4.
2. Goody, J., *The Expansive Moment: Anthropology in Britain and Africa 1918–1970*, Cambridge: Cambridge University Press, 1995, pp. 109ff.
3. Harris, W. T., and Parrinder, E. G., *The Christian Approach to the Animist*, London: Edinburgh House Press, 1960, p. 26.
4. Sanneh, L., 'Theology of Mission', in Ford, David F. (ed.), *The Modern Theologians*, Oxford: Blackwell, 1997, p. 570.
5. See Shorter, A., *African Christian Theology: Adaptation or Incarnation*, Maryknoll, New York: Orbis, 1975, p. 20.
6. Letter to writer from Eugene A. Nida, 18 July 1994.
7. Letter to writer from the Revd Dr Colin Morris, 4 April 1996.
8. Colson, E., and Gluckman, M., *Seven Tribes of Central Africa*, London: Oxford University Press, 1951, p. ix.
9. *The Times*, 8 January 1958.
10. Letter to writer from Sir Raymond Firth, 28 June 1994.
11. *The Times*, 8 January 1958.
12. Obituary, 'Edwin Williams Smith', *Africa* 28 (1958), p. 94. See also *Linguistic Survey of the Northern Bantu Borderland*, vol. i, London: Oxford University Press, 1956, p. 4.
13. McVeigh, *God in Africa*, Cape Cod: Claude Starke, 1974, p. 2. Malcolm McVeigh in a letter, 28 July 2001, revealed that he, like Smith, was a victim of a publisher's whim. His 1971 Ph.D. dissertation was entitled, 'The Interaction of the Conceptions of God of African Traditional Religion and Christianity in the Thought of Edwin W. Smith'.

Bibliography of Edwin Smith

Primary sources

Edwin Smith's Bible. Interleaved Bible, with notes and preaching record, 1895–1901. Property of Mrs J. Smedley.

Letter to his mother, 13 March 1900, SPMMS.

Edwin Smith Diaries

   1909 End of furlough, Kasenga, SPMMS.

   1915 War diary, SPMMS.

   1929–30 Palestine and Sudan, SPMMS.

   1938–9 India, SPBSC.

   1939–43 USA, SPMMS.

   1946–7 Southern Africa, SPMMS.

   1948–9 Southern Africa, SPMMS.

   1953–4 South Africa, SPMMS.

Edwin Smith Photograph Collection, SPMMS.

'An African Odyssey', 1952, unpublished manuscript, SPMMS

Tape by Edwin Smith of early memories, made c.1957. Copy in author's possession.

'Reminiscences'. Reminiscences of Edwin Smith, used in tape, extending to c.1902, written c.1957, SPMMS.

Also in SPMMS: Microfiches, covering mainly 1895–1914 – includes diary, translation work, journalistic material. The other items mentioned above under SPMMS were added to the collection after 1995.

Bible Society Archives, Cambridge. Smith Papers.

Hartford Seminary Archives. Smith Papers.

United Church of Zambia Archives, Kitwe.

Methodist Archives, Manchester. Smith letters to A. S. Peake.

Macmillan Archives, Reading. Smith Correspondence.

Baptism Certificate of Edwin Smith.

Marriage Certificate of Edwin Smith.

Death Certificate of Edwin Smith.

Death Certificate of Julia Smith.

Books, articles and major reviews by Edwin Smith

1895   *The Record*, Report on visit of Khama.

1896

1897   'British Central Africa', *Primitive Methodist Magazine*, pp. 752–8. (Review article of book of that title by Sir Harry Johnston.)

1898   'M. Coillard's New Book – "On the Threshold of Central Africa"', *Primitive Methodist Magazine*, pp. 37–43. (Review Article.)

        'Among the Mushukulumbwe', *Primitive Methodist Magazine*, pp. 689–94. (Review article of A. St H. Gibbons, *Exploration and Hunting in Central Africa, 1895–6*, 1898.)

1899

1900

1901

1902   'Sayings of the African'. Series of articles in *The Record*, *c*.1901/2.

        1. Introductory.

        2. Some Sesuto Proverbs.

        3. Some Sesuto Proverbs – Continued.

          A Sesuto Tale – The Assembly of the Birds.

        4. A Sesuto Tale: 'Ma-Molitsane the Witch.

          A Sesuto Tale: Limo and 'Ma-Liepetsane.

        5. Some Sesuto Proper Names.

        6. Some More Sesuto Proverbs – Continued.

        7. Sayings of the African.

1903

1904   'A Plea for a Forward Missionary Movement in Central Africa', *PMQR*, January, pp. 1–15.

1905   'The Ethiopian Church Movement in South Africa. First Paper', *PMQR*, pp. 328–39.

        'The Ethiopian Church Movement in South Africa. Second Paper', *PMQR*, pp. 504–17.

1906   *St Mark in Ila*, London: BFBS.

1907   'The Religion of the Bantu', *PMQR*, January.

        A Handbook of the Ila Language, London: Oxford University Press (pp. xii, pp. 488).

        'Coillard of the Zambezi', *PMQR*, July, pp. 461–79.

        'The Secret of the African', Primitive Methodist Book Room, October (pp. 32).

        'Holman Bentley, D.D., Pioneer and Linguist', *PMQR*, ?October, pp. 613–30.

1908   'A Great Missionary Explorer' (George Grenfell and the Congo), *PMQR*, ?October, pp. 602–15.

        Nanzela: Some Personal Experiences in Central Africa, London: Edwin Dalton, n.d., *c*.1908.

1909   'Stewart of Lovedale', *PMQR*, January, pp. 1–18.

        'Uganda: A Fairy Tale', *PMQR*, July, pp. 384–401.

1910 'African Folk Tales', *PMQR*, April, pp. 234–50.

        'Henry M. Stanley', *PMQR*, ?July, pp. 403–22.

1911 'The Story of our Central African Mission, ch. X, A Sketch of Missionary Activity', *Aldersgate Magazine*, pp. 224ff.

        'The Story of our Central African Mission, ch. XI, Missionary Activity', *Aldersgate Magazine*, pp. 296ff.

        'The Story of our Central African Mission, ch. XII, The Beginnings of the Ila Language', *Aldersgate Magazine*, pp. 380ff., 485ff.

        Ila Phrase Book for the Use of Sportsmen and Settlers, Livingstone: 'Administration Press'.

1912 *Matthew's Gospel in Ila. Makani Mabotu a Jesu Kristi mbwa kananwa kwa Mateyu.*

        'The South African Mission Field', *PMQR*, ?January, pp. 105–22.

1913 'The Sententious Wisdom of the African', *PMQR*, ?April, pp. 225–37.

        'Cecil Rhodes', *PMQR*, ?July, pp. 401–20.

1914 *Ila Made Easy*, Book Room of the Baila-Batonga Mission (pp. 96).

        'The Bantu Conception of God', a lecture delivered at the First General Missionary Conference of NW Rhodesia, by Revd E. W. Smith, the President, July.

1915 *Intestemente Impya oya Mwami Mufutudi wesu Jesu Kristu. The New Testament in Ila.*

1916

1917

1918

1919 'La Bibbia in Italia', paper given in Rome, 26 June 1919 (pp. 24).

1920 (with A. M. Dale) *The Ila-Speaking Peoples of Northern Rhodesia*, 2 vols, London: Macmillan.

1921 'The Ila-Speaking People of Northern Rhodesia', *JRAS* 20 (January), pp. 89–94.

1922 'The Sublimation of Bantu Life and Thought', *International Review of Missions*, January, pp. 83–95.

        'An Italian Life of Christ', *PMQR*, ?1922, pp. 159–69. (On Papini's *Storia di Cristo*.)

1923 Articles in *The Bible in the World* and *For Every Land*.

        BFBS Popular Report, *The Bridge Builders*.

        The Religion of Lower Races, as Illustrated by the African Bantu, New York: Macmillan (pp. xiii, pp. 82).

        'Papini's Life of Christ', *Outward Bound*, June, pp. 667ff. (Review of English translation of Papini.)

        'The Education of the African', *Holborn Review*, July, pp. 302–14. (On the Phelps-Stokes Commission.)

        'An Unbroken Fellowship: The Story of 120 Years' Close Co-operation', *Church Missionary Review* 74 (December), pp. 212–20.

1924 Articles in *The Bible in the World* and *For Every Land*.

        BFBS Popular Report, *Like Unto Leaven*.

'The Bible in the Empire', in *The Native Races of the Empire*, ed. Godfrey Lagden, London: Collins.

'An Unbroken Fellowship: The Story of 120 Years' Close Co-operation', *Church Missionary Review* 75 (March), pp. 18–26.

'The Disintegration of African Society', *The East and the West*, April, pp. 143–60.

'Northern Rhodesia', *Empire Review*, April, pp. 436–44.

'Social Anthropology and Missionary Work', *International Review of Missions*, October, pp. 518–31.

'Leaves from my Journal', *Aldersgate Magazine*.

1925   Articles in *The Bible in the World* and *For Every Land*.

BFBS Popular Report, *The Seekers*.

'The Avengers', *Holborn Review*, January, pp. 12–22.

Robert Moffat, One of God's Gardeners, London: SCM Press (pp. 256).

'These Fifty Years in Africa: 1875–1925', *Church Missionary Review* 76 (December), pp. 296–308.

1926   Articles in *The Bible in the World* and *For Every Land*.

BFBS Popular Report, *The Everlasting Doors*.

'Some Periodical Literature Concerning Africa', *International Review of Missions* 15 (July), pp. 602–7.

The Golden Stool: Some Aspects of the Conflict of Cultures in Modern Africa, etc. (The Twenty-Sixth Hartley Lecture), London: Holborn Publishing House, 1926 (pp. xvi, pp. 328).

The Christian Mission in Africa: A Study Based on the Work of the International Conference at Le Zoute, etc., London: The International Missionary Council (pp. viii, pp. 192).

1927   Articles in *The Bible in the World* and *For Every Land*.

BFBS Popular Report, *The Immortal Story*.

1928   Articles in *The Bible in the World* and *For Every Land*.

BFBS Popular Report, *The Glory of the Garden*.

Tales of God's Packmen, London: BFBS (pp. 133).

The Way of the White Fields in Rhodesia: A Survey of Christian Enterprise in Northern and Southern Rhodesia, London: World Dominion Press (pp. 172).

'Exploring the African's Soul', *Missionary Review of the World* o.s. 51 (October), pp. 793–8.

1929   Articles in *The Bible in the World* and *For Every Land*.

BFBS Popular Report, *Another Milestone*.

Exploration in Africa, ed., London and Toronto: Dent & Sons (pp. 253).

Aggrey of Africa: A Study in Black and White, London: SCM Press (pp., xii, pp. 292, with plates, including portraits).

The Shrine of a People's Soul (on the literary work of the missionary), London: Church Missionary Society (pp. 208).

The Secret of the African (lectures on the religion of the Africans), London: SCM Press (pp. 142).

1930   Articles in *The Bible in the World* and *For Every Land*.

BFBS Popular Report, *In the Mother-Tongue*.

The Story of the B.F.B.S., Little Books on Religion 68, London: SPCK (pp. 31).

1931   Articles in *The Bible in the World* and *For Every Land*.

BFBS Popular Report, *Dust of Gold*.

1932   Articles in *The Bible in the World* and *For Every Land*.

BFBS Popular Report, *The Impossible*.

1933

1934   'Indigenous Education in Africa', in *Essays Presented to C. G. Seligman*, ed. E. E. Evans-Pritchard et al., London: Kegan Paul, Trench, Trubner & Co., pp. 319–34. (Cf. 'La Langue Indigene et l'Education Africaine', *Le Monde non-Chretien* 2 (March 1938), pp. 21–8.)

Anthropology and the Practical Man (Presidential Address), reprinted from the *Journal of the Royal Anthropological Institute*, London (pp. xxxvii).

The Story of the Institute (i.e. the International Institute of African Languages and Cultures), IAI Memo. no. 12, Oxford University Press (pp. 27); also: *Africa* 7, pp. 1–27. A survey of seven years.

Sectional Proceedings of the International Congress, Ethnography, Africa. *Man* 34.

1935   'Africa: What do we know of it?' (Presidential Address), *JRAI* 65 (pp. 81).

'Inzuikizi', *Africa* 8 (October), pp. 471–80.

1936   *African Beliefs and Christian Faith: An Introduction to Theology for African Students, Evangelists and Pastors*, London: United Society for Christian Literature (pp. 191).

'Land in Kenya', *JRAS* 35 (July), pp. 246–50.

1937

1938   *The Basic St John* (John's Gospel in Basic English), Psyche Miniatures – General Series 92, London: Kegan Paul & Co.

'The South African Protectorates', *JRAS* 37 (April), pp. 199–205.

'The Language of Pygmies of the Ituri', *JRAS* 37 (October), pp. 464–70.

1939   *The Mabilles of Basutoland*, London: Hodder & Stoughton (pp. 382).

'Polygamy and African Marriage Customs', paper presented to a missionary conference on Africa, called to follow up the recommendations of the Tambaram Conference, New York, 9 December 1939. (Mimeographed.)

1940   'The Function of Folk Tales', *JRAS* 39 (January), pp. 64–83.

1941   'Association and Assimilation in the Christian Mission', paper given at the Fellowship of Professors of Missions, Princeton, October 1940, printed in *IRM* 30 (July), pp. 324–36.

1942   *Events in African History*, a chronologcal table for the USA Committee on Africa, the War and Peace Aims (pp. 67).

'The Indigenous African Church', in *The Church Conference on African Affairs*, Westerville, Ohio: Otterbein College, pp. 1–32.

1943
1944
1945 *Intestemente Impya yamwami Mufutuli wesu Jesu Krisitu*, trans E. W.
    Smith and J. W. Price.
    'Religious Beliefs of the Akan', *Africa* 15, pp. 23–8. Review article of J. B.
    Danquah's book, *The Akan Doctrine of God*.
    'Lord Lugard the Man', *Africa* 15 (July), pp. 112–13.
    'A School for Translators', *IRM* 34 (July), pp. 243–52.
1946 *Knowing the African*, London: Lutterworth (pp. 194).
1947
1948 *Plans and – People! A Dynamic Science of Man in the Service of Africa*,
    The Frazer Lecture in Social Anthropology delivered before the Univer-
    sity of Liverpool on 23 October 1946, London: Lutterworth (pp. 70).
1949 *The Life and Times of Daniel Lindley, 1801–80, Missionary to the Zulus,
    Pastor of the Voortrekkers*, London: Epworth (pp. xxx, pp. 456). (Also
    listed as 1942, which seems to have been an earlier draft (pp. 575), but
    the 1949 edition includes material gathered in post-war visit to Africa.)
    Foreword to Geoffrey Parrinder, *West African Religion*.
    'Addendum to the "Ila-Speaking Peoples of Northern Rhodesia", Part I',
    African Studies, 8.1 (March), pp. 1–9.
    'Addendum to the "Ila-Speaking Peoples of Northern Rhodesia", Part II',
    African Studies, 8.2 (June) pp. 53–61.
1950 *The Blessed Missionaries*, the Phelps-Stokes Lectures delivered in Cape
    Town in 1949 etc., Cape Town: Oxford University Press (pp. xx,
    pp. 146).
    African Ideas of God: A Symposium, ed. E. W. Smith, London: Edinburgh
    House Press (pp. x, pp. 308).
1951
1952 'African Symbolism', the Henry Myers Lecture, RAI, *JRAI*, pp. 13–37.
1953 Review of 'A Survey of African Marriage and Family Life', *Journal of
    African Administration* 5.3 (July), pp. 102–12.
1954
1955
1956
1957 *Great Lion of Bechuanaland. The Life and Times of Roger Price, Mission-
    ary*, London: Independent Press (pp. xvi, pp. 444).
1958 Review of Lord Hailey, *An African Survey Africa* 28 (April), pp. 168ff.

Books by other Smiths

Smith, John, *Christ and Missions*, London: Primitive Methodist Publishing House,
    1900.
Smith, Julia A, *Sunshine and Shade in Central Africa*, London: Primitive Methodist
    Publishing House, 1908 (pp. 107).

Obituaries

Doke, Clement M., *African Studies* 17.2 (1958), pp. 116–18.
Forde, Daryll, *Africa* 28 (April 1958), pp. 93–4.
Schapera, I., *Man*, 1959, p. 213.
Shaw, J. R., *Rhodes-Livingstone Journal* 23 (1958), pp. viii–ix.
Minutes of the Methodist Conference, 1958, pp. 182–3.
The Times, 28.12.57, 8.1.58.

Communications to the author

W. R. Booth, Bar Harbour, USA, 6.3.93, 18.6.93.
Andrew M. Dale, Lusaka, 26.5.95, 10.9.95.
Mr D. Davies, Wells, 28.10.95.
Professor Sir Raymond Firth, London, 28.6.94.
Mrs Priscilla Hannam, Brixham, Devon, 15.1.95.
Revd Fergus Macpherson, Thornhill, Scotland, telephone interview, 1.12.95.
Revd Dr Malcolm J. McVeigh, 17.2.94, 25.9.96, 28.7.2001.
Revd Dr Colin Morris, Lewes, 4.4.96.
Eugene A. Nida, Savannah, Ga., USA, 18.7.94.
Professor Roland Oliver, Placida, Fla., USA, 4.2.96.
Revd Professor Geoffrey Parrinder, Orpington, 5.11.77, 30.5.92, 21.9.94.
Miss J. Potter, Gaborone, 25.2.96.
Professor I. Schapera, London, 8.8.92.
Mrs June Smedley, Loughborough, 19.11.92.
Mrs Muriel Stamp, Winchester, 28.7.91, 9.2.94, 15.7.94.
Rt Revd J. V. Taylor, Oxford, 20.3.93.
Revd Merfyn Temple, Reading, 17.6.92.
Ernst Wendland, Lusaka, 12.9.94.
Revd Denys Whitehead, Livingstone, Zambia, 26.4.95.

Other authors

Anderson, Gerald H., *Biographical Dictionary of Christian Missions*, Grand Rapids: Eerdmans, 1999.
Cocks, P., '*Musemunuzhi*: Edwin Smith and the Restoration and Fulfillment of African Society and Religion', *Patterns of Prejudice* 35.2 (2001).
Dictionary of National Biography, Missing Persons, Oxford: Oxford University Press, 1993. Article on 'Edwin Williams Smith' by J. D. Y. Peel.
Douglas, J. D. (ed.), *The New International Dictionary of the Christian Church*, Exeter: Paternoster, 1974. Article on 'Edwin William Smith' by D. G. L. Cragg.
Fielder, R. J., 'Social Change among the Ila-speaking Peoples of Northern Rhodesia', unpublished MA thesis, Manchester University, 1965.
Johnson, Thomas P., 'Anthropology and History in Northern Rhodesia: Changing Approaches to the Study of Subsistence and Environment', unpublished paper, 1992.

—— 'A Vanishing People? Population, Fertility and Venereal Disease among the Ila of Northern Rhodesia, 1900–1960', presented to the University of Kent, Canterbury, 17 October 1995.

Lucheya, Revd Matthew S., unpublished paper on Pioneer Missionaries, *c.*1976.

McVeigh, M., *God in Africa: Conceptions of God in African Traditional Religion and Christianity*, Cape Cod, Mass.: Claude Starke, 1974.

Moreau, A. Scott (ed.), *Evangelical Dictionary of World Missions*, Grand Rapids: Baker Books, 2000. Article on 'Edwin Williams Smith' by Kevin Roy.

Rinsum, Henk J. van, ' "Knowing the African": Edwin W. Smith and the Invention of African Traditional Religion', paper presented to the Centre for the Study of Christianity in a non-Western World, University of Edinburgh, 25 February 1997.

—— *Slaves of Definition: In Quest of the Unbeliever and the Ignoramus*, Maastricht: Shaker Publishings BV, 2001.

Rutherford, J., 'W. C. Willoughby of Bechuanaland: Missionary Practitioner and Scholar', unpublished Ph.D. thesis, University of Birmingham, 1983.

Tilbe, Jim, 'The Descendants of William Smith'. Ongoing genealogical information.

Vickers, John A. (ed.), *A Dictionary of Methodism in Britain and Ireland*, Peterborough: Epworth, 2000. Article on 'Edwin William Smith'.

Young, W. John, 'Edwin Smith: Pioneer Explorer in African Christian Theology', *Epworth Review*, May 1993.

—— ' "For Services to Africa": The Contribution of Edwin W. Smith to African Studies', unpublished paper, 1994.

—— 'The Contribution of Edwin Smith to the Study of African Traditional Religion', unpublished paper, 1994.

—— 'The Integrative Vision of a Pioneer Africanist: Edwin W. Smith (1876–1957)', unpublished M.Phil. thesis, University of Bristol, 1997.

—— 'The Legacy of Edwin W. Smith', *International Bulletin of Missionary Research* 25.3 (July 2001).

General bibliography

Ackerman, R., *J. G. Frazer: His Life and Work*, Cambridge: Cambridge University Press, 1987.

Alexander, P. F., *Alan Paton: A Biography*, Oxford: Oxford University Press, 1994.

Allen, R., *Missionary Methods: St Paul's or Ours?*, London: Robert Scott, 1912.

—— *The Spontaneous Expansion of the Church: And the Causes which Hinder It*, London: World Dominion Press, 1927/1960.

Anderson, Gerald H., and Thomas F. Stransky, *Christ's Lordship and Religious Pluralism*, Maryknoll, New York: Orbis Books, 1981.

Andrews, C. F., *The Renaissance in India: Its Missionary Aspect*, London: United Council for Missionary Education, 1914.

—— *What I owe to Christ*, London: Hodder & Stoughton, 1932.

Appiah-Kubi, K., and Sergio Torres (eds), *African Theology en Route*, Maryknoll, New York: Orbis Books, 1979.

Ashton, Edmund Hugh, *The Basuto*, London: Oxford University Press, 1952.

Awoniyi, T. A., *The Teaching of African Languages*, London: Hodder & Stoughton, 1982.

Baker, R. S., *American Chronicle*, New York: C. Scribner's Sons, 1945.

Baldwin, A., *How We Entered Central Africa*, Centenary Series 8, London: Edwin Dalton, ?1907.

Banana, C. S. (ed.), *A Century of Methodism in Zimbabwe, 1891–1991*, Harare, 1991.

Bannister, R. C., Jr., *Ray Stannard Baker: The Mind and Thought of a Progressive*, New Haven: Yale University Press, 1961.

Barber, B. A., *A Methodist Pageant*, London: Holborn, 1932.

Barnard, Alan, and Spencer, Jonathan (eds), *Encyclopedia of Social and Cultural Anthropology*, London: Routledge, 1996.

Bédarida, F., *A Social History of England, 1851–1975*, English trans. A. S. Forster, London: Methuen, 1979.

Beetham, T., *Christianity and the New Africa*, London: Pall Mall Press, 1967.

Belmont, N., *Arnold van Gennep*, Chicago: University of Chicago Press, 1979.

Bible in Basic English, Cambridge: Cambridge University Press, 1949.

Blakely, Thomas D., van Beek, Walter E. A., and Thomson, Dennis L., *Religion in Africa*, London: James Currey, 1994.

Bolink, P., *Towards Church Union in Zambia*, Franeker: Wever, 1967.

Bosch, D., *Transforming Mission: Paradigm Shifts in Theology of Mission*, Maryknoll, New York: Orbis Books, 1991.

Bouquet, A. C., *Comparative Religion*, Harmondsworth: Penguin, 1941.

—— *The Christian Faith and Non-Christian Religions*, Welwyn: Nisbet, 1958.

Bowran, J. G., *The Life of Arthur Thomas Guttery*, London: Holborn, n.d.

Bruce, F. F., *The English Bible: A History of Translations*, London: Lutterworth, 1961.

Brunner, Emil, *Revelation and Reason: The Christian Doctrine of Faith and Knowledge*, trans. Olive Wyon, London: SCM Press, 1947.

Bryce, James, *Impressions of South Africa*, London: Macmillan, 1897.

Butler, Mrs T., *Missions as I Saw Them*, London: Seeley, Service, 1924.

Butt, G. E., *My Travels in North West Rhodesia: Or a Missionary Journey of Sixteen Thousand Miles*, London: E. Dalton, ?1910.

Cassell, *Illustrated History of the Boer War*, n.d.

Chapman, W., *A Pathfinder in Central Africa*, London: Hammond, ?1910.

Chidester, David, *Religions of South Africa*, London: Routledge, 1992.

Clements, Keith, *Faith on the Frontier: A life of J. H. Oldham*, Edinburgh: T. & T. Clark, 1999.

Clifford, J., *Person and Myth: Maurice Leenhardt in the Melanesian World*, Durham, N.C.: Duke University Press, 1982.

Colson, Elizabeth, *The Plateau Tonga of Northern Rhodesia (Zambia): Social and Religious Studies*, Manchester: Manchester University Press, 1962.

—— *The Social Consequences of Resettlement: The Impact of the Kariba Resettlement upon the Gwembe Tonga*, Manchester: Manchester University Press, 1971.

—— 'Introduction', 1968 edition of *ISP*.

Colson, E., and Gluckman, M. (eds), *Seven Tribes of Central Africa*, London: Oxford University Press, 1951.

Comaroff, John, and Comaroff, Jean, *Of Revelation and Revolution*, Chicago: University of Chicago Press, 1991.

Cook, C., *A Short History of the Liberal Party, 1900–1984*, London: Macmillan, 1984.

Cox, James L., *Expressing the Sacred: An Introduction to the Phenomenology of Religion*, Harare: University of Zimbabwe, 1992.

Cracknell, K., *Towards a New Relationship: Christians and People of Other Faiths*, London: Epworth, 1986.

—— *Justice, Courtesy and Love: Five Early Scottish Contributions to the Theology of Inter-Faith Dialogue*, St Colm's Public Lecture, 1991.

—— *Justice, Courtesy and Love: Theologians and Missionaries Encountering World Religions 1846–1914*, London: Epworth, 1995

Cripps, Arthur S., *An Africa for Africans*, London: Longman, 1927.

Crawford, D., *Thinking Black: 22 Years without a Break in the Long Grass of Central Africa*, London: Morgan & Scott, 1912.

Dante Alighieri, *The Divine Comedy*, trans. Dorothy Sayers (*Paradiso* completed by Barbara Reynolds), 3 vols, Harmondsworth: Penguin, 1949–62.

—— *The Divine Comedy*, trans. C. H. Sisson, Introduction and notes by David H. Higgins, Oxford: Oxford University Press, 1981/93.

Dante Alighieri, *Inferno*, trans. John Ciardi, New York: Mentor, 1954.

Davenport, T. R. H., *South Africa: A Modern History*, Johannesburg: Macmillan South Africa, 1978.

Davies, R. E., George, A. R., and Rupp, G. (eds), *A History of the Methodist Church in Great Britain*, 3 vols, London: Epworth, 1965–83.

Derricourt, Robin, *Man on the Kafue: The Archaeology and History of the Itezhitezhi Area of Zambia*, London: Ethnographica, 1985.

Dickson, Kwesi A., *Theology in Africa*, London: Darton, Longman & Todd, 1984.

Douglas, J. D., *The New International Dictionary of the Christian Church*, Exeter: Paternoster, 1974.

Du Bois, W. E. B., *Writings*, New York: Library of America, 1986.

Eliade, Mircea, *Images and Symbols: Studies in Religious Symbolism*, ET, London: Harvill, 1961.

Eliade, M. (ed.), *The Encyclopedia of Religion*, 16 vols, New York: Macmillan, 1987.

Evans-Pritchard, E. E., *Social Anthropology*, London: Cohen & West, 1951.

Fairbairn, A. M., *The Place of Christ in Modern Theology*, London: Hodder & Stoughton, 1893.

——*The Philosophy of the Christian Religion*, London: Hodder & Stoughton, 1903.

Farmer, Alan, *Britain: Foreign and Imperial Affairs 1919–39*, London: Hodder & Stoughton, 1992.

Farquhar, J. N., *The Crown of Hinduism*, London: Oxford University Press, 1913.

Firth, R., *Elements of Social Organisation*, London: Watts & Co., 1951/61.

Ford, David F., *The Modern Theologians*, Oxford: Blackwell, 1997.

Forster, Peter G., *T. Cullen Young: Missionary and Anthropologist*, Hull: Hull University Press, 1989.

Fortes, M., and Evans-Pritchard, E. E., *African Political Systems*, London: Oxford University Press, 1940.

Forward, Martin, *A Bag of Needments: Geoffrey Parrinder and the Study of Religion*, Bern: Peter Lang, 1998.

Fraser, Agnes R., *Donald Fraser of Livingstonia*, London: Hodder & Stoughton, 1934.

Fraser, Donald, *The Future of Africa*, London: Young People's Missionary Movement, 1911.

Gallo, M., *Mussolini's Italy: Twenty Years of the Fascist Era*, London: Abelard-Schuman, 1974.

Garrett, A. E. F. (ed.), *South African Methodism: Her Missionary Witness*, Cape Town: Methodist Publishing House, n.d.

Germond, R. C. (trans. and ed.), *Chronicles of Basutoland*, Morija: Morija Sesuto Book Room, 1967.

Gibellini, R. (ed.), *Paths of African Theology*, London: SCM Press, 1994.

Gilbert, M., *The First World War in Maps*, London, 1970.

——*Second World War*, London: Fontana, 1990.

——*First World War*, London: HarperCollins, 1995.

Goldenweiser, A., *Anthropology: An Introduction to Primitive Culture*, London: Harrap, 1937.

Gollick, Georgina A., *Sons of Africa*, London: SCM Press; New York: Negro Universities Press, 1969.

Gollwitzer, Helmut, *Karl Barth's Church Dogmatics: Selections*, trans. G. W. Bromiley, Edinburgh: T. & T. Clark, 1961.

Goody, J., *The Expansive Moment: Anthropology in Britain and Africa 1918–1970*, Cambridge: Cambridge University Press, 1995.

Gray, S. Douglas, *Frontiers of the Kingdom in Rhodesia: The Story of Wesleyan Missions in Rhodesia*, London: Cargate Press, 1930.

Grayson, D., *Adventures in Contentment*, London: Melrose, 1907.

—— *The Friendly Road*, London: Melrose, n.d.

Groves, C. P., *The Planting of Christianity in Africa*, 4 vols, London: Lutterworth, 1948–58.

Guthrie, M., *The Classification of the Bantu Languages*, London: Oxford University Press, 1948.

Hailey, The Lord, *An African Survey: A Study of Problems Arising in Africa South of the Sahara*, London: Oxford University Press, 1938.

Harris, I., et al., *Longman Guide to Living Religions*, Harlow: Longman, 1994.

Harris, W. T., and Parrinder, E. G., *The Christian Approach to the Animist*, London: Edinburgh House Press, 1960.

Hastings, Adrian, *A History of African Christianity*, Cambridge: Cambridge University Press, 1979.

—— *A History of English Christianity, 1920–1985*, London: Collins, 1987.

—— *African Catholicism: Essays in Discovery*, London: SCM Press, 1989.

—— *The Church in Africa: 1450–1950*, Oxford: Oxford University Press, 1994.

Hastings, J. (ed.), *A Dictionary of the Bible*, 5 vols, Edinburgh: T. & T. Clark, 1898–1904.

—— *Encyclopaedia of Religion and Ethics*, 12 vols, Edinburgh: T. & T. Clark, 1908–21.

Hayward, Victor E. W., *African Independent Church Movements*, London: Edinburgh House, 1963.

Henkel, R., *Christian Missions in Africa: A Social Geographical Study of the Impact of their Activities in Zambia*, Berlin: Reimer, 1989.

Higgs, Catherine, *The Ghost of Equality: The Public Lives of D. D. T. Jabavu of South Africa, 1885–1959*, Athens, Ohio: Ohio University Press, 1997.

Hinnells, J. R., *A Handbook of Living Religions*, London: Penguin, 1984.

Hobsbawm, E. J., *The Age of Empire, 1875–1914*, London: Cardinal, 1989.

Hodgson, Janet, *The God of the Xhosa*, Cape Town: Oxford University Press, 1982.

Hoernlé, R. F. Alfred, *South African Native Policy and the Liberal Spirit: Being the Phelps-Stokes Lectures, delivered before the University of Cape Town, May 1939*, Johannesburg: Witwatersrand University Press, 1945.

Hogg, William Richey, *Ecumenical Foundations: A History of the International Missionary Council and its Nineteenth-Century Background*, New York: Harper, 1952.

Holmes, Oliver Wendell, *The Professor at the Breakfast Table*, London: Dent, 1902 (first published 1859).

Hopgood, C. R., *A Practical Introduction to Chitonga*, London: Longman, Green, 1940.

Huddleston, T., *Naught for your Comfort*, London: Collins, 1956.

Hugon, A., *The Exploration of Africa, from Cairo to the Cape*, London: Thames & Hudson, 1993.

Idowu, E. Bolaji, *Olodumare: God in Yoruba Belief*, London: Longman, Green, 1962.

——*Towards an Indigenous Church*, London: Oxford University Press, 1965.

——*African Traditional Religion: A Definition*, Maryknoll, New York: Orbis, 1975.

Ila Hymn Book, 1907.

Inglis, K. S., *Churches and the Working Classes in Victorian England*, London: Routledge & Kegan Paul, 1963.

Intestemente Impiya (Ila New Testament), Lusaka: Bible Society of Zambia, 1978.

James, E. O., *Comparative Religion*, London: Methuen, 1938/61.

James, Wendy, and Johnson, Douglas H., *Vernacular Christianity: Essays in the Social Anthropology of Religion*, Oxford: JASO, 1988.

Jones, A. M., *African Music in Northern Rhodesia and Some Other Places*, Livingstone: Rhodes–Livingstone Museum, 1958.

Jones, Thomas Jesse, *Education in East Africa: A Study of East, Central and South Africa by the Second African Education Commission under the Auspices of the Phelps-Stokes Fund, in Cooperation with the International Education Board*, London: Edinburgh House Press, 1924.

Judd, Denis, *The Boer War*, London: Hart-Davis MacGibbon, 1977.

Junod, H. A., 'Should Heathen Games be Preserved in a Christian Community? A Bantu Speaks', *IRM* 1920, pp. 274ff.

Kato, Byang H., *Theological Pitfalls in Africa*, Kisumu, Kenya: Evangel, 1975.

Kay, George, *A Social Geography of Zambia: A Survey of Population Patterns in a Developing Country*, London: University of London Press, 1967.

Keltie, Sir John Scott, and Samuel Carter Gilmour, *Adventures of Exploration*, iv: *Africa*, London: Philip, 1929.

Kendall, H. B., *The Origin and History of Primitive Methodism*, 2 vols, London, 1906.

——*History of the Primitive Methodist Church*, London: Primitive Methodist Publishing House, 1919.

Kerswell, K., *Romance and Reality of Missionary Life in Northern Rhodesia*, London, n.d.

Knappert, Jan, *African Mythology: An Encyclopedia of Myth and Legend*, London: Diamond Books, 1990.

Kraemer, H., *The Christian Message in a Non-Christian World*, London: Edinburgh House Press, 1938.

——*World Cultures and World Religions*, London: Lutterworth, 1960.

Kraft, C. H., *Christianity in Culture: A Study in Dynamic Biblical Theologizing in Cross-Cultural Perspective*, Maryknoll, New York: Orbis Books, 1979.

Kuklick, Henrika, *The Savage Within: The Social History of British Anthropology 1885–1945*, Cambridge: Cambridge University Press, 1993.

Kuper, A., *Anthropology and Anthropologists: The Modern British School*, London: Routledge, 1983.

Lane, W., *Jesuits in Zambia, 1880–1991*, Lusaka, 1991.

Latourette, K. S., *Christianity in a Revolutionary Age*, vol. v, New York: Harper & Row, 1962.

Leary, W., *Directory of Primitive Methodist Ministers and their Circuits*, Loughborough: Teamprint, 1990.

Lidgett, J. Scott, and Reed, Bryan H. (eds), *Methodism in the Modern World*, London: Epworth, 1929.

Link, Arthur S. (ed.), *The Papers of Woodrow Wilson*, vol. 53, Princeton, N.J.: Princeton University Press, 1986.

Livingstone, D., *Missionary Travels and Researches in South Africa: Including a Sketch of Sixteen Years' Residence in the Interior of Africa*, London: Ward, Lock & Co., 1857.

Lloyd, A. B., *Apolo of the Pygmy Forest*, London: Church Missionary Society, n.d.

Luck, Anne, *African Saint: The Story of Apolo Kivebulaya*, London: SCM Press, 1963.

Luig, Ulrich, *Conversion as a Social Process: A History of Missionary Christianity among the Valley Tonga, Zambia*, Hamburg: LIT, 1997.

Machin, Noel, *'Government Anthropologist': A Life of R. S. Rattray*, Centre for Social Anthropology and Computing, The University of Kent at Canterbury, 1998.

Mackintosh, H. R., *Types of Modern Theology: Schleiermacher to Barth*, London: Nisbet, 1937.

Macmillan, Hugh, 'Return to the Malungwana Drift', *African Affairs* 94 (1995), p. 62.

Macmillan, Hugh, and Marks, Shula (eds), *Africa and Empire: W. M. Macmillan, Historian and Social Critic*, Aldershot: Gower, 1989.

Macmillan, W. M., *Africa Emergent: A Survey of Social, Political and Economic Trends in British Africa*, Harmondsworth: Penguin, 1949.

Macquarrie, J., *Twentieth Century Religious Thought*, London: SCM Press, 1988.

Mair, L., *An Introduction to Social Anthropology*, Oxford: Oxford University Press, 1972.

—— Comments on 'Anthropologists versus Missionaries', in C. E. Stipe, 'Anthropologists versus Missionaries', *Current Anthropology* 21.2 (April 1980), p. 172.

Malinowski, B., *The Dynamics of Culture Change: An Enquiry into Race Relations in Africa*, New Haven: Yale University Press, 1945/61.

—— *A Scientific Theory of Culture, and Other Essays*, New York: Oxford University Press, 1960 (originally 1944).

Mandela, Nelson, *Long Walk to Freedom: The Autobiography of Nelson Mandela*, London: Abacus, 1995.

Marett, R. R., *The Threshold of Religion*, 3rd edn, London: Methuen, 1914.

Marquand, Leo, *The Peoples and Policies of South Africa*, 3rd edn, London: Oxford University Press, 1962.

—— *Liberalism in South Africa*, Johannesburg: South African Institute of Race Relations, 1965.

Martey, Emmanuel, *African Theology: Inculturation and Liberation*, Maryknoll, New York: Orbis Books, 1993.

Marwick, Arthur, *Britain in the Century of Total War: War, Peace and Social Change 1900–1967*, Harmondsworth: Penguin, 1970.

Marwick, Max (ed.), *Witchcraft and Sorcery: Selected Readings*, 2nd edn, Harmondsworth: Penguin, 1982.

Mason, P., *Christianity and Race: The Burroughs Memorial Lectures, 1956*, London: Lutterworth, 1956.

—— *The Birth of a Dilemma: The Conquest and Settlement of Rhodesia*, London: Oxford University Press, 1958.

Mathews, Basil, *The Clash of Colour: A Study in the Problems of Race*, London: Edinburgh House, 1925.

Matthews, Z. K., *Freedom for My People: The Autobiography of Z. K. Matthews: Southern Africa 1901 to 1968*, Claremont, South Africa: David Philip, 1983.

Mbiti, John S., *An Introduction to African Religion*, London: Heinemann, 1975.

Mews, S. (ed.), *Modern Religious Rebels*, London: Epworth, 1993.

Moore, R. J. B., *Man's Act and God's in Africa*, London: Livingstone, 1940.

Morris, Brian, *Anthropological Studies of Religion: An Introductory Text*, Cambridge: Cambridge University Press, 1987.

Murray, A. Victor, *The School in the Bush: A Critical Study of the Theory and Practice of Education in Africa*, London: Longman, 1929.

Myers, Adolph, *Basic and the Teaching of English in India*, Bombay: Times of India Press, 1938.

Needham, D. E., *From Iron Age to Independence: A History of Central Africa*, London: Longman, 1974.

Neill, Stephen, *A History of Christian Missions*, Harmondsworth: Penguin, 1967.

Nida, Eugene A., *Religion Across Cultures: A Study in the Communication of Christian Faith*, New York: Harper & Row, 1968.

Nightingale, E. G. (ed.), *The Widening Way*, London: Cargate, 1952.

Notes and Queries on Anthropology, London: Royal Anthropological Institute, 1929.

Nowell-Smith, S., *Edwardian England*, London: Oxford University Press, 1964.

Oldham, J. H., *Christianity and the Race Problem*, London: SCM Press, 1924.

—— *Florence Allshorn*, London: SCM Press, 1951.

—— *New Hope in Africa*, London: Longman, Green, 1955.

Oliver, John, *The Church and Social Order: Social Thought in the Church of England, 1918–1939*, London: Mowbray, 1968.

Oliver, Roland, *The African Experience*, London: Pimlico, 1991.

Oliver, Roland, and Fage, J. D., *A Short History of Africa*, Harmondsworth: Penguin, 1966.

Oman, John, *Grace and Personality*, 3rd edn, London: Cambridge University Press, 1925.

Otto, Rudolph, *The Idea of the Holy*, trans. John W. Harvey, Harmondsworth: Penguin, 1959.

Packenham, Thomas, *The Scramble for Africa: 1876–1912*, London: Abacus, 1991.

Parrinder, Geoffrey, *West African Religion: Illustrated from the Beliefs and Practices of the Yoruba, Ewe, Akan, and Kindred Peoples*, London: Epworth, 1949.

—— *Witchcraft*, Harmondsworth: Penguin, 1958.

—— *Religion in Africa*, Harmondsworth: Penguin, 1969.

—— *African Traditional Religion*, 3rd edn, London: Sheldon, 1974.

Parratt, John (ed.), *A Reader in African Christian Theology*, London: SPCK, 1987.

Paton, A., *Cry the Beloved Country*, Harmondsworth: Penguin, 1958.

—— *Hofmeyr*, Cape Town: Oxford University Press, 1964.

Pauck, Wilhelm, *Harnack and Troeltsch: Two Historical Theologians*, New York: Oxford University Press, 1968.

Payne, D. (ed.), *African Independence and Christian Freedom*, London: Oxford University Press, 1965.

Peake, A. S., *Plain Thoughts on Great Subjects*, ed. L. S. Peake, London: Allenson, n.d.

—— *The Bible, its Origin, its Significance, and its Abiding Worth*, London: Hodder & Stoughton, 1914.

—— *The Nature of Scripture*, London: Hodder & Stoughton, 1922.

—— *The Life of Sir William Hartley*, London: Hodder & Stoughton, 1926.

—— *The Servant of Yahweh*, Manchester: Manchester University Press, 1931.

Peake, A. S. (ed.), *A Commentary on the Bible*, London: T. C. & E. C. Jack, 1929 edition.

Peake, Leslie S., *Arthur Samuel Peake: A Memoir*, London: Hodder & Stoughton, 1930.

Perham, Margery, *African Apprenticeship*, London: Faber, 1974.

Phillips, James M., and Coote, Robert T. (eds), *Towards the 21st Century in Christian Mission*, Grand Rapids: Eerdmans, 1993.

Platt, W. J., *From Fetish to Faith: The Growth of the Church in West Africa*, London: Cargate, 1935.

Powdermaker, Hortense, *Stranger and Friend: The Way of an Anthropologist*, London: Secker & Warburg, 1967.

Puisano: Suto–English Phrase-book, Morija: Morija Sesuto Book Room, 1983.

Quarles, Benjamin, *The Negro in the Making of America*, New York: Collier, 1964.

Radcliffe-Brown, A. R., and Forde, Daryll (eds), *African Systems of Kinship and Marriage*, London: Oxford University Press, 1950.

Ranger, T. O. and Weller, John (eds), *Themes in the Christian History of Central Africa*, London: Heinemann, 1975.

Ranger, T. O., and Kimambo, Isaria (eds), *The Historical Study of African Religion*, London: Heinemann, 1972.

Ritson, J., *The Romance of Primitive Methodism*, London: Dalton, 1909.

Roberts, A., *A History of Zambia*, London: Heinemann Educational, 1976.

Roe, James Moulton, *A History of The British and Foreign Bible Society, 1905–54*, London: British and Foreign Bible Society, 1965.

Roscoe, John, *The Baganda*, London: Macmillan, 1911.

Rotberg, Robert I., *Christian Missionaries and the Creation of Northern Rhodesia, 1880–1924*, Princeton: Princeton University Press, 1965.

Rouse, Ruth, and Neill, Stephen Charles (eds), *A History of The Ecumenical Movement*, 2nd edn, London: SPCK, 1967.

Rumscheidt, H. M., *Revelation and Theology: An analysis of the Barth–Harnack Correspondence of 1923*, Cambridge: Cambridge University Press, 1972.

Sampson, R., *They came to Northern Rhodesia*, Lusaka, 1956.

Sanday, Rev. William, and Headlam, Rev. Arthur C., *A Critical and Exegetical Commentary on the Epistle to the Romans*, 4th edn, Edinburgh: T. & T. Clark, 1900.

Sanders, P. B., *Moshoeshoe, Chief of the Sotho*, London: Heinemann Educational, 1975.

Sanneh, L., *Encountering the West: Christianity and the Global Cultural Process: The African Dimension*, London: Marshall Pickering, 1993.

Schoffeleers, Matthew, 'Black and African Theology in Southern Africa: A Controversy Re-examined', *Journal of Religion in Africa*, 1988.

Scotland, Nigel, *Methodism and the Revolt of the Field: A Study of the Methodist Contribution to Agricultural Trade Unionism in East Anglia, 1872–96*, Gloucester: Alan Sutton, 1981.

Seligman, C. G., *Races of Africa*, London: Thorton Butterworth, 1930/39.

Setiloane, Gabriel, *The Image of God among the Sotho-Tswana*, Rotterdam: Balkema, 1976.

Sharpe, E. J., *Not to Destroy but to Fulfil: The Contribution of J. N. Farquhar to Protestant Missionary Thought in India before 1914*, Uppsala: Almqvist & Wiksells Boktryckeri AB, 1965.

——*Comparative Religion: A History*, London: Duckworth, 1975.

Sharpe, M. R. L., *Everyday Sesotho Reader*, Morija: Morija Sesuto Book Room 1987.

Shaw, Mabel, *God's Candlelights: An Educational Venture in Northern Rhodesia*, London: Edinburgh House, 1932.

Shaw, R., 'The Invention of African Traditional Religion', *Religion* 20 (1990), p. 341.

Shorter, Aylward, *African Christian Theology: Adaptation or Incarnation?*, Maryknoll, New York: Orbis Books, 1977.

Sills, L. (ed.), *International Dictionary of the Social Sciences*, New York, 1969.

Smalley, William A., *Translation as Mission: Bible Translation in the Modern Missionary Movement*, Macon, Ga.: Mercer University Press, 1991.

Smalley, William A. (ed.), *Readings in Missionary Anthropology*, South Pasadena: William Carey Library, 1974.

Smith, Huston, *The Religions of Man*, New York: Harper & Row, 1958.

Smuts, J. C., *Jan Christian Smuts*, London: Cassell, 1952.

Snelson, Peter Desmond, *Educational Development in Northern Rhodesia, 1883–1945*, Lusaka: National Educational Co. of Zambia, 1974.

Stanley, Brian, *The Bible and the Flag: Protestant Missions and British Imperialism in the Nineteenth and Twentieth Centuries*, Leicester: Apollos, 1990.

Steer, Douglas V., *God's Irregular: Arthur Shearly Cripps*, London: SPCK, 1973.

Stipe, C. E., 'Anthropologists versus Missionaries', *Current Anthropology* 21.2 (April 1980), pp. 165–79.

Stock, Eugene, *A Short Handbook of Missions*, London: Longman, Green, 1904.

Sundkler, Bengt G. M., *Bantu Prophets in South Africa*, 2nd edn, London: Oxford University Press, 1961.

Syabbalo, Enock, and Syatakali, Jemusi, *Mukristo Muzambezi*, Lusaka: United Church of Zambia, n.d.

Syed Ameer Ali, *The Spirit of Islam*, London: Chatto & Windus, 1922 edn.

Taylor, A. J. P., *The First World War: An Illustrated History*, London: Penguin, 1963.

Taylor, H. J., *From Cape Town to Kafue*, London: Hammond, 1915.

Taylor, John V., *Christianity and Politics in Africa*, Harmondsworth: Penguin, 1957.

—— *The Primal Vision: Christian Presence Amid African Religion*, London: SCM Press, 1963.

Taylor, John V., and Dorothea Lehmann, *Christians of the Copperbelt: The Growth of the Church in the Copperbelt*, London: SCM Press, 1961.

Tempels, Placide, *Bantu Philosophy* (ET of *La Philosophie Bantoue*, 1945), Paris: Présence Africaine, 1959.

Till, Barry, *The Churches Search for Unity*, Harmondsworth: Penguin, 1972.

Torrend, J., *An English–Vernacular Dictionary of the Bantu-Botatwe Dialects of Northern Rhodesia*, Mariannhill, 1931; reprinted Farnborough: Gregg, 1967.

Townsend, W. J., Workman, H. B. and Eayrs, George, (eds), *A New History of Methodism*, 2 vols, London: Hodder & Stoughton, 1909.

Trimingham, J. Spencer, *The Influence of Islam upon Africa*, Harlow: Longman, 1968.

Tucker, A. N. et al., *Linguistic Survey of the Northern Bantu Borderland*, London: Oxford University Press, 1956 onwards.

Turnbull, Colin M., *The Forest People*, London: Reprint Society, 1963.

Turner, John Munsey, *The People's Church: Primitive Methodism, From Counter-Culture to Transformer of Values*, Englesea Brook Chapel and Museum, 1994.

Turner, V. W., *The Forest of Symbols: Aspects of Ndembu Ritual*, New York: Cornell University Press, 1967.

UNESCO General History of Africa:

—— vol. i: Ki-Zerbo, J. (ed.), *Methodology and African Prehistory*, abridged edn, London: James Currey, 1990.

—— vol. vii: Boahen, A. Adu (ed.), *Africa under Colonial Domination 1880–1935*, abridged edn, London: James Currey, 1990.

—— vol. viii: Mazrui, Ali A. (ed.), *Africa since 1935*, Oxford: Heinemann, 1993.

Underhill, Evelyn, *Mysticism: A Study in the Nature and development of Man's Spiritual Consciousness*, 12th edn, London: Methuen, 1930; Woking: Unwin, 1960.

van der Geest, S., 'Anthropologists and Missionaries: Brothers under the Skin', *Man* n.s. 25 (1990), p. 588.

van Gennep, A., *The Rites of Passage*, London: 1960/77.

Walshe, Peter, *The Rise of African Nationalism in South Africa: The African National Congress 1912–1952*, London: Hurst, 1970.

Ward, Kevin, 'Even God is not Wise Enough (Some Issues in African Christian Theology)', *Epworth Review* January 1994.

Warren, Max, *Social History and Christian Mission*, London: SCM Press, 1967.

—— *To Apply the Gospel: Selections from the Writings of Henry Venn*, Grand Rapids: Eerdmans, 1971.

Wearmouth, R. F., *Methodism and the Struggles of the Working Classes 1850–1900*, Leicester: Edgar Backus, 1954.

Welbourn, F. B., *East African Christian*, London: Oxford University Press, 1965.

—— *East African Rebels: A Study of some Independent Churches*, London: SCM Press, 1961.

Welbourn, F. B. and Ogot, B. A., *A Place to Feel at Home: A Study of Two Independent Churches in Western Kenya*, London: Oxford University Press, 1966.

Werner, Alice, *Africa: Myths and Legends*, London: Harrap, 1933; Senate, 1995.

Westermann, D., *The African To-day and Tomorrow*, 3rd edn, London: Oxford University Press, 1949.

Westermann, D., and Ward, I. C., *Practical Phonetics for Students of African Languages*, London: Oxford University Press, 1933.

Wilkes, Arthur, and Lovatt, Joseph, *Mow Cop and the Camp Meeting Movement: Sketches of Primitive Methodism*, Leominster: Orphans' Printing Press, 1942.

Wilkinson, John T., *Arthur Samuel Peake: A Biography*, London: Epworth, 1971.

Willett, Frank, *African Art: An Introduction*, rev. edn, London: Thames & Hudson, 1993.

Willoughby, W. C., *Race Problems in the New Africa: A Study of the Relation of Bantu and Britons in those Parts of Bantu Africa which are under British Control*, London: Oxford University Press, 1923.

—— *The Soul of the Bantu: A Sympathetic Study of the Magico-Religious Practices and Beliefs of the Bantu Tribes of Africa*, New York: Doubleday, 1928; Harper, 1969.

World Missionary Conference, *Report of Commission IV, The Missionary Message in Relation to Non-Christian Religions*, Edinburgh and London: Oliphant, Anderson & Ferrier, 1910.

Zwemer, Samuel, 'The British Empire and Islam', *The East and the West* 22.86 (April 1924), pp. 108–24.

Index